STRATEGIES

FOR DEVELOPMENT OF FOREIGN LANGUAGE & LITERATURE PROGRAMS

by

Claire Gaudiani

with

Carol A. Herron and others

The Modern Language Association of America
New York   1984

The author wishes to acknowledge gratefully grant support from the
Exxon Education Foundation for the preparation of this book. Grants
from both the Exxon Education Foundation and the National
Endowment for the Humanities made possible the four Workshops
for Development of Foreign Language and Literature Programs.

Copyright © 1984 by the Modern Language Association of America

Library of Congress Cataloging in Publication Data

Main entry under title:

Strategies for development of foreign language and literature
programs.

  Includes bibliographies.
1. Philology, Modern—Study and teaching
(Higher)—United States. I. Gaudiani, Claire.
PB38.U6S78 1984   418'.007'1173   83-17370
ISBN 0-87352-124-2 (pbk.)

Published by The Modern Language Association of America
62 Fifth Avenue, New York, New York 10011

To Congressman Paul Simon,
with gratitude and admiration.
Your efforts to reestablish the
importance of the study of foreign languages,
literatures, and cultures have benefited us all.

Contents

A Professional Collaborative Team: The Holston Language
  Charles W. Byrd, Jr.

Chapter Ten:
**A Case for the Study of Literature in
Foreign Languages**

Bibliographies

Index

Foreword

The concepts and examples of program development described in this book had their first incarnation in a faculty workshop held at the Modern Language Association's 1979 Convention. In retrospect, we can say that for faculty in language and literature the event marked the end of a decade of decline and retrenchment and the beginning of an era of rebuilding. In four successive annual workshops and in the meetings, projects, and collaborative activities the workshops helped generate, faculty have learned to take a fresh look at approaches to basic language instruction, to the integration of language and culture studies, to languages for special purposes, and to the study of literature as an outgrowth of language study. At the same time, our profession has also witnessed a remarkable revival of spirit and of purpose. Faculty have discovered new forms of creativity, new ways to achieve consensus, new sources of support, new styles of leadership—all in the service of our traditional educational mission.

New learning and new attitudes go hand in hand. For those directly involved in these programs and for others with whom they have had contact, a vital and sustaining sense of renewal has emerged. Individually and collectively, these colleagues have found the resources to persevere through a period of low demand and to prepare themselves for an eventual resurgence of interest in language and literary study. The response has been strong in part because of the leadership vacuum left by the traditional vanguard—the foremost universities and their faculties—and in part because of a sudden flowering of leadership ability among individuals who had not been challenged before. This process has stimulated an astonishing increase in energy, and the results offer hope for an extended period of growth and activity in the years ahead. The need for our profession's services is substantial, well documented, and now almost universally acknowledged. Though we should not underestimate the complexity of our task, it is primarily one of organization and integration of ends and means. If our profession can learn to understand its needs, reclassify its priorities, and re-

distribute its rewards, it will emerge stronger than before and well prepared to face the new century.

Richard I. Brod
Modern Language Association of America

Preface

Several factors strengthen my conviction that foreign language departments can grow again. The President's Commission on Foreign Language and International Studies in 1979 certainly drew needed attention to this area of the curriculum. The field still benefits from the new awareness of many citizens to the importance of FL studies. More significant in the long run, falling SAT scores have impelled parents and educators to study curriculum changes from 1970 to 1980. The decline in the study of foreign languages now appears to have affected students' performance on both verbal and mathematics sections of the tests. These and other realizations about the 1970s' curriculum have caused a swing back toward requirements in many subject areas, among them foreign languages. (See Requirements insert, p. 67.) The great increase in enrollments in proprietary language schools indicates that more adults are returning to FL study for professional or personal reasons. Finally, the number and range of language teaching methods currently being used ensures that most learners can find an approach that will meet their needs. It is important that FL faculty and curricula are ready to satisfy the expectations of those with a new interest in our discipline.

The disintegration of FL departments into their present state took a number of years. Building them back, especially in times of diminishing resources and possibly falling enrollments in many institutions, will likewise take years. It can be done if departments believe they can and should rebuild.

This book aims to support the development of foreign language and literature (FLL) departments. Departments vary widely in size and in mission, and some have already put into practice many of the suggestions in each chapter. I include examples of how these suggestions operate and thank those who have provided them. Other ideas emerge from work I and my colleague-authors have done in connection with the Workshops for Development of Foreign Language and Literature Programs and from our experience as teachers and consultants.

I intend this text to serve as a handbook to assist faculty in their efforts to improve FLL departments; therefore I have purposely avoided lengthy footnotes and have placed practical examples of syllabi, polls, and information packets alongside the descriptions of their use. I hope that all faculty will find many good ideas in this volume.

After an introduction that describes the four Workshops for Development of Foreign Language and Literature Programs, part 1 focuses on the management of change. This section suggests ways to build enrollments, establish long- and short-term planning models, improve opportunities for faculty development, and encourage teamwork among department members. Part 2 focuses on the foreign language classroom and opens with two articles on the place of FLL study in general education. The papers that follow cover the so-called five skills—speaking, understanding, reading, writing, and cultural understanding—and include a draft of the provisional ACTFL Stepladder descriptors. The next chapter offers information on course testing and placement and proficiency testing and reviews evaluations in the foreign language curriculum. Part 2 closes with six exemplary reports on departmental change. Part 3 concerns building departmental strength beyond the college or university framework, on the one hand with funding agencies and other external resources and on the other with academic institutions in the community or region. A postscript offers some cautionary remarks on future directions of the profession in general and on the literature component of the curriculum in particular. Following is a set of bibliographies to guide further efforts in a range of areas related to each aspect of development described in the volume.

This book does not cover foreign languages and careers. This important aspect of the revised curriculum did not receive significant attention during the NEH–Exxon Education Foundation-sponsored workshops.

Some FLL faculty may find certain suggestions and perceptions impractical, impossible, outrageous, or opposed to their personal philosophies. Nonetheless, many of the ideas reflect the experience and wisdom of the chairpersons and faculty with whom I have worked, and in fact most of the suggestions in part 1 have been tried successfully at different institutions. Individual faculty members and institutions will of course need to adapt and transform suggestions according to their specific situations. My experience with more than two hundred departments tells me that few suggestions—whether for complete curriculum revision, writing or culture course changes, or language clubs—can be imported into a department without adjustment to local conditions; therefore no part of this book should be accepted in a doctrinaire fashion.

All through this volume, readers will see that I have insisted on using the term "foreign language and literature" departments. Other denotations seemed cumbersome. Romance, Germanic, Slavic would have entailed too long a list. "Foreign language departments" would have separated language from literature—a dangerous game already being played on many campuses (see ch. 10). In my view, this separation removes the content area from the discipline and makes no more sense than introducing a new friend to a group of people by presenting only his or her clothes without the person. The denotation "foreign language, culture, and literature" was appealing, but in many institutions the social science faculty will object to our taking over the term culture until we are better prepared formally to address it. That time has not yet arrived. "Commonly taught languages" would have correctly limited the range of languages dealt with in this book but would also have brought problems. In some areas of the country there are no "commonly taught languages"—all languages are "less commonly taught." And upholding my commitment to keeping "literature" in the titles would have rendered that denotation awkward: "commonly taught languages and literatures."

Therefore, despite the range of different names by which departments are known, I hope this title designation will find some favor with the faculty whose work centers on the foreign languages, cultures, and literatures commonly taught in this country.

Acknowledgments

This book is dedicated to the foreign language faculty who attended the four Exxon Education Foundation–National Endowment for the Humanities Workshops for Development of Foreign Language and Literature Programs and to the foreign language and literature departments I have worked with in various capacities over the past four years. The energy, creativity, and intelligence of all these faculty members have helped to improve foreign language study in their institutions. Many faculty have had a broader regional or national impact on strengthening teaching and learning in our discipline. It has been my privilege to work with them.

The consultants who conducted each workshop not only gave presentations, but committed themselves to helping participants personally. Their dedication indicates their faith in the future, in the project participants, and in their own capacity to make a difference. I feel fortunate to have learned so much from them and appreciate their willingness to make their work available for this volume.

Richard Brod has been the godfather of the four workshops. At various stages he, Blanche Premo, H. Gene Moss, and Arnold Shore argued with me, criticized, advised, encouraged, and praised, thereby providing invaluable help. Their concern for improvements in humanities education in general and in foreign language and literature departments in particular guarantees a brighter future for teachers and students.

I am particularly grateful to Carol Herron, my friend, my collaborator on this book, and the associate project director of the second Workshop for the Development of Foreign Language and Literature Departments (1980–81). She maintained careful daily stewardship of the project during the year I was on a research fellowship at the National Humanities Center, Research Triangle Park, North Carolina. Her intelligence, attention to details, and good humor provided an inestimable asset to the project.

I am grateful for support from the National Endowment for the Humanities and the Exxon Education Foundation. Funds from these two sources made possible all four workshops and the preparation of this book.

Finally, I wish to thank Giulia Fitzpatrick, who provided priceless administrative assistance to me during the third and fourth years of the workshop project and in the preparation of this manuscript.

For all their confidence, patience, and encouragement, I thank my husband, David Graham Burnett, my first and best collaborator, and our children, Graham and Maria.

C. G.

Introduction

This introduction describes and evaluates the actual grant model that serves as the basis for this book. Many of the papers presented during the workshops appear in this volume to provide guidance to other departments embarking on improving their programs. The ideas for the first workshop in 1979 resulted from the volume of mail received by me and the eight other teachers featured in *Change* magazine's special issue *Report on Teaching* (January 1978). Many of the faculty members who wrote us expressed concern about their few professional contacts and their isolation from opportunities to bring their knowledge and skills up-to-date. The workshop was a response to their needs. I sought an NEH–Higher Education Projects Grant and assistance from Exxon Education Foundation to fund the first four-day workshop, which was planned to coincide with a regular MLA Convention. After seeing impressive improvements in most of the participating departments (see table 1, p. xxiv), I amended the 1979 grant and invited Carol Herron to act as associate project director and pedagogical consultant. This amendment permitted a second workshop, which took place in 1980 in Houston, Texas. The third and fourth workshops, modeled after workshops one and two, took place in 1981 and 1982 at the MLA Convention sites.

The design of the workshop emerged from my belief in a four-part plan as the best way to strengthen language departments. Foreign language and literature (FLL) faculty would need to improve curriculum and teaching, but they would also need to manage their departments more effectively, especially as resources and student population decline in many colleges. In addition, faculty would need to know how to raise their own funds as well as establish continuing opportunities for faculty development for themselves and their colleagues. I felt that improving one of these four areas while leaving the others weak would benefit the department little. The 1970s were destructive times for most FLL programs. Improving them would mean reversing a serious decline; it would also require enormous force, not simply a tinkering with a course here or a new brochure there. I had (and still have) great faith that many FLL faculty had the energy, determination, and intelligence to develop and fulfill a four-part plan to strengthen their programs. My faith has been amply rewarded by the faculty participants in the workshops.

The project began each year by calling for proposals nationwide in the *Chronicle of Higher Education* and through a direct mailing to all institutions on the MLA's list of foreign language department chairmen. Eligibility was restricted to tenured faculty from two- and four-year institutions with limited financial and educational resources, few opportunities for faculty development, and no Ph.D. programs. Chairpersons received preference because they were most likely to lead departments through development.

Interested faculty wrote the required two-page double-spaced proposal, which included the following information:

1. a brief description of the institution and FLL department
2. the current state of FLL education and requirements at the institution
3. the two or three most pressing problems in the foreign language area
4. the department's involvement with regional or national professional organizations
5. recent grants or fellowships
6. benefits the faculty member could reasonably expect to derive from the workshop experience
7. the method the applicant would use to share the experience on return to the department

The grant provided small stipends to cover daily living expenses ($200 in 1979, $260 in 1980, $270 in 1981 and 1982) to fifty participants in each of the workshops. Each participant's institution shared costs by paying travel expenses from a budget outside the FLL department. ADFL, Purdue University (1979), Emory University (1980), and the University of Pennsylvania (1981 and 1982), together with Exxon Education Foundation and NEH, contributed to the financial support of the programs.

The project directors and a panel of three faculty members from the grant-administering institutions reviewed all proposals and selected fifty that most nearly matched the criteria and that indicated the department's readiness to make the changes the project would suggest. An average of 150 faculty members applied each year for the fifty available spaces. In 1979 twenty additional faculty members participated at their own (and their department's) expense as observers. They or their academic officers saw the potential value in the workshop experience and arranged for their participation even without stipend support. Observer status was requested by twelve faculty members in 1980, by sixteen in 1981, and by eleven in 1982.

Letters mailed in late October informed participants of their acceptance into the project. The project director sent the academic officer speci-fied by the faculty participant a congratulatory letter announcing the faculty member's award and explaining the goals of the project. The intent of this letter was to draw administrators' attention to the faculty members' NEH–Exxon Education Foundation grant, to raise administrative consciousness about the impending effort to strengthen the FL program and department, and to enhance the chances of the grantees' success by preparing the admin-istrators to expect changes resulting from new expertise of the faculty. Aca-demic officers were offered a copy of the final report of the project so they could assess the project's overall impact. Many even wrote to request the report when it became available. The information in the final report helped to bring many academic officers up-to-date on the FLL field.

A month prior to the workshop each faculty member received a packet containing a bibliography of required readings for each workshop session, a brief descriptive statement on each of the other participant's departments, and biographies introducing the project staff, master teachers, and consul-tants.

Each workshop began at 7:30 a.m. on 27 December. At the first ses-sion each participant received a packet containing:

1. outlines related to each section meeting
2. addresses of regional and national groups dedicated to improving under-graduate foreign language teaching
3. names of leaders of MLA divisions devoted to improvement of literature and language teaching
4. description of regular MLA sessions that addressed participants' specific problems
5. information on grant sources
6. forms to assist in development of participants' work plans
7. short evaluation form
8. three- and six-month progress report forms
9. names, addresses, and telephone numbers of workshop faculty partici-pants, teachers, grant officers, observers
10. daily workshop schedule and other pertinent information

The first plenary session consisted of a one-hour review concerning the state of FLL departments and the philosophy of development guiding the grant project. This session was followed by four sessions of $1\frac{1}{2}$ hours each with the master teachers. The fifty grantees were divided into two equal sections to increase the opportunities of individual participation and atten-tion. Master teachers gave forty-five-minute presentations, which they then discussed for the rest of the session. This format permitted the teachers to share new and useful information and still left time for specific problem solving. The grantees were repeatedly encouraged to consider how they could apply suggestions to their departments. Those making presentations had received grantees' lists of problem areas and were instructed to address those concerns specifically. Grantees took notes, which they referred to in private and small group consultations with master teachers. Grantees reported that they benefited from the solutions they found as much as from the knowledge that they shared problems with many other institutions across the country. Each year grantees listed the following problem areas in their proposals: lack of financial support, professional isolation, understaffing, low enrollments, outdated or inadequate foreign language courses and curricula, and ineffective management.

The major workshop sessions each year addressed these problems by offering guidance in the four crucial categories that I suggested at the outset of this introduction.

1. *Curricular design and evaluation.* While the workshops did not advocate any one teaching method, the following faculty participated by sharing their expertise with grantees:

Intensive language approach: John Rassias (1979, 1980, 1981, 1982)

Teaching FL composition: Claire Gaudiani (1979, 1980, 1981, 1982)

Teaching grammar and communicative skills: Carol Herron (1980, 1981, 1982)

Teaching reading: Janet Swaffar (1981, 1982)

Program and student evaluation: Renate Schulz (1980)

Testing oral proficiency: Judith Liskin-Gasparro (1981, 1982)

Teaching culture: Howard Nostrand (1979, 1980, 1981, 1982)

2. *Creative Management of FLL departments.* Master teachers shared specific suggestions designed to encourage dynamic leadership in FL departments. Jean-Charles Seigneuret (1979), Richard Preto-Rodas (1980), and Claud DuVerlie (1981, 1982) chaired these sessions. Among topics considered were the responsibility of the FLL department to institutional mission; the production and use of polls and surveys to assess needs and strengths in faculty, students, and community; suggestions for improving public relations; approaches to organizing faculty development within the department; advice on how to reinstate the foreign language requirement; discussion of advantages of proficiency as opposed to "seat-time" language requirements.

3. *Resource development.* Faculty explored the large variety of external and internal, public and private, sources of support for language programs. Speakers represented the National Endowment for the Humanities, the Fund for the Improvement of Post-Secondary Education, the International Communications Agency, the U.S. Department of Education, and the Délégation du Québec.

Program officers described their agencies, grants, and potential services to FLL departments. Participants received brochures and other materials about the agencies, advice on how to seek grants, and names, addresses, and telephone numbers of program officers to facilitate future contacts. Program officers made private appointments with those who wished them.

4. *Collaboration in ongoing faculty development.* Participants left with responsibility to carry their development plans forward within their departments and also to involve their local, regional, and state-wide foreign language colleagues. They created networks of their own and joined the network of advisers and consultants who had worked with them. (See ch. 9, Professional Collaborative Development Programs, for further information.) Many faculty set up consortia in their regions and gave joint papers about the workshop experience at the state FLTA meetings. Some visited one another's schools and helped one another redesign courses.

Special seminars were also planned for the workshop days. The selection of topics was based on an evaluation of participants' needs by the project staff and by the previous year's workshop participants. Issues discussed over the three-year period included foreign language contributions to general and liberal education, foreign language responsibilities in international education, foreign languages and business, foreign languages and continuing education, foreign languages and student literacy, enrollment building and restoration of the foreign language requirement and faculty development. During the second and third days grantees also had the chance to attend regular MLA and ADFL convention sessions and individual consulting sessions with project staff, master teachers, consultants, and former workshop participants. In the consulting sessions, faculty received assistance in developing their detailed work plans, as well as additional specific information on workshop sessions. In preparing their work plans, the grantees, of course, drew on all the resources of the project.

During the closing workshop session held on the last day of the MLA Convention, participants gave five-minute talks describing their plans for their departments' development and the steps they would take when they returned to their institutions. This final experience of sharing solutions served as a review of the project sessions. Grantees also stimulated one another's imaginations as they indicated how they expected to adapt general suggestions to their situations. Many grantees evaluated this session as one of the most helpful events of the workshop. This response was especially heartening since the final session was a witness to the benefits of professional collaboration and a significant opportunity for participants to move away from the isolation they had signaled as a major problem.

Grantees were all encouraged to share their carry-over work plans with their department colleagues as soon as possible on their return. They were also advised to share their plans with their academic officers and to begin collaborative work with them to strengthen the department. Many faculty reported enthusiastic responses from their deans and presidents. A number of faculty were invited to report on the workshop to their faculty senate. A few even gave reports to the boards of trustees of their institutions.

Finally, grantees were obliged to submit three- and six-month progress reports to the project directors. These reports, along with revised course descriptions, new departmental grant proposals, and related documents, form the basis of our evaluation of the impact of these workshops. All participants' reports, as well as the overall final project reports of each workshop, are on file at the Education Programs Division of NEH under grant number EH-20022-80-1429.

Results for Workshops One and Two

The participants in workshops one and two represented a cross section of institutions: state-supported schools, four-year private liberal arts institutions, community and junior colleges, and black heritage institutions. Twenty-seven states were represented in 1979 and twenty-eight in 1980. A high rate of return of progress reports greatly facilitated general evaluation of the project. At three- and six-month intervals after the workshops, 79% of workshop one participants returned three-month reports, and 83% sent in six-month information. Only four of the forty-eight participants (two became ill and did not attend) sent no reports. For workshop two the return was equally encouraging: an 80% return of both three- and six-month reports. Five of the fifty attending participants sent no reports. A summary of the achievement of objectives (as indicated by three- and six-month progress reports) appears in table 1 (p. xxiv). The analysis of these reports was done by 1980 Associate Project Director Carol Herron.

The statistics in table 1 indicate how many participants at the workshops reported acting on each of the listed suggestions. Interesting in themselves, these facts are useful to FLL faculty in two significant ways. The lists contain suggested activities that many departments could try as they strengthen their programs. Departments that have already embarked on some of these efforts will be gratified to know that other departments chose to make similar changes.

In reviewing the data, it is important to remember that faculty reported on accomplishments they had achieved within six months of the grant workshop. Each participant returned to campus with many tasks to do. Obviously, the different needs of their institutions and departments forced faculty to emphasize different areas of change in those first six months. Therefore, the number of faculty attempting each kind of change is less significant, especially to nonparticipants, than the range of changes.

CURRICULAR REVISIONS

Table 1 indicates that participants clearly responded to the specific suggestions for curricular changes suggested by the master teachers. New or modified composition and culture courses tended to be the modifications most preferred by the two groups: 30% of the 1979 and 1980 respondents experimented with new composition courses, and 20% with culture courses. Another popular option for the 1979 group (33%) was developing one-credit courses in conversation and culture. The one-credit model has been suggested to encourage students to pursue FLL study after their required or nonrequired introductory courses. (See One-Credit Conversation Courses insert, p. 22.) Advanced conversation and grammar courses made up the bulk of new upper-division curricula.

The most popular new first-year courses developed by workshop one participants were in French and Spanish, while workshop two participants reported a growth in less commonly taught language courses in Russian, Chinese, and Arabic at the beginning level. New programs in foreign languages consisted of a new B.A. in Spanish, a new modern language major, a new French major from workshop one, and a new Russian studies program and an individualized Spanish program from workshop two.

MANAGEMENT STRATEGIES

Changes in the second category, approaches to management of FL programs, were most exciting and suggested the potential for continued growth of the FLL programs in participants' institutions. A significant increase in student enrollments was mentioned by 30% of the reporting participants from workshop one and 20% from workshop two. These statistics reflect many factors, not all of which can be credited to workshop activities. Yet many suggestions offered by the workshops do appear in participants' reports: writing new departmental brochures and sending them to incoming freshmen; initiating FLL clubs, festivals, symposia, and information centers; reinstating or creating study-abroad programs; developing a system of certificates of proficiency for students who complete a number of courses fewer than a minor but beyond the requirement (this helps draw students to postintroductory courses); and using student apprentices to assist faculty. Regional and local high schools were also contacted by 31% of workshop two participants. By sharing workshop materials, speaking about the future of the profession and about the President's Commission, and holding local workshops, participants extended the benefits of their workshop experiences to their colleagues at the high school level.

As for public relations, participants did an excellent job of presenting their departments to their various colleagues. Sixty-eight percent of the participants in both workshops reported that they shared their work plans and workshop-related materials with FLL faculty colleagues, with deans and presidents, and with appropriate institutional committees. For example, one 1979 participant was asked by his president to address the board of regents because the president wished to illustrate the vigorous approaches being used to solve the enrollment crisis in the humanities. Of the 1979 group 57% distributed all or parts of the President's Commission report on campus, and 32% of the participants in both groups used school newspapers, local and regional press, radio and tv, and public lectures to discuss the importance of FLL study and the implications of the President's Commission.

The area of data development in the management category received enthusiastic responses: 55% of the 1979 group and 41% of the 1980 group returned home and designed surveys to determine FLL-related needs, interests, and opinions of students and of the business and academic community.

RESOURCE DEVELOPMENT

In the third major category, the pursuit of external funding, 68% of the 1979 group and 40% of the 1980 group applied for grants and fellowships related to some aspect of their experience with this project. In 1979 the largest number (13) stated that they were applying for NEH consultant grants. In 1980 the favored form of funding (12 applicants) was in special development leave or special travel opportunities. It is not surprising that private funding was a preferred source of support for workshop two participants since they met soon after President Reagan had warned of cuts in the federal budget.

Participants received specific instructions on where, how, and when to apply for grants. They learned how to plan program developments to discover first the materials and personnel support within their institutions. This research usually reveals unexpected resources. It also strengthens the case made in a subsequent proposal for external funding to supplement the resources on hand. Faculty expressed an increase in confidence and optimism in seeking grant support when they had gathered data, the step that precedes worthwhile curricular design.

COLLABORATION

The fourth general aim of this project was to assist faculty in finding colleagues with similar problems and challenges. In addition, we had hoped to put faculty in contact with consultants and others who could help to improve their development plans. According to reports from grant consultants, 25% of the participants did contact them. The project office continues to receive calls and letters from former participants with news on their recent accomplishments.

Tables 2 and 3 rank achievements made by at least 25% of the reporting participants of workshops one and two. A comparison of tables 2 (workshop one) and 3 (workshop two) shows that most advances were made toward meeting the workshop objective of building approaches to management, growth, and development of FLL programs. An analysis of workshop one indicates that nine activities in all were achieved by at least 25% of the responding participants. Of these nine activities, four fell under the objective of approaches to management, three under curriculum remodeling, one under resource development, and one under professional collaboration. A similar analysis of the accomplishments from workshop two shows that seven activities in all were achieved by at least 25% of the responding group: five in the area of management; one in curriculum remodeling; one under resource development; and none under professional collaboration. Moreover, the three top-ranked accomplishments for workshop one fell within the objective of approaches to management and growth, and the five top-ranked achievements for workshop two fell within the same objective. Within this area three activities were accomplished by at least 25% of the groups from both workshops: sharing work plans and materials with colleagues, administrators, and committees; designing surveys; and using the media and public lectures to discuss the importance of FLL study. The reason for the reported success in this category may be that strategies for improving public relations and visibility within an institution and in the community are feasible goals to attain within a short period of three to six months.

In the area of curriculum remodeling, it usually takes six months to a year or more for a new course or program to pass through various committees before a recommendation is made. The one curriculum change that was accomplished in a six-month period by at least 25% of participants in both groups was the remodeling of traditional composition courses. Also, at least 25% of both groups did apply for external funding within six months of returning to the home institution: 30% of the 1979 group applied for NEH consultant grants; 27% of the 1980 group requested special development or travel leaves.

The three- and six-month progress reports from the 1979 and 1980 groups indicated such an exciting range and number of FLL development activities in participants' institutions that I applied for a grant from Exxon Education Foundation to repeat the workshops in 1981 and 1982 for another fifty faculty participants each year. The project was approved and funded. Data from these Exxon-sponsored workshops appear to be as encouraging as the analysis of workshops one and two. Publication of this book, however, preceded final evaluation of workshops three and four. The results to date encourage consideration of this successful model project as a springboard to major redevelopment in FLL departments throughout our educational system.

Table 1. Analysis of Progress Reports from Workshops 1 and 2

	NO. OF PARTICIPANTS WHO ACHIEVED THE OBJECTIVE	
	Workshop 1 (44 respondents)	Workshop 2 (45 respondents)

FLL METHODOLOGIES AND CURRICULUM REMODELING

	Workshop 1	Workshop 2
1. Experimented with intensive language acquisition model	20	7
2. Planned new culture courses	10	10
3. Implemented new composition course	13	13
4. Developed 1-credit course in conversation, text reading, or culture	15	6
5. Developed language courses with career focus	5	8
6. Reported new upper-division courses	4	5
7. Reported new or additional first-year courses	5	9
8. Reported a new program in FL study	3	2

NEW APPROACHES TO MANAGEMENT, GROWTH, AND DEVELOPMENT OF FLL PROGRAMS

Student Enrollment

	Workshop 1	Workshop 2
1. Revised or wrote new departmental brochures, course descriptions	9	10
2. Initiated FLL clubs, international clubs, FLL information centers, festivals, symposia	8	19
3. Began FLL awareness weeks or public celebrations of national FL week	3	10
4. Initiated summer, interim, or year abroad program	6	2
5. Initiated awards or certificates of FL proficiency	2	1
6. Used student apprentices to aid slow or advanced group	3	4
7. Initiated contacts with local or regional high schools	5	14

Public Relations

	Workshop 1	Workshop 2
1. Shared workshop materials with colleagues, administrators, committees	30	30
2. Distributed copies of President's Commission report on campus	25	2
3. Used school newspapers, press, radio, to discuss importance of FLL study	14	14

Data Development

	Workshop 1	Workshop 2
1. Designed questionnaires or surveys to establish FLL-related needs, interests, and opinions of faculty, students, and community	24	18

PURSUIT OF EXTERNAL FUNDING

	Workshop 1	Workshop 2
1. Applied for NEH consultant grant	13	4
2. Applied for NEH pilot grant	2	1

Table 1. (*cont.*)

	Workshop 1 (44 respondents)	Workshop 2 (45 respondents)
3. Applied for special development leave or travel opportunities	6	12
4. Made a fellowship application	9	1

PROFESSIONAL NETWORKING

1. Contacted fellow workshop participants after the workshop	12	5

ADDITIONAL BENEFITS DESCRIBED BY PARTICIPANTS

1. Increased administrative support and interest	15	10
2. Embarked on rebuilding language requirements	10	5
3. Built up laboratory, library, or audiovisual resources	8	10
4. Promoted or read Paul Simon's book, *The Tongue-Tied American*	(not yet published)	7

Table 2. Ranking of Accomplishments by at Least 25% of Workshop 1 Participants

ACTIVITY	OBJECTIVE	% OF RESPONDENTS WHO ACCOMPLISHED THE ACTIVITY
1. Shared workshop materials with colleagues, administrators, committees	Management, growth, development	68%
2. Distributed copies of President's Commission report on campus	Management, growth, development	57%
3. Designed and ran surveys	Management, growth, development	55%
4. Experimented with intensive language acquisition model	Curriculum remodeling	45%
5. Developed 1-credit courses	Curriculum remodeling	34%
6. Used press, radio, tv, public lectures to discuss FLL study	Management, growth, development	32%
7. Experimented with new composition courses	Curriculum remodeling	30%
8. Applied for NEH consultant grant	External funding	30%
9. Remained in contact with other participants	Professional networking	27%

Table 3: Ranking of Accomplishments by at Least 25% of Workshop 2 Participants

ACTIVITY	OBJECTIVE	% OF RESPONDENTS WHO ACCOMPLISHED THE ACTIVITY
1. Shared workshop materials with colleagues, administrators, committees	Management, growth, development	68%
2. Initiated FLL clubs, information centers, festivals, symposia	Management, growth, development	43%
3. Designed and ran surveys	Management, growth, development	41%
4. Initiated contacts with high schools	Management, growth, development	32%
5. Used press, radio, tv, public lectures to discuss FLL study	Management, growth, development	32%
6. Experimented with new composition courses	Curriculum remodeling	30%
7. Applied for special development leave or travel opportunities	External funding	27%

Participating Institutions

1979

Aquinas College (Mich.)
Armstrong State College (Ga.)
Austin Peay State University (Tenn.)
Berry College (Ga.)
Birmingham-Southern College (Ala.)
Buena Vista College (Iowa)
Cabrillo College (Calif.)
Catawaba College (N. C.)
Central College (Iowa)
Central Florida Community College
Central Washington University
Clark College (Wash.)
David Lipscomb College (Tenn.)
Eastern Kentucky University
Elmhurst College (Ill.)
Garland County Community College (Ark.)
Grossmont College (Calif.)
Hiram College (Ohio)
Hollins College (Va.)
LeMoyne-Owen College (Tenn.)
University of Maine
McMurry College (Tex.)
Minot State College (N. D.)
Mississippi University for Women

University of Missouri, Rolla
Moorhead State University (Minn.)
Muskingum College (Ohio)
Nazareth College of Rochester (N.Y.)
North Carolina A&T State University
Northern Michigan University
Prairie View A&M University (Tex.)
Ripon College (Wis.)
Saginaw Valley State College (Mich.)
St. Mary's College of Maryland
College of St. Teresa (Minn.)
University of San Diego (Calif.)
Santa Ana College (Calif.)
Sauk Valley College (Ill.)
Southern University (Baton Rouge, La.)
Southwestern University (Tex.)
Texas Women's University
Thornton Community College (Ill.)
Wayne State College (Neb.)
West Virginia State College
Western Kentucky University
Western Maryland College
Wiley College (Tex.)
University of Wyoming

Participating Institutions (*cont.*)

1980

Alcorn State University (Miss.)
Allentown College of St. Francis de Sales (Pa.)
Baker University (Kans.)
Bethel College (Kans.)
University of Colorado
Delaware State College
University of Detroit (Mich.)
Dillard University (La.)
Drury College (Mo.)
Eastern Washington University
Edinboro State College (Pa.)
Fort Hays State University (Kans.)
Graceland College (Iowa)
Hawaii University
Iowa Central Community College
Lehigh University (Pa.)
Lincoln University (Pa.)
Louisiana State University, Shreveport
Manhattanville College (N.Y.)
University of Maryland
McPherson College (Kans.)
Metropolitan State College (Colo.)
Midway College (Ky.)
Morningside College (Iowa)
State University of New York

North Dakota State University
North Shore Community College (Mass.)
Northeast Louisiana University
Northern State College (S. D.)
Notre Dame College of Ohio
Oklahoma State University
School of the Ozarks (Mo.)
Pace University (N.Y.)
Pacific University (Oreg.)
University of Puget Sound (Wash.)
Radford University (Va.)
Russell Sage College (N.Y.)
St. Augustine's College (N. C.)
St. John Fisher College (N.Y.)
San Jacinto College (Tex.)
Southeast Missouri State University
Southern University in New Orleans (La.)
Southwest Missouri State University
Somerset County College (N.J.)
Talladega College (Ala.)
Texas Tech University
Tougaloo College (Miss.)
Tuskegee Institute (Ala.)
West Virginia University
Westminster College (Mo.)
Wheeling College (W. Va.)

1981

Abilene Christian University (Tex.)
Arkansas State University
Atlanta University (Ga.)
Bethune-Cookman College (Fla.)
University of Central Arkansas
Concordia College (Minn.)
Culver-Stockton College (Miss.)
East Stroudsburg State College (Pa.)
Fayetteville State University (N.C.)
Georgia Southern College
Gonzaga University (Wash.)
Grambling State University (La.)
Hampden-Sydney College (Va.)
Jacksonville State University (Ala.)
Keene State College (N.H.)
Luther College (Iowa)
Marywood College (Pa.)
University of Michigan, Flint
Millikin University (Ill.)
University of Minnesota, Duluth

Morehead State University (Ky.)
Morgan State University (Md.)
Napa College (Calif.)
New Mexico Highlands University
North Carolina Central University
University of the Pacific (Calif.)
Pacific Lutheran University (Wash.)
Ricks College (Idaho)
St. Lawrence University (N.Y.)
Seton Hill College (Pa.)
University of the South (Tenn.)
South Carolina State College
University of South Dakota
Sweet Briar College (Va.)
Texas Christian University
Texas Southmost College
Tennessee State University
University of Tulsa (Okla.)
Wesley College (Del.)
Westminster College (Pa.)

Participating Institutions (*cont.*)

1982

University of Alaska, Fairbanks
Allegheny College (Pa.)
Augustana College (S.D.)
Barber-Scotia College (N.C.)
Bentley College (Mass.)
Butler University (Ind.)
California State University, Sacramento
California State College, Stanislaus
DePaul University (Ill.)
Drew University (N.J.)
Florida International University
Florida Memorial University
Fullerton College (Calif.)
Guilford College (N.C.)
Indiana University, Southeast
John Carroll University (Ohio)
Los Angeles City College (Calif.)
Marymount College (N.Y.)
Mesa College (Colo.)
Mills College (Calif.)

University of Minnesota, Morris
University of Mississippi, University
University of Missouri, Kansas City
Mount Mary College (Wis.)
Newmann College (Pa.)
Panhandle University (Okla.)
Phillips University (Okla.)
Providence College (R.I.)
Rocky Mountain College (Mont.)
St. John's University (Minn.)
City College of San Francisco (Calif.)
Seattle University (Wash.)
Southern Oregon State College
Stetson University (Fla.)
Stockton State College (N.J.)
Tyler Junior College (Tex.)
Virginia Union University
Western Oregon State College
West Georgia College

Part One

PLANNING AND MANAGEMENT

Chapter One

Strengthening Foreign Language and Literature Departments

In many colleges and universities, improving the foreign language department is impossible to separate from building enrollments. They are in fact two different issues. After all, there are ways to build enrollments that would not improve the department: giving all students A's regardless of their performance, avoiding use of the foreign language to help ensure universal comprehension in the classroom, offering free airplane tickets to Munich, Paris, or Madrid to students who sign up for advanced literature seminars. Each of these enrollment-building ideas would cost more than it would contribute morally, academically, or financially. Consequently even in the darkest days of the 1970s the profession has, to my knowledge, avoided these methods. This chapter deals with four major ways to build enrollments that do improve departments and vice versa. They are (1) improving teaching, (2) revising curriculum, (3) strengthening public relations, and (4) restoring the language requirement. Considered in this fashion, the task may seem more appropriate and less odious. The task of increasing enrollments seems to be particularly distasteful to faculty, mainly, I think, because it is contemplated in isolation and quickly transforms itself to a task akin in teachers' minds to hawking snake oil or selling used cars.

Before turning to the four topics cited above, a few remarks on the nature of enrollment building per se seem appropriate. (See DuVerlie, pp. 88–90.) Each year of the NEH-Exxon Education Foundation Workshops for Development of Foreign Language and Literature Programs, more than half of the participants note enrollment building as their greatest challenge. Most find it unappealing. FL requirements make the task a bit easier in some institutions. Even with requirements, however, the department must show enrollments in advanced-level courses. This job presents the kinds of tasks most faculty have nightmares about and others refuse even to acknowledge. Nightmares and insouciance notwithstanding, faculty certainly could look at their efforts to build enrollments as one way to fulfill their responsibility of guiding the student's choice of academic courses. It is the

3

faculty's responsibility to explain the benefits of foreign language study and to encourage students to take FLL courses. Somehow, though, it often goes against the grain for many faculty to "sell" their discipline, although in recent years some language faculty have indeed developed excellent marketing skills.

Other factors also make enrollment building unappealing. Many faculty teach overloads and therefore resist helping to stimulate enrollment. Often they teach these overloads because the departments have lost faculty positions, not because of a dramatic increase in student enrollment. Faculty can justly perceive no advantage in attracting more students to their already overcrowded classes. As a consultant to departments like these, I ask faculty to enter into an agreement with the dean or president. The agreement might state that if through excellent teaching, curriculum and course design, and public relations, the department increases the enrollments by twenty percent for three semesters in a row, a two-year full-time contract will be offered to bring a new faculty member to campus. If enrollments warrant keeping the new person after two years, that position could become tenure track. If not, it would dissolve. Or the agreement might state that if improvements in the curriculum create four new sections enrolled at ten or more for two or three semesters, one of the part-time faculty positions used to cover the increased enrollment will be changed to a full-time one on the same contractual basis as referred to above.

Unappealing or not, building enrollments remains an important task for pragmatic as well as philosophical reasons. Moreover, it can be effec-

---

Incentives: Signs of Encouragement

1. Administrators should ask faculty what special incentives would help to motivate them.
2. Administrators can write letters of appreciation.
3. Administrators can feature active faculty in alumni publications, give them awards (alumni can often endow modest amounts for prizes) or raises (often no longer offered on a merit basis).
4. Administrators can invite active faculty to address the board of trustees or community organizations and describe the special work the department is doing.
5. Administrators can award small grants ($200–500) for summer work on course development or on departmental curricular revision or for scholarly work, especially for faculty who teach twelve hours or more.
6. Administrators can provide single-course release or teaching-hour reduction for faculty embarked on projects like those suggested above.
7. Administrators can often arrange to have neighboring institutions give faculty members expanded privileges at libraries and AV and computer departments and reduction or elimination of fees for courses. Reciprocal agreements already exist between many schools. Faculty requesting and meriting special privileges can be designated college fellows during the period of their award.

tively done only by faculty. Excellent programs draw students to our institutions and our departments. Administrators must give faculty tangible incentives for the extra work and time that enrollment building and consequently larger classes entail. As a consultant I have found that faculty, even those who have done little for years, can be motivated to make greater efforts if incentives are clear. (See Incentives insert, p. 4.)

Finally, enrollment building and strengthening departments require team effort (see C. DuVerlie, p. 85, on team building). Different members of the department will find themselves naturally disposed toward certain tasks and repelled by others. Obviously, where possible, faculty should embark on the tasks they feel best qualified to do; but everyone should play an active role in the effort. Given four different kinds of work to choose from, every faculty member should be able to find a reasonably appealing assignment.

Improving Teaching

At institutions like Dartmouth College, Middlebury College, and Earlham College, the excellent teaching in the language departments attracts many students to courses they might never have been tempted to take. Good teaching matters. Regardless of how well a department designs its curriculum or how successful its public relations are, courses will rarely have large enrollments unless the teaching is exemplary and enables students to achieve the goals advertised in the course descriptions.

Good teachers capitalize on their personal styles. It is a cliché to say that not everyone can explode into the drama of John Rassias. Good teachers also know themselves, their material, and their students and have realistic goals for their courses. They know how to evaluate and hold to high standards. Through the 1970s, many good teachers gave grades away too easily. Some did so to retain students in their classes, to become popular, to indicate their discomfort over passing judgment on students whom they sought to elect to peer status. Evidence of this spirit still pervades many departments despite the years of negative press on grade inflation. Good teachers accept the role of mentor—one who knows more about the subject than the students do and who guides and nurtures students in their attainment of skills and knowledge. Passing judgment is an important part of this nurturing process. Faculty who shrink from the hard job of grading firmly commit an act of cowardice. On the other hand, those who grade firmly and rarely offer students the opportunity to revise, rewrite, and recommit themselves to the learning task reduce the act of teaching to one of simply evaluating. In most classes, students should have the opportunity to revise and resubmit for regrading at least half of all written work. In this system, the teacher can hold high evaluation standards and give students the chance to recoup and meet those standards. (See p. 160 on teaching writing.) For years many college students had to take FL courses to qualify for the degrees they wanted. Many still do. More will have to in the future as language requirements return. If we can judge by informal reports from adults, our colleagues, our students' parents, and our contemporaries, really good teaching in language classes has not been as widespread as we might wish. We must focus on this issue in the next ten years. First, it is our moral obligation to do so. It is also the best way to meet the challenge of returning language requirements and to use that challenge to strengthen our contribution to the general curriculum and improve our departments.

Teaching well is everyone's responsibility. Faculty, like members of other professions, tend to shelter their colleagues from criticism, even when poor professional work occurs regularly. No good comes of this protectiveness. The department should foster and support excellent teaching and tolerate nothing less than good teaching. Moral suasion is one powerful tool, especially if it is backed up by opportunities for colleagues to help one another.

Many people teach poorly because they lack the skills to analyze and criticize their teaching and then to plan appropriate action to improve. Many teach poorly because they are discouraged. They lack commitment to what they teach and to whom they teach. They have, in a sense, lost their faith. They no longer remember why they wanted to become teachers and would not make the choice a second time if they could begin their careers over again. They are alienated from their work and trapped in it. Many others teach poorly because they are teaching a curriculum that no longer works for the students they teach. They are using materials and methods that put off rather than attract student confidence.

These statements reveal nothing new to FLL teachers. The reasons for the malaise have been studied extensively. The important message here is to begin to make changes. A good way for a department to begin is for them to decide to teach better. The central question is: How can we better fulfill our responsibilities as FLL teachers?

CLASS VISITATION

Class visitation provides an excellent way for department members to assist one another to improve teaching. Most of the faculty I have worked with in the NEH-Exxon Education Foundation grant project and my NEH consultancies initially dislike the idea of visiting one another's classes—probably because they associate it with student teaching, graduate supervision, or some other mildly distasteful event in their professional training.

A very fine older teacher once suggested to me, in a somewhat tongue-in-cheek way, that she thought that most faculty dislike visiting their colleagues as well as being visited by them because visitation violates the spirit of intimacy between teacher and students. Faculty, my colleague told me, seem somehow quite unconsciously to have created a mental model that equates the act of teaching with the act of lovemaking. Consequently, they have a need for privacy, and naturally, feel uncomfortable with visitors present. In fact, she went on, teaching is not inherently a private act. It is analogous to acting, so visitors of any sort are perfectly appropriate.

Whether or not my colleague is correct about the lovemaking analogy, her view of teaching as a kind of acting does make the thought of class visitation more bearable. John Rassias and many others have made this analogy. To please and to instruct are goals that transfer easily from classroom to theater but with difficulty to the bedroom. Once teachers change the metaphors they use to structure their thinking, they find class visitation much more natural. When students become accustomed to visitors in the room, the class performs normally in their presence. In addition, teachers should note that doctors and lawyers regularly call their colleagues in for professional consultations. As the academic profession sees its work in new ways, exchange visitations will become less threatening and will greatly enhance teaching.

Faculty should also exchange visits to language programs in neighboring departments. Departmental or intradepartmental brown-bag lunches offer faculty in many institutions fine occasions to share suggestions for improving teaching gleaned from visitation trips. In some institutions faculty can arrange for videotaping of FLL classes. This is an excellent way for faculty to work on their teaching.

GOOD MATERIALS AND METHODS

Good teaching improves with availability of good materials and methods. (See Methods insert, pp. 9–11, and Howard Nostrand's suggestions for evaluating textbooks for their culture component, p. 181.) Departments contemplating changes in texts should contact publishers or authors to locate reviews of the books under consideration. Language pedagogy specialists offer insightful reviews in *Modern Language Journal, Foreign Language Annals,* and the language-specific AAT publications. In addition, book publishers can tell faculty where their texts are in use so that faculty can consult colleagues in those institutions for reactions to the books.

GOOD COURSE OUTLINES

Many fine methods exist to teach elementary and intermediate foreign language courses. (See Methods insert, pp. 9–11.) Most specialists in pedagogy, regardless of their methodology, agree that course planning and evaluations are vital to good teaching. Construction of a detailed outline helps ensure accomplishments in class. A good one contains not only a listing of the pages, chapters, and exercises for each week but also a list of initial and revised learning objectives, teaching strategies, evaluation methods, and materials appropriate for each week's work. Such an outline becomes a script complete with stage directions that the teacher uses to shape each class. (See How to Set Up a Course Outline, p. 11.) Instead of restricting creativity, this script encourages it. The learning objectives in a grammar class, for example, should determine the teaching strategies. Certain games, drills, and activities support specific learning objectives, and good planning will bring these objectives and strategies together. (See Carol Herron's article, pp. 123–28.) Detailed outlines allow the teacher to allot time for films, slides, and tapes for use with certain chapters of grammar study and to balance the practice students get in all four skills.

Many departments do not require faculty to prepare detailed outlines. I strongly advise that faculty begin to produce them by doing one new one each semester. Thus the department will gradually accumulate a store of them. Colleagues should share good ideas by exchanging course outlines.

EVALUATIONS

Midsemester evaluations help students and faculty to focus on improving the teaching and learning atmosphere while time still exists for all to benefit. A simple form with four or five questions suits most classes well. (See Sample Questions, p. 11.) Most institutions now have some process of final course evaluation. Students certainly need to have a constructive way to comment on their language courses. I do suggest to many departments, however, that they have students prepare an additional evaluation (by mail if necessary), which is distributed to students from six months to a year after completion of the language requirement or course sequence. Students' immediate reactions to a course carry important information to faculty. But perceptions students later develop often provide insights on the long-term benefits of the knowledge gained from a course. In fact, faculty and courses that students might initially have adjudged difficult and demanding often receive much better ratings with the passage of time. Follow-up evaluations would certainly assist departments contemplating changes in their programs.

TESTING

Entry testing, teaching-learning, review and practice, retesting: this is the structural model of foreign language classes. Testing holds a significant place in the curriculum for all the obvious reasons, such as the need to give grades and to ascertain students' levels of competence. Now, however, proficiency testing helps FL departments demonstrate some accountability for the learning that occurs in class. It shows that students actually attain the goals described in brochures and catalogs. (See ACTFL-ETS section, pp. 184–94.)

Entry-level testing helps ensure that students will bring manageably similar ranges of experience and ability to their language class. (Renate Schulz's article, pp. 196–200, discusses ways to design and use entry tests.) Course testing should include opportunities for students to demonstrate their attainment of course goals. For instance, if a course aims to advance students' abilities to read, write, speak, and understand the language and to improve their knowledge of the cultures where people speak the language, the final examination must test each of these areas. This means that the final exam should include an oral-aural section. Most teachers use dictations or responses to oral questions and find them easy to administer even to large groups. Group interviews also work. (See Group Interviews insert, p. 12.) Material for the reading section of the final might come from literature or from current press, travel brochures, or other written materials. In addition, the test should include a writing passage. Even first-semester students should be able to write five to ten sequential sentences on a topic they have learned about in their course. Finally, the course final should include a substantive question on culture. I have evaluated a number of FL curricula where none of the courses required students to demonstrate what they knew about other cultures or how their global perspectives had changed during the course. Students quickly learn "what is going to count." Cultural awareness counts, and I believe that students should answer significant questions, in English if necessary, on the culture elements covered in their FL courses. (See Sample Test, pp. 16–17.)

Renate Schulz and Judith Liskin-Gasparro have addressed the major issues related to testing in the FL classroom and program. (See pp. 196–209 and pp. 210–21.) Their work makes most of us realize that although we were not trained to design tests, we can and should design them well.

Methods in College Foreign Language Instruction

(Excerpts from the article by David P. Benseler and Renate Schulz, *Modern Language Journal*, 64 [1980], 86–96.)

1. *Audiolingual method.* This method originated in the Army Specialized Training Program during World War II. It emphasizes the development of speaking skills. Much attention is given to pronunciation and colloquial everyday language. Oral skills are practiced before reading or writing skills. Students don't say or write anything they have not said or written. Errors are corrected immediately. Translations are avoided and formal grammar plays a minor role in this method.

The premise for this method lies in the belief that language is a set of habits. These can be acquired through mimicry and memorization of dialogues, and various mechanical pattern drills conducted at "normal" speed to overlearn the structural patterns of the target language. This enables students to make automatic responses to various verbal stimuli.

Major criticism of the audiolingual method is that it prepares students only for mechanical manipulation of linguistic elements and not for spontaneous communication and interaction.

Methods (*cont.*)

2. *Cognitive method.* The method teaches the system of language through formal grammatical explanations and analysis, and through cognitive exercises (including translations), which necessitate understanding of the meaning at all times. The assumption behind this method is that language is a creative activity utilizing mental processes in a conscious, analytical manner.

3. *Direct (or natural) method.* The direct method makes exclusive use of the target language for instruction and interaction in the classroom. Other techniques include avoidance of mechanical pattern drills and translations, heavy use of question-answer exercises, and emphasis on inductive learning of grammatical patterns.

This method is currently in use at Yale University, Emory University and the University of Pennsylvania, among others.

4. *Grammar-translation method.* This approach focuses on formal and extensive grammatical analysis of the target language and on translation. The main objectives are development of reading and writing skills.

FL learning is considered an intellectual discipline and the method is a means to "develop the mind." It is rooted in the teaching of classical languages.

5. *Confluent approach.* The confluent approach borrows from values clarification and sensitivity training movements in psychotherapy. It stresses the emotional development of students. The target language serves as the vehicle for self-awareness, self-expression, and self-affirmation. It uses special group interaction techniques to enhance development of interpersonal communication.

6. *Community language learning.* The theoretical foundation of this method lies in the recognition of the fundamental human need "to be understood and to be aided in the search to fulfill personal values and goals" in a community with others.

Students work in small groups seated in a circle with the teacher sitting outside the circle. The learning process consists of five phases that guide the students to the point where they and the teacher interact freely in the target language, offering corrections and stylistic improvements on what is being said.

7. *Psycho-generative method.* This method was developed at the University of Northern Iowa. It teaches grammatical structures inductively within certain frames of references. The approach is primarily oral; it stresses high frequency vocabulary and grammatical structures through situational questioning.

8. *"Silent way."* It was developed by British mathematician and psychologist Caleb Gattegno. Visual aids (e.g., colored rods) are very important in this method. Used in specific ways, these aids lead students to language production and to inductive insights about linguistic patterns of the target language.

The target language is used exclusively in class. Students take greater responsibility for their own learning. Their creativity in developing original utterances from minimal vocabulary and aid is stressed. This method is used at Earlham College, Richmond, Indiana, among other institutions.

9. *Suggestology (the Lozanov method).* Suggestology originated in Bulgaria under the direction of physician and psychotherapist Georgi Lozanov. This method aims to put students in a mentally relaxed state, which is to make them more receptive to language learning.

It uses the target language exclusively during classroom review practice. New material is presented in context of practical and interesting dialogues with grammatical explanations and translations in the mother tongue. Through specific environmental settings (decorations, music, etc.) and readings by the teacher of new materials in various modes, memorization takes place via unconscious absorption of vocabulary.

Methods (*cont.*)

10.   *Total physical response method.* This method was developed by psychologist James Asher. The premise of the response method is that listening comprehension should be developed before stressing active oral performance and that "the assimilation of information and skills can be significantly accelerated through use of the kinesthetic sensory system."

The method uses oral commands that are carried out by students, showing that the directions were understood. Understanding should be developed through movements of the student's body.

How to Set Up a Course Outline

Course outlines should divide the course into discrete modules or units. Teachers retain outlines for their own use and hand out the simple course syllabus. For each unit, the outline should state:

1.   the new learning objectives with items for review
2.   specific teaching strategies appropriate for the grammar items being taught and reviewed
3.   evaluation methods, especially those that permit students to verify their own and one another's understanding and growing mastery of the unit lessons
4.   experiential materials, such as games, films, tapes, slides, computer programs, interviews or guest presentations, and trips

Sample Questions for Midsemester Evaluations

1.   This course is/is not fulfilling my expectations because . . .
2.   The best feature(s) of the course so far has (have) been . . .
3.   This course would be better if . . .
4.   In general, my reaction to the _____ books has been . . .
     I found the grammar book to be . . .
     the worksheets to be . . .
5.   As for my progress in this course, I . . .
6.   I think that assignments . . .
7.   My professor's attitude to the class as a group is . . .
8.   I feel that the teacher's treatment of me as an individual is . . .
9.   When I talk about this class to other people, I often tell them . . .
10.   In conclusion, I would like to say that . . .

Entry Testing

One age-old testing problem faced by FL departments involves placement. Students who want an easy grade either place themselves at the 101 level despite years of adequate second language training or purposely fail to disclose their ability on the placement test. Three measures have been tried at institutions:

1. The program can be designed so that students gain additional credit if they take a course above the elementary level: one credit for a B or two additional credits for an A in a second-semester-level course. Three additional credits are given for an A or B in intermediate-level courses. This obviously encourages students to place themselves where they belong. Students pay for the earned credit hours.

2. The department can reserve the right to deny credit to students whose performance in a 101 class indicated significant prior language experience. Students may remain at the lower level but do so at the risk of receiving no credit or reduced credit.

3. The department can design a course for students who have studied the language but need review. This method helps both students who have been away from language study for several years and those who fear that their language training was inadequate.

Group Interviews

The faculty member asks three to five students to come in for a twenty- to thirty-minute conversation on subjects studied in the course. Students can prepare vocabulary, review their course materials for the selected chapters or subjects, and even meet together beforehand. They should come prepared to speak and to ask two questions of their classmates. This enables the teacher to create a more natural conversation. The test can occur at any time in the last two weeks of class. Faculty who teach more than one hundred students in a semester will find interviews a strain on their already burdensome schedule. At the rate of five students a half hour, these faculty will spend over ten hours in oral testing. More than five hours each week in oral testing in the last two weeks may prove too much of an effort. Faculty teaching fewer than one hundred students should find interviews feasible. Oral testing is a great motivator for both faculty and students.

TEACHING CULTURE BETTER

In teaching culture, I encourage students to do independent work in the library. Each class should, in fact, meet once in the library near the beginning of each semester. The librarian, given advance notice, will probably delight in showing students relevant elements of the collection. I send the librarian a copy of the culture capsule I will use with the students so that the library staff will be prepared to help them find the materials they need. (See culture insert, pp. 14–17.) In the first year, students often do some or all of this work in English as part of weekend assignments. As they are able, they begin to write in the target language. I permit rewrites on the same basis as I do with my other writing assignments. As the student rewrites each draft, I strike out the previous grade and note the new grade. When possible, FL courses, even elementary sections, should be paired with social science or humanities courses related to the culture where the target language is spoken.

Scholars have produced excellent work on teaching culture in the past ten years. Howard Nostrand's "Emergent Model" is a leading example (*Contemporary French Civilization,* 2 [Winter 1978], 277–94). Ned Seelye's book, *Teaching Culture* (Skokie, Ill.: National Textbook, 1974), will appeal to those who prefer a more behaviorist approach. Genelle Morain and Rebecca Valette have made fine contributions. Departments might want to consider a year-long project in which faculty meet every two weeks to discuss ways to improve the teaching of culture in the FL curriculum: the focus could be on reading and reviewing the work of scholars in the field, demonstration classes taught by and to faculty, and the development of teaching materials. FLL faculty have received a serious charge to assume partial responsibility for widening students' cultural perceptions.

Using the list of identifiable universals (see p. 14) and a list of areas of the world where the target language is spoken, the teacher simply assigns or lets students choose a culture capsule subject. Students do the library research using social science research materials, documents from the United Nations, and articles in the current press. Like all writing assignments, the capsules should be rewritten until they reflect the students' best work. I suggest that faculty tell students that the information they are collecting is important and that the capsules go into a permanent departmental file to help future students learn about world cultures. I also stress how important good bibliographies are to next year's classes. This tactic makes students see their work not simply as a school exercise but as an important part of a larger effort that others will benefit from.

(See Howard Nostrand's article, p. 000, and the ACTFL Stepladder Project, p. 184.)

Suggestions for Improving the Teaching of Culture

IDENTIFIABLE UNIVERSALS

A checklist for organizing the study of human cultures

Material Culture
- a. Food
- b. Clothing and Adornment of the Body
- c. Tools and Weapons
- d. Housing and Shelter
- e. Transportation
- f. Personal Possessions
- g. Household Articles

The Arts, Play and Recreation
- a. Forms of the Arts, Play and Recreation
- b. Folk Arts and Fine Arts
- c. Standards of Beauty and Taste

Language and Nonverbal Communication
- a. Nonverbal Communication
- b. Language

Social Organization
- a. Societies
- b. Families
- c. Kinship Systems

Social Control
- a. Systems and Governmental Institutions
- b. Rewards and Punishments

Conflict and Warfare
- a. Kinds of Conflict
- b. Kinds of Warfare

Economic Organization
- a. Systems of Trade and Exchange
- b. Producing and Manufacturing
- c. Property
- d. Division of Labor
- e. Standard of Living

Education
- a. Informal Education
- b. Formal Education

World View
- a. Belief System
- b. Religion

SOURCE: "Global Responsibility: The Role of the Foreign Language Teacher," *Northeast Conference Reports, Foreign Language and International Studies: Toward Cooperation and Integration,* ed. Thomas H. Geno (Middlebury, Vt.: Northeast Conference, 1981), p. 72.

TEACHING CULTURE THROUGH INDEPENDENT STUDY

A. Use the list of identifiable universals to select topics or to suggest other topics that demand more complex analysis. Examples:
  1. kinship relations; family, age, sexes
  2. definition of the hero/heroine
  3. definition of the good
  4. uses of time
  5. regard for work
  6. modes of verifiability or ways of determining truth
  7. concept of progress

B. Have students at all levels prepare culture capsules/assignments.

   Elementary level: Two or three capsules a semester. They should be shared at the end of the semester. English *may* be used in the first semester or term.

   Intermediate level: Four or five capsules with a short summary paper. Target language should be used.

   Advanced level: Four or five capsules. Have the students work in peer groups to develop a project covering either one topic through different cultures speaking the same language or various topics on one culture or country.

SOURCE: *Northeast Conference*, p. 72.

SAMPLE CULTURE CAPSULE

A writing-research assignment for use in foreign language and culture classes. The length of the capsule section will vary from a paragraph to several pages depending on class level.

Topic:
Country:
Geographical Region—climate, terrain, neighboring countries:
Economy—dependencies, growth rate:
Ethnic Diversity:
Population Density:
Political Status:
Languages Spoken:
Religion:
Signal Features:

Capsule: (specify topic chosen from the list of identifiable universals, p. 14.)

Bibliography:
For further information, consult:

[Students should do drafts for the teachers' and classmates' reviews and evaluations.]

SAMPLE TEST OF CULTURAL UNDERSTANDING
(to be included on final course exams at elementary and intermediate levels)

Answer one of the following questions in a three- or four-paragraph essay.

1. Describe family structures in any black African country you choose. Name the country and describe its geographical area. You may wish to mention facts about male-female relations, regard for old-age, responsibilities of mother and father to family life, education of children, and so forth.

2. In what black Hispanic culture would you most like to live? Describe what you consider its most important features? How is it different from American black culture as you know it? How is it similar? Why does it appeal to you? What are its strong and weak points? What special contribution could these people offer the world community?

3. Compare any two black Hispanic cultures with which you are familiar. What are the most important features of each one? How does each culture show the value it places on work? on religion? Contrast any pieces of art or literature that you know come from these cultures. How is each culture unique? What do they share?

SAMPLE TESTS INTEGRATING LANGUAGE AND CULTURE SKILLS

The following tests not only exercise students' reading, writing, and comprehension skills but also test students' ability to use the language creatively and to write in coherent paragraphs.

Students should of course have class practice and homework practice on each kind of question to be given on a test. Tests should both tell the teacher what students have learned and provide an opportunity for students to show off their growing language skills.

Hour Test 1—First-Semester FLL Course

1. Dictation   (7 minutes)

2. Reading: Read the following paragraph and write a three-sentence summary of it in good English.   (8 minutes)

3. Fill in the blanks in the following paragraph.   (20 minutes)
   (Paragraph with grammar and vocabulary fill-ins for students to do. This is the major part of the test and contains perhaps twenty blanks. Teachers may prefer two shorter paragraphs.)

4. In a short paragraph in English, explain what you have learned about family relationships in Haiti (or Martinique or whatever country students have studied).
                                                                                        (10 minutes)

Hour Test 2—First-Semester FLL Course

1. Dictation   (7 minutes)

2. Reading and Writing   (30 minutes)
   Fill in the blanks in the following essay. Use the most appropriate grammar and vocabulary. Be sure you understand the meaning of the paragraph. Then in complete sentences in (foreign language) answer the five questions at the end of this page. These questions will help you show that you understand tha paragraph.

   (The essay should consist of several paragraphs about the culture of a people who speak the language being studied. It may be two hundred words long and have thirty blanks. Students may need a vocabulary list if there are new words.)

   Questions in the FL (to be answered in the FL)
   1.
   2.
   3.
   4.   (10 minutes)
   5.

Hour Test 3—First-Semester FLL Course

1. Dictation   (10 minutes)

2. Essay fill-in (shorter than test 2 but similar in format)   (15 minutes)

3. Create a story (guided composition):
   I have begun a story, indicating the first words of some sentences. Complete these sentences using correct syntax. You will find a list of vocabulary (without English translation) to help inspire you. Make sense and use your new language creatively.   (25 minutes)

   I am an executive from Haiti.
   Today I _____ New York.
   I _____ .
   Americans often _____ .
   In Haiti, _____ .
   My family _____ .

READING LIST

Another good teaching practice is to give students a long-range reading list to accompany the course syllabus. Required reading lists and suggested readings have long been a part of syllabi in intermediate and advanced courses. I believe, however, that all course outlines should include readings, even elementary language courses. The long-range reading list should contain articles and books and perhaps names of journals that students could refer to profitably after the course is over—possibly even when they are permanently ensconced in their careers. I often tell my students to put the long-range reading list with their tax records or anywhere they would be likely to discover it in the future. With this list I wish to imply my belief that their capacity to read and profit from texts in their second language will endure. I create a link for students between their present and future intellectual lives. I indicate my expectation that regardless of their career orientation some texts will remain significant to them as educated persons. This practice takes little time and has important implications for the FL study and for students' humanities education.

SUMMARY

Good teaching is the single most important factor in building enrollments and strengthening departments. Creating better language proficiency in class and increasing the intellectual content in elementary and intermediate FL courses will both have a positive effect on enrollments. At Western Maryland College, William Cipolla has found that many students from the intensive French courses go on to major and minor in the language. They feel *able* to do so with success. I have long felt that the language class unnecessarily frustrates students. It is true that they are more conscious than younger children are of losing their personalities, senses of humor, and self-confidence when they must check their native language at the door and wade into childishness to express themselves. I encourage faculty to mitigate some of this frustration by giving weekend assignments of significant readings in English on the cultures of the peoples who speak the target language. These assignments create an intellectual context for the daily work and give students material that is more sophisticated and more easily read than texts in the foreign language. The readings compete intellectually with the students' assignments for other courses, thus helping to close the gap in sophistication of content between the FL course and other courses. The students may also become more interested in the people and cultures being studied in the language class.

Another way to raise the intellectual level of the class is to commit students to more frequent reading and writing assignments. As part of the FL teachers' program to improve general English literacy, such assignments help students appreciate the broader advantages of the course.

Many schools with language requirements do not have higher enrollments in postrequirement courses than do similar schools without language requirements. When so many students are exposed to the subject and faculty, one might expect more of them to go on to advanced course work. Of course, students have many obligations to fulfill—in basic educational requirements and in their majors. Let us assume, though, that most institutions could add even a ten percent enrollment increase to their postrequirement courses by improving language proficiency levels achieved by students and by creating more dynamic FL courses. Students would pursue FL studies because they chose to and because the FLL faculty would be doing their jobs with more vigor, interest, and appeal. Most important, there would be a higher-quality curriculum. (See pp. 9–11 for a synopsis of current FL teaching methods; see also ch. 4, "Curricular Change," and Earl Stevick's book *Teaching Language: A Way and Ways* [Rowley, Mass.: Newbury, 1980], for a most insightful review of approaches to teaching foreign languages.)

Curriculum Revisions

A curriculum that meets students' needs and builds on faculty strengths can greatly improve enrollments. Theodore Higgs' recent publication will help departments whose curriculum is out-of-date. Curriculum design concerns both structure and content of course offerings. Revisions must of course be based on the faculty's professional determination of what constitutes an appropriate course of study in their institution for their students. (See ch. 2 for ways to determine appropriate curriculum.)

(See Theodore V. Higgs, ed., *Curriculum, Competence, and the Foreign Language Teacher* [Skokie, Ill.: National Textbook, 1982].)

STRUCTURAL CHANGE IN CURRICULA

Variable content–variable credit courses. These courses are designed to accompany the elementary and intermediate language sequence. The course meets once a week for one class period with one instructor and eight to ten students. A variety of games and learning activities fit into the course format. (See Games insert, pp. 22–26.) For more advanced levels, faculty make photocopies of articles from foreign publications, gloss the texts for difficult vocabulary or turns of phrase, and give glossed copies to students to read and discuss in the conversation class. The advanced course could be established to follow one of the core business courses or a popular social science course. In that case, the texts chosen should relate to the subject under study.

Proficiency maintenance courses. Versions of the variable credit courses should be available for students who have finished the early language sequence and who wish a "low cost" way to maintain their language proficiency. These courses demand no heavy homework assignments but permit students to remain in contact with the FL faculty and other students who are interested in languages. The only prerequisite is evidence of past enrollments in an FL course.

When Sidney Pellissier began these courses at Purdue University, he arranged one section to be taken after first-year FL, another to be taken after the second year, and a third to be taken after requirements. The first time it was offered, he expected nine students to sign up. Ninety enrolled. Nine sections were necessary.

When a student has taken two or three of these courses and has an elective course slot open in a given semester, the student is much more likely to attempt an introduction to French literature or a Latin American culture and civilization course in the FL department than if the student's last contact with the FL department occurred three or four semesters before. This technique is pedagogically sound, helps students maintain FL proficiency whether or not they take the advanced-level course later, and does in fact build enrollments.

Modular courses. In some institutions modular courses work well. For instance, three one-credit courses on introduction to the francophone world can form one well-integrated course that could easily be subdivided into discrete units: (1) France, (2) the Caribbean, and (3) Africa. The course might also be subdivided into (1) Paris, (2) three provinces, and (3) the French-speaking world outside France. A student could take the entire three-sequence course or just one part of it. Modular courses in introduction to business in Germany might subdivide into (1) banking, (2) marketing, and (3) diplomacy and government service. As enrollments increase, the department might offer regular three-credit courses in any one of the modules. Non-foreign-language majors can choose one of the units and try out the language course with less fear of failure than a full course commitment entails. In addition, some students could take one module as an extra course by arranging the module during a less demanding segment of the semester.

Pairing with non-FL courses. FL courses can be scheduled back to back with related non-FL courses. For example, a Latin American history course at 10:00 A.M. might precede a Spanish course on contemporary issues in Latin America or perhaps on the contemporary Latin American press. Readings could be chosen from such journals as *L'Economista* or *Excelsior.* The readings can be glossed for difficult vocabulary or syntactical arrangements before copies are handed out to students. A European history course might be matched with a one-credit conversation course designed on the modular or maintenance structure. For instance, if enrollments justified the arrangement, a one-credit Spanish course might meet Mondays following the history class meeting; the French course could meet Wednesdays, and the German course Fridays. Students in each FL section could read some short selection from a document related to the week's readings in the history course. Discussion of the course topics in the foreign language would reinforce students' work in the history course as well as help students maintain their contact with their second language. After some experimentation, faculty teaching the history course and the conversation courses should meet to discuss ways that the readings assigned in the FL courses could be placed on an optional reading list in the history course. Richard Lambert ("Language Learning and Language Utilization," *ADFL Bulletin,* 13, No. 1 [Sept. 1981], 7) has wisely noted that often the only place in the curriculum where students see a need for knowledge of a foreign language is in the FL classroom. Course pairing and shared reading lists offer excellent ways for faculty to indicate the interrelatedness of liberal studies and the importance of foreign languages to the rest of students' education.

The kind of piggybacking described above can work with many courses already being taught. Some faculty teaching the non–foreign language course may wish to attend the FL conversation section and certainly should be invited to do so. Faculty outside the FL department often have little occasion to keep up their language skills and value such opportunities. Course pairing costs nothing to administer and requires little extra work for FL faculty. In fact, instead of the courses being taught on overload, faculty can often be allowed to accumulate three such units over a certain number of semesters and then be credited with having taught a full course; following the completion of the three courses, they can take a "course release." Enrollments in the three courses taken together (at nine or ten students each) may even surpass the average departmental course enrollment figures. Faculty members could benefit from the lighter course load that this system would provide by doing further course development work, by taking a new course, or by doing research. Here again, designs for enrollment building serve students and faculty and make sense in the general design of the curriculum in the institution.

Pairing with composition courses. In another form of course pairing the English department can be brought closer to the FL department through a comparative composition course. Foreign language and English faculty should work together to create a common approach to the acquisition of writing skills. Elaine Maimon's work in writing across the curriculum combines well with my own efforts in this area. (See Bibliography at the end of the book.) Writing well is not basically a language-specific skill. It involves attention to the word, the sentence, the paragraph, the whole unit. Looked at and in fact taught from this perspective, composition skill development becomes a natural common ground for FL and English faculty. The two departments can often join forces in the effort to develop students' competency in writing. In some schools, a mandatory two-semester composition course requirement stipulates that students must take one semester in English but allows them to take the other either in English or in a foreign language. (See "Teaching Writing in the Foreign Language Curriculum," p. 151.)

One-Credit Conversation Courses

Some institutions have developed one-credit conversation courses to help students develop oral skills while they are taking foreign language courses or after they have completed their foreign language courses. In the first case, students have an extra chance to use their second language; in the second, they have the opportunity to maintain some contact with their second language. These courses also help students use the language with more confidence, keep them in touch with the foreign language department, and may influence them to fill in an elective course slot with a foreign language course in their junior or senior years.

FORMAT

There are eight to ten students in the course, probably enrolled on a pass-fail basis. The teacher chooses an authentic text that has been glossed for difficult vocabulary or construction. Current pieces of journalism are usually most useful and stimulating. Students read the text in class with the teacher and discuss it together in the foreign language. Controversial topics work very well. The teacher may give out next week's text in class, but students probably should not have homework assignments. Class may last one or two hours, may meet once or twice a week, and may include students of varying ability. Generally it works to have a first level for students with elementary training, a second for those with intermediate training, and a third for those no longer taking foreign language courses. (See pp. 19–20.)

Games

In January 1981 the Modern Foreign Language Department of High Point College, a small private liberal arts college in High Point, North Carolina, began a series of one-hour elementary conversation courses in French, German, and Spanish. These courses, taken concurrently with the second semester of language study, intend to afford the student maximum opportunity to converse in the language, and hence enrollments do not exceed ten students.

To encourage spontaneous and creative conversation, the atmosphere of the class is relaxed, somewhat unstructured, and activity oriented. The teacher's preparation for the class is, however, very structured, with activities designed to elicit the vocabulary and reinforce the grammar being taught in the regular three-hour beginning language course.

What follows is a description of those activities that have been most successful at High Point College. Some of them, "games" if you will, are the result of informal chats about the classes. Most, however, have been borrowed from other sources, such as the Instructor's Manual to John Rassias' *Le Français, Depart-Arrivée* (New York: Harper and Row, 1980) and the student teaching assistants at Earlham College in Indiana. Most of the activities are done in pairs or small groups, and no activity is pursued longer than ten minutes. In many games, pairs or teams compete with each other or against the clock. Winners receive sticks of gum or jelly beans.

VOCABULARY-ORIENTED GAMES

1. Password: Each student takes a partner, and the students place their desks so that partners face each other, one student (a) facing away from the blackboard and the other (b) facing it. The instructor writes a list of five to seven words on

Games (*cont.*)

the board, and (b) explains the first word to (a) until (a) can guess the word. (b) then proceeds to the next word, and so on. When the students have finished the list, (a) changes places with (b), and the procedure is repeated with a new list of words. This game works well when it is played competitively with a strict time limit.

2. Opposites: The instructor has prepared on a large poster a list of unrelated words in the target language. On another poster is a list of the opposites of these words in a different order. The instructor points out a word, and the student finds its opposite. This game can be played with teams and a scorekeeper.

"CONTROLLED" EXPRESSION

1. What's my line?: The instructor gives the students a mimeographed list of jobs and their definitions and another list of questions that can be used to ask about someone's job. The students take partners, and the instructor gives student (a) a three-by-five card with the name of a job on one side and the words "what's my job?" on the other side, both written in the target language. Student (b) asks (a) questions (only those with yes or no answers) until (b) is able to guess the job. Alternative: (a) gives clues to (b) until (b) discovers the job.

2. Pantomime quiz: Students are in pairs. Student (a) receives a three-by-five card with a verbal description of an action (e.g., "Je me brosse les dents"); (a) then pantomimes the action until (b) discovers it (and says, "Vous vous brossez les dents").

3. Who am I?: The instructor describes someone in the class until the students guess who it is. The students then take partners and follow the same procedure demonstrated by the instructor.

4. What am I?: The instructor shows the class a picture with vocabulary already familiar to the students. One student chooses a person or object from the picture. The other students ask "yes/no" questions until they can guess what the student has identified.

5. Directions: The instructor gives the students mimeographed city maps, having all the buildings and streets labeled. With an established point of departure the instructor gives directions to a location (without naming it); the students must follow the directions and call out the location when the description is finished. The students then take partners and proceed in one of two ways: (1) (a) asks (b) how to get to X, and (b) gives the directions; (2) (a) gives a point of departure, then directions to an unnamed destination, and (b) guesses the destination.

"FREE" EXPRESSION

1. Interview: Students are in groups of two. (a) interviews (b) and writes down the information given. Then (a) talks to the class about (b), based on the information he noted. Students then switch roles.

2. Themes: The instructor has written settings on large pieces of paper and five or ten minutes before class has taped them to the blackboard. On entering the classroom, the instructor asks a student to choose any topic and give two or three sentences that might be heard in that setting (e.g., restaurant, hotel, soirée de dance).

Games (*cont.*)

3. Open-ended sentences: The instructor starts a sentence, and the students shout out any logical end to the sentence.

4. Variable comments: The instructor gives a sentence, and the students give any appropriate comment or answer.

5. At the flea market: Students are in pairs. Student (a) wants to sell something (an article of clothing, a book, a desk, etc.) to (b) and gives as many reasons as possible to convince (b) of the value of the article. Alternative: The instructor brings articles to class and creates a specialty store, such as a kitchen store, a clothing store, a sports store.

6. Picture series description: The instructor brings a series of related pictures that convey an obvious story (in the manner of a comic strip). The students choose partners and take five minutes to write appropriate dialogues for the scenes. Then they read the dialogues to the class. These dialogues are usually humorous and enjoyable.

7. Sketchalog: Students are grouped in twos, (a) having his or her back to the blackboard and (b) facing the board. Another student draws a sketch on the board, and (b) describes it to (a), who must draw the scene according to the description given.

8. Catch-a-story: Students stand in a circle. The instructor gives the first sentence or so of a story and pitches a tennis ball to a student at random. This student then adds a sentence to the story and pitches the ball to another student, who does likewise, and so on.

9. Picture story: The instructor gives each student a picture, taken from a magazine. The students are given five minutes and asked to write a story (not a mere description of the picture) in which the picture is one scene. The students then show their pictures and tell their stories to the rest of the class.

STICK GAMES

The sticks used here are Algebrics (available from Educational Solutions, 80 Fifth Ave., N.Y., NY 10003). These rectangular sticks come in various sizes and colors. They stimulate and facilitate creative expression by giving students something concrete with which to work.

1. Preposition game: Students are in pairs. The instructor gives both members of each pair duplicate sticks. Student (a) sets up his sticks and hides the arrangement from (b) with a paper or book. (a) then describes the placement to (b) and watches as (b) places his or her sticks until (a)'s has been exactly duplicated.

2. Construct-a-city: Students may work in pairs or alone. Each student takes various sticks and constructs a city. The student then describes the city to the class, naming the buildings and roads, giving reasons for their placement, and so on. (This activity is also successful done on the blackboard).

3. Traffic problem: Pairs or alone. Students take various sticks and design a traffic situation, such as a collision, a traffic jam, or a right-of-way problem. The student then explains the situation to the class.

4. My dream house: Pairs or alone. Using the sticks, students create their dream houses, which they then describe to the class.

Games (*cont.*)

5. Additional scenes: Students can use the sticks to create many other scenes, such as inside the supermarket, on the beach, at the hotel, at the discothèque, taking a trip.

In all these games the instructor becomes an animator and observer, helping when necessary, and giving encouragement and praise while listening. Students become very excited, enjoy the competition, and are generally reluctant to leave the classroom. The goal of these courses is communication, not perfection, and grammar is therefore not stressed. Such an atmosphere naturally enhances the creative process and produces rewarding experiences for both students and teachers.

While most of the activities stress meaningful communication, some are designed to improve understanding of grammatical points.

GRAMMAR GAMES

1. Verb games: Teams of two or three students have cards with ten infinitives on them. After each infinitive a subject and a tense is indicated. Each group puts the verbs in the designated tenses with the subjects given. This game is run as a contest to see which team finishes first with the correct answers. There is a strict time limit. At the end the teacher goes over the answers and announces winning teams.

2. Tense recognition: The class is divided into two groups for a "Verb Bee." The teacher has a corpus of five-by-seven cards with verbs conjugated in different tenses. Each team gets points for identifying the tense. The teacher can also check for meaning as well. At the end of the time limit, the team with the most correct responses wins.

3. Relative pronoun game: The format is similar to the first verb game. Each group of two or three students has a card with ten sentences in which the relative pronouns have been deleted. Students compete to finish first with the correct responses.

4. Objet: The game is based on Bingo; the cards have five columns and one free space in the middle. Each space is filled by one of the many configurations of direct object pronouns, indirect object pronouns, adverbial pronouns, including the configurations for the affirmative commands. The teacher has a separate group of three-by-five cards with sentences using these pronouns. They are tossed in a box and called out one by one. The student who fills the spaces calls out "Object" and verifies the pronouns. As a review tool this game can be played a little differently. The teacher reads out the entire sentence and the student must decide which pronouns would be used.

5. Object pronoun Christmas activities: There is a packet of activities that work with the indirect object. In one, the students are asked to create their own versions of the "twelve Days of Christmas" using the target language version of "... my true love gave to me." A second activity in this packet is to make up a Christmas gift list following this model in target language: Je lui donne deux disques parce qu'il aime danser. "To my brother I will give two records because he likes to dance." A third activity is to make New Year's resolutions. A fourth is to teach seasonal carols.

Games (*cont.*)

6. "Binder" games: There are a set of notebooks arranged with three-by-five cards to work on different grammar points. The students, in groups of two or three, flip through the cards to form correct sentences.

   Relative pronoun binder game: three groups of cards on rings: beginnings of sentences; relative pronouns; relative clause. The students are given two relative pronouns to work with and can choose a third in a ten-minute period. The teacher circulates as the groups work. Correct sentences are put on the board and discussed at the end of the time limit.

   Other binder games that work in the same fashion are the direct-indirect object game, the partitive game, and the interrogative adjective-pronoun game.

OTHER VOCABULARY-ORIENTED GAMES

1. Grid game. The teacher draws a three-by-three-feet grid on the board. Categories are placed across the top and letters down the side. The students in groups of two or three work to complete the grid in five minutes. There are many possibilities, and the groups like to find different answers.

2. "After the hurricane": Each group has a sheet with five or six store names on it. Under each store are listed ten items. But there has been a hurricane, and all the merchandise is in the wrong stores. The groups have five to ten minutes to put the items back where they belong.

3. Live sentences: This is an icebreaker. It can be used with different grammatical structures as well as with vocabulary items. The teacher has written each word of a sentence on a five-by-seven card and passed the cards out to a group. There may be two or three groups. Each group tries to put its sentence together first.

4. Picture game: Each student or group of students has a picture to describe to the class in story form. The pictures reflect the vocabulary lesson being done in the regular class.

5. Pass-photo: Students are in groups of two. One student holds a card with a famous person's picture on it and gives clues to the other student, who tries to guess who the person is. At the end of the time limit whichever group has guessed the most wins.

6. "The ideal voyage": Students are in groups of two. Each traveler must pick a destination from a box. The travel agent praises the country in detail to make the traveler want to go there. The traveler must in turn ask pertinent questions.

These games were developed by Carole Head and Barbara Long, Modern Foreign Language Department, High Point College, High Point, NC 27262. For additional suggestions, see bibliography, p. 312.

CONTENT CHANGE IN CURRICULUM

The world of language. Another excellent way to build enrollments in FL programs is to create a "flagship" course. The course need not be part of the foreign language requirement. It introduces students to concepts related to language, touching on the history of human language, etymology, other codes that convey meaning, problems and challenges posed by language, and animal and machine communication. (See Claud DuVerlie and

Alan S. Rosenthal, "How to Prosper during a Foreign Language Crisis," *ADFL Bulletin,* 12, No. 1 [Sept. 1980], 17.) For further information on course design, write Chair, Dept. of Modern Languages and Linguistics, University of Maryland, Catonsville, MD 21228.

The flagship course may enroll fifty or sixty students and may be team-taught with significant use of films. Once attracted to the department through this course, students may elect to study a foreign language. The heavier enrollments in the flagship course boost departmental figures and help support smaller enrollments in other courses. The course itself fills an important educational need by teaching students about the nature and function of language.

Career-oriented language courses. The current interest in business and computer science courses has stimulated a fine response from the language profession. Many FLL programs include a career language track. Excellent materials are available to support the teaching of these courses. As an NEH consultant, I have helped set up multicultural studies and international business programs. They can be designed in a number of ways (see International Business insert, pp. 29–31, and Multicultural Studies insert, pp. 32–33), but the essential elements are a business background, a foreign language proficiency, and a set of elective humanities courses related to world affairs with an area studies concentration. Business department chairmen sometimes welcome the chance to broaden their programs. I explain it using a diagram.

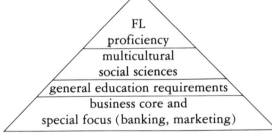

For the business major with a special focus in management, advertising, banking, or computer science, the course load and primary course work remain almost unchanged. A careful selection from among courses being taught at the college forms the multicultural unit. Some of these courses will have a global focus: world history, world religions, international relations. Others will take an area focus appropriate to the language the student chooses: Latin American history, economic development in the Hispanic world, or Latin American geography. These courses satisfy most general education requirements and improve the student's global perspectives. Finally, the language courses should offer business-specific preparation after the elementary level (see Bibliography insert, p. 34). Courses in writing as well as conversation should aim students toward an ACTFL-ETS proficiency of advanced plus. (See ACTFL Proficiency Guidelines, pp. 184–194, for details.) The writing course should use methods that reinforce English composition skills (see my article, pp. 151–52). A work experience in the summer in a multilingual or bilingual setting, either in the United States or abroad, will further strengthen the student's language proficiency and understanding of a variety of cultures.

The academic integrity of such a program is easy to defend. The brochure designed to advertise the program ought to explain how the course of study relates to the broad-based thinking and problem-solving skills that employers value. It should also stress the proficiency in English and FL communication skills that employers so often find lacking. The area studies focus creates some links between elective courses and required general education courses, which together often constitute a grab bag.

While business remains a principal career direction for FL students, other professions also appeal to students. Many departments now offer Spanish designed for medical and health personnel, social workers, and law and justice program trainees. These offerings provide important career advantages and also help professionals to serve the public with more compassion and intelligence. Besides language proficiency, these programs, like the rest of the FL curriculum, should focus on imparting significant cultural understanding. (See Howard Nostrand's article, p. 172.)

REVISIONS OF MAJOR PROGRAMS

Curricula in many institutions now permit a major in "modern languages." It consists of a dual language proficiency combined either with business or with education minors. Many students will find it easier to secure employment with two languages and an adjacent skill.

As more high schools and grammar schools return gradually to more significant FLL offerings, job applicants with dual language skills, teaching certificates, and the capability to run a learning resource center will be very appealing. Students would take the following kinds of course in *two* languages. (Students should attain ACTFL-ETS proficiency of Level 3 in one language and "advanced" in the other.)

Elementary and intermediate conversation courses

Culture courses

Pedagogy courses

Professional options language courses (business, health science, law, etc.)

Phonetics courses

Word elements (etymology) courses

Audiovisual internship

Apprentice teacher at college under supervision

Study-abroad experience

In one or both languages, two courses in advanced reading on culture, literature, or linguistics

International Business with a Humanities Approach
Frances Hoch

The Modern Foreign Language Department and the School of Business at High Point College, a small private college in central North Carolina, have developed an interdisciplinary program in international business with a humanities approach. Aided by a consultant grant from the National Endowment for the Humanities, the pilot program was in Spanish and was followed by a similar program in French. The Spanish curriculum represents a cooperative effort of the entire college, combining a core of general business courses, twelve hours of Spanish beyond the intermediate level (including one course in business Spanish), and fifteen hours of supporting courses selected from history, literature, geography, economics, political science, religion, and cultural anthropology. Moreover, in the senior year students participate in a seminar to bring together all areas in a culminating experience.

This program should be of interest to other small colleges for the following reasons:

1. It uses the existing college curriculum and gives the student a strong humanities background in accordance with the liberal arts tradition.

2. It was instituted with virtually no additional expenditure of money.

3. It received strong support from all areas of the college, including the administration, because everyone took part in the planning process from the beginning.

4. It uses community resources through the organization of an advisory committee of local leaders in international business, particularly in textiles, furniture, and finance. They will advise on the curriculum, help in finding internships for students, and may participate in an actual course on international marketing and finance at no charge to the college.

B.S. in Business Administration
with a Concentration in Multinational Studies

Business Core:
    Economics 207–208—Principles of Economics
    Economics 317—Statistics
    B.A. 203–204—Principles of Accounting
    B.A. 311—Marketing
    B.A. 321—Management
    B.A. 301–302—Business Law
    B.A. 351—Administrative Communications

Foreign Language Core:
    Spanish/French 223—Conversation
    Spanish/French 226—Civilization
    Spanish/French 312—Advanced Grammar
    Spanish/French 318—Business Spanish or French

Senior Seminar in Multinational Studies

BS in Business Administration (*cont.*)

Supporting Courses:

Three hours in literature: either English 215–216 or literature in the foreign language

Twelve hours from the following:

      Economics 243—Comparative Systems

      Economics 346—International Economics

      History 171—The World in the Twentieth Century

      History 222—Latin American History

      Political Science 101—U.S. Government

      Geography 101—Political and Regional Geography

      Sociology 205—Cultural Anthropology

Suggested four-year curriculum for B.S. in business administration with a concentration in multinational studies (beginning with Spanish or French 101)

Freshman Year

First sem.	Hrs.	Second sem.	Hrs.
English 101	3	English 102	3
Economics 207	3	Economics 208	3
Sp./Fr. 101	3	Sp./Fr. 102	3
Religion	3	Math 131	3
Elective	3	Elective	3
P.E.	1	P.E.	1
	16		16

Sophomore Year

First sem.	Hrs.	Second sem.	Hrs.
Sp./Fr. 201	3	Sp./Fr. 202	3
B.A. 203	3	B.S. 204	3
B.A. 311	3	Support course	3
Support course	3	Support course	3
Nat. Sci. or math	3 or 4	Elective	3
	15 or 16		15

Junior Year

First sem.	Hrs.	Second sem.	Hrs.
B.A. 321	3	Econ. 317	3
B.A. 301	3	B.A. 302	3
Sp./Fr. 223 or 226	3	Sp./Fr. 312 or 318	3
Support course	3	Literature	3
Elective	3	Elective	3
		Elective	1 or 2
	15		15 or 16

Senior Year

First sem.	Hrs.	Second sem.	Hrs.
B.A. 351	3	Seminar	3
Sp./Fr. 223 or 226	3	Sp./Fr. 312 or 318	3
Elective	3	Elective	3
Elective	3	Elective	3
Elective	3	Elective	3
	15		15

BS in Business Administration (*cont.*)

Suggested four-year curriculum for B.S. in business administration with a concentration in multinational studies (beginning with Spanish or French 201)

Freshman Year

First sem.	Hrs.		Second sem.	Hrs.
English 101	3		English 102	3
Economics 207	3		Economics 208	3
Sp./Fr. 201	3		Sp./Fr. 202	3
Religion	3		Math 131	3
Elective	3		Elective	3
P.E.	1		P.E.	1
	16			16

Sophomore Year

	Hrs.			Hrs.
Sp./Fr. 223 or 226	3		Sp./Fr. 312 or 318	3
B.A. 203	3		B.S. 204	3
B.A. 311	3		Literature	3
Support course	3		Support course	3
Nat. Sci. or math	3 or 4		Elective	3
	15 or 16			15

Junior Year

	Hrs.			Hrs.
Sp./Fr. 223 or 226	3		Sp./Fr. 312 or 318	3
B.A. 301	3		B.A. 302	3
B.A. 321	3		Econ. 317	3
Support course	3		Support course	3
Elective	3		Elective	3
			Elective	1 or 2
	15			16 or 17

Senior Year

	Hrs.			Hrs.
B.A. 351	3		Seminar	3
Elective	3		Elective	3
Elective	3		Elective	3
Elective	3		Elective	3
Elective	3		Elective	3
	15			15

Foreign Language–Multicultural Studies

This course of studies was developed by Earlene Frazier and the foreign language faculty at Morris Brown College, Atlanta, Georgia, in conjunction with social science and religion faculty during the NEH consultancy I led in 1980–81. No new courses were added to the catalog to complete these programs.

AREA STUDIES PROGRAM: SOUTH AMERICAN/AFRO/FRENCH

General Studies

101–102	English Communications
107	Public Speaking
101	Math
101	Physical Education
100	Freshman Orientation
101	Biology
101	Chemistry
221–222	Humanities
223–224	Humanities
228–229	Lit. & Drama
	Total credits: 37

History

201–202	History of Africa
307	Peoples of Africa
100	Man-in-Society
320	Recent Afro-American History
405	Comparative Government (pol. sci.)
393	Comparative Government (pol. sci.)
311	Geography of Europe (geo.)
312	Geography of Asia (geo.)
412	Cultural Geography of Afro-America (geo.)
308	Culture and Personality (soc.)
407	Sociology of Economic Development (soc.)
314	Foods of Various Cultures
301–302	Human Behavior (social welfare)
	Total credits: 45

Multicultural

331	Geography of Africa
320	History of the Afro-American
307	Sociology of the Black Experience in the Americas
304	Economic Geography
304	Urban Anthropolgy
364	International Law
391	International Relations
417	Political Anthropology
	Total Credits: 24

French

101–102B	Basic French for Business
201–202	Business Composition & Conversation
204–205	Advanced Conversation in French
309	French Civilization
308	French Culture in Other Countries
	Total credits: 24

AREA STUDIES PROGRAM: LATIN AMERICAN/SPANISH

General Studies		History and Social Science		Multicultural		Spanish	
101–102	English Communications	201–202	History of Africa	302	Geography of Latin America	101B–102B	Basic Spanish for Business
107	Public Speaking	307	Peoples of Africa	251–252	Latin American History	310–311	FL for Diplomacy & Communication
101–102	Math	100	Man-in-Society	307	Sociology of the Black Experience in the Americas	301–302	Spanish Conversation, Reading & Composition
101	Physical Education	320	Recent Afro-American History	304	Economic Geography	308	Latin American Civilization
100	Freshman Orientation	405	Comparative Government (pol. sci.)	304	Urban Anthropology	316	Latin American Thought
101–102	Biology	311	Geography of Europe (geo.)	372	U.S. Foreign Policy		Total credits: 18
101	Chemistry	312	Geography of Asia (geo.)	391	International Relations		
221–222	Humanities	412	Cultural Geography of Afro-America	417	Political Anthropology		
223–224	Humanities	308	Culture and Personality (soc.)		Total credits: 24		
228–229	Lit. & Drama	407	Sociology of Economic Development (soc.)				
	Total credits: 32	314	Foods of Various Cultures				
		301–302	Human Behavior (social welfare)				
			Total credits: 45				

Bibliography on Career Language Programs

Teacher training: Goethe Institute
(offices located in New York, Houston, Boston, Chicago, San Francisco, Atlanta)

Chambre de Commerce et d'Industrie de Paris
27, avenue de Friedland
75382 Paris

Franco-American Chamber of Commerce
1350 Avenue of the Americas
New York, NY 10019

Textbooks: D. C. Heath Publishers (inquire about their Spanish series)
125 Spring St.
Lexington, MA 02173

Patricia Cummins. *Commercial French.* Englewood Cliffs, N.J.: Prentice-Hall, 1982.

Other readings: See pp. 307–09, "Internationalizing the Curriculum"

Other resources: Continuing Education Cassette Library
North East Conference
P.O. Box 623
Middlebury, VT 05753

ERIC/Clearinghouse on Languages and Linguistics
User Services
Center for Applied Linguistics
3520 Prospect St., N.W.
Washington, DC 20007

Internationes, e.V.
Audiovisuelle Medien
Arbeitsgruppe: Kultureller Tonbanddienst
Kennedyallee 91–103
5300 Bonn 2
W. Germany

Public Relations

Anyone outside the FLL department becomes part of its public. This public divides into six segments: administrators, non-FL faculty, students, alumni, FL teachers in the surrounding schools and postsecondary institutions, and the community the college serves. Several general suggestions can help improve the department's relations with all its constituencies. First, develop an attractive, well-organized, informative departmental brochure. An appropriately talented student may agree to design it. If costs become a problem, the department might seek support from an interested alumni major. Often a bank, restaurant, bookstore, or other local concern seeking students' business will agree to cover printing costs in return for a small advertisement space on the brochure. The brochure should explain the course offerings, lab and extracurricular activities, and other departmental features, and it should outline career directions for students with language majors and minors. Quotes from recent language-major graduates employed in various fields may help answer questions students and parents have about language study. These brochures can become part of the packet carried by college recruiters, given out by admissions officers, and mailed to graduates through the alumni office. The department should arrange to send copies of brochures to new matriculants and to local businesses. They also clearly belong in the offices of academic advisers and in the lounges of student housing and recreation units.

In addition to well-designed brochures, many departments now publish a newsletter once or twice a year. Large departments like the one at Purdue University produce long and comprehensive publications. Many other institutions do less ambitious newsletters. In any case, these publications keep others informed of changes in the department's curriculum, awards to faculty and students, publications, grants, new projects, teaching techniques, and developments in the FL field. The newsletter circulates widely on and off campus. Alumni FL majors, regional FL teachers in all sectors of education, interested community members and local clubs and business groups, as well as regional officers of FL groups, all receive copies.

Departments should also consider the image they project. Department members who meet the public should be pleasant, helpful, and positive in speaking about the field. Jean-Charles Seigneuret, the very successful past chairman at Washington State University, Pullman, made a special point of ensuring that the department offices offered an attractively decorated, well-lit setting for business. He also insisted on courteous telephone and personal treatment of callers and guests.

Making these three obvious public relations gestures will not repair the serious and longstanding negative image of some FL departments. The unhappy fact remains that language departments do not always enjoy the affection and respect of their colleagues in other departments. Administrators have often expressed to me special frustration with their FLL faculty. As I see it, there are three major reasons for this situation. One is that many administrators and colleagues outside FLL have painful memories of their own second language experience. Not only do they remember the pain, they also realize that they have little remaining language proficiency to show for their pain. No matter that they may have agonized through zoology and can no longer remember the Krebb's cycle, or that they studied mathematics for years and can no longer say anything coherent about conic sections or solve quadratic equations. Our colleagues outside our departments usually believe that they should still have some fluency in the foreign languages they studied, even though they have not used them for years. Their memory of painful learning and their lost skills often plague their feelings about our discipline. They remember frustration and remain frustrated.

The second reason arises in part from the first: many administrators and non-FL colleagues now fear that imposing or even encouraging FL study will reduce student enrollments at their institutions and in their programs. For the foreseeable future, stable enrollments will be a very great challenge in many institutions. All college requirements that are believed to bring students pain are likely to lose the support of those fearful of dropping enrollment figures. The history faculty designing a program for European or Latin American history majors, which should clearly require a well-developed foreign language proficiency, will not insist on one if they feel that doing so will reduce the number of history majors. Our colleagues' perceptions of the long-term benefits of language learning and the short-term unpleasantness do not encourage them to risk enrollment drops, even if they believe that "educated people should know more than one language."

Finally, fairness demands that we admit that we are often our own worst enemies when it comes to building a common purpose and forming alliances. A great many FL departments live in states of chronic divisiveness. The possible divisions are many: the American-born and the non-American born; the aristocrat, the bourgeois, and the worker-class ancestries; the northern and southern temperaments within the languages; the futurists with their computers and those who yearn for the *bon vieux temps* and the *ancien régime:* the scholars and the pedagogues; the deadwood and the activists. Added to these are the century and theoretical school–related divisions and the language divisions themselves, which are fraught with long-standing national and cultural animosities. With all this potential for divisiveness, it is amazing that language departments can function at all. When they do not, it is easy for outsiders to comment ironically on the advantages of foreign language study in developing global understanding and appreciation of other cultures.

Despite or perhaps because of the disadvantages of our colleagues' memories, their fears of declining enrollment, and our internecine divisions, it is clear that developing good public relations must occupy a central place in any program of improvement for an FL department. It is also clear that this task will involve very hard work.

PUBLIC RELATIONS WITH ADMINISTRATORS

Higher enrollment figures are probably the best way to establish good PR with administrators. The department that embarks on improving teaching and redesigning curriculum to increase enrollment enhances its relations with academic officers. A large proportion of participants in the NEH-EEF project identified better support from their administrators as one of the outstanding benefits of project participation. As I review their documents, I notice that most of them made special efforts to keep their administrators informed about their FL discipline and the department's plans to improve. The following approaches are being used in many institutions:

1. The FL department sends a single-page information sheet to academic officers and heads of other departments once a month. The sheet might reproduce a recent newspaper article on a language-related subject. It might contain a nonscholarly review of a book related to the foreign language field. Many grant participants did reviews or synopses of Paul Simon's *Tongue-Tied American* and of the President's Commission report, *Strength through Wisdom.* Earl Stevick's book, *Language Teaching: A Way and Ways,* should join this list.

As the department begins to improve enrollments, wins an NEH planning grant, launches a flagship course or a business track, or begins using the ACTFL-ETS proficiency scale, short descriptive articles should appear on the monthly information sheet. Who should keep the administration up-to-date on the FLL field and on the FL department? Certainly not the physics faculty. (See How to Develop Publicity Packets, p. 42.)

2. As the department evolves a plan to strengthen its program, academic officers should be kept abreast of the plan and its development. In the early stages, the FL department chair should inquire how the department can help advance the institution's short- and long-term goals. For instance, if improvement of contacts with alumni or with the business community rates high on the list of institutional goals, the FL department can move toward supporting that goal, usually without greatly altering its strategies.

In later stages, the department should provide academic officers with the rationale for departmental changes, an explanation of costs and funding sources, details on recruitment and assessment procedures, and of course a careful outline of how the curriculum will improve. In short, the outline of strategies for planned change (ch. 2) will help the department organize its efforts *and* transmit them to academic officers in a form that will engender their confidence and respect. With these two elements, the department can often expect improved administrative support.

PUBLIC RELATIONS WITH NON-FL FACULTY COLLEAGUES

1. Find out where your strengths are. Do a survey among colleagues in other departments and discover what languages they know, how proficient they are, and how foreign languages could help them (do help them) in their professional work. What countries have they visited? What courses do they teach that have multicultural or multilingual content? Are they interested in brushing up their language skills or in learning a new language? The number of questions should not exceed ten, or faculty may be discouraged from responding. The survey results will permit the FL faculty to find and develop links to the rest of the curriculum. I have seen struggling history and sociology departments jump at the chance for course pairing with the FL department. I know of an overburdened business department that needed to begin an international business specialty and leaped at the interest and support offered by the FL department. Many FL departments have become accustomed to resistance by other departments in the last twelve years of dropping requirements and of competition for bodies in the headcount battles. Resistance still exists, but surprising support also exists just waiting to be discovered. (See Sample Faculty Polls inserts, pp. 42–44.)

2. Encourage faculty to take FL courses. If they feel welcome, they may decide to sit in on an elementary course or on a conversation course. This approach serves non-FL faculty while soothing the bad memories they may have of their past language training. These faculty often discover that they are more proficient than they had thought.

This public relations gesture has enormous potential to affect the curriculum. (See course pairing, pp. 20–21.) FL faculty may ask to take social science and history courses to teach culture more knowledgeably, while faculty from these areas take FL courses. An NEH-funded project providing for this kind of crossover has been in progress at Earlham College, Richmond, Indiana, under the direction of Richard Jurasek. Its success bodes well for the future of undergraduate curriculum and faculty development. The same kind of exchange may be workable between FL departments and business departments or computer science departments.

3. Arrange opportunities for non-FL faculty to take trips abroad supervising students. FL faculty in some schools hold advantages in international travel with students. Sharing may generate broader interest in foreign study among both faculty and students.

4. Interdisciplinary colloquiums at many institutions improve relations between FL and non-FL faculty. They may be brown-bag lunches or more formal events. They sometimes result in new team-taught courses,

area studies, and an interchange of majors and faculty as guest lecturers at each other's classes. These interactions always encourage the sense of a community of scholars.

PUBLIC RELATIONS WITH STUDENTS

Students need to learn in our classes, and to enjoy at least part of the process. They also need to understand the reasons for language study and to believe it will be a useful and satisfying part of their future lives. The first two issues—learning and enjoying—concern pedagogy and curriculum design. The last two—understanding and believing—fall under public relations.

1.   At Purdue, Sidney Pellissier developed "Why Study a Foreign Language" packets for students taking the required language courses. These packets contained several short articles or synopses of articles related to teaching and learning languages and using languages in careers. Students read the articles, answered short questions at the end, and received some extra credit units in the course. (See Why Study a Foreign Language insert, pp. 45–51.) Others have adopted this idea. If students receive one packet a month, they have time to do the reading, which is in English, and to respond to questions without straining their academic schedules. Faculty might use these packets as the subject of a short class or language club discussion. Like most good ideas, this one must be adapted to individual settings.

2.   Offering students a chance to introduce themselves to the teacher has become standard in most good programs. (See Personal Assessment Questions insert, p. 52.) This idea can build good will and help students achieve. Faculty can create links among students and between the course and the students individually. Faculty also know where they need to minister to past anxieties and feelings of failure. I find that students succeed better in courses where the teacher takes cognizance of their past experience while still demanding the very best achievements now.

3.   Where no FLL requirements exist, the FLL department should do a survey of student attitudes on foreign language learning. (See Ripon Poll insert, pp. 52–54.) This information helps faculty plan for curriculum development and reveals what kind of obstacles students face in broadening their global outlook. (See section on planned change, pp. 80–82, for the kinds of data that are useful in preparing new curricula.)

4.   Establishing a foreign language–multicultural studies center or lounge is an excellent way of fostering good public relations with students. A center of this sort should provide information on careers and languages, study abroad, work internships in foreign countries and with U.S. multinationals as well as American businesses in bilingual areas. It should also have literature about travel abroad and a selection of foreign magazines, newspa-

pers, and journals for student use. The center might also house duplicate issues of FL journals for faculty to refer to or for faculty to ask students to use in doing certain class assignments. If possible, the center should also have refreshments daily. An occasional social event will attract student interest as well. The language club can often help set up such a center and may even decorate it if that proves necessary and feasible. If the center is large enough, it can show films, house a drop-in tutorial service run by majors, or organize the National FL Week activities for the campus and the region (see pp. 54–56).

5.   Well-run language houses, or corridors, language tables, and language clubs (see pp. 56–57) create a positive feeling about FL study. The houses and tables have worked well for years, but in many institutions the language clubs have fallen onto hard times. Volunteers from the community, especially retired persons, can often provide excellent leadership for international club activities and relieve overburdened faculty.

6.   A part-time placement officer in the FL department does a lot to bolster the confidence of students. Here again a retired professional person may be of great assistance. In small departments this officer may initially work to develop leads for internships and contacts with businesses and government offices where foreign language knowledge is preferred. The officer can help students prepare their résumés, write letters of inquiry, develop skills for interviews, and learn how to do job searches. Most institutions have placement offices that provide some or all of these services, but good departments are taking increasing responsibility for assisting their students in finding summer and full-time employment.

7.   FL faculty should help students prepare compositions in their second language for publication in college creative writing journals. Many of these journals publish solely in English. If an undergraduate journal of criticism exists, it should also publish works in foreign languages. If there are no journals on campus, FL faculty should encourage their development.

Public Relations with Alumni

Alumni should receive information through the appropriate channels. Elements from the administrative news sheet, from the student "Why Study a Foreign Language" packets, and from the new brochure can be sent to the alumni office for publication. A description of the new FL program will interest alumni. They should be informed that the department seeks work and study opportunities for its students and asked for suggestions.

Alumni majors and minors are an important group. By surveying them and a sampling of non-FL-major alumni, a department can discover what FL needs they have and how they feel about the usefulness and importance of foreign language and culture study. One school running a survey promised alumni who returned the completed surveys a two-year subscription to the department newsletter.

PUBLIC RELATIONS WITH REGIONAL FL FACULTY

Neighboring elementary, high school, and postsecondary language faculty should know about one another's programs, resources, and needs. For information on how to set up professional development groups analogous to county bar societies and medical associations, see chapter 3.

PUBLIC RELATIONS WITH THE COMMUNITY

Good community relations are vitally important to a healthy language program. Intelligent dissemination of departmental publications will easily keep the public informed of departmental progress.

Enlisting the services of volunteers, as suggested above, also creates links between the community and the department. Retired FL teachers in the area may agree to tutor language students or to supervise language club activities.

Many departments have set up advisory boards for their multicultural studies and business programs or for the departments in general. Composed of civic and business persons, local alumni, and regional FL faculty, the board helps the department find the support it needs to locate jobs for its students and raise prize money for faculty and students and makes suggestions on extracurricular opportunities for students with an FL background. (See Community Polls, pp. 58–62.)

(Attention: In some institutions the activities of boards engaging in fund raising must be checked through the college or university development office. Some schools like Princeton University find that coordinating fund raising with the departments brings a gratifying response from alumni. In many institutions development offices do not do much coordination of fund raising from alumni with the departments. They should. The FL department can lead the way in these institutions.)

Public relations work takes time. It is vitally important. The chairperson and faculty can share some of it with students and some with volunteer help. Some of it becomes standard operating procedure eventually. Good public relations in the FL field supports the importance of humanities education and higher education in general.

How to Develop Publicity Packets

Each FL faculty member should take responsibility for one or two major journals in our field (*Modern Language Journal, Foreign Language Annals, French Review, Hispania, ADFL Bulletin,* etc.). Each quarter the faculty should write short abstracts of the best or most useful articles and photocopy the table of contents and interesting Notes pages. This material should be collected into a "professional update packet" just for the foreign language faculty.

INDIVIDUAL PACKETS

From the wealth of information available in the professional journals and in the national and local press (*Time, Newsweek, Business Week, New York Times,* etc.), create one-page "Language Update Sheets." Some items may particularly suit *student* interests; others may be more appropriate for *administration* and faculty outside the department. Most information will help the *admissions and alumni* understand the place of our field in higher education and in American culture. The community newspapers may print other updates. Keep your constituencies up to date. Do not forget high school foreign language teachers in your region. Make sure the article you select will suit its intended audience. Keep it short.

Sample Faculty Polls
State University College of New York, Potsdam

The following questionnaire was distributed to faculty by the Department of Foreign Languages, State University College of New York, Potsdam. Of the 278 faculty surveyed, 92 completed and returned the forms.

1. Did you find your language requirement in graduate school an asset to your professional preparation?
2. If no, was it because
   a. you could not at that time apply the language to your field or graduate study?
   b. the language instruction provided was poor?
   c. Other (specify)
3. What foreign language(s) do you read or speak?
   a. French
   b. German
   c. Spanish
   d. Other (specify)
4. Do you feel that knowledge of a foreign language would help you professionally?
5. If yes, would you be interested in language courses designed for faculty?
6. Are you considering a year abroad as part of Potsdam's exchange programs?
7. If yes, is it with (a) Mexico, (b) Taiwan?
8. If no, would you participate in the exchange if your language skills were improved?

Faculty Polls (*cont.*)

9. In what way(s) would language instruction at Potsdam College improve your own courses?
    a. It would enable students to make use of material rendered inaccessible due to its being in a foreign language.
    b. Knowledge of a foreign language is in itself important for a greater appreciation of your field.
    c. Knowledge of a foreign language on the part of students would give you the opportunity to make comparisons with English not only in terms of syntax and vocabulary but also in terms of concepts.
    d. Other (specify).

10. Your field and major interests are in (a) Natural Sciences, (b) Social Sciences, (c) Humanities, (d) Music, (e) Education, (f) Mathematics, (g) Physical Sciences, (h) Art, (i) Management.

11. Would you wish to have a foreign language faculty member attend your classes to find common areas of interest in the curriculum?

12. Would you be interested in attending foreign language courses for the same purpose?

13. What do you feel to be the major role of the Foreign Language Department at Potsdam College as it is presently organized?
    a. To offer courses that contribute to liberal arts education.
    b. To offer courses that provide a service to other academic areas.
    c. To prepare students for a career or graduate school.
    d. No real function as far as you can see.
    e. Other (specify).

14. If you could change the curriculum or direction of the Foreign Language Department, what would you like to see accomplished?
    a. Make the Foreign Language Department curriculum emphasize the interrelationship of cultures.
    b. Have the courses emphasize practical skills, such as reading.
    c. Prepare the students for a career in which a foreign language would be helpful.
    d. Teach literature and linguistics.
    e. Provide a service to the college by developing courses for general education requirements, e.g., the nature of language.
    f. Other (specify).

Faculty Polls (*cont.*)
Morris Brown College

The following minisurvey was administered by the Department of Foreign Languages at Morris Brown College, Atlanta, Georgia, to determine how many faculty are involved in foreign travel or study and assess the interest in multicultural activities.

1. Would you like an International Studies Program at Morris Brown College?
    Place an X in the appropriate block(s).
    ☐ Yes, I would like to participate in such a program.
    ☐ No, I don't see the significance of such a program.
    ☐ No, I am not familiar with the area.
    ☐ Yes, I think the program will enhance the college curriculum at large.

2. In what multicultural activities and/or programs are you now involved?
    a. _____
    b. _____
    c. _____
    d. _____

3. What other languages do you speak?
    Place an X in the appropriate block(s).

		Write	Read	Understand
☐	French	☐	☐	☐
☐	Spanish	☐	☐	☐
☐	Swahili	☐	☐	☐
☐	Others	☐	☐	☐

4. How do you rate your ability to use the language?
    ☐ Excellent
    ☐ Good
    ☐ Fair

5. What foreign countries have you visited?
    Place an X in the appropriate block(s).

☐	Mexico	☐	Germany
☐	Martinique	☐	Canada
☐	Haiti	☐	France
☐	Panama	☐	Spain
☐	India	☐	Nigeria
☐	Brazil	☐	Others

Why Study a Foreign Language?
A Self-Study Unit
Developed by *Sidney Pellissier*

There are two self-study units in French 101 and 101A. Each unit contains material related in subject, theme, or content to the course. You may elect to take either or both of the self-study units, since each one is *optional.* There is a quiz based on each self-study unit that is worth *twenty course points.* Your instructor will announce the date of the quiz two weeks in advance. The quiz will be administered in the monitored laboratory class session in SC 219. (There is no prequiz.)

INTRODUCTION

In this self-study unit all the readings are in English. There are no study tapes to accompany the readings.

Please note that the readings are in two different locations:

1. There are excerpts from articles and books written by Asher, Chastian, Cook, and Grittner. These readings are on the mimeographed sheets you are now reading.
2. There is a thirty-one-page pamphlet by Lucille J. Honig and Richard I. Brod entitled "Foreign Languages and Careers." The pamphlet is on reserve in the *Reserved Book Room* of the main campus library.

These readings are intended to inform you in a general way about:

1. Acquisition of one's native language
   a. Physiology: how we learn to form words
   b. Psychology: how we learn what words mean
   c. Manipulation: how we learn to use our language
2. Learning a foreign language
   a. Rationale: reasons for studying a foreign language
   b. Methodology: brief history of trends of foreign language instruction in the United States
   c. Comparisons: native language acquisition vs. acquisition of a foreign language
3. Career opportunities
   a. Foreign language as an auxiliary skill
   b. Foreign language as a primary skill

The readings in this self-study unit will enhance your understanding of some of the problems encountered by teachers and students of foreign languages. Learning a foreign language is never easy, but it can be rewarding to both your personal and professional development. It is hoped that the readings in this unit (which has been kept purposely brief) will serve as a general introduction to foreign language study and will help you to gain new insights.

PERFORMANCE OBJECTIVES

1. You should know the factual contents of all readings in the self-study unit well enough to be able to:
   a. Answer true-false statements in English based on the readings.
   b. Write short-answer (one-paragraph) essays in English based on the readings.
2. You *do not* need to memorize which authors made which statements. For example, if you read a true-false statement on the quiz such as: "Smith maintains that French is the language most commonly spoken in Paris," you may assume that Smith is indeed the person who made the statement, and then decide whether the statement is true or false.

Why Study a Foreign Language? (*cont.*)

3. You should be able to answer all content questions given in this unit *in your own words*. Your opinions and personal ideas are encouraged—you do not have to agree with everything you read—*but* you must demonstrate that you have assimilated the factual content of the material you read in this Self-Study Unit.

QUIZ

The quiz for this self-study unit is worth thirty course points, and will follow this outline:

Part 1.   True-false statements based on writings of Asher, Chastain, Cook, Grittner. *Fifteen* statements.   (15 points)

Part 2.   True-false statements based on "Foreign Languages and Careers" by Honig and Brod. *Ten* statements.   (10 points)

Part 3.   Short-answer question in English, based on *all* readings in this self-study unit. *One* question.   (5 points)

If your quiz score is:	Then you earn:
27–30 = A	20 course points
24–26 = B	16 course points
21–23 = C	14 course points

Note: You must earn a grade of C or better (21 points or more) to be given any credit for this self-study unit.

READINGS

Chastain, Kenneth. *Developing Second Language Skills: Theory to Practice.* 2nd ed. Boston: Houghton, 1976, pp. 46–47.

N. M. Lewis, a recognized authority on infant speech, has based the beginnings of the long speech process on ideas of Charles Darwin. According to Darwin, a baby's cry can be compared to the bleat of a hungry lamb. This cry of hunger is just one among several movements which the lamb makes in his urgent desire to attain nourishment. This cry is not deliberately produced, but is part of the newborn's bodily struggle as it reacts to its discomfort. Therefore, in response to the question of when a child begins to learn to speak . . . "The answer is, if not at the moment of birth, then certainly during the first day. For as soon as a child cries and someone pays attention to his cry, the first step has been taken; the essentials of language are there: one person makes a sound which another person interprets." Other writers agree with this statement. Most feel that the first vocalizations of the newborn baby, his first cries at birth, are the beginning of language. Even in his first vocal reactions to his new and uninviting environment he is using his lungs to produce sounds.

The earliest noises which a child makes are the discomfort sounds, and these sounds are the result of his agitated body state and his struggles for relief. These sounds are shrill, nasalized vowel sounds. . . . These early cries are involuntary responses to hunger, pain, etc. Toward the end of this early period, the cries begin to have differences in vocal tones and mother can begin to identify the reasons for his crying.

In addition to the discomfort sounds, the baby learns to make comfort sounds. These sounds are relaxed, deeper, and without a nasal quality. Like the discomfort sounds, these sounds are produced naturally as a result of the body state of the baby. . . .

Why Study a Foreign Language? (*cont.*)

Next, consonant sounds begin to appear when the child is uncomfortable. Since the need to cry in a state of distress is much more powerful than the comfort sounds, consonant sounds are first noticed when a baby is in a state of discomfort. The early consonants in discomfort cries are as follows:

wa . . . wa . . . wa . . . wa
la . . . la . . . la . . . la
nga . . . nga . . . nga . . . nga
ha . . . ha . . . ha . . . ha

Lewis explains the appearance of these sounds as being a result of the fact that distress cries come in bursts. Each pause for breath will cause a constriction of some part of the air passage. . . . Later, the child will add the sounds "ma" and "na" to his repertoire of discomfort sounds.

The second stage in the development of language is generally referred to as babbling. Berry and Eisenson state, "The babbling stage may be considered a training and preparatory period for later articulate utterance." In other words, it is during this stage that the baby really begins to practice the variations of the sound system. Lewis emphasizes the relation of the babbling stage to the later comfort situations in which the baby, after a feeding and lying on his back, begins to add consonants to his collection of vowel sounds used when he is comfortable. He has saliva in his mouth and is perhaps making swallowing movements. As a natural result of this situation, the baby begins to make some of the . . . consonant sounds such as gu, ga, ka, cha, and ru. The later consonant sounds of a satisfied baby include ma, na, pa, ba, ta, and da. . . .

Up to this point, all babies everywhere make the same sounds. One investigator, by recording a baby's vocalizations during the first year, concluded that a baby makes all possible sounds and gradually loses them as he is reinforced by the sounds he hears in his environment. . . .

The next stage is lalling. Beery and Eisenson give the following description: "Lalling, which usually begins during the second six months of the child's life, may be defined as the repetition of heard sounds or sound combinations." For the first time, then, hearing others becomes important in the speech-development process. However, the repetition of sounds heard is merely for the pleasure of oral activity and is not an environmental response.

The speech-learning process soon develops into constant imitations of sounds in his environment. This stage, called echolalia, is further practice in sound manipulation and preparation for actual talking. It is during this stage, which begins about the age of nine or ten months, that parents first hear the "dadas" and "mamas." However, as of yet the child has no real comprehension of the significance of what he is saying. . . .

Babies speak pretty much the same first words, but doting and anxious parents give their words different meanings. For example:

German: dada (there it is), baba (father), wow-wow (dog), mama (mother)
French: papa (father), mama (mother), non-non (no), wa-wa (dog)
Russian: mama (mother), tata (father), baba (grandmother), da (give)

Why Study a Foreign Language? (*cont.*)

Content Questions

1. What is the first step in a baby's struggle to communicate?
2. What are the conditions surrounding this first step?
3. If a baby's first cries are involuntary, how can we say then that language is creative? (What are the differences between creative language and a baby's cry?)
4. How do the consonant sounds originate?
5. What is the second stage of language acquisition?
6. In what way can babbling be considered a "trial run" for actual speaking?
7. How many sounds does the baby make during the babbling stage?
8. What happens to all these sounds?
9. Do you consider the term "reinforcement" an inadequate description of the way a baby eliminates sounds from his repertoire? Why or why not?
10. What is the third stage of language acquisition?
11. What kind of role does hearing and listening play in the lalling stage? What kind of role does it play in the babbling stage?
12. Up to this point, how much significance does a child intentionally put into the sound he makes?

Asher, James J. "Implications of Psychological Research for Second Language Training." *ACTFL Review of Foreign Language Education,* ed. Dale L. Lange, 4 (1972), 169–72.

Experiments indicate that immediately from birth, human infants can respond with selectivity to different auditory signals. Infants are not passive recipients of stimuli, but can act to select certain stimuli and exclude others. In a study . . . one-day-old infants showed reliable preferences for different types of music by turning the music on by sucking on a pacifier nipple, and off by not sucking. . . . others have mounted on the infant's crib a toy called a "Playtest" which the infant operates by touching either of 2 large . . . switches that played a preprogrammed selection on a two-channel stereo tape. This toy has shown that the preverbal infant prefers listening to a longer rather than a shorter story, a lullaby rather than a hum, . . . and nursery songs with the full range of frequencies in the signal rather than with some frequencies filtered out. . . .

A response system that has important implications . . . is "meaning" of "thought." . . . a recent theoretical article . . . presents the thesis that infants use meaning as a clue to the linguistic code. When infants begin to develop language, their thought is more developed than their use of the linguistic code. . . . at the age of one year, an infant has thoughts that are quite independent of language. The infant has made observations about himself, his environment, and people who interact with him; and he can classify many things and see the relationship between his own activities and the movement of objects. . . .

In learning one's native language, listening skill develops when language is synchronized with the location, orientation, and action of the young child. Evidence to support this . . . showed that about 50 percent of all utterances directed at the 12-month-old infant were commands such as, "Don't make a fist when I'm trying to put on your coat."

Why Study a Foreign Language? (*cont.*)

Content Questions

1. What is the meaning of "stimuli"?
2. The fact that infants have definite preferences right from the start and can classify things even before they can speak indicates what?
3. What is a "linguistic code"?
4. How does listening develop in a child?
5. Asher's theory of listening skill has been labeled the "total physical response." Why?
6. How, then, according to the article, does a young child learn the meaning of words?
7. How would someone learning another language, according to this theory, learn the meanings of the foreign language words?

Grittner, Frank M. *Teaching Foreign Languages.* New York: Harper, 1969, pp. 135–38.

To the cognitive theorist, language learning is problem solving. And conversation ... is achieved by speeding up the problem-solving process, not by bypassing it. ... Studies of infant language learning seem to indicate that a child does not acquire language by imitating complete utterances from adult speech. Instead he appears to draw selected ... items from the language environment and to manipulate these items according to simple grammatical rules. Thus, according to this line of thought, the fractured language called "baby talk" is different from adult speech precisely because the child is following basic ... patterns in applying his limited repertoire of words. His ability to combine these items into all sorts of nonadult patterns indicates that he is applying rational principles rather than merely imitating adult speech. The fact that he can form hundreds of meaningful utterances from a few dozen words seems to attest to that fact. A number of linguists suspect that children possess an innate capacity for producing the basic structures of language. ...

For example, any normal 5-year-old can demonstrate his control of grammar in test situations such as the following:

Adult: Today I am glinging. I did the same thing yesterday. What did I do?
Child: You glinged (or: You glung.)
Adult: (*Holding up a picture of an imaginary beast*) This is a gick. Now I have two of them; what do I have?
Child: You have two gicks.

The first reply shows that the child has mastered the system for changing regular verbs to the past tense. The second example demonstrates an ability to form regular plurals. The fact that the child can perform these operations with nonsense words proves that he has not merely memorized the forms from the adult speech community. The child has never heard of a "gick" nor has he ever seen anyone "glinging." ... Yet he quite correctly and instantly treats "gick" as a noun and "gling" as a verb. ...

It appears that all normal children develop this ability to integrate new ... lexical items into the native language system which they have largely mastered ... during the first five years of life. ... In the great majority of cases, the preschool child has developed a listen-speak communications system which is infinitely expandable to all the tens of thousands of vocabulary items which exist in his language and those which will later be created during his lifetime.

Why Study a Foreign Language? (*cont.*)

Content Questions

1. What is language according to the cognitive theory?
2. What do the words "cognitive theory" mean, and how does this definition apply to learning language?
3. What role does imitation of adult speech play in the child's acquisition of language?
4. How does a child manipulate the language?
5. How does this fit in with the definition of language as problem solving? With the definition of language as creative?
6. How is language control illustrated? What happens when a child is confronted with an unfamiliar word?
7. How does the child's treatment of unfamiliar words show that he mastered some basic principle?
8. What kind of a listen-speak communications system are you developing in your study of French?

Grittner. *Teaching Foreign Languages.* Pp. 24–25.

The writings of Sapir and Whorf and the investigations of various cultural anthropologists have produced a new humanistic rationale for the study of languages. In essence ... the hypothesis asserts (1) that the native language determines how a person views the world and (2) that he is unaware of his mental entrapment if he remains monoligual. Thus the American who grows up speaking only English is never conscious of how thoroughly his ability to think is circumscribed by the way his language compels him to structure his thoughts. Just as a deep-sea creature would be unaware of the nature of water because he has never experienced non-water, a monolingual American is unaware of the nature of English because he has no significant contact with non-English. His ethnocentric mind set traps him into believing that English is the only reasonable way to express reality. Actually English, like all languages, causes distortions by the way it structures expression. For example, the language of the Hopi Indians is more accurate [regarding] certain natural processes. In English we say, "John is dying." The Hopi language, by contrast, would say something like, "Dying is taking place in John." The Hopi language more accurately expresses the fact that John is really not doing anything, whereas the Anglo-American by the very nature of how his language symbolizes actions in the real world, is forced to attribute agent power to John, even though John is passively, and perhaps unwillingly, in the process of dying. ...

It follows that the study of a second language is essential to understanding what language is all about. The American student can develop a clearer understanding of his native English by comparing it with a non-English communication system. But this understanding can come only by means of a thorough immersion in a totally new system of oral and written symbols. He must to some degree become conversant in the mother tongue of some non-Anglo-American culture.

Why Study a Foreign Language? (*cont.*)

Just how powerful this attachment to the mother tongue is was demonstrated by the riots in India during the winter of 1965, when Prime Minister Shastri signed a parliamentary decree making Hindi the sole official language. According to newspaper reports at the time, Tamil-Bengali-speaking citizens reacted with such violence that more than 70 people were killed in the rioting and over two million dollars worth of property was destroyed. In an effort to calm the angry mobs, Shastri proposed elevating English to the status of an associate language. This only served to infuriate the one group which had theretofore remained calm. The 40 percent of India which speaks Hindi was incensed at the prospect of elevating an alien tongue to such a position of recognition. They began rioting, burning English books, and effacing signs written in English. . . .

The American will never really penetrate the thinking of people in a new country until he has first penetrated the language which carries, reflects, and molds the thoughts and ideas of that people. . . .

Anyone who views education as a way to get a better job or to improve his social standing or to solve economic or social problems has a nonhumanistic outlook. . . . Through most of history, the foreign language community kept the nonhumanists on the outside.

The time arrived, however, when the language people themselves took up the habit of ascribing utilitarian values to the learning of a language. . . . The first Russian Sputniks had been launched . . . and the event led to widespread criticism of America's schools and focused public attention upon education in Russia and America.

The same article points out some "utilitarian" values of learning a foreign language:

International understanding: by using the foreign language to penetrate another culture, to understand the world from another viewpoint, and to promote international understanding.

Foreign language and business: opportunities for foreign-language-speaking personnel are almost limitless: import-exporting, airlines, advertising, hotel service, librarians, scientific research, travel and tourism industry, secretarial work, government. Although knowledge of a foreign language is not necessary to obtain employment in any of these fields, knowledge of at least one foreign language puts a person in a much better position to progress upward in the company ranks.

Content Questions

1. What is humanism? How is the study of a foreign language related to humanism?

2. In what way does speaking only one language "trap" a person?

3. You have read about the difference in idea between the Hopi way of seeing death and the Anglo-American way. Name at least one difference in expression of an idea between English and French.

Personal Assessment Questions

1. Why have you chosen the class?
2. What are your specific goals for this course?
3. What do you expect the content of this course to be?
4. What prior knowledge of the subject do you feel you bring to this course?
5. What do you feel are your special strengths and weaknesses related to the course subject?
6. How does the course fit both in time commitment and in content with the broader objectives of your major fields of interest?
7. What pedagogical methods in your experience best enhance your learning and why?
8. What are your outside interests or skills?
9. Is there any part of this statement you wish kept confidential?

**Ripon College
Student Poll on Language and Literature**

Please answer carefully the following questions: Yes   No   Don't Know

Do you wish this to be kept confidential?_____ ☐ ☐

1. Name_____
2. Home Address_____
3. School Address_____
4. Year in School: Fr. ☐ Soph. ☐ Jr. ☐ Sr. ☐
5. Female ☐ Male ☐
6. Present G.P.A._____
7. Do you plan to go on to graduate study?   ☐ ☐ ☐
   If so, which field?_____
8. What are your future career goals?_____   ☐ ☐ ☐
   _____
9. Do you expect to use an FL in your career?   ☐ ☐ ☐
   In your private life?   ☐ ☐ ☐
10. Would you elect to study an FL if it were not a requirement for graduation?   ☐ ☐ ☐
11. If you have already completed the FL graduation requirement, are you now happy to have had this exposure?   ☐ ☐ ☐
12. Do you feel FL study is encouraged by other disciplines or departments?   ☐ ☐ ☐
    What is your opinion of graduation requirements?
    _____
13. Would you welcome
    a. two-year FL graduation requirement?   ☐ ☐ ☐
    b. abolition of FL graduation requirement?   ☐ ☐ ☐
    c. no change in the requirement?   ☐ ☐ ☐
    d. abolition of *all* graduation requirements?   ☐ ☐ ☐

Ripon Student Poll (*cont.*)

		Yes	No	Don't Know

14. Years of study of FL: High School _____
    College _____
    Other _____

15. Have you resided or traveled abroad? ☐ ☐ ☐
    If so, in which countries?_____
    How long?_____

16. Are you an FL major? ☐ ☐ ☐
    If so, which language? _____
    If not, what is your major?_____

17. Are you now taking an FL course? ☐ ☐ ☐
    If so, which one?_____

18. Do you feel your exposure to FL has enhanced your appreciation and command of English? ☐ ☐ ☐

19. Was the emphasis in your FL course on
    a. listening and speaking? ☐ ☐ ☐
    b. reading and translation? ☐ ☐ ☐
    c. grammar and writing? ☐ ☐ ☐

20. Has your exposure to FL grammar been useful to your understanding of language as a tool? ☐ ☐ ☐

21. Has your exposure to literary criticism and literary history (FL or English) been a valuable experience? ☐ ☐ ☐

22. Has your exposure to foreign culture and civilization (in FL courses) been a valuable experience? ☐ ☐ ☐

23. How would you grade the FL instruction you have received at Ripon?
    ☐ A ☐ B ☐ C ☐ D ☐ F

24. Would you be interested in taking
    a. a one-hour, one-credit FL conversation course? ☐ ☐ ☐
    b. a half-semester, two-credit minicourse that addresses:
       (1) one author ☐ ☐ ☐
       (2) one period ☐ ☐ ☐
       (3) one problem ☐ ☐ ☐
       (4) one work ☐ ☐ ☐
       (5) other_____

25. Do you see a need for new courses in the following areas:
    a. Advanced grammar and stylistics ☐ ☐ ☐
    b. Literary translation ☐ ☐ ☐
    c. Scientific and technical translation ☐ ☐ ☐
    d. Comparative literature ☐ ☐ ☐

26. Would you welcome the opportunity to write in English more
    a. Essays ☐ ☐ ☐
    b. Compositions ☐ ☐ ☐
    c. Research Papers ☐ ☐ ☐
    d. Journals (personal) ☐ ☐ ☐
    e. Letters ☐ ☐ ☐

Ripon Student Poll (*cont.*)

	Yes	No	Don't Know
27. Would you welcome the opportunity to write in FL more			
a. Essays	☐	☐	☐
b. Compositions	☐	☐	☐
c. Research Papers	☐	☐	☐
d. Journals (personal)	☐	☐	☐
e. Letters	☐	☐	☐
28. Do you perceive a value or use to foreign language study?	☐	☐	☐
29. Would you like to see other languages taught besides German, Spanish, French, Latin, Japanese, and Italian? If so, which? _____	☐	☐	☐

30. How would you characterize your perception of learning a foreign language?

exciting ☐
stimulating ☐
interesting ☐
noncreative ☐
dull ☐
boring ☐
too much memorization ☐

Thank you for completing this poll.

Activities for National Foreign Language Week
Frank Longoria

1. Arrange for exhibits in school or community libraries. The librarians welcome the opportunity to take an active part in promoting the literature and culture of other countries. They are able, because of their resources, to provide striking displays that effectively communicate the key ideas.

2. Place posters in prominent places on campus as well as in civic centers and municipal buildings.

3. Present assembly programs planned by the students of foreign languages or by interested language groups. The programs should attempt to emphasize one or two main ideas rather than just entertain.

4. Plan panel discussions on such subjects as "The Contribution of Languages to Modern Living." The panelists should represent different professional fields, the more varied, the better, to demonstrate that the value of languages is recognized in just about every facet of our lives.

5. Foster contests sponsored by the department of foreign languages, with prizes awarded to the author of the best essay, poem, or short story on an appropriate theme. To bring in other students, it is, of course, advisable to conduct this competition in English. This does not obviate the possibility of having a similar contest conducted in the languages taught in a particular institution. The latter can be an especially valuable learning experience.

6. Schedule movies, film strips, and travelogues.

Activities (*cont.*)

7. Have language tables where only a foreign language may be spoken during the luncheon hours. There should be a capable individual at each table who can sustain the activity if it begins to languish. This is an excellent activity for both the students who speak the language and the "outsiders" who can only listen enviously.

8. Print editorials and other items of interest relevant to National FL Week in the school paper. The cooperation of the school paper and of other school publications is essential for the success on campus of the NFLW activities; it is a cooperation that, fortunately, they are very willing to give. This medium of communication should be exploited to the utmost; it should be saturated with articles, cartoons, jokes, and editorials, all dealing with or having reference to the points we are trying to get across. Start the publicity campaign early and build up to the week's activities in such a way that the student body will be waiting for it with anticipation.

9. The amount of space devoted above to using the school paper or publications is not to say that the community publications should be neglected. If anything, they should be exploited even more, as much as they will permit. In most cases, they will be glad to mention the planned school and community activities.

10. Contact radio and television stations. Most of them have a definite amount of time that they allot for public service features and announcements. An outstanding news commentator on the local level will often be more than happy to devote some of his air time to the discussion of various aspects of foreign languages, travel, brotherhood, and so on.

11. Arrange for the printing and distribution of stickers carrying an appropriate slogan. These may be placed in windows, on car bumpers or bus sides, and so on.

12. Arrange for slogans on metered mail sent out by companies in our area.

13. Sponsor language contests for local high school students.

14. Set up a miniature world conference, as represented by the different languages, to discuss problems and disputes.

15. Display the various national flags in a centrally located spot.

16. Have a special day on which the student body in general may wear foreign costumes if they wish. Have a fashion show. Have a parade. There are many things of this sort that can be done and that lend color and vivacity to the campus and to the proceedings.

17. Have a "Singarama" at which members of the community sing familiar and popular songs from other lands. This is one of the more pleasant and more satisfactory ways of arousing the interest of students. These Singaramas can be held practically anywhere; the words of the songs can be duplicated and passed out, or they can be put on slides and projected on a screen or wall. Classes, choral groups, or even individuals can provide the vocal impetus to get the audience singing. As an added touch, costumes can be worn by the people leading and singing. There are all sorts of possibilities in this activity.

18. Hold sales of foreign delicacies.

Activities (*cont.*)

19. Have popular or traditional songs from other countries played on the public address system during the noon hour or between classes. Music has the ability to speak universally. In conjunction with the music, it is an excellent idea to have students introduce each song with a few remarks in the language of the country that the song represents.

20. Invite individual foreign students to come and speak in the classrooms.

21. Have a noon dance with exhibitions of traditional dances, or present a program after school that will include folk music, folk dances, and entertainment typical of other countries. There are few colleges that do not have in their student bodies a number of students from foreign lands. And strangely enough, these students not only seem to be extremely talented but also demonstrate a gracious willingness to perform.

22. Collect cartoons or jokes that have something to do with other countries or languages, and blow them up to poster size for distribution. Humor is often far more effective than a straight conventional approach in awakening interest.

23. Contact local foreign groups or clubs to urge their participation in the week's activities.

24. Set up "man on the street" programs during the course of which interviews with foreign students could be broadcast, mention could be made of planned programs to tease the curiosity, little quiz programs could be carried out with foreign delicacies as prizes, opinions of passing students could be taped and broadcast, and so on.

Foreign Language Clubs

In most institutions an international club with interest areas in the separate languages works better than separate clubs for each language. Regardless of how the club is formulated, its activities should combine reinforcement of language skills with students' other interests, be they career or avocational. Students should consider a range of possible groups within the language club.

1. *Great books.* Students choose and read texts that they discuss with or without a teacher. Faculty might guide the process of selection, but the focus of the group might be on learning to enjoy reading in the students' second language—a habit that if once formed and practiced has a better chance to become part of the student's life experience. Not all students need to be at the same level. Those not enrolled in an FLL course should be welcome. Those who have never taken an FL literature course should be particularly welcome. The group might decide to read one book in sections and in depth each semester instead of several books. The point is that students experience recreational reading in the FL.

2. *Research group.* Students interested in psychology can attempt to replicate studies showing how to enhance retention of language skills. James Asher's work offers accessible and interesting guidance for this project.

Clubs (*cont.*)

3. *Journalism.* Students write a weekly column in English or the FL foreign languages and cultures for the school paper. Possible topics are news events, teaching methods, campus activities touching international issues, and activities of the student speakers' bureau. Occasionally, a particularly well-written culture capsule or a piece of creative writing might appear. This project prepares students for possible work with foreign language journalism in American cities and keeps international issues before the student body.

4. *Speakers' bureau.* Students visit local schools, churches, and community groups to speak about FL study, global awareness, or FL and the professions; they may do skits or give slide or tape presentations on foreign countries, careers and languages, or methods of language teaching. Students use their English and foreign language skills. Those interested in forensics are particularly interested in this opportunity.

5. *Materials development.* Students interested in graphics, art, engineering, crafts, films, photography, and so forth might find challenge in creating teaching and learning materials for language classes, such as games, toys, puzzles, and posters.

6. *Language and careers.* Students arrange for speakers, organize trips, and so forth to learn about opportunities and placement approaches.

7. *Gourmet group.*

8. *Foreign film group.*

9. *Study-abroad group.* Students can be of great help to one another in preparing for study abroad and in making post-trip readjustments. Those hoping to go abroad before they graduate and those with firm plans can both participate. Readings and other activities will enhance the impact of the study-abroad experience.

Only three or four students may be involved in each group. It is quality of the activity that determines its worthiness to be a part of the program. Students often do not see how they can engage their interest in FL with the rest of their interests and obligations. Faculty need to show leadership in indicating these potentialities.

Community Polls

HIGH POINT COLLEGE COMMUNITY POLL

High Point College recently has instituted an international business program and would like your input to make the curriculum suitable to the needs of today's business community.

Name_____ Address_____

Business Affiliation_____

Part 1

1. Does your company do business in foreign countries?

    Yes_____   No_____

2. If yes, in what international business dealings is your company currently involved?

    _____a. Purchasing raw materials abroad
    _____b. Manufacturing products in other countries
    _____c. Selling finished goods in other countries
    _____d. Other (please explain)

3. In what foreign countries do you do business?_____

4. Do you have anyone on your staff with a usable knowledge of foreign languages?

    Yes_____   No_____

    If yes, what languages?_____

5. If you do not currently have anyone on your staff proficient in languages, would you be interested in hiring someone with this ability?

6. If you have international business dealings, would you be willing to consider having one or more of our students in your organization as a student intern?

    Yes_____   No_____

Part 2: Questions on curriculum

7. Do you think international concepts and practices should be integrated into existing business coursework?

    Yes_____   No_____

8. Do you think international business concepts should be offered as a separate body of course work?

    Yes_____   No_____

9. Which of the following business subjects do you think should be integrated with international concepts and practices?

    _____Business communications   _____Accounting
    _____Business internship   _____Finance
    _____Marketing   _____Policy
    _____Advertising   _____Others (please explain)
    _____Management   _____

10. As a corporate business person, do you think the study of business communications in a foreign language should consist mainly of the following: (Rate according to importance)

    _____Communication   _____Exercises in grammar
    _____Business letters   _____Syntax exercises
    _____Annual reports   _____Others (please explain)

11. In addition to a basic knowledge of business principles and practices and a foundation in foreign language, what other areas of study would be useful preparation for an international business career?

Community Polls (*cont.*)

MORRIS BROWN COLLEGE COMMUNITY POLL

Name_____ Address_____

Business Affiliation_____

This is a survey administered by the Business and Foreign Language Departments at Morris Brown College to assess the interest in multicultural activities in the business community.

1. Do you think students should be given an opportunity to co-op or intern in international business?

    Yes_____   No_____

2. Is your business an international corporation?

    Yes_____   No_____

3. In what multicultural activities and/or programs are you now involved?

    a. _____

    b. _____

    c. _____

    d. _____

4. Have you traveled abroad to a foreign country?

    Yes_____   No_____

5. What foreign countries have you visited?_____

6. Place (X) in the correct blank.

    _____within the last six months   _____within the last two years

    _____within the last year   _____within the last three years

7. Do you have or do you think you have adequate bilingual language mastery to cope with an international society?

    Yes_____   No_____

8. What foreign language do you speak? Check one or more items.

    _____French   _____Spanish   _____Swahili

    _____German   _____Others

9. How do you rate your ability to use the language?

    Excellent_____   Good_____   Fair_____

10. Do you think the type of course work presently available in most undergraduate college business departments adequately prepares students for positions in international business?

    Yes_____   No_____

11. Do you think some exposure to international business concepts and practices should be required of all business undergraduate students?

    Yes_____   No_____

12. Do you think international concepts and practices should be integrated into existing business course work?

    Yes_____   No_____

13. Do you think international business concepts should be offered as a separate body of course work?

    Yes_____   No_____

Community Polls (*cont.*)

14. Which of the following business subjects do you think should be integrated with international concepts and practices?

    _____Business Communications   _____Accounting
    _____Business Internship   _____Finance
    _____Marketing   _____Policy
    _____Shorthand   _____Typewriting
    _____Office Procedures   _____Office Management
                                          _____Others

15. In your business or in the business you work in, is there a need for persons to be exposed to international business concepts and practices?
    Yes_____   No_____

16. In the community in which you live or work, have you been in contact with a foreigner in the last six months?
    Yes_____   No_____

17. As a corporate business person or lender, do you think business communications should consist mainly of the following? (Rate according to importance)

    _____Communication   _____Exercises on grammar
    _____Business letters   _____Syntax exercises
    _____Annual reports   _____Others

18. Do you think that you might be interested at some time in the future in contributing $500 or $1,000 for partial scholarships for students in foreign languages who specialize in a multicultural program?
    Yes_____   No_____   Contact me_____

19. Did you study a foreign language in school?   Yes_____   No_____

20. Do you believe that students in college should study a foreign language/culture?
    Yes_____   No_____   I don't know_____
    Which one(s)?
    Spanish_____   French_____   Japanese_____   German_____
    Swahili_____   Other(s)_____

21. Are you satisfied with the literacy levels of new college graduates you work with (5 years or less postcollege)?
    Yes_____   No_____   Undecided_____

22. Would the level of professional work at your office improve if your employees had better writing skills? better speaking skills?
    Yes_____   No_____   Undecided_____

23. Suggestions:_____
    _____
    _____
    _____
    _____

NORTH SHORE COMMUNITY COLLEGE COMMUNITY POLL

As we contemplate the redesign of some of our modern foreign language courses at North Shore Community College, we would like to take into consideration your possible need for manpower with knowledge of a language besides English.

If you would take the time to reply to the following questions, it would guide us in a meaningful redesign of some of our programs to better serve your needs. A business reply envelope is provided for a postage-paid return.

1. Do you service a clientele that speaks a language other than English?
   Yes_____ No_____

2. Do you do business internationally? Yes_____ No_____
   If your answer was yes to either of these questions, please answer the rest of the questionnaire where applicable.

3. Do you have commercial dealings with people in the following countries?
   _____Mexico
   _____Canada
   _____France
   _____Japan
   _____West Germany
   _____Latin America (please specify)_____
   _____People's Republic of China
   _____Soviet Union
   _____United Arab Republic (please specify)_____
   _____Other (please specify)_____

4. Which two languages would be most practical for your employees to know, based on your present international commerce?
   French_____ German_____ Spanish_____ Other_____

5. Would executives and/or their wives need to be prepared to live abroad?
   Yes_____ No_____

6. Do your executives need training for multinational management?
   Yes_____ No_____

7. Would you be willing to offer training to your executives in intercultural understanding if such courses were made available in English?
   Yes_____ No_____

8. Would it be helpful for other employees to know a language other than English?
   Yes_____ No_____
   Which one? French_____ German_____ Spanish_____ Other_____

9. If your answer is yes, in which occupational category would these employees belong?
   _____Secretarial
   _____Child care
   _____Health care
   _____Factory worker
   _____Shop foremen
   _____Supervisor
   _____Sales
   _____Management
   _____Other

Community Polls *(cont.)*

10. Would you be willing to offer foreign language training to these employees?
    Yes_____ No_____ Maybe_____
    If your answer is yes, would you offer
    French_____ German_____ Spanish_____ Other_____

11. Would you be interested in classes at your business facility? Yes___ No___
    At North Shore Community College? Yes_____ No_____

12. Could your employees take a course in the
    morning_____ afternoon_____ evening_____ weekend_____
    intensive 2- or 3-week seminar_____

13. Would your company be willing to fund such courses?
    Yes_____ No_____ Maybe_____

14. Could you use bilingual secretaries? Yes_____ No_____

15. Which of the following skills would such a secretary require? Check pertinent skills.
    _____Typing in a foreign language (use of IBM Selectric with accent element)
    _____Translation of foreign correspondence
    _____Composition of letters in a foreign language
    _____Telephone, telex communications

16. Could you give short-term internship outside the United States to one of our students who may be fluent in a foreign language? Yes_____ No_____

Respondent's Name and Title

_____

_____

Good Ideas for FLL Program Building

1. Appoint a teaching consultant: have students nominate and faculty elect an FL faculty member to assist in developing courses, modules, syllabi, and study questions.

2. Put the teaching consultant in charge of circulating a list of teaching tips to faculty each month or each term.

3. Draw up a list of suggestions to help students improve their language learning and give it to all FLL students. Faculty should note additional hints as the semester progresses and put them in a box in the departmental office.

4. Investigate language teaching on computers. More and better programs become available each year. Students should become familiar with computers during their humanities education. Word processors offer enormous advantages to students in composition courses in foreign languages. See Michael J. Collet, *Computers in Language Teaching,* Canterbury Monographs for Teachers of French, University of Canterbury, New Zealand (1980). See also bibliography in *Computers in the Humanities,* a journal of general interest on the subject.

5. If possible, all departments should belong to the Association of Departments of Foreign Languages, the American Council on Teaching of Foreign Languages, and the Modern Language Association. Total costs are *under $100* and bring three very important publications quarterly to the department: the *ADFL Bulletin,* the *Foreign Language Annals,* and, of course, *PMLA.* Departments should also subscribe to *Modern Language Journal* and the principal language-specific journals like *French Review, Hispania,* and *Unterrichtspraxis.* Although these publications may be in the library, they typically are not well used by faculty. Copies should be available right in the department office.

   These journals should be shared by all faculty and can be sent·from one to another on a routing slip—if the number of faculty permit. If not, the journals should be placed on a shelf accessible to all. In addition, one faculty meeting a month should be devoted to reviewing the contents of these and the major language-specific journals. Faculty should each report on the major articles of interest to their colleagues (see details in section on professional update teams, pp. 000–00).

6. Use departmental faculty meetings for substantive discussions of teaching methods and course content. In many institutions, faculty meetings get bogged down in administrative detail.

Restoring the Language Requirement

On some of the campuses I have visited, the FL faculty themselves remain indifferent to the advisability of FL requirements. Many say flatly, "It would never pass faculty senate." I hope this book helps them to rethink their views. Some have a philosophy of education that condemns a prescriptive curriculum. Others feel that unwilling students detract from their classes. These faculty usually say that they want to "teach students who really want to learn." This position is particularly disappointing. On the one hand, it seems quite naive to me. Do students take economics, statistics, or organic chemistry because they really want to learn these subjects? I hope some do, but many enroll in these and other courses because they are necessary for an M.B.A. or admission to medical school or because they will enhance job prospects. Professors in those courses must teach students regardless of what motivated enrollment. On the other hand, it is, I think, both arrogant and selfish to wish to teach only those who really want to learn. Our obligation is to help educate citizens who enroll in our institutions. A faculty member might certainly decide that being an educated citizen does not entail knowing a second language and culture. Or a faculty member might believe that each student has the right to determine what an "educated" person should know. For these faculty, no FL requirements at all would remain appropriate. Another principle that moves people to decide against language requirements is the belief that "not everyone can learn a language." Of course, most everyone already knows one, and I do not know of a study that affirms that those who know one cannot learn another. But, in any case, these reasons for opposing FL requirements seem to me to move from principles and beliefs, whereas the reason based on whom one likes to teach seems to move from personal convenience. I also think of the impact of this selfishness on the English faculty who must regularly teach composition to the unwilling. Few of us would accept their refusal to teach any students save those who really want to learn how to write. In short, there are reasons to oppose FL requirements, but FL faculty who want to teach only those who want to learn do not express one that does them or their profession much service.

It is more of a challenge to teach well under a requirement system. Bright and interested students can indeed lose interest in a required class where their abilities disappear in a morass of indifference generated by their classmates. An artful teacher using a carefully prepared lesson plan and well-chosen materials can meet this challenge successfully. Some of the excellent work by experts in pedagogy offers guidance to teachers in dealing with varying ability and interest levels. Part of our job is to make students care about the ideas, texts, and subjects we teach, just as a good actor and script make us care about characters we did not know before the curtain rose, just as John Steinbeck made us care about Lenny and George. To accept only students who want to learn is to forget a large part of our responsibility.

The process of restoring the language requirement consumes huge amounts of time and energy, and faculty should probably not attempt it unless they believe the institution is in a state of readiness. Often the chances of passing the language requirement increase as the department grows in strength and in enrollments. Justification for a requirement should obviously proceed from academic reasons rather than from an effort to save faculty positions or departmental prestige.

When the department has engineered improvements like those suggested in this book, it will have developed a wider cadre of support, overcome some long-standing institutional resistance, and begun to make language study both profitable and attractive to students and faculty.

The arguments for a language requirement come down to one issue: the definition of an educated American citizen. In a world increasingly experienced as McLuhan's global village, educated citizens in this powerful democracy will bear serious responsibilities for the quality of leadership and decisions. More than ever before, Americans need to be familiar with other languages, cultures, and people. We must vote and perform professionally and personally with a global consciousness. Moreover, in an age of omnipresent communication, Americans need to understand what language is and how it works. The rhetoric supporting FL study presents a convincing case for FL requirements. The President's Commission report and Paul Simon's book *The Tongue-Tied American* offer excellent support for faculty attempting to restore the requirement on their campuses. The National Council on FL and International Studies (605 Third Ave., N.Y., NY 10022) has information to help as well. Skepticism, however, also operates very broadly, hence my own preference for first making sure that the FL courses in the department really do produce some of the heralded benefits of FL study before introducing suggestions to restore or increase language requirements. Right now, many FL classrooms teach foreign language phrase manipulation skills, not communicative proficiency. Many also do not substantially broaden students' cultural outlook or global perspective. Our major responsibility as FLL faculty lies in creating and teaching the courses that do in fact impart the skills and knowledge we and others expect from FL study and then in proving that our students have acquired these benefits from our programs. My work in the grant project, in my consultancies, and in this book indicate my confidence in this approach.

Once the department has determined that its program can impart the benefits associated with FL study, it should initiate a series of guest visits by members of the faculty and administration. If departmental class visitation has, as suggested (p. 6), become commonplace, students will function normally in class despite visitors. Even in institutions where the FL department consists of only one or two faculty, this approach can greatly enhance a substantial reassessment of FL study. A great many faculty now teaching voted to eliminate FL and other requirements in the past ten to twelve years. They deserve an opportunity to reverse those votes. But they need to know from personal experience what FL study can do for students and, moreover, what it *is* doing in their institutions. Problems of competition among departments intensify in periods of declining enrollments and resources. Therefore FL faculty on each campus have a serious obligation to prove to their community the value and importance of the work they do. Seeing can encourage believing even in our skeptical world. Class visitation can show our colleagues how things have changed since they did their foreign language study. A review of precourse and postcourse proficiency tests also enhances outsiders' confidence in the worth of the courses we teach. With personal experience as a basis for decision making, our colleagues may begin really to hear the rhetoric that supports so well the need to increase FL study throughout the country.

A large number of colleges and universities have returned to FL requirements. (See Preliminary Report insert, p. 67.) Language study committees often can help in the process of reinstating the requirement. These committees can combine faculty from English, FL, and all departments that have courses relating to language. They should also include student advisers or counselors. The charge of this interdisciplinary committee centers on studying the status and quality of language instruction at the institution and the need for improvements. The committee can offer an important first step in broadening the constituencies that know about and support the FL department and that eventually may support the requirement.

One excellent way to return to requirements involves establishing a short-term seat-time requirement that will become a proficiency requirement as soon as proficiency tests become available and faculty learn to give them reliably. For instance, an institution could approve an intermediate-level requirement that can be satisfied by three semesters of the language or the equivalent. This requirement would remain in place for three years while the FL faculty norm the standardized tests to the institution and attend workshops that teach faculty how to give the ACTFL-ETS proficiency tests. (See Judith Liskin-Gasparro's article, p. 211.) By the end of the three-year period, the institution would convert to a proficiency requirement of "intermediate" or "advanced" or whatever level the faculty judged appropriate. A review of this proficiency requirement would occur at the end of the next three-year period.

Another aspect of requirements pertains to the context of FL courses. An FL requirement standing alone and unconnected to the rest of a student's educational experience may breed frustration. The FL requirement should lock into a cluster of other courses. The institution might require that students choose two or three courses related to the language they select to study. The courses could be in non-American history, art, philosophy or religion, political science, economics, sociology, geography, or anthropology. If students have selected one of the commonly taught languages, they might also be required to elect a two-course non-Western sequence in one of the humanities or social science fields. In such a context, language study becomes part of the institution's efforts to broaden global outlook.

(For additional strategies to support a return to the FL requirement, see my article " 'Cultivons notre jardin': Strategies for Building Foreign Language and Literature Programs," *ADFL Bulletin,* 11, No. 3 [March 1980], 21–26.)

Preliminary Report on College and University Entrance and Degree Requirements in Foreign Languages, 1980–1981

In an effort to supply information concerning the status of college-level foreign language requirements for entrance and for the B.A. degree, the MLA undertook in the spring of 1981 a survey of approximately 850 departments that are members of the Association of Departments of Foreign Languages. Responses were received from 713 departments at 553 colleges and universities. A preliminary tally shows that 20 institutions, or 3.6%, report the establishment or reestablishment (since 1975) of an entrance requirement; 49, or 8.9%, report establishment or reestablishment of a requirement for the B.A. degree. The MLA's last comprehensive survey of requirements, undertaken in 1974–75 (see *ADFL Bulletin* 7, No. 1 [Sept. 1975], 43–48), showed that 239, or 18.6% of the 1,285 institutions surveyed, still had an entrance requirement in foreign languages, while 684, or 53.2%, had a requirement for the B.A. degree. An interim survey taken in 1978 elicited the names of 15 institutions that had restored a requirement for the B.A. degree or that had strengthened an existing requirement between 1975 and 1978.

The current list of public-supported institutions that have restored or strengthened an entrance requirement includes Univ. of California, at Berkeley, Davis, Irvine, Riverside, and Santa Cruz; Univ. of North Carolina, Chapel Hill; Minot State Coll.; Montclair State Coll.; Douglass Coll. and Rutgers Coll. of Rutgers Univ.; and the universities of New Mexico, Vermont, and Washington.

Private colleges that have restored or strengthened the entrance requirement are Allentown, Kenyon, LeMoyne, MacMurray, Seton Hill, Smith, and Williams,

Public-supported institutions that have reestablished a college-wide requirement for the B.A. degree include Northern Arizona Univ.; Univ. of California, Berkeley and Santa Cruz; Florida International Univ.; Iowa State Univ.; Indiana Univ., Bloomington, and Northwest Emporia State and Kansas State universities; Univ. of Minnesota, Duluth; Univ. of Missouri, Kansas City and St. Louis; North Carolina State Univ. and Univ. of North Carolina, Greensboro and Wilmington; William Paterson Coll.; Queens Coll., City Univ. of New York; State Univ. of New York, Binghamton, Buffalo, and Stony Brook; Univ. of Toledo; Univ. of Rhode Island; East Tennessee State Univ.; Texas Woman's University; and Univ. of Wisconsin, Milwaukee.

Among the private colleges and universities, the following report restoration of a requirement for the B.A. degree (in alphabetical order, by state): Connecticut Coll., Georgetown Univ., Emory Univ., Kennesaw Coll., Luther Coll., DePauw Univ., Transylva-

Entrance and Degree Requirements *(cont.)*

nia Univ., Centenary Coll., Tulane Univ., Regis Coll., Alma Coll., Augsburg Coll., Coll. of St. Catherine, St. John's Univ. (Minnesota), Millsaps Coll., Duke Univ., Caldwell Coll., New York Univ., Univ. of Rochester, Syracuse Univ., Xavier Univ., Chestnut Hill Coll., Duquesne Univ., Rosemont Coll., Newberry Coll., and Lambuth Coll. In addition to the institutions listed above, the following colleges and universities reported to the MLA in 1978 that they had restored a requirement for the B.A. degree: Asbury Coll., Old Dominion Univ., Rider Coll., and Southern Illinois Univ., Carbondale; a strengthened requirement was reported in 1978 at Brandeis Univ.; Univ. of Illinois, Chicago Circle; St. Francis Coll. (Pa.); and St. Patrick's Coll. (Calif.).

A final report on the results of the 1980–81 survey will be released in July 1981, giving a breakdown of the number of institutions reporting establishment or reestablishment of a language requirement, no requirement, or no change in the status reported in 1974–75. Since there is little evidence of any continuing trend to abolish requirments, it is reasonable to assume that the status of requirements nationwide has changed relatively little since 1975, having risen perhaps to 20% (from 18.6%) for entrance requirements and possibly to 60% (from 53.2%) for degree requirements.

REPORT UPDATE

Since the publication of this report, the following institutions have restored or strengthened their foreign language requirements: Univ. of Tennessee, Univ. of Wyoming, and Yale Univ. The following institutions, arranged by zip code, have added a degree requirement: Boston Coll., MA 02167; Stonehill Coll., MA 02356; Univ. of Maine, Presque Isle, ME 04769; Upsala Coll., NJ 07019; Drew Univ, NJ 07940; Brooklyn Coll., NY 11210; Marist Coll., NY 12601; Colgate Univ., NY 13346; Duquesne Univ., PA 15282; Lehigh Univ., PA 18015; Swarthmore Coll., PA 19081; Alvernia Coll., PA 19607; Ferrum Coll., VA 24088; Univ. of South Carolina, Aiken, SC 29801; Eckerd Coll., FL 33733; Southwestern at Memphis, TN 38112; Anderson Coll., IN 46011; Michigan Tech Univ., MI 49931; Morningside Coll., IA 51106; Univ. of Wisconsin, Eau Claire, WI 54701; Air Force Academy, CO 80849; Univ. of Southern Colorado, CO 81001; Southern Utah State Coll., UT 84720; New Mexico Highlands Univ., NM 87701; Biola Coll., CA 90638; Westmont Coll., CA 93108; Stanford Univ., CA 94305; Central Washington Univ., WA 98926.

The following institutions have added an entrance requirement: Anna Maria Coll., MA 01612; Boston Univ., MA 02215; Bucknell Univ., PA 17837; Wake Forest Univ., NC 27109; Wittenberg Univ., OH 45501; Biola Coll., CA 90638.

Chapter Two

Strategies to Support Planned Change in Foreign Language and Literature Departments

Productive and effective departments remain in a constant state of development. Development means change. College and university departments in all subject areas have a common and primary goal: to teach better the students who enroll in their classes. Teaching better means more than preparing for classes carefully. It means keeping up-to-date with current professional literature. It means helping one another improve syllabi, teaching strategies, and curricular materials. It means taking the lead in developing course offerings and major, minor, and special programs. Finally, we teach better when we take seriously the contributions we make to the lives of our students, our colleagues, our institutions, and our society. Many departments have other goals as well, such as pursuing research on literature, on language learning, and on linguistics. Some departments must take major responsibility for preparing professionals who will work abroad in agriculture, pharmacology, or engineering. Many departments still prepare high school language teachers. Fulfilling departmental responsibilities, including those concerned with research, depends on the faculty's belief that teaching well makes a difference to learners and teachers alike.

This preamble to a chapter on strategies to support planned change in humanities curricula should underline my belief that FLL faculty have a primary responsibility for improving the quality of the teaching in the humanities in general and in foreign language classrooms in particular. An elegantly designed curriculum that fails to improve teaching and to motivate teachers and students to achieve the course objectives fails in a crucial way.

Regardless of differences, all plans for change should reflect team effort, capitalize on each person's strengths, and consistently assess the positive impact on teaching and learning. Claud DuVerlie's suggestions for building faculty teamwork begin on p. 85. It is true that humanities faculty have never been known for their ability to work in teams. We are supposed to project the image of eccentric lonely scholars pushing away at a seemingly intractable wall of ignorance. Our departments are often a col-

69

lection of individuals pursuing very different quests, not a unit in any real sense. The expectations and pressures of the current academic scene suggest that we should review this model. In any case, regardless of our scholarly orientations, members of departments and institutions have certain obligations. The time has come for better orchestrated, well-researched teamwork to plan changes in our departments. Nothing stops us from pursuing the individual quest Mondays, Wednesdays, and Fridays and playing a team sport on Tuesdays and Thursdays. At many of the best schools scholars do just that.

How to Plan Change in FLL Departments

I advise departments planning substantial development to begin by setting up ten folders marked with headings found in the outline beginning on p. 80. Whether or not the department plans to seek extramural funding, a conscious, common understanding of the task ahead will facilitate future work.

1. INSTITUTIONAL SETTINGS

The Institution

Institutions change over time. Many colleges in 1983 have very different missions and even values than they had in 1968. Faculty members must plan to improve their programs with these changes clearly in mind. A comparison between a current catalog and one from, say, ten years ago will help to define these transformations. How has the mission statement changed? Requirements? Majors? Numbers of courses? In some institutions a quick telephone survey of departments may reveal how many courses all across the curriculum are actually being taught and how often. In other institutions, variable content course numbers conceal curricular opportunities and diversities not apparent in the catalog (Poli Science 399: Special Topics, or History 400: Seminar on Selected Subjects). Study of one's institution leads to an assessment of the current mission and values. Harder to isolate but not less important are questions about the institution's popular image. What is the ratio of applicants to acceptances to student arrivals? Or, more to the point on many campuses, how hard do recruiters work to keep the enrollments at acceptable levels? How far do they travel? Do they recruit abroad? How many alumni children attend? How many students from out of state? Study these figures for the ten years. (Much of this data exists at the admissions office or in the dean's or provost's office.)

What is the history of the college in the community it serves? Does the college draw strength from and offer help to the community? In this respect many smaller historically black schools have changed dramatically in the past fifteen years as many black students opt for admission to majority institutions. Costs as well as changing societal values have altered enrollments at many small church-related schools.

What is the institution's style at present? If general faculty morale is a major problem, your development plan would do well to include non-FLL faculty in a summer workshop. If administrators seem at odds with faculty over directions for change, you may wish to build in some source of funds for faculty and administrators to travel to other institutions and develop some common understanding about what works well. Or you may wish to bring an expert or consultant to campus who can help you plan a better curriculum while also alleviating the stresses that alienate faculty from administration. (See possible sources for funding, consultant assistance through various programs at NEH, p. 263.)

If your institution is in a particularly dynamic mode, you may wish to hold a regional workshop for faculty and administrators from high schools, community colleges, and colleges and universities to show them your successes and recommend ways to build better FLL programs in your region. *Know thyself* and plan accordingly.

Students

Collect information on your students to be sure you design a curriculum to meet their needs. From what geographical areas do your students come? What are their family incomes? What is the educational level of their parents? Why do they come to your institution? Where do they go? How many go directly to graduate school? How many are in preprofessional programs? How many find employment in the careers for which they prepare? Are there special groups on your campus?

Although it takes a little more time, I prefer FL departments to develop some of these answers on their own instead of relying totally on college sources. Run a survey of one hundred recent graduates. Besides asking some of the questions outlined above, try to ascertain how content the graduates are with the education they received. What would they change? What are their contacts with non-English speakers? What do they value most (and least) in their undergraduate experience? Did they admire or tolerate their professors?

No faculty group will have difficulty preparing a list of questions that will satisfy their need to know students better before planning a curriculum. I should note parenthetically but emphatically that the reason to know students is not to design a curriculum they will like. The responsibility of faculty is to design a curriculum that is academically sound and, if possible, to interpret to students and their families a compelling rationale for this curriculum. To do these tasks, faculty must know their students' needs, abilities, expectations, and goals.

Faculty

An outline of faculty strengths and weaknesses within the FL department will suggest important elements of the new program. A predominantly tenured faculty has years of experience in teaching to offer a new curriculum. They should list and describe all the courses they have ever taught. Some of the approaches and materials they have used in the past may provide special inspiration to a new curriculum. For instance, former courses in civilization may serve as a fine basis for an updated history and contemporary affairs course in the foreign language, or for a course on "the fifties in France," or for the collection of new materials for a course contrasting American and foreign contemporary affairs. Old materials on literary texts may be useful in FL writing courses as bases for pastiche exercises (see p. 163). Reviews of old grammar or composition books may offer interesting assignments for writing or conversation courses. How did those books see the culture and the world? In what ways are current texts different? What is the global perspective of the old texts? A mature faculty has special strengths that are often ignored in the race to modernize. And by using old materials creatively, the language curriculum can help students to use their judgments and learn about recent history.

Institutions that experienced the collapse of FL departments in the seventies along with retirements often have a group of younger faculty. In many I have visited, no one is tenured, not even the chairman. The strengths of these faculty may lie in their energy and ambition rather than in their experience. Their more recent training may have better prepared them to teach the language. They may have fewer fixed ideas about what does and does not work in the classroom. They may not foresee problems, however, and may be unrealistic about students' abilities. Some may feel less committed to the institution where they teach. They may hope to move on or move up to a department oriented more toward research and thus be less willing to commit time and energy to curriculum design.

Whether the department is mostly tenured, mostly young, or a mix, faculty members should list their individual interests, areas of special strength, and the curricular areas in which they would like to develop expertise in the future.

Administration

Any plans for change should take cognizance of administrators' goals and concerns. While faculty and administrators often find themselves acting like adversaries, they share many goals. I suggest that departments preparing for change ask their administrators what they consider to be the current goals and greatest challenges to the institution. What is their prognosis on these subjects for the next five years? A modification in the FL department can often help advance larger goals beyond that unit. Strong institutions attract good students and keep good faculty.

State System

Finally, a study of the institutional setting will often involve some investigation of the state education system. In some states new courses cannot be proposed at state-funded institutions unless old ones are targeted to be dropped. Instituting a curriculum plan that includes a major or a minor may also demand special permission or trade-offs. Such restrictions should not discourage change and development. They simply indicate the kind of battle that must be waged and the kind of data that will be needed to win the engagement.

2. PRESENT CURRICULUM

All departments have lists of courses given, though faculty often do not know one another's approaches to teaching the courses, what texts are read, or how testing is conducted. Like members of a group medical practice, teachers in the same department should know one another's work. The planning period is a perfect time to develop this familiarity. Beyond the department, the non-FL curriculum bears study by FL faculty. How has it changed in the last four years? To what degree are students expected to create the links among courses and fields of inquiry? To what degree could links be forged by faculty? For instance, could the readings in a social science course (or courses) be the subject of the foreign language conversation course? Does the business program lack any strong international dimension that the FL and social science faculty could help to provide?

In general, are faculty both in and out of the FL program content with the present curriculum and with the contribution of the FL department to it? I suggest that FL departments take a poll among non-FL faculty to determine their interest and ability in FLs, their sense of its importance in their professional and personal lives, and their willingness to integrate languages into their curricula. (See Faculty Poll insert, ch. 1, pp. 42–44.)

Perhaps the most important work of this section is to develop new information about the curriculum, student needs, and institutional mission. None of the items mentioned in the outline is significant alone, and none should determine curriculum, but together they do permit faculty to explain academic decisions to their constituencies coherently and persuasively. Many mistakes can be avoided, and features can be built into courses to address the needs of special groups. For instance, students who enter with low verbal SAT scores may benefit from a frankly comparative grammar unit every two weeks in the FL course. (See Jacqueline Morton's *English Grammar for Students of French* [Ann Arbor, Mich.: Olivia and Hill, 1979]. Editions are available in other commonly taught languages.) In schools where many students major or minor in business, some business-oriented reading and writing assignments can be included in the elementary course even before the intermediate-level business language course.

3. THE NEW CURRICULUM

The new curriculum or course sequence will be the result of an honest look at faculty strengths, student needs, institutional mission, and a consensus on what is academically sound. Faculty should read about successful programs for inspiration. NEH will send descriptions of successful grant projects, which can be modified for use at other institutions. FIPSE also has information on its projects. Current journals may have articles describing model programs. It is obviously a good idea to write to chairpersons at other institutions and ask them for curricula and course descriptions. Attendance at professional meetings and keeping up-to-date with professional literature also help. Interested faculty both in and outside the FL department should be invited to brainstorming sessions. The basic data that the department has developed should be reviewed for all to hear. The group, which might also include high school teachers, should exchange ideas on how to improve the FL curriculum. The chairperson or someone designated by the faculty may head a language advisory committee, on which interested members from departments such as business or the sciences serve. Administrators and chairs of other departments should become involved as early as possible in the planning stages.

An exciting range of curricular options now exist. Some have received attention in Theodore Higg's *Curriculum, Competence, and the Foreign Language Teacher* (1982) and in Sims and Hammond's *Award-Winning FL Programs* (1981). (See bibliography, pp. 298, 299. Both are available from National Textbook, Skokie, IL 60077. See additional suggestions in ch. 1, pp. 19–21.)

The only serious dangerous trend that I see in FLL curriculum changes involves the move away from the skills and content of the humanities. As the emphasis on teaching oral-aural competency meets the demands of career-oriented FL programs, faculty may find themselves distracted from teaching reading and writing, which are the fundamental skills of humanities education. Currently most English faculty teach these skills in English courses not because they expect students to become literary critics or professional writers but because they believe that building these skills supports general literacy in English and helps develop students' ability to think critically. Faculty should teach reading and writing in the target language as ways of building literacy, which includes oral-aural proficiency. We have omitted teaching these skills well in many classes because we say "students won't need to write German." This is true. Many people do not need to write English either, but practicing this skill improves the ability to use the language. (See the sections on teaching reading and writing, pp. 129, 151.) FL study at each level should also continue to bring students into contact with the content of humanities education. The humanities includes productions that describe and assess the human condition. FL teachers can use many different vehicles for this contact, such as literary and other texts, films, tapes, magazines, journals, newspapers, and oral testimony. The FL curriculum should offer students opportunities to encounter these materials and to consider throughtfully their implications through class discussions and writing assignments.

Curricular redesign can aim to strengthen students' skills in and knowledge of the humanities, create strong links to other departments, or improve FL proficiency levels. If any or all of these are major goals of the redesigned courses, the department will want to ensure that program plans indicate clearly how these objectives will be reached.

As the new curriculum or course series begins to evolve, the person responsible for guiding the changes should keep track of activities in a copybook. The project needs a history, but, more important, many good ideas that develop as the program gets started cannot be integrated into the early stages. They can escape everyone's attention unless the chair keeps track of them. The faculty will, of course, proceed to develop bibliography, syllabi, detailed course outline (see p. 11), and descriptions of course content and aims, evaluation methods, teaching strategies, and materials. In addition, the faculty should write a short cogent rationale relating the new program to the needs of students, the institution's mission, and existing curriculum. The department will also need an outline of methods intended to prepare faculty to teach the new courses. These plans should include some judgments on the likely short- and long-range (four or five years) impact of the revised curriculum on faculty members, on student learning, on administrative goals, and on the community the institution serves (outreach). The department should also consider the project's effect on other departments or schools, on recruitment efforts and the admissions office, on the way the advising staff views the FL departments, and on alumni. Considering these constituencies while developing the new curriculum may help the department ensure not only a program responsive to constituents' needs but a receptive audience as well.

Planning for the promotion of the new curriculum will help faculty evaluate the program. Brochures, information sheets, newspaper articles, and class discussions often do not provide a sufficiently striking forum in which to introduce a program designed to have a significant impact on the department and the institution. A faculty colloquia may be effective, or an open "town meeting" with students and faculty. Finally, the new curriculum design should set forth the incentives you and your administrators have developed to encourage and support participating faculty (see incentives, pp. 4–5).

4. HUMANITIES EDUCATION

Since FLL departments represent a discipline usually classified as one of the humanities, good planning should deal with the way the new curriculum strengthens humanities education. The faculty will need to ask themselves these kinds of questions: Are students reading enough in the new courses? What are they reading? How are they being asked to assess the texts? Are students writing enough? Are they rewriting their essays? What kind of faculty and peer guidance do students receive on their writing?

What is the philosophy behind the faculty's choice of materials? Do students have the opportunity to assess this selection? Does the course offer occasions for students to witness and participate in a community of educated people reflecting intelligently on significant subjects? The criteria for good humanities education can be met in varying degrees in *all* well-designed FLL courses, from the elementary language courses to the most advanced, highly specialized seminars. They will be met more often as the result of conscious planning. Creating a high-quality academic program means addressing these issues early and vigorously.

5. RESOURCES

As plans develop, faculty will confront two pragmatic issues that touch the rate and quality of progress: the availability of support and resources and an assessment of the needs the program will create. Faculty awareness of the support and resources at the institution may significantly reduce costs. Resources fall into three categories: personnel, equipment, and spendable funds.

Personnel

Faculty will want to note the special skills that each faculty member will bring to the program (in fact, these skills may actually help to shape the program). A short paragraph outlining the rationale for each faculty member's participation will keep these special skills and interests in the forefront of planning deliberations. Certain institutions have additional resources in the student body and community. For instance, even a short history of college recruiting efforts in South American countries not only creates a pool of native informants for Spanish conversation classes, it may also create links to business and industry in Spanish-speaking countries. Internships for American students, guest lecturers from the Latin American country, and a study-abroad program may all develop quite naturally from this pool. The community around a college often has resources ready to be tapped. The international furniture industry near High Point College (N.C.) enabled the foreign language department to branch out toward business internships through their multicultural studies and business program. The Spanish-speaking communities of many large American cities offer excellent opportunities for student internships in bilingual settings and may lead to the participation in the program of Spanish-speaking professionals from newspapers, hospitals and clinics, and social service and legal aid agencies. One faculty member and several majors might wish to do a survey of the personnel resources on hand in the community. The results may surprise even the long-tenured faculty.

Non-FL departments and offices in the institution provide another kind of personnel resource. Administrative support and suggestions should be sought early and nurtured. The admissions, alumni, and student advising offices all offer potential sources of support for the new program. How these units react to FL development plans should be on record in the department, as should efforts to improve relations. If the department decides to seek outside funding, this kind of information will be helpful in articulating the need for financial support.

Equipment

Most institutions have some major pieces of equipment on hand, though often their existence is a well-kept secret. The FL department should check with the audio-visual center, the radio and tv departments, and other units that might have underutilized or usable equipment that is being replaced and that could be reallocated to an experimental phase of the FL project. In one program for which I was consultant, tv camera equipment was made available to FL students so that they could film interviews in social welfare settings and in health clinics. These films helped students use their foreign language skills to improve their professional work. In the early stages of the project, the students borrowed equipment from the social work and radio and tv departments during hours when it was not in use. The FL department may decide to make a call for equipment in general faculty meetings or in some faculty publication. A memo to all chairpersons may do as well. The point is to discover all the equipment resources that might be brought to the support of the new program.

Spendable Funds

Finally, what institutional expenditures can the department count on? Can the dean provide course release or summer stipends for faculty developing the new program? Does the dean have funds to hire a consultant for the department? The extreme budget restrictions that characterize so many institutions may prohibit such outlays. Funding may be more forthcoming for certain categories of support, such as consultation on curriculum development materials, especially in the state college and university systems.

6. Needs

Once the support and resources are clear, the needs will become obvious to the department's planning team. An outline of needs should describe the kind and amount of faculty development and retraining necessary to support the new program. It should state how many faculty will participate in retraining and how its impact will be evaluated. Will faculty need released time or summer support to prepare for the new program? Will new faculty or support personnel be necessary? When? How will the department assure the dean that hiring will be cost-effective? What consultants or specialists will be necessary and why? What new material and equipment will be required? How will you decide what to buy? Who will train faculty to use this equipment? What programs at other institutions should faculty visit? These trips are costly, but in my experience they bear high dividends in exposing faculty to new and different ways of teaching. Finally, in outlining needs, describe how you plan to overcome the obstacles you expect to meet. I find that preparing for resistance to change reduces the sense of disenchantment faculty feel as they encounter opposition to programs. The need for diplomacy, patience, and persistence are as real as the need for a language lab or course release if the new program is to succeed.

7. Evaluation

Evaluation of the new project is a vital part of the planning process. The department should have a fully developed plan to evaluate the program and its various components in both the short and the long range. Evaluation concerns two levels, the pedagogical and the institutional. On the pedagogical level, do you intend to administer pretests or posttests? Will they be exams with national norms or will you norm the tests to your institution? Will you develop your own tests? How will course testing change? Will the tests measure mastery of specific content, skill development like speaking or writing, or attitude changes? Contact specialists like Judy Liskin-Gasparro at ETS for information on proficiency testing. Find out from Global Perspectives in Education (218 East 18th St., New York, NY 10003) about ways to test for cultural awareness. What will the faculty consider a successful performance by a student? How would current FL students do on the tests for the new program? Do you wish to develop and use the tests before you change the curriculum to obtain some baseline data? What will administrators consider a successful pedagogical outcome?

At the institutional level, find out the basis for the evaluation process used at your college. Do student enrollments or retention rates tell the story? Do consultant teams or visiting committees evaluate programs regularly? What criteria do they use? Academic officers can often advise on these points and help the department build appropriate evaluation plans.

Finally, who will evaluate? Must students' judgments play as important a role as those of faculty participants? Will the evaluation of the student advisers be based on reactions they receive from FL students or from their own observations of classes? Administrators, non-FL faculty, community contacts, and, of course, outside evaluators can all contribute to the adjustments needed by any new program.

8. Schedule of Activities and Duties

A schedule of activities and duties for each FL faculty member and outside participant will help the program run smoothly. (See Claud DuVerlie, p. 93.) This schedule, written up each semester, or an outline of activities and duties written on a time line, will give the group a sense of what it intends to achieve and by what date. Monthly update sheets will describe advances and delays in the schedule. Should the team decide to seek a grant, this schedule will strengthen the proposal by indicating that a serious and well-organized faculty is ready to undertake additional responsibilities. The proposal itself should, of course, include a time line displaying the schedule of activities and objectives to be pursued and an additional outline of duties of faculty and other participants. This permits reviewers to understand the dimensions of the project at a glance.

9. BUDGET

Most new projects will need a well-prepared budget whether or not outside funding is involved. The budget should contain a breakdown of costs and the basis of cost projections using the institution's standard categories. I encourage faculty to include a short budget narrative with paragraphs numbered like the budget items. Each paragraph should explain briefly the importance of the item and outline any other pertinent details, such as where funding will come from. (See ch. 6 for more information.)

10. RESOURCE DEVELOPMENT

Readers interested in how to get grants and other support for the new program should see chapter 8, "Securing Outside Funding," and number 10 in the outline on p. 82. NEH and some colleges offer funds for planning. Faculty may need financial support at this early stage, an important one in program development.

This detailed discussion of strategies for planning change should not overwhelm a faculty member or team. The idea of collecting ten folders and beginning to move carefully through the steps breaks a complex task into discrete parts, encourages teamwork, and helps to attract the confidence of others. None of the categories must necessarily be studied extensively. Institutional setting will determine the order of activities and degree of effort needed under any one of the ten rubrics. In my experience with helping departments develop, thoughtful planning for change enhances the success of the project considerably. Organized proposals that arrive in the dean's office or in the faculty senate with their evaluation plans, budgets, resources, and schedules of duties and activities accompanying course or curriculum descriptions make convincing reading.

Should the department ultimately decide to seek outside funding, the ten folders contain the information needed for most grant proposals. Methodical planning greatly lightens the task of preparing a proposal. This kind of academic planning is not common in FL or humanities departments. FL faculty and, in fact, humanities faculty have not been trained to work as a team, hold tenaciously to deadlines, or conceive of an overall game plan and then proceed to fulfill it. Our approach to discovery and change is more often solitary and eclectic. While it works for scholarly research, it is less dependable as a way to achieve sound curricular revisions and program development. Nothing impedes most of us from working eclectically on our research and strategically in our departmental planning. We must simply begin to expect this dual ability from ourselves and then practice it.

General strategies that support planned change make more sense when accompanied by an example of how one department actually progressed through significant changes. The Modern Languages and Linguistics Department at University of Maryland–Baltimore County proceeded through a full-scale development under the direction of Alan Rosenthal and Claud DuVerlie. I appreciate Dr. DuVerlie's contribution to this book, in which he describes the management strategies used during the development period.

Strategies to Support Planned Change in Humanities Curricula

1. The institutional setting
   a. Describe your institution: its mission, its values, its image and history in the community it serves, its institutional style (conservative, dynamic, confident, demoralized).
   b. Describe your students—their backgrounds and objectives—and any special target groups, e.g., students with particular career goals.
   c. Outline faculty strengths and weaknesses (turnover rate in humanities, tenure levels, etc.).
   d. Outline administrative officers' primary goals and concerns and your institution's administrative structures.
   e. How does educational change occur within existing state structure? How does your state's coordinating board for education affect your institution? (In some states, a new course cannot be added unless a current course is dropped.)

2. Present curriculum
   a. Describe existing educational structures, programs, courses.
   b. Explain problems, challenges, gaps in humanities curriculum as it now stands. Describe the degree of integration among humanities courses.
   c. Clarify the degree of consensus in the institution about elements in 2 b.
   d. Describe any data you have collected relative to student needs and institutional mission (student interest surveys, class evaluations, surveys of faculty or community needs, student test profiles, etc.)

3. The "new idea," or program, or course series
   a. Sketch a short history of how the new idea developed.
   b. Include description of course content, bibliography, syllabi.
   c. Describe various teaching strategies to be used.
   d. Outline rationale for the program in terms of community needs and existing curriculum.
   e. Outline the short- and long-range (4–5 years) impact on faculty development, student learning, administrative goals, and community.

Strategies to Support Planned Change (*cont.*)

    f.   Project program's effect on other departments or schools in your institution, on the admissions office, on *advising* staff, etc.

    g.   Outline the ways that different units in your institution will be introduced to the new program (colloquia, "town meetings," etc.). How will you *promote* this new feature of the curriculum?

    h.   Involve administrators and department chairs as early as possible in the planning stages.

    i.   Describe the incentives you and your adminstrators have developed to encourage and support participating faculty: released time, summer stipends, letters of recognition, merit raises, etc.

4. Humanities education
    Explain how this curriculum will improve teaching and learning in the humanities.

5. Support and resources
    a.   Explain special personnel resources presently on site (i.e., specially prepared faculty, students, or community members).

    b.   Give rationale for participation for each faculty member on the project.

    c.   Describe administrative and departmental support (show deans and chairs your plans, get their advice, and secure specific letters of support from them).

    d.   Describe support from other units in your institution (admissions, alumni, student advising).

    e.   Describe community support, if relevant (business leaders, civic groups, etc.).

    f.   Describe equipment and other material resources on hand to support project.

    g.   Describe institutional cost sharing (how much financial support the institution can offer, in-kind, cash, etc.).

6. Needs
    a.   Describe faculty development and retraining necessary to support new program (how many faculty will be involved? how significant will training be?).

    b.   Describe rationale for any hiring of new faculty or support personnel (TAs, etc.).

    c.   Explain released-time needs for current faculty, staff.

    d.   Describe materials necessary (equipment, software, etc.).

    e.   Outline needs for consultants or specialists, describing the kind of assistance you need and why you need it.

    f.   Explain other costs that will need to be covered (travel by faculty to other institutions).

    g.   Describe the materials and approaches you need to use to overcome the obstacles you expect to encounter. (List obstacles, individual as well as general problems like student resistance, administrative reluctance, etc., and then explain the approach you will need to meet each one.)

7. Evaluation plans (include in-process shorter-range and longer-range plans)
    a.   Pedagogical level: Do you plan to administer pre-post course tests? Will they be exams with national norms or specially prepared tests? Will they reflect mastery of specific content? skill development? changes? or all of these?

    b.   Institutional level: Discover the basis for the evaluation process used at your institution. How are decisions made about the worth of a program? Is it the student retention rate? outside evaluators' judgment? national tests (CLEP, etc.)? new enrollments attached to institution by the new program? Administrators can help you develop this information and build appropriate evaluation plans into your program.

Strategies to Support Planned Change (*cont.*)

   c. Who will evaluate? Students? Faculty participants and nonparticipants? Counselors and advisers? Related community contacts? Administrators? Are any outside consultants or evaluators necessary?

8. Schedules of activities and duties

   a. Prepare a time-line summary plotting the schedule of activities and objectives to be pursued during different phases of change.

   b. Outline the duties of all faculty and participants.

9. Budget (see ch. 8)

   Prepare a budget and budget narrative (explain in paragraph form the details of each line item, breakdown of costs, and the basis of cost projections).

10. Financial resource development (see ch. 8)

   Most good ideas involving curriculum change and development can be undertaken without external support and as ongoing facets of college or university business. When the projected changes rise beyond the resources of routine growth and development, outside funding may provide an answer. Be sure to plan how the program will continue under institutional funds after grant funds run out. Be prepared to explain these plans clearly in any planning document or grant proposal you write. Additional suggestions on grants include:

   a. Find out what private and federal agencies have grant programs that your program is eligible to compete for (ask your grants or development office; write Department of Education, NEH, FIPSE, or your state office of education; or consult the *Catalog of Federal Domestic Assistance*).

   b. Send for descriptions of grant programs, deadline dates, and copies of forms.

   c. Does the granting agency read preproposals? If so, send one.

   d. *Read* directions and suggestions from granting agency. Refer often to the information you have received from the agency. Follow directions, suggestions, and guidelines carefully.

   e. Some agencies publish descriptions of successful programs they have funded. In addition, some send copies of successful grant applications (without budget information). These materials will guide and inspire you. Find out the size of the average grant in the agency's program you are applying to.

   f. Make sure you understand the review process. Ask for the ratio of proposals funded to proposals received. Also find out whether or not reviewers' comments will be available to you after the competition. These can help you be more successful next time.

   g. Be prepared to fail at grantsmanship. Many fine proposals need two, three, or more chances to compete before they yield funds. Humanists need to learn from their colleagues in the sciences who keep right on doing proposals, regardless of their success ratio, learning from the rejected proposals how to make a more competitive proposal the next time.

   h. The "strategy for planned change" that you are developing could be used as a basis for your preproposal or proposal to the funding agency (excluding certain details [6 g.] and adding ones an agency may request).

Strategies, Tactics, and Activities in Department Development

Claud DuVerlie

It seems fit to start with two observations that, without being directly related, are of some consequence to the organization and management of departments.

First, the term "management" is not frequently used in academic circles; indeed, the word usually has negative connotations for academics. Professorial dislike for the business world is nearly proverbial. The pervasive disdain for "management" in many departments may help account for the serious problems they are experiencing today.

Second, it is necessary to recognize at the outset that there are many variations in the unit of organization called "academic departments." Their composition ranges from one to some sixty faculty members. Their status in the college or university and their methods of operations also vary greatly. Despite this diversity, it is my hope that my practice at the University of Maryland–Baltimore County (UMBC), a medium-sized state university, will reflect our common concerns, questions, and problems and provide a useful model for strategies, tactics, and activities that others can follow for department development.

A concrete picture of what management has accomplished at UMBC can best be given by comparing the states of the department in 1977 and in 1982. After university requirements were liberalized in 1970, students no longer had to take a foreign language, and department enrollments slid unremittingly down to a crisis point in 1977. Since then, we have worked vigorously to reverse the decline and have produced not only the sought-after recovery but substantial growth as well. Here are the two states of the department five years apart:

1977	1982
13 faculty members	15 faculty members and 6 language counselors
Scheduled to lose 4 or 5 positions because of overstaffing and underenrollment	Understaffed by 3 positions

1977	1982
Part-time lab director	Full-time lab director
Low departmental enrollments	Long student waiting lists
15 language majors	About 70 majors
No graduate program	M.A. in bilingual education
Very low budget	Budget increased eight-fold, although still inadequate
No resources	Dept. of Education grant for bilingual education (3 yrs.)
	NEH pilot grant (1979–80)
	NEH implementation grant (1982–86)
	Technical assistance grants from Md. State Dept. of Education
Aging language lab	State-of-the-art Language Center
Poor image	Department perceived positively by university and community

What accounts for this drastic change? Obviously, it took energy, innovation, and *management.* The "management" encountered in most colleges and universities bears little resemblance to that of departments in other kinds of organizations. Management of the academic department typically rests on faculty governance and collegiality, an arrangement that often puts the manager in a straitjacket. As Jean-Pierre Barricelli writes, "The problem of personnel management is greatly intensified by a chair's powerlessness and severely limited authority, now compounded by the steady state of staffs locked in by tenure." ("Managing a Zoo: The Total Foreign Language Department," *Profession 81* [New York: MLA, 1981], p. 41).

Despite the peculiarity of the academic world, it seems to me that we must take lessons from the business world. We must be willing to look at the department as any generic department whose fate is determined by its internal strengths and weaknesses. My impression is that few departments have shown a readiness to assume that responsibility. Most seem to depend on university administrations, particularly the deans. But deans do not solve departmental problems; at best, they may help departments in solving problems or meeting objectives.

One point cannot be overstressed: a department should take its destiny in its own hands, should develop its internal strengths and strive to become self-sufficient and self-reliant. Deans not only appreciate but also respect departments that leave them alone. And when such a department does have to see the dean, he or she is all the more likely to grant a request.

The hallmark of the eighties will probably be its abundance of regressive measures. A particularly unfortunate result is that the department has become the chairperson's castle. In a period of scarcity and budget cuts, internal reallocations have become a general practice. The scrambling for resources has led to a Darwinian form of management by which the weakest lose or even perish. The tools used include enrollments, institutional priorities, overall productivity, and needs and demands for programs. In these circumstances, wisdom precludes weakness and the appearance of weakness. The time has therefore come for us all to practice department development.

Department development involves the evolution, change, and improvement of systems and subsystems. It focuses on short-and medium-term organization missions and goals and aims to increase organizational health and effectiveness.

From the diagnosis of departmental systems and processes emerges a strategy for change, which will probably include the following types of "interventions":

Communications system and team building

Organizing

Goal setting and planning

Activating and controlling

Problem solving

These headings reflect five basic functions of management. An examination of these functions and suggested tactics for carrying them out follow.

Communications System and Team Building

Team building may be seen as a corollary of sorts to communications. Two needs in this area are an open departmental communications system and good intergroup collaboration. Excessive competition among individuals and groups causes major dysfunctional expenditure of energy in many departments.

COMMUNICATIONS

How does the chairperson ensure a fast flow of information in the department? Traditional ways of communicating are memorandums and faculty meetings. But even assuming a smoothly functioning system, these means often have limited value. The following typology suggests the range of standard means at one's disposal.

Techniques	Advantages	Disadvantages
Private conversations	Persuasive	Inefficient 1-to-1 ratio
Meetings other than faculty meetings (curriculum committee, coordinators, etc.)	Better efficiency, information tailored to group	Somewhat formal
Faculty meetings	Maximum efficiency, effective decision-making mechanism	Formal and cumbersome, limited availabilty

Techniques	Advantages	Disadvantages
Mail boxes for exchanging information	Easy to use, fast	Impersonal, unreliable
Brown-bag lunch	Relaxed setup, easy communication	Precludes some topics
Departmental happy hour	Ideal for socializing	May preclude serious questions and topics
Social events	Group spirit, team building	May preclude business

One could add to this list special arrangements such as the departmental retreat, which usually allows an entire faculty to spend a weekend brainstorming and planning. The question is not so much which activities as it is how many and how satisfactorily they are carried out. Since many of them complement and reinforce one another, departments should consider whether they practice enough of the activities—at least four or five—covering the full range from formal communication to socializing.

INTERGROUP COLLABORATION

The typical structure of a language department often makes collaboration among groups difficult. At UMBC we realized that our department—administratively organized as a series of departments within a department—was inefficient for the following reasons:

1. It generated substantial overlapping, which we could ill afford. For instance, the traditional course of textual analysis had five students in each language.
2. It encouraged the segregation of French, Spanish, and German students for no other reason, it seems, than territorial jurisdiction.
3. It led to faculty provincialism and competition among language areas.

There are two ways to foster interaction among faculty and interrelations among languages. One operates at the level of the language curriculum (the way used at UMBC), whereby faculty from different language divisions team-teach departmental courses, or even a multioption departmental major. In the second way, which works through the departmental organization, "the basic idea is to create many faculty overlaps, as many as the qualifications of your colleagues permit, so that a professor of Spanish may be not only on the Spanish program staff but also, say, on the classics program staff" (Barricelli, p. 42). Such changes result in a renewed sense of unity. In most institutions faculty members cannot function cohesively because language programs are not coordinated. Each area focuses on its own interests. A divided faculty cannot plead its case effectively in the university. An FL department needs to have an identity beyond its constituent fields of specialization, and it needs to have a unified sense of mission. Only then can we work effectively in furthering the cause of foreign languages.

Organizing

DEPARTMENTAL STRUCTURE

Is the department clearly organized as to roles, responsibilities, and the assignment of various tasks? Does everybody know who is in charge of what and when?

One way to clarify how a department is organized uses an organizational chart identifying responsibilities for each faculty member. The ground rule for establishing such a chart is to have every faculty member fulfill a departmental (internal) function and a university-wide (external) function. An organizational chart—a public document perceived as contractual—helps a department attain the following goals:

1. Fair division of labor and responsibilities. This systematic approach to governance makes it particularly difficult to evade service to the department.

2. Instilling faculty members with a sense of responsibility first to the department and secondarily to the chair. Faculty who put the department first are more likely to discharge their responsibilities conscientiously, especially if faculty meetings include time for regular reports.

3. Clarity of lines of communication. A department with three language coordinators, one of whom serves as assistant to the chair, might have an organizational chart like the one on p. 93.

I favor a system that requires tenured faculty members to carry a larger share of responsibilities than nontenured faculty. Thus most of the persons who appear on the chart with no functions are junior faculty members working toward their tenure. Our department also decided to exempt one or two tenured faculty from administrative assignments each year, depending on individual circumstances. A yearly rotation ensures fairness.

FACULTY MEETINGS

To increase the effectiveness and make the most of faculty meetings, it is important to lay out a clear framework.

1. To hold faculty meetings at regular intervals (e.g., the third Wednesday of each month).

2. To publish and distribute the schedule of faculty meetings at the start of each semester.

3. To circulate at least two days before the meeting a full agenda with the names of people who will give a report.

4. To structure the agenda with care. Include many details. Does it allow for the three types of activities: old business, reports of various committees, and new business?

5. To make sure that faculty meetings fulfill their two major goals: exchanging information and generating action. Is it clear to faculty members which part of the agenda is for their information and which requires action?

6. To establish a decision-making process. The most obvious one is to submit everything to a vote and to operate under a simple majority rule. Once the group has reached a decision in a faculty meeting, the chair assumes the responsiblity of having it implemented. See sample agenda highlighting the information and action parts of a meeting, p. 94.

Goal Setting and Planning

External Norms and Goals

If in the past few years chairpersons have learned that goal setting does not rest on self-determination, the faculty at large still cling to the idea of autonomy. In reality outside factors determine many goals for us. Therefore, departments must learn the "rules of the game." Faculty must know how their university administration evaluates programs. What criteria do administrators use when making decisions about budgets, priorities, and support? At UMBC we have ascertained these criteria through various university documents that have circulated, as well as from memos, letters, and statements emanating from the Maryland State Board for Higher Education. We found that institutional commitment depends largely on the following considerations:

1. The need and demand for a program (overall enrollment)
2. The relationship of a program to institutional goals and missions (how the program fits into the spectrum of university offerings)
3. Program productivity (number of majors)
4. Indications of potential program quality (outside recognition, grants, etc.)
5. Resources needed and their availability (cost of the program in terms of personnel, equipment, etc.)

Although qualitative considerations count, we know from experience that quantitative considerations generally come first. In other words, how we assess the academic quality of our programs makes no difference if we lack the enrollment.

A chairperson should educate departmental faculty in at least three areas:

1. Institutional measures of productivity, that is, total student credit hours expected from each faculty member if they are in use in the institution. (At UMBC the number is 270; assuming a three-credit course, that means three classes with thirty students in each.)

2. Formulas used by administrations to compute operations budgets of departments.
3. University, board of regents, or higher education criteria used in the evaluation of academic programs.

A good way to educate the faculty about the first topic is to circulate departmental enrollment statistics each semester. (See the charts on pp. 94 and 95; the first provides department enrollments, and the second breaks down the numbers by instructor.) These statistics do not constitute an endorsement of the university's norms of productivity; they only inform faculty regularly about its standing in relation to those norms. The breakdown of data by faculty member is sensitive information since it makes public everybody's FTEs. But it creates a salutary awareness about the politics of numbers and may also generate a certain amount of healthy peer pressure.

Lest one think that I advocate abandonment of academic standards in pursuit of student numbers, let me state my basic assumption: curricular quality and impressive enrollment do not have to be mutually exclusive.

To educate the department about these quantitative and qualitative norms, one has only to give faculty the proper information. Discussing the criteria at a faculty meeting will generate an atmosphere of awareness in the department.

The question of departmental resources also clearly concerns faculty members. We all share the experience of seeking and not finding help or funding for a project. Consequently, I have found it productive to review administrative criteria and formulas for budgets at a faculty meeting coinciding with the start of the budget cycle. I introduce the subject with a chart contained in the memo on p. 96. The ensuing discussions, sometimes passionate, have generally enabled the department to make the best possible decisions in terms of schedules, course offerings, and overall planning.

QUALITATIVE GOALS AND PROGRAM DEVELOPMENT

(See pp. 5–19, ch. 1, on teaching better.) The above rules of the game clearly establish that FL programs cannot rest on abstractions or idealistic objectives but must incorporate the specific needs of the student population. Serious departmental enrollment problems are often the result of isolation and insulation from other disciplines. Any FL department concerned about goal setting and planning might do well to consider the following questions:

1. Does the present FL program serve the needs of nonmajors as well as majors? Every department should offer not only language courses but also courses that address the needs of students in other fields and that these students can take in their freshman or sophomore years. At UMBC we established a series of three core courses that introduce students to (1) the

phenomenon and nature of language itself, (2) its structure and relation to meaning, and (3) its social context. Thus the core provides the common ground that underlies our discipline. This core, taught in English, is to be taken by all language majors, but since it consists of introductory courses, it can also be taken as electives by nonmajors. In addition to making ourselves accessible to the nonspecialists, we have effected a bridge between the nonmajor and the major. Quite a few students started with the core courses as electives and then continued with foreign language classes. Other courses such as Themes in Literature in Translation or Studies in International Film have also helped build our enrollment.

2.   Does the major program accommodate different student needs? Only a few language majors plan to go on to graduate studies in languages or into teaching. Most envisage careers with government agencies and businesses. FL skills have increasingly been regarded as an invaluable career tool. We need to recognize this awareness and to respond to the overwhelming student interest in language and culture studies. The response at UMBC was to transform the various language majors into one B.A. in modern languages, with options for specialties in one language, two languages (a major and a minor), and literary studies.

3.   Is the existing FL program sufficiently linked to other academic disciplines? Have the possibilities of links with other academic programs been fully tapped? The easiest and fastest way to link programs is to explain how FL competencies can benefit other fields of study. The emerging patterns should hold few surprises: students in social work, sociology, and nursing will most likely choose Spanish; those in economics, managerial sciences, African-American studies, psychology, biological sciences, and music find French or German a useful elective. Some even choose a double major.

4.   What opportunities exist for new programs? Especially those based on collaboration with other departments? Many institutions develop and periodically update a five-year academic plan that lists new programs under consideration. Such a plan can offer growth opportunities for language departments. Proposed new programs often involve interdisciplinary studies and thus lend themselves to the participation of foreign language departments.

5.   Has the teaching of elementary and intermediate foreign language courses improved over the last two years? If the answer is negative or not clear, then the issue should be looked at with concern. Beginning courses in language require constant improvements and innovations.

To conclude, working with other departments not only brings in new curricula but also builds understanding, empathy, and positive feelings. The congeniality enormously facilitates the work of the language department in all other university committees and with the administration as well.

Activating and Controlling

Questions to consider under this rubric include: How do you implement departmental decisions and plans? What mechanisms do you have at your disposal? Where and how do you get the resources? How do you get the necessary feedback? What monitoring procedures can you use?

Once decisions have been made at the departmental level, their implementation will be the responsibility of a faculty member, a committee, or the chairperson. Implementation may take place at either the intradepartmental or interdepartmental level.

THE INTRADEPARTMENTAL LEVEL

Going back to the organization chart and the second intervention, organizing, one can see that progress can be adequately monitored through direct reports to the chair but much more effectively monitored through regular reports to faculty meetings. The faculty know that they are due to report at the coming meeting and that they will be accountable to the whole department. Consequently, few failures occur since most people avoid embarrassment if they can.

THE INTERDEPARTMENTAL LEVEL

You will remember that the department has a member sitting on every major university committee thanks to a systematic deployment of its members who have a double assignment, one inside and one outside the department. As a result, the department is always well informed of activities campus-wide and can react adequately to any issues or situations that concern the group.

On the question of resources, let me just say that one faculty member should act as resource coordinator. Of course the first step is to identify as many sources of funding as possible, local as well as national. Although most faculty in a department may know the main grant foundations, few will be aware of the less familiar ones. These sources may range from technical assistance grants from a state department of education to funding by community groups.

An in-house information specialist can become an invaluable catalyst and can influence the number of projects and grant applications emanating from the department.

Problem Solving

ADVISORY BOARD

Many problems and crises crop up in the daily business of departments. Their resolution depends largely on the negotiation skills and talents of chairpersons. Department heads, however, should not see problems as their solitary burden or trust only their own skills. I suggest establishing an advisory board not only to become "a cushion or a buffer" between the chair and other parties, as Barricelli puts it (p. 42), but also to offer genuine help and support. For instance, in a crisis having an external cause, a department advisory board could act as a writing team to produce the necessary documents and studies needed to make a response. An intervention of this kind not only provides needed assistance but also, through collective involvement, generates support and unity.

TEAM INTERVENTION

On really important matters, it is often more productive if the chair goes to the administration accompanied by the leadership of the department, e.g., the area coordinators. In this way a department can bring more clout to the negotiations. An administrator is likely to be more responsive when talking to the group that assumes departmental responsibilities. Furthermore, the team approach, which represents the collective voice of the department, provides a buffer for the chair.

DEPARTMENTAL RETREAT

When the department faces a severe crisis or an unusually difficult issue, a weekend retreat will probably work best. If the retreat is in a nice country setting, few colleagues will resent having to sacrifice their weekend. They may even find the novelty of it appealing. The work accomplished during a two-day retreat can sometimes carry a department for three or four years. At one such retreat, for example, we systematically listed all our ideas about improving public relations for the department. Four years hence, we have implemented many of the ideas but by no means all of them.

In general, when it comes to problem solving, I follow a cardinal rule: *Involve the department,* especially the leadership. A department chairperson should not attempt to solve serious problems all alone. Since they inevitably concern the welfare of the group, colleagues should team up to identify immediate solutions or to study long-range answers. This approach draws faculty members together, makes them close ranks, and generates departmental unity.

Conclusion

The difficulty in the art of managing academic departments concerns the balance between productivity and quality. I hope it is obvious by now that all the managerial and technical skills described do not simply serve the god of productivity. Rather, they ensure the healthy level of productivity that releases resources for the development of quality. The feature that distinguishes the academic department from the generic department lies precisely in the dynamics of productivity and quality. In the academic department, however, no gains can result from opposing these two key aspects, and we should strive to relate and integrate them.

Organizational Chart
Modern Languages and Linguistics Department, 1979–80

Claud D., Chairman
Council of Chairpersons
Graduate Council
Member, Curriculum Com-
mittee (ex-officio)
Property Officer

Alan R. Assistant to Chairman Scheduling Officer NEH Liaison Member, Curriculum Com- mittee		Victor A. Director, Language Media Center Member, Curriculum Com- mittee
Alan B. Coordinator for Spanish Member, Curriculum Com- mittee Advisement Coordinator Member, GDR Committee	Angela M. Coordinator for French Chairperson, Curriculum Committee Member, Chancellor's Commission on Status of Women at UMBC	May R. Coordinator for German Member, Curriculum Com- mittee Undergraduate Council Senate 1979–80
Ricardo P. Library Representative	Ronald S. Bilingual Education Devel- opment Liaison with City, State	Bob S. Public Affairs Officer Affirmative Action
Wolfgang F. Senator-at-large Departmental Liaison with English (M.A.)	Mary O. Exchange and Internship Programs	Olga P.
Tom F.	Martine P. Renate E. (Sabbatical)	Jack S.

Memo

Date: 31 October, 1978

To: MLL Faculty

From: Claud DuVerlie

Re: Agenda for Departmental Meeting, Wednesday, 1 November at 3:00

A.   Information

A few remarks on the state of MLL:
Graduate Council: M.A.'s in humanities—Claud
Bilingual education: Instructional Systems Development—Ron S.
Undergraduate Council: General Distribution Requirements, Comparative and
World Literature—Alan R.
Curriculum Committee—Angela
Progress on the new schedule for Fall '79—coordinators
Foreign language requirements models

B.   Action

1. A revised schedule of faculty meetings for the remainder of the semester.
2. A departmental policy concerning the scheduling and cancellation of courses
with particularly low enrollment.

New Business

Quote from the Graduate Council minutes on M.A. in English Studies.
Reference: UMBC Graduate Council, minutes of meeting, 23 October 1978

**Enrollment Statistics for Modern Languages and Linguistics
Department, Fall 1981**

Total enrollment	1,265	
Total credit hours	4,553	
1. Total student credit hours, lower level	3,128.00	
2. FTE faculty justified by lower-level credit hours (#1 ÷ 300)	10.43	
3. Total student credit hours, upper level	1,425.00	
4. FTE faculty justified by upper-level credit hours (#3 ÷ 216)	6.59	
5. FTE faculty justified by total student credit hours (#2 + #4)	17.02	
6. Actual FTE faculty	14.58	
7. Comparison of actual FTE faculty with justified FTE faculty	2.44	*understaffed*

Enrollment Statistics (*cont.*)

Breakdown by Subject Area

Subject	Enrollment	Credit Hours
French (9 courses)	322	1,253
German (8 courses)	171	649
Russian (2 courses)	14	56
Spanish (11 courses)	444	1,655
MLL, etc. (8 courses)	314	940
Total	1,265	4,553

Enrollment Statistics by Instructor, Fall 1978

FACULTY NAME	FAC. EQUIV.	NO. OF COURSES	ENROLLMENT	CREDIT HOURS	COMMENTS
B., B.	1	3	81	301	
B., M.	.5	2	44	176	p/t
C., M.	1	2.33	78	234	
D., C.	.75	2.25	32.50	110.50	dept. chair
F., O.	1	3	32	116	
F., R.	.5	1	35	105	½ LWOP
F., W.	1	3	39	150	
M., A.	1	2.58	88.50	313.50	
O., M.	1	3	57	225	
P., R.	1	3.5	73.50	249.50	
P., A.	1	3.25	77.50	296.50	
B., M.	1	3.25	28.50	90.50	
S., V.	.5	2	46	173	p/t
S., R.	1	3	77	292	
S., J.	—	—	—	—	sabbatical
S., R.	1	3.5	69.50	264.50	
Independent Studies	—	—	8	21	
Workshops		—	68	68	
Total	13.25	40.66	935	3,186	

Average credit hours per faculty member	240.45
Average courses per faculty member	3.06
Average class size	22.99

Memo

Date: 19 September 1978

To: MLL Faculty

From: Claud DuVerlie

PLEASE BRING TO DEPARTMENTAL MEETING OF 9/20 AT 3 IN LANG. LAB.

Following are the data used to compute the operating budget for this year.

Operating/Instruction Formula: $500 per faculty member
100 per lab credit—Biol., Chem.
50 per lab credit—Physics
25 per lab credit—Geo., Psych., Educ.
10 per lab credit—Arts, Mod. Lang.

# Faculty	Per-Faculty Allocation	Credit Hrs.	Lab Credit Allocation	Total	Difference from Fiscal Year 1978	Adjustments	Difference	Total Fiscal Year 1979 Budget
13	$6,500	851	$8,510	$15,010	+$10,082	−$1,500	+$8,582	$13,510

Labor and Assistance Instructional Formula: $200 per faculty member
5 per lab credit—Bio., Chem., Mod. Lang., Physics
3 per lab credit—Music, Theater, Dance, Visual Arts, Educ., Geog., Psych.
2 per lab credit—Philo., Math

# Faculty	Per-Faculty Allocation	Credit Hrs.	Lab Credit Allocation	Total	Difference from Fiscal Year 1978	Adjustments	Difference	Total Fiscal Year 1979 Budget
13	$2,600	851	$4,255	$6,855	−$145	+$645	+$500	$ 7,500

Part Two

CURRICULUM DESIGN

Chapter Three

Foreign Language and General Education

This chapter examines the relation of foreign language study to the idea of "general education." The authors of both articles use the term to mean the part of the curriculum outside the major field of study, the learning experiences in which the student is expected to master general thinking skills, basic epistomological concepts, and other concerns that are not discipline-specific.

This topic is both important and complicated. Foreign language departments are often confused about undergraduate pedagogical goals. Should all our efforts go toward improving the linguistic proficiency of our students? Are literary theory and history the basics of our field? What about cultural studies and civilization? How can we articulate our contributions to the general education of students, especially if the institution has a core curriculum or distribution requirements to which the department contributes only through first- and second-year FL courses?

Departmental predicaments in this area are usually a microcosm of larger institutional considerations. There is inevitably much politicking and competition when individualistic departments attempt to deal with the collective ideal of general education. FL departments will need many skills in institutional processes if they wish to avoid having their fortunes rise and fall solely on the willingness of their colleagues to vote in or keep an FL requirement.

The authors of this section are concerned with both departmental and institutional considerations. David Burnett details FL departmental concerns. He sees the department's responsibility for elementary foreign language instruction not as a detriment to general education contributions but as an opportunity. He reviews a variety of successful programs that have incorporated broad objectives concerning the nature and function of language into the elementary and intermediate FL classroom. In his analysis of these efforts and their rationale, he provides an abundance of reasons to justify an expanded role for FL departments in the provision of general education to the heterogeneous student body of the eighties.

Clifford Adelman considers the institutional context, analyzing various general education models and internal interest groups that are potential allies for FL departmental initiatives. His message is a difficult one. Faculty members must put the time and energy into analyzing their environment, the students, the curriculum, and the institutional mission. Only then will they be able to devise effective ways to make a substantive contribution to general education reform.

Exploring Language in Elementary Foreign Language Courses

David Graham Burnett

Defining the contributions of individual academic departments to the "general" education of students is not simple. Disciplines are, by definition, specialized fields of inquiry, and faculty members are rewarded on the basis of their contributions to this specialized understanding. The objectives of undergraduate general education—whether defined as analytic and synthetic thinking skills, as moral and ethical development, or, most grandly of all, as the ability to acquire and utilize knowledge—are clearly transdisciplinary. While a few institutions have sought to overcome this tension by creating nondisciplinary core curricula or by abolishing departments altogether, most still rely on introductory-level departmental courses to furnish students with the general educational experience.[1]

Foreign language departments have thus been placed in a particularly difficult position by the recent wave of reforms and by the growing concern about general educational outcomes. Like our colleagues in English who have been obliged to invest more and more time in training students in the fundamentals of applied writing, we have faced students with less and less basic training in foreign languages and have responded by increasing our efforts to transmit rudimentary linguistic competence to these inexperienced learners. This challenge has occupied us profoundly in recent years and has left little time for reflection on our role as contributors to general education. Yet there is considerable evidence that the role assigned to foreign language departments in the general education mission does not always correspond to the goals of foreign language faculty members and their course offerings. This insidious problem is becoming more serious, because academic departments, particularly in the humanities, are becoming increasingly interdependent. It is essential that each department articulate its contribution to overall institutional purposes to avoid the dangers of reduced support, internal isolation, and reduced curricular responsibility.

Elementary foreign language courses offer myriad opportunities to contribute to broad educational goals. Moreover, because language is the key to all learning strategies in all disciplines, we have a special responsibility to students and colleagues in other disciplines to provide leadership in developing broad educational goals for students and in conceptualizing departmental roles to achieve these objectives. To do so, we need (1) to be aware of the problems we face in our departments, (2) to learn a bit about the successes and failures of colleagues at other institutions, and (3) to develop a strategy for implementing whatever changes are necessary to bring departmental efforts in line with institutional priorities.

Defining the Problem

When the MLA created a task force on Institutional Language Policy in 1979, the group found that many institutions had high expectations of foreign language departments in the general educational area. The inculcation of second language skills in students was a less frequently cited mission than was the transmission of cultural pluralism:

> Traditionally, foreign language departments are charged with a primary responsibility to provide a major share of the humanities thrust in general education and liberal arts programs. Usually, the role of the department is to develop in students a range of general understandings, attitudes, and values needed by broadly educated persons to cope and survive in a multinational, multicultural world. The emphasis here has tended to be upon exposure to the language, literature and culture of foreign societies, *not* necessarily upon developing linguistic competence.[2]

As an example of the institutional role that a group of colleagues from a variety of disciplines might foresee for foreign languages, the following definition may be considered typical. It is taken from the February 1979 report of the Standing Committee on General Education at the State University of New York, Buffalo:

> The expectation of the committee is that elementary language programs will consider it their serious responsibility to adjust their formats, especially for students intent on minimal compliance with the [foreign language] requirement, to stress reflection on language structure, linguistic and cultural identities and differences, and the relation between language, perceptual world view, and categories of thought. (p. 7)

The justification that accompanies this charge to the foreign language departments relies, for the most part, on the testimony not of businesspersons or poets but of philosophers such as Wittgenstein and Merleau-Ponty. Language in the view of these philosophers does more than convey messages; it defines the sender, the receiver, and the message itself. For Merleau-Ponty the study of another language transforms us with respect to ourselves, thus creating a critical distance that allows the reflective process to function. The Committee on General Education calls on foreign language faculty to take up questions that, in today's specialized academic environment, one might have expected to be the purview of linguists (language structure), anthropologists and sociologists (linguistic and cultural identities), and psychologists and philosophers (language world views and categories of thought). In short, foreign language departments are challenged to present substantive issues in the elementary foreign language classroom, to broaden the vision of language to include its analytical, esthetic, and perceptual functions as well as its communicative ones.

Such a wide-ranging mandate may well be met with skepticism by foreign language faculty hard pressed to impart basic factual information. There is a tendency, for instance, to view such grandiose notions as attempts to cover up a lack of precise objectives in other disciplines. The comments of the MLA Task Force on their findings seem to imply such an attitude:

> The role of foreign languages in general education and liberal arts studies would seem to be clear and straightforward were it not for the persistent inability of the academic community to articulate a coherent and cogent philosophy of general education and liberal arts.   (Brod, p. 10)

Yet, more often than not, foreign language faculty members do seem intent on limiting their task to dealing with the pragmatic or communicative aspects of language. Reinhard Kuhn writes, "it is obvious that the health of a department of languages and literatures depends first and foremost on the linguistic competence of its students."[3] The report of the President's Commission on Foreign Language and International Studies strikes a similarly pragmatic note: "Foreign language instruction should concentrate on speaking and understanding before other foreign language skills are developed."[4] The appeal of this line of reasoning derives in part from a belief that linguistic competence is what students want. Maria Alter asserts, "Pragmatic students will judge us on their actual experience in our language courses, on the simple fact of whether they really acquired that linguistic edge. . . ."[5]

Certainly the President's Commission, which heard hours of testimony about foreign language skill deficiencies in America, was understandably concerned with practical solutions. TWA testified that sixteen thousand résumés were reviewed in a search for four hundred positions requiring second language proficiency, underscoring the gravity of the problem and providing a sense of urgency so often missing in the study of the humanistic disciplines.[6] But foreign language faculty concerned about a lasting contribution to students' educational development must reserve the right to go beyond student desires and socioeconomic needs.

Elizabeth Barber has pointed out that her students express a preference for learning how to speak a foreign language (as opposed to learning how to read or write it).[7] This preference, she feels, stems from their developmental concerns at age seventeen to twenty. As a social instrument, spoken language is the "only" language, and socially minded seventeen-year-olds are unlikely to be interested in language as an analytical tool, aesthetic object, or perceptual frame. It is for this very reason that we should attempt, despite the difficulties and fears involved in reaching beyond one's training and expertise, to deal with language in its broadest possible definition in the foreign language classroom. Moreover, we should do so even at the risk of incurring a small initial loss in linguistic proficiency. An extra verb tense or vocabulary lesson can more readily be acquired independently than can complex substantive notions.

SOME INSTITUTIONAL INITIATIVES

There are, of course, faculty members in foreign language programs who accept this vision both of language and of their pedagogical mission. An eloquent statement of the broadly conceived mission of the elementary foreign language curriculum has been provided by Carolyn Dunham:

> I believe in teaching not language as communication, but language as *culture.* I believe the primary function of second language learning within a liberal arts curriculum, and the foundation of teaching language as culture, to be to give students an understanding of the *nature of language* as such, its powers and limitations. Language is the primary medium through which the members of a given community perceive and understand the world. My underlying objective in the foreign language classroom is to teach students to view reality in a different way, to understand how a linguistic system shapes values and attitudes.[8]

Dunham's beliefs lead her to rely on explicit comparisons of English and the target language as a regular part of her teaching.

This philosophy of language teaching and the natural connections of foreign language and native language study have also inspired a collaborative effort of foreign language and English faculty at the Indianapolis campus of Indiana University. Students in selected sections of Elementary French, Elementary German, English Composition, and Introduction to English meet periodically to explore topics of common interest to language students. Participating faculty members have prepared a source book divided into four sections: (1) Adult and Child Language Acquisition, (2) The Game of Language (language rules and communication systems), (3) Development of Written and Spoken Language Systems, and (4) Language and Society (horizontal and vertical social relations in language). The essays and suggested outside readings in the book are supplemented by periodic major presentations to the assembled students by faculty or guests. Each participating faculty member then follows up in his or her section with specific exercises and examples based on the target language or on the particular native language skill sought in the course. In the process no new "courses" or positions have been created.[9]

Perhaps the most ambitious and developed initiative that reflects a broadened mission in general education for the foreign language department is the program at the University of Maryland-Baltimore County.[10] This program, which has attracted substantial attention and has resulted in such tangible rewards as increased departmental enrollments, consists of a departmental core of courses on the nature and function of language. The two-semester course, The World of Language, is supplemented by additional offerings entitled Textual Analysis and World Language Communities. All are required of language majors; more important, the courses are offered to all students as part of the general education distribution requirements. (See pp. 26–27 for further information on the UMBC program.)

The existence of such programs, especially those like the one at Indiana University, does not guarantee their continuation or "success." Efforts to enrich the elementary foreign language curriculum are not new. Elizabeth Barber, for example, used lectures and supplementary materials on various aspects of language at Occidental College during the 1970s.[11] Despite her remarkable devotion and imagination, there was little evidence that students' linguistic competence was in fact enhanced by additional general information on language.

Another ambitious program recently conducted at Pomona College likewise failed to demonstrate a relationship between skill improvement in English composition or in foreign language acquisition and the study of the nature and function of language. In this program, dubbed Prolan, faculty members in English, philosophy, and foreign language sought to integrate their teaching efforts and to develop supplementary materials, and then to track a group of students through a coordinated first-year program in the hope of achieving a cumulative effect. The preliminary evaluative efforts, however, did not attest to significantly greater achievements in any of the areas in question by the select group when their accomplishments were compared with those of a control group. At the same time, the project did result in the development of substantial enrichment materials.[12]

The Institutional Context

These results make an essential point for those who might wish to broaden their departmental focus. Despite the appeal of the argument that a better understanding of language in general will lead to improved performance in second language acquisition, the premise remains unproved. The commitment to broaden the focus of the elementary language classroom must, in my opinion, be made because the information is important to the general education of students, not because it will improve student scores on language proficiency tests.

The institutional environment will dictate the precise content and form of any new program. The initiative of the foreign language department must be consonant with overall institutional goals for general education, and the connection must be made explicit. Likewise, the format must integrate the new project into existing general education program structures, whether distribution requirements, competency models, worked-base models, or any other type. Institutional mission statements may provide a starting point, but the advice and counsel of colleagues in other disciplines and on the support staff are also essential. Not only may some of them have already taken up the topic of language explicitly in their own departmental offerings, but also all will have valuable information on student attitudes toward language as seen through their classroom or counseling experiences. As we have seen, collaboration across disciplinary lines is both a logical and beneficial dimension of curricular approaches to language study. General education must be built on the general resources of the institution.

This is not to say that every effort must be formally inter- or multidisciplinary. The design of such efforts is difficult enough, but their implementation is often slow and frustrating. The momentum of the planning process must not be destroyed by undue delays. Common sense dictates a modest initial effort. Such simple devices as the concurrent scheduling of an elementary foreign language course and an already extant introduction to linguistics will permit periodic joint meetings. Only slightly more complex is a course-pairing arrangement in which instructors of Foreign Language 101 and English Composition, or Foreign Language 101 and Child Development, coordinate all or part of their course outlines for the benefit of students (not necessarily all in each class) simultaneously enrolled in both courses.

Such initiatives, even those of a single faculty member who might be granted the liberty to experiment with a section of 101 and to exempt students from the departmental final, will provide a testing ground for new possibilities. The results, in turn, can be vigorously evaluated, and unsuccessful ideas quickly discarded. In this way the quality of foreign language programs will never be seriously jeopardized, while individual initiative and creativity will be fostered. The approach does require careful evaluation. Faculty members, especially those working alone or in small groups, may lack the time or expertise to establish an extended implementation plan. Such obvious questions as "What will be the criteria on which we judge success or failure?" "How long can the experiment continue before a binding decision is made?" and "What will happen if 'success' is in fact achieved and demonstrated?" must be answered before faculty members proceed with an experiment.

Conclusion

A number of arguments justify recognition in the elementary foreign language classroom of the many functions of language beyond simple denotation. The most important, I believe, is the value of language as a heuristic device. George Levine expresses the curricular mission of language study exceptionally well: "The primary function of the humanities within college curricula today should be the exploration of the enterprise of learning. And the basis of that exploration must be the study of language."[13] Virtually all institutions of higher education aspire to develop "life-long" learners, motivated graduates who have and use the ability to learn independently, to convert information into knowledge. Such an active, problem-solving orientation to life requires a polyvalent conception of language.

The strategies of conceptualizing, analyzing, evaluating, and synthesizing new experience demand the use of language as an information channel, a sorting device, a tool for social adaptation, and a unifying force for the individual consciousness. In this circumstance, the understanding of language is inseparable from the understanding of self. Unlike a tool that exists only to hammer nails or to clamp arteries, human language is not definable in relation to something other than its user. A psychoanalyst does not apply the tools of Freudian analysis to the body of experience provided by a patient and thereby effect a cure. The analyst is part of this experience and thus cannot act independently of himself or herself in dealing with the experience. Highly disciplined effort is required to manage such an ambivalent relationship successfully.

The same level of discipline is required for self-directed learning that leads to intellectual development. As a writer's style is a verbal expression of a particular way of living in the world, so the knowledge creator's solutions reflect a personal relationship to language.[14] The more sophisticated this understanding, the more profound the sense of self in the act of learning. The foreign language classroom is the ideal environment in which to explore the multiple roles of language and the multiple benefits of language study.

Notes

[1] Arthur Levine, *Handbook of Undergraduate Curriculum* (San Francisco: Jossey-Bass, 1978), offers a detailed review of many structural and functional models of general education.

[2] Richard Brod, ed., *Language Study for the 1980s* (New York: MLA, 1980), p. 10.

[3] Reinhard Kuhn, "German Studies Today: Some Signs of Sanity in Bedlam," *ADFL Bulletin*, 8, No. 4 (May 1977), 3.

[4] *Strength through Wisdom: A Critique of U.S. Capability: A Report to the President from the President's Commission on Foreign Language and International Studies* (Washington, D.C.: U.S. Government Printing Office, 1979), p. 11.

[5] Maria Alter, "A Modern Case for Foreign Languages," *ADFL Bulletin*, 7, No. 1 (Sept. 1975), 31.

[6] *New York Times*, 23 February 1980, p. 20.

[7]Elizabeth Barber, "Language Acquisition and Applied Linguistics," *ADFL Bulletin,* 12, No. 1 (Sept. 1980), 26–32.

[8]Carolyn Dunham, "Language as Culture," *French Review,* 54, No. 2 (1980), 221.

[9]The *Reader on Language* and additional information are available from Professor Rosalie Vermette, Dept. of French, IUPUI, 925 West Michigan St., Indianapolis, IN 46202.

[10]C. DuVerlie and A. Rosenthal, "How to Prosper during a Foreign Language Crisis," *ADFL Bulletin,* 12, No. 1 (Sept. 1980), 17–22; also "Climbing the Ladder of Institutional Priorities," *ADFL Bulletin,* 12, No. 2 (Nov. 1980), 4–7.

[11]Barber, "Language Acquisition and Applied Linguistics."

[12]These very cursory remarks, which do not do justice to the vigor and promise of the Pomona effort, are based on readings of the pilot grant proposal and final report to NEH, generously shared with the Language Study Group of Indiana University by Dean Robert T. Voelkel of Pomona.

[13]George Levine, "Notes toward a Humanist Anti-curriculum," *Humanities in Society,* 1, No. 3 (1978), 234.

[14]J. Hillis Miller, *Charles Dickens: The World of His Novels* (Cambridge: Harvard Univ. Press, 1958), p. viii.

Language Study and the New Reform in General Education

Clifford Adelman

In the face of the old aphorism that changing a curriculum is harder than moving a cemetery and on the assumption that general education—like the Grail—must exist, because it has something to do with salvation, I want to discuss general education reform from an organizational perspective, to describe the various environments in which general education and foreign language education might coalesce, and to recommend a range of institutional strategies for fostering such a fusion.

In all discussions of reform, a standing metaphor prevails: in the curricular contortions of the 1960s we managed to throw the baby out with the bathwater; in the reconstructions of the 1970s, we seemed hell-bent on bringing back the bathwater. The 1980s may be the decade in which we finally learn how to save the baby; and I suggest that existing research—both basic and institutional—can provide some strong clues for us in that regard. Indeed, the research argues that determining the most equitable and effective form of language study in a general education curriculum requires a knowledge of key elements of the institutional setting.

Understanding Student Constituencies

The first element is the student constituency, which, as we know, has become increasingly heterogeneous and which will become even more so within a decade. But knowing one's student constituency requires more than demographic data, test scores, and the like. It requires ethnographic work by faculty to produce three-dimensional portraits, or topologies, of students' assumptions about the learning environment, of students' educational goals, and of actual learning behaviors. For example, if we can determine that certain groups of students assume discontinuities between home and campus and if they come from homes where second languages have been spoken, their attitudes toward collegiate language learning will obviously be affected. Or, if we can observe and document adversary and gaming relations between students and instructors and ascertain that students expect the same kind of totalitarian classrooms they experienced in high school, then we know that to teach foreign languages merely as advanced skills and to follow expected patterns of classroom activities will both reinforce the students' sense of security in the classroom and fail to challenge or motivate them. Or if we can describe the learning resources that different types of students are wont to use if left to their own devices (printed media, other people, electronic media, recollected experience, etc.), we may have some hints as to what vehicles will be most successful in classrooms.

On a deeper level, such student traits as preference for and fluency in various communication systems (written, oral, symbolic, graphic), perceptual habits (generalized or concrete, patterned or fragmented, descriptive or judgmental, speculative or familiar), and conceptual habits (tolerance for ambiguity and complexity, theoretical orientation)—all tell us something greater about the goals of a general education curriculum and how foreign language study might advance that curriculum than do the deductive approaches we have taken to date.

We have the tools for making such measurements, for drawing the three-dimensional map. Some are testing instruments, such as the Omnibus Personality Inventory; others are survey instruments, such as the American Council on Education–Cooperative Institutional Research Program survey of entering freshmen; and still others are experimental assessment instruments, such as the Academic Competences in General Education examination developed by Jonathan Warren at Educational Testing Service, Berkeley. But the most formidable tools in our possession are the powers of observation and analysis of faculty. Those powers, along with a substantial number of faculty participating in the descriptive institutional research, will guarantee a proprietary interest in reforms based on analysis and will strongly suggest a process of faculty learning that is essential for perceiving the nature and place of language study in general education.

A Typology of General Education Programs

The second major component of the institutional setting is the type of general education program either in effect or likely to be in effect in the near term. I propose that there are four types of general education programs; each of them presents boundaries and conditions under which foreign language education might operate. These types may or may not be appropriate to the collegiate sectors in which they are found.

1.   The first type I call fundamentalist. It is the most widespread paradigm and can be described as the entry-level portion of liberal education. It is the rite of passage, the acculturating transition to higher learning. Be-

cause it functions at the entry level, it tends to include—if not exclusively—introductions to the various disciplines. Whether by a core or distribution formula (i.e., closed or open), this model assumes that secondary schools give students fluency in the basic skills. It is a convenient formula for faculty since it allows them to make a case for their disciplines (which, in an atmosphere of enrollment-driven departmental competition, faculty are all too happy to do), to teach subject matters of which they are masters, and to maintain their traditional work roles in the institution. It is also the most politically digestible of general education models, since it respects an academic organization based on departments and branches of knowledge.

2. The second model, the synthetic, focuses on specific content or ideas that can bring together a diversity of knowledge. This model understates disciplinary instruction and minimizes the roles of departments as curricular arbiters. The synthesists tend to favor core curricula, normative statements of the knowledge most worth having, even though the underlying assumptions of their curricula are not inimicable to quasi-distribution patterns based on ideas, temporal periods, and so on. The synthetic model requires either separate general education faculties or faculties of generalists (which amount to the same thing in an academic organization), and they are not easy to find in an age of specialization. The model also assumes that students entering college are synthetic thinkers who, in Charles Wegener's words, can have "enlarged" and "stabilized" within them "the capacity to have purposes" that are necessary for synthetic thinking.[1] But recent research on cognitive development and styles strongly disputes this assumption.

3. The third paradigm, which I call "modal," advances the idea that the deepest objectives of liberal learning—flexibility of mind and self-reflection—can best be developed by teaching forms of thinking, rather than by introducing students to specific disciplines or taking them on a grand tour of all thought. Faculties are extraordinarily adept at identifying generalized modes of thinking—analytic, synthetic, critical, wholistic, inductive—that are or should be the goals in general education programs. And some of them can speak fluently of the search for languages and symbol systems as keys to those modes. But because they are as adept at defending their individual disciplines as they are at meeting those objectives, the curricular emanations of this otherwise Platonic model often use courses in the disciplines (introductory or advanced) as vehicles. Needless to say, the relation between the objective and the vehicle is assumed to be self-evident. In theory, then, the modal paradigm relies heavily on what Phillip Phoenix once called the architectonics of knowledge, on the superstructures of thought processes and ways of investigation that are held to be common among groupings of disciplines (as if to say, "ask not what the scientist knows, rather what the scientist does"). In practice, the delivery of this form of general education is determined far more by the organization of

academic work, and the embodiments are left to be justified by the epistemologists.

4. When, in the 1960s and 1970s, curriculum construction was passed to the psychologists, a logical extension of the modal idea of general education emerged: from a hierarchy of ways and languages of knowing, we moved to a hierarchy of cognitive tasks and statements of precise learning objectives for students. This developmental model of general education carefully articulates a series of learning experiences from the genotypic to the phenotypic, though the experiences are not necessarily tied to specific courses.[2] Indeed, the developmental model, anchored by a language of outcome statements that, as Thomas Ewens observes, "is not always constrained by a sense of modesty,"[3] is difficult to translate into curricular form. Not surprisingly, the model is allied with competency-based education, individualized and experiential education, contract learning, and so on, no matter how dubious a shape some of these allies take and no matter how much faculty time is drained off in certifying (as opposed to enabling) activities under these rubrics.

But, by the same analysis, the developmental idea seems well-suited to a new generation of college students entering with deficiencies in training and with a skepticism of the instructor as the repository of all knowledge. Indeed, a logical extension of the developmental model is the notion that faculty are master learners whose job is to model and guide the process of learning for students. The departmental base of curriculum is thus undercut in favor of new processes and organizational forms of general education within institutions. Traditional faculty work roles radically change.

There is no rule, of course, that only one of these models is to be found in any one institution. Those institutions employing self-paced contractual approaches to general education, for example, might make all four forms possible. In fact, a more institutionally informed general education program should provide for competitive models, the number of which would depend on the size and organizational complexity of the institution, a strong sense of multiple constituencies, and the talents and inclinations of the faculty. As I note later in this discussion, language study not only fits into all the models but is also essential to each.

Institutional Niches

The third component of setting involves the existing niches of language study in postsecondary institutions. Research has demonstrated that the power of departments and programs depends on the clarity of the disciplinary-knowledge paradigm.[4] The foreign language paradigm—unless linked with what we now call language sciences—is not particularly strong. At the same time, the paradigms of general education are chimeras, and the intrinsic power of general education programs is limited and dependent. While the power of foreign language programs is also weak (and hence, enrollment-driven), they do inherit an established institutional niche, and it may be heartening to recall that history has worked on the process of expansion of niches. In a provocative analysis, Kenneth Boulding proposes that such expansion is coordinated by three agents: prices, policemen, and preachments.[5] In an academic community, that trinity becomes the curriculum market, the governance structure, and the cultural environment of institutions.

The curriculum market is a far more complex place than we have made it out to be—an observation underscored by the aptness of the market metaphor, since curriculum involves the allocation of resources. We like to simplify things to student drives for employability, and we tend to oppose utilitarian motivations. We have been both classicists and Keynesians about such matters, accepting supply and demand curves and calling for administrative intervention (or bidding for soft money) when we find ourselves with sagging faculty lines. Alternatively, we have engaged in entrepreneurialism, seeking and adapting to new markets with such vehicles as French for air traffic controllers and Japanese for hotel managers and using such mechanisms as continuing education programs and individualized home study to bolster our FTEs.

The governance structure has tolerated these activities. Faculty senates maintain enough collegiality to respect established niches, however weak the bases. And while administrators and boards of trustees may consolidate language departments, they leave the niches intact. The value placed on language study is too strong a tradition to deny, in part because faculty were required to study languages for their degrees. But the tradition may also be influenced by ties with community and regional organizations that evidence either an ethnic base or an international orientation. In this respect, too, institutional culture may be more receptive to language study if a noticeable percentage of the student body comes from second-language households and if that constituency seeks to maintain its ethnic visibility. All these features create a rhetorical environment in which the niche of language study might be expanded.

General Education and Niche Expansion

As long as expanding one's personal language and rendering it more efficient can be clearly connected with developing the capacities and knowledge covered by general education, we have an entry to the use of foreign language studies in basic skills courses, in freshman English courses, and in other general education courses that focus on communication.

Our current preoccupation with basic communications skills illuminates that symbolic ecology of language through which the structure of the world is developed, maintained, and controlled. A student's sense of self—let alone knowledge of things out there—is determined by his or her language environment, and it is an enduring insight of anthropology that language is the most elaborate and efficient set of artifacts we have for negotiating the world, expressing our values, and creating the reality of tribe or social organization. And, as Joseph Schwab wisely pointed out, linguistic intercourse, in general education, "is not simply efficient or powerful" but "indispensable, for the same reason that the act of swimming is indispensable to teaching that art and practice on the piano indispensable to learning that." That is, discussion is necessary not merely for the intellectual content of general education but for "the arts and skills and habits and attitudes" without which neither the student nor the enterprise could function.[6]

Hypotheses and Contexts

Persuasive hypotheses should ideally indicate what each of the major features of second language learning—for example, code switching, visual literacy, and cultural formation—would yield under each type of general education program and what kinds of faculty resources and changes in faculty roles would be necessary. That task would be complex enough in itself, tantamount to writing a classic curriculum cookbook. At the risk of apparent superficiality, I beg the task, but I do so principally because I believe the key element in such a speculative analysis must be a topology of student constituencies. That topology should be drawn by those who know it. Thus the purpose of the following thin examples is only to prod faculty to think through local general education reform in the light of what they know and can determine about their students.

Under the fundamentalist model, it is possible to build foreign language units on culture formation into core courses such as the classic Western civilization or the neoclassic non-Western civilization. To minimize faculty work-role strain, the language chosen should be both appropriate to the course content and one that the faculty member presented for his or her doctorate. If foreign language faculty teach such courses, so much the better; if not, there is a touch of the master-learner model that would need to be supplemented by language laboratories. In institutions using a distribution scheme, introductory courses in appropriate disciplines could be reconstructed to reflect language study broadly conceived, for example, metalinguistic approach to introductory philosophy, a psycholinguistic approach to general psychology, or an introduction to anthropology that focuses on the relation of language and culture. These approaches are recognized traditions within the disciplines, do not violate either faculty or student expectations, and bring students into the world of language.

Depending on the student constituency, the synthetic model of general education is most likely to use clusters of courses, including language courses, organized around ideas, temporal periods, global problems, or policy issues. The particular idea, period, problem, or issue determines the form, timing, and delivery of the language component. Since the synthetic model does not limit general education to entry-level studies and since synthetic thinking requires integration and extrapolation (clear messages drawn from discrete bodies of information), a teacher has the flexibility to bring students through a sequence of language units to a level of competence at which they can seek at least factual information in the printed word. The synthetic model inevitably involves faculty in language instruction, and those from other disciplines may require some review. I believe that the generalists who tend to be engaged in synthetic general education programs are more amenable to such a regimen than others are and that when careers depend on the strength of the general education program in the local institution, mere amenability will turn into enthusiasm. This enthusiasm will, in turn, heighten the rhetorical environment (preachment) for language study, since students are more likely to be persuaded of the value of languages when they see non-foreign language faculty using them.

The modal paradigm tends to regard language learning more as a creative process than as patterned behavior. The major features of language study can thus be addressed directly in courses on semiotics (e.g., by comparing a natural language, a psychomotor language, and a visual language), through social science research methods (e.g., by studying the impact of second language learning on native language skills), or in course units that call on students to gather language information by field study or to analyze the presentation of a foreign language in a textbook. In each of these and similar cases, a foreign language forms a discrete block of the subject matter as both an illustration and a vehicle for predisposing students to further language study. Alternatively, since the modal paradigm respects disciplinary groupings, foreign languages themselves can be presented within broader analytical frameworks, like linguistics, or synthetic frameworks, like anthropology. Either way, the only significant change in faculty work may be that new groupings of curricular entrepreneurs emerge as the context of language study is reformulated.

Oddly the developmental model can integrate foreign language learning with general education most directly and naturally, but to do so it requires a significant shift in faculty work roles and expectations. The developmental model respects the notional-functional approach to language learning and the needs of students—from gathering information to suasion—in real cultural contexts. The drive of the developmental model is toward student autonomy, toward tolerance for ambiguity and complexity, and toward the perception of an instructor as a resource (not as an external, authoritative repository of knowledge). In Arthur Chickering's words, the model drives toward the capacity to generate "paradigms, insights, judgments" and to "reorganize past conceptions on the basis of new experiences." The role of curriculum under that model, Chickering would say, is to "pose key dilemmas" to students.[7] The notional-functional approach to language learning is ideally suited to this process, but only after students have been challenged into entering the world of language.

How does one effect this challenge? A single example suggests a range of possibilities. The course level should be introductory and the constituency "transitional," that is, entering or reentering students whose assumptions about the learning environment are in flux. The teacher should take the role of master learner, that is, someone who is presenting a subject outside his or her area of expertise, preferably a subject never before studied. A language—particularly one of the less commonly taught languages and even more particularly a language that does not rely on a romanized alphabet—is an ideal vehicle for modeling the process of learning: organizing a wholly strange territory, identifying (and using and evaluating) various resources, setting learning objectives, and judging whether goals have been achieved. The situation poses a three-way predicament for students: one of role, one of ambiguity, and one of reflection on learning itself. Both to limit the situation and to induce a wider perspective, the course might focus on language functions, on the relation between language and culture, or on the nature of language itself. I have witnessed such experiments using ancient Greek, Chinese, Russian, and Sanskrit. That students generated their own research projects on such subjects as the origin of gender, the evolution of symbols, the relation of language to family structure, or the transformations of language in economic transactions indicates to me that there is joy in this approach. Follow-up testing showed that students who participated in these experiments performed better in basic English skills than their peers did, though I am sorry that no data are available on how many subsequently took foreign language courses.

The problem with the master-learner work role is that it violates the norms of faculty behavior and specialization, threatens other faculty, and requires high risk takers. To take on such a role, as the sociologist Arthur Stinchcombe once observed, you have to know that "you can't build a railroad within the law," that new organizational forms and functions rise to meet environmental conditions only when there is "some disrespect for traditional standards."[8] That posture is difficult to maintain in a period of increased formalization of the governance process in colleges and universities.

There are, in fact, both personal possibilities and institutional limitations in each of the four illustrations above. They all indicate that through language study, general education can be infused with the enthusiasm necessary to transform the student's experience from either a trench of learning or a rite of passage to an opening out into the world. Under each model, language study can provide precisely those moments of reflection—

a thinking about what we are doing in the process of learning—that are necessary for general education itself to exist. In fact, it is extraordinarily difficult in language study to isolate the teaching of the subject from the teaching about the subject. General education reformers tend to engage in such isolationism, "reducing," as Charles Wegener observed, "the whole curriculum to the teaching of philosophy"(p. 137). They also further antagonize the organizational forces arrayed against such reforms.

Prove It to the Police

Efforts to adapt the forms of language study to student constituencies within general education paradigms go to the heart of institutional mission, to the heart of custom and usage in curriculum trading, and, in most institutions, to the heart of the governance system. It is not surprising opposition is so formidable. Curriculum is a genuine organizational element in postsecondary affairs. It is a structure that conditions student and faculty expectations, making and reconciling demands, offering a web of choices, and determining flows of resources. More than any other group, faculty attempt to control that structure. They have become policemen and require proof that any innovation works better than the structure to which they are accustomed.

For this reason, comparative, longitudinal assessment studies must be built into any reform of general education in an institution. What kinds of assessments might address the impact of an expanded role for language study in general education programs? Three or four come to mind, depending on the student constituency. The first—and most applicable—derives from contrastive linguistics and identifies the impact of the four types of language study on basic English skills, using Cummins' cognitive-academic language proficiency (CALP) as the basis for an individual's academic development.[9] Such an assessment has an obvious rhetorical purpose: collegiate faculty tend to be impressed by integrated procedures that will contribute to students' lexical and syntactical sophistication.

If one takes a heuristic approach to language learning, such as that suggested in the master-learner model, it may also be possible to assess the impact on students' inductive and creative thinking (in the sense of generating hypotheses, using a variety of contexts to extend an idea in new directions, etc.). While our knowledge of what constitutes creativity and how to measure it is limited,[10] both science and social science faculty are naturally intrigued by potential contributions to students' creative thinking skills. Such allies would certainly be welcome.

If a foreign language is taught in the context of culture studies or of communication problems (i.e., as a subordinate vehicle), then one may assess skills of identifying and codifying patterns of information, of perceiving and organizing detail. The study of literary texts in second languages (even when considered cultural artifacts) in general education programs do not achieve such ends because at the basic level of language study it is difficult for students to perceive literature in other than idiosyncratic terms. In addition, as Roger Pillet has noted, the texts normally chosen are "beyond the linguistic capabilities of the class," thus generating a frustration that extends to hostility toward foreign language learning in general.[11]

But the impact of culture studies as a context for foreign languages may also be reflected in students' sensitivities to other times and places, their "negative capability," if you will. Warren's experimental Academic Competences in General Education instrument has made some fascinating strides in this regard, identifying and successfully measuring a characteristic he calls "awareness," although the term "differential perspective" is perhaps more accurate. One of Warren's questions assumes that the rotation of the earth is about to slow from twenty-four to twenty-six hours a revolution and asks the student to draw up a brief environmental impact statement. My experience with faculty who read and score this examination suggests that a student's ability to perceive the broad ramifications of such questions may be considerably heightened by experience studying a language in a cultural context.

I raise the issue of assessment to make two points: first, that faculty are often called on to justify their claims of effectiveness and, second, that participation in the design and execution of assessments in the context of general education reform may be its own reward. At a time when rewards for such participation are not institutionally visible, we need to recall that from all we know about professional values and collegiate organization, faculty will find ways to adapt to changing conditions while simultaneously expressing personal interests through their work. They may use participation in general education program reform to achieve other ends (to escape departmentally based pressures, to build constituencies among students, or to reshape their working groups of colleagues, for example), but participation in simultaneous assessment activities can both seal their commitment to second language study and expand their understanding of how we get from here to there in general education.

In the process, faculty will have the opportunity to mobilize other allies for expanding the niche of language study. Nonteaching professionals in academic administration, for example, are critical allies in this respect, and their advancement in the institution depends strongly on stretching the boundaries of their jobs. To the extent to which registrars, directors of continuing education, and associate deans for research can be involved in a reformulation of general education that includes language study, the greater the chances for niche expansion. After all, it is the nonteaching professionals who develop and execute the organizational processes necessary to modify existing programs of all kinds. Admissions officers, too, can be of considerable assistance, particularly as they can determine how much second language experience entering freshman classes have. Where there is also a concern for increasing minority representation in the student body, faculty might urge admissions officers to look at school systems that have alternative programs to produce bilingual students with an international orientation. Cincinnati (where 1,800 native speakers of English, 30% of them black, are involved in such a program), Milwaukee, and Atlanta all have made notable efforts, though they have yet to start graduating students from these programs. The point is that a significant percentage of an entering student constituency already attuned to second language learning is a positive preachment in itself.

External allies can be mobilized as well, but it is important to choose them from expanding sectors of the society and economy, like minority language populations or international business. Such connections can strengthen the contributions of language faculty to the resources of the institution and thus substitute for other internal political weaknesses. To the extent that external parties can contribute to international or language study aspects of general education programs, regardless of form, the hand of language faculty in organizational development will become more visible.

A Widening Agenda

If there is advocacy for change in all this, it calls for imaginative faculty development programs that are integrated into broader institutional processes. It is an advocacy for organizational development with language consciousness at its core. Organizational development, as Warren Bennis observed a decade ago, is a mind-boggling, resource-draining "complex educational strategy intended to change the beliefs, attitudes, values, and structure of organizations themselves,"[12] not to focus on the improvement of merely one group in the organization. It is a task requiring a level of energy and creativity that is paradoxically lacking in a period of pressure and decline. But it is precisely such a period, as Boulding said, that calls for "the creative widening of agendas,"[13] for both empathy (for student constituencies) and realism, and for a keen vigilance to avoid the mistakes that are not easily forgiven in difficult times. For the sake of the baby, we should rise to that task.

Notes

This article appeared in slightly different form in *ADFL Bulletin,* 13, No. 2 (Nov. 1981), 13–19.

[1]Charles Wegener, *Liberal Education and the Modern University* (Chicago: Univ. of Chicago Press, 1978), p. 103.

[2]Gary A. Woditsch, *Developing Generic Skills* (Bowling Green, Ohio: Bowling Green State Univ., 1977).

[3]Thomas Ewens, "Analyzing the Impact of Competence-Based Approaches on Liberal Education," in Gerald Grant et al., *On Competence* (San Francisco: Jossey-Bass, 1979), p. 172.

[4]See, e.g., Janice M. Beyer and Thomas M. Lodahl, "A Comparative Study of Patterns of Influence in United States and English Universities," *Administrative Science Quarterly,* 21 (1976), 104–29; and Gerald R. Salancik and Jeffrey Pfeffer, "The Bases and Use of Power in Organizational Decision Making: The Case of the University," *Administrative Science Quarterly,* 19 (1974), 453–73.

[5]Kenneth Boulding, *Ecodynamics* (Beverly Hills, Calif.: Sage, 1978), pp. 22–24.

[6]Joseph J. Schwab, "Eros and Education," in Ian Westbury and Neil J. Wilkof, eds., *Science, Curriculum, and Liberal Education: Selected Essays of Joseph Schwab* (Chicago: Univ. of Chicago Press, 1978), p. 106.

[7]Arthur W. Chickering, "Developmental Change as a Major Outcome," in Morris T. Keeton et al., *Experiential Learning* (San Francisco: Jossey-Bass, 1976), pp. 90–91.

[8]Arthur L. Stinchcombe, "Social Structure and Organizations," in James G. March, ed., *Handbook of Organizations* (Chicago: Rand-McNally, 1965), p. 174.

[9]James Cummins, "The Cross-Lingual Dimensions of Language Proficiency," *TESOL Quarterly,* 14 (1980), pp. 175–87.

[10]See, e.g., Norman Frederickson and William C. Ward, *Developmental Measures for the Study of Creativity* (Princeton, N.J.: Educational Testing Service (ETS RB 75-18), 1975); and Norman Frederickson, *Assessment of Creativity in Scientific Problem Solving* (Princeton, N.J.: Educational Testing Service (ETS TB 78-9), 1978).

[11]Roger A. Pillet, *Foreign Language Study: Perspective and Prospect* (Chicago: Univ. of Chicago Press, 1974), p. 45.

[12]Warren Bennis, *Organizational Development* (Reading, Mass.: Addison-Wesley, 1969), p. 2.

[13]Kenneth Boulding, "The Management of Decline," *Change,* 7, No. 5 (June 1975), 64.

Chapter Four

Curricular Change

In this chapter master teachers and consultants for the grant workshops suggest guidelines to formulate a college foreign language program. From the onset, we, the authors, acknowledge a seeming contradiction between our long-standing relationship with a general liberal arts education on the one hand and on the other the recent curricular emphasis of our profession on special student needs and interests and on language and culture for specific purposes. But the history of college foreign language instruction indicates that teaching has generally been limited to language—that is, grammar, literature, and civilization courses—and to an on-again, off-again time-based foreign language requirement (the completion of a given number of semester hours). Thus the inclusion of special areas in the curriculum—such as balanced skill courses, cultural issues traditionally covered by the social sciences and a proficiency-based requirement—represents an expansion and not a narrowing of perspective.

Our new clientele, the students who major in other subjects and study a second language as an ancillary skill, also suggests curriculum growth. In emphasizing that we have more to offer to more students for more purposes, we are not limiting ourselves to vocational pragmatism but are seeking to widen our focus and to make a liberal arts discipline indispensable to American higher education. Furthermore, by stressing the refinement of cognition as well as recognition and recall processes in the second language acquisition process, the authors aim to keep the intellectual level of the foreign language curriculum on a par with students' other academic courses. The curricula suggested in the following papers is intended to ensure that the foreign language learning experience will have a life-long impact on students.

Carol Herron treats the fundamental issue of oral skill development and grammar analysis in the beginning and intermediate college foreign language classroom. She urges teachers interested in developing functional

121

second language ability in their students to strive in each class period to create a balance among habit formation, rules analysis, and communicative practice. She also suggests a student-centered discovery approach to error correction.

Janet King Swaffar presents techniques that any adult reader, regardless of language level, can apply to achieve comprehension of a text. These techniques are based on the assumption that readers comprehend a text by actively and analytically restructuring information.

Claire Gaudiani turns her attention to the improvement of student writing skills. The objective of her student-centered text-editing approach is to help learners write coherently in the target language and to become sensitive to the dynamics of good expository writing in general.

Howard Nostrand reminds us of the unique international and cross-cultural contribution that language learning can make in the general American education system. The cultural element in foreign language study is not only essential for successful communication; according to Nostrand, it is also the subject's most broadening, most humanizing contribution to the inner life of the learner.

Though the papers in this section treat different aspects of a balanced foreign language curriculum, they are complementary in perspective. An expanded curriculum, formulated along the authors' suggested lines, emerges as one in which students discover and apply new cognitive processes and skills, while the teacher guides learning and affirms or adjusts the students' conclusions.

Building Communicative Skills in the Foreign Language Classroom

Carol A. Herron

Since the 1960s, the trend away from audiolingualism and its mimicry-memorization approach has contributed to a renewed interest in the use of language as communication in oral activities. This does not mean, however, that rote learning of basic structures can be entirely replaced by spontaneous personal expression in beginning foreign language courses. Free conversation is a continually developing skill rooted in reproducing language patterns and in understanding the rules that generate those patterns. Today researchers suggest that foreign language teachers interested in developing conversational skills in their students should strive to maintain a balance among habit formation, rule analysis, and communicative practice. As Rivers wrote:

> There has been much controversy on whether, in using a language, we operate according to rules we have internalized or habits we have acquired. Much of this discussion has been at cross-purposes. Understanding of grammatical rules and practice of rules with changes in lexical content and in different combinations and variations are both essential if the language user is to operate freely and effortlessly in the expression of meaning.[1]

In this paper I suggest some basic techniques that encourage students to internalize rules, to develop skills or habits, and to communicate personal meaning. These strategies pertain to teaching grammar, a fundamental activity in all college foreign language classes, and to correcting students' errors in a meaningful and communicative fashion.

If we turn first to the oral practice of new linguistic units, research generally suggests that the grammar lesson should have three basic parts: a repetition stage, an explanation phase, and communicative practice.[2] Their precise ordering depends on the theoretical bases subscribed to by the materials designer or the teacher. For example, if a teacher chooses to present a certain grammar point deductively, the explanation, or rule analysis stage, will precede the drill (repetition) phase. If the teacher uses an inductive approach, students will repeat eight to ten examples of the new linguistic pattern before they are asked to formulate the rule underlying the pattern. It is true that the audiolingual (inductive presentation) versus the cognitive (deductive presentation) discussion has not yet been resolved.[3] But research does emphasize that both methods of ordering the grammar lesson should be followed by a communicative transfer stage in which students try to use the new rule in analogous sentences to express personal meaning. This last stage aims to help students advance from repetition to free speech and to help teachers and check students' progress.

Various techniques have been suggested for each of these phases. Repetition is an essential part of a language learning at the rote, or skill-getting level. Thus both Grittner[4] and Rivers (p. 100) argue that structured pattern drills remain an effective strategy for teaching orally the observable, fixed interrelationships of a language. These two authors discuss many different kinds of drills (substitution, replacement, transformation, completion, etc.) that can be adapted easily to any textbook or method. Knop emphasizes that when teaching a pattern practice, four important principles can create interest and add meaning: visualization (pictures, objects), personalization of repeated sentences (using students' names or famous people), physical activity (acting out the meaning of repeated sentences, using gestures and facial expressions), and the use of humor.[5] When cuing a drill, Knop says, teachers may use repetition of the rote type (straight repeating after the teacher's model), but repetition will usually appear more meaningful if it occurs in a question-answer sequence and if pictures or accompanying sentences are used as faded cues:

1. *Fullest cue:* Teacher teaches the answer and then asks the question with the answer in it.

    E.g.,   *Teacher:*   I am going to the bank.
             Students: I am going to the bank.
             Teacher: Are you going to the bank?
             Students: Yes, I am going to the bank.

2. *More faded cue:* Either-or question.

    E.g.,   *Teacher:*   Are you going to the bank or to the stadium? (shows picture of bank to class)
             Students: I am going to the bank.

3. *More faded cue:* Visual cue.

    E.g.,   *Teacher:*   Where are you going? (holds up picture of bank)
             Students: I am going to the bank.

4. *More faded cue:* Accompanying statement.

    E.g.,   *Teacher:*   To cash my check . . .
             Students: To cash my check, I am going to the bank.

5. *Most faded cue:* General question (personalized).

    E.g.,   *Teacher:*   Really, after class where are you going?

Student 1:   I am going to the bank.
Student 2:   Not me, I am going to the cafeteria.
Student 3:   I am going to the bookstore.

This last, general question is an important one to position at the end of a mechanical drill since students are asked to respond with a personal, meaningful choice from the eight to ten variations presented in the drill.

In the rule analysis stage, a grammatical explanation should be kept as simple as possible so that students will understand it and be able to provide examples of its use. Knop suggests teaching the rule in the target language so that students can restate it without breaking the cultural island established in the classroom.[6] She encourages teachers to introduce the rule by a model sentence students already know so that they will be aware that the rule is both useful and actually used. This sentence could be lifted from a previously learned dialogue, drill, or reading. Whereas the repetition stage is primarily oral, I have found it effective in the explanation phase to provide at least three written examples of the rule (in addition to the model sentence) in contextual sentences. Key points can be underlined in colored chalk on the board for review and emphasis.

In the transfer, or communicative practice phase, teachers ask students to create examples of a concept that has just been repeated and analyzed. New vocabulary in context enters naturally at this stage. This step reinforces a pattern already practiced orally and can serve as a diagnostic check on students' learning. Whereas the class as a rule performs the drill phase orally, the reinforcing may occur in an oral or written mode. A written check does provide a change in routine and a break from oral work. Some examples of oral and written transfer activities follow.

1. Give the students an infinitive, and they make up a whole, meaningful sentence, practicing the grammar point recently learned:
   Tell your teacher to do certain things.

   a. *to eliminate*   and students say   *Eliminate quizzes!*
   b. *to finish*   *Finish this exercise.*

   or
   Tell your classmates what you used to do often when you were in high school.

   a. *to play*   and students say   *I used to play football.*
   b. *to drink*   *I used to drink beer.*

2. Give question-answer drills, asking students for a personal response to a learned structure:

   a. *Do you like*   and students say   *Yes, I like it.*
       ice cream?

       or
       No, I don't like it.

3. Ask the students for a quick translation of sentences already practiced in the target language or analogous to learned ones. This

idea works best for idioms and verb tenses that conflict with a native language pattern.

    a. *I am thirsty.*   French: *J'ai soif.*

    b. *I am ten years old.*   *J'ai dixans.*

4. Do a written or oral exercise from the textbook.

5. Look in other textbooks for a communicative activity in which students transfer a concept learned by repetition to a realistic situation.

6. Give students a list of infinitives, and they select the verb that makes sense in a group of sentences with verb blanks. Students can be told to conjugate each verb in a certain tense, or they can decide on the appropriate tense from key words in the sentences. Sentences should be realistic and personalized:

    parler   danser   regarder   jouer

    a. Nous_____très bien français.

    b. Les Américains_____beaucoup de télévision.

    c. Les "Yankees"_____au baseball.

7. Use a personalized learning activity for communicative practice. Guidebooks with such activities are often organized around specific grammar points in the target language. See for example:

Boylan, Patricia, and Alice Omaggio. *Strategies for Person-Centered Language Learning.* Detroit: Advancement Press of America, 1976.

Christensen, Clay B. "Achieving Language Competence with Affective Learning Activities." *Foreign Language Annals,* 2 (1977), 157–67.

Disick, Renee. "Developing Communication Skills through Small-Group Activities." *American Foreign Language Teacher,* 3 (1972), 3–7.

Knop, Constance. "Toward Free Conversation." *American Foreign Language Teacher,* 2 (1972), 5–9.

Moskowitz, Gertrude. *Caring and Sharing in the FL Classroom.* Rowley, Mass.: Newbury, 1978.

Wattenmaker, B., and V. Wilson. *A Guidebook for Teaching Foreign Languages: Spanish, French, and German.* Rockleigh, N.J.: Allyn and Bacon, 1980.

Of course, real communication needs realistic situations outside the classroom. Activities might include language clubs, language tables, interviewing native speakers, and study-abroad experiences.

Linked closely to the issue of how to provide maximum reinforcement of the new concept is the question of which student errors to correct. Researchers are now indicating that correction is important for three kinds of errors: errors that impair communication, errors that stigmatize the learner, and errors that students produce frequently with respect to a particular pedagogical focus.[7] Examples of errors that might impede the intelligibility of a message are the misuse of a preposition or pronoun or the omission of a word. Examples of errors that could stigmatize a language learner from the perspective of a native speaker include phonological mistakes and the misuse of a formal or familiar pronoun. An example of an error pertaining to a specific pedagogical point would be the incorrect formation of the *passé composé* in French after the teacher has spent several class periods discussing it.

Teachers use a wide variety of techniques to correct errors in a meaningful way. Although no extensive empirical research substantiates whether any of these strategies reduces errors significantly, recent research indicates that indirect procedures are more effective than direct ones, in which the teacher immediately supplies a correct response. A discovery approach to error correction can help students make inferences about the target language and fix this information in their long-term memory. Teachers are encouraged to remind a student of a relevant rule or recue the question so that the student can self-correct and develop an inner monitor.

Here are some specific suggestions for correcting errors indirectly:

1. When a student hesitates in answering, the teacher can say or do nothing for five to ten seconds, giving the student a chance to replay the information. Stevick calls this the "silent method."[8]

2. A teacher can rephrase a question, if possible reducing the number of words.
   Teacher: Why did he arrive home so late last night?
   Student: Ummm. . . (hesitation)
   Teacher: Why is he late?

3. The teacher can cue the student visually or linguistically. For instance, if the teacher makes a backward gesture over one shoulder or points to a time line drawn on the board, the student gets the cue that the response occurred in the wrong tense and needs restatement in the past. Or a simple communicative "Comment?" or "Pardon?" in French can warn the student that an error was made. Giving more help, the teacher can provide a grammatical rule or hint:
   Student: Hier, j'ai allé au cinéma.
   (Yesterday, I went to the movies.) Student used wrong helping verb with past participle.
   Teacher: Bon, au cinéma. Mais est-ce que le verbe *aller* est conjugué avec *avoir* ou *être?* (Oh, to the movies. Good, but is the verb *aller* conjugated with *avoir* or *être* in the past?)

In this last example of student self-correction, note that the teacher praised the factual accuracy of the student's message while indicating a grammatical inaccuracy. This helps the beginning student to distinguish between communicating an idea and making a grammatical error. Of course, giving such a grammatical hint is appropriate only if the student has already learned the particular grammatical structure. Otherwise, the teacher should simply ignore the mistake, if it does not involve a pedagogical focus at that stage in language acquisition, or supply the correct grammatical form by rewording the student's statement.

Moreover, indirect correction strategies should still be supported by general teaching principles and techniques that can help alleviate the problem of teacher-induced errors. Students may make mistakes because the teacher has failed to create awareness and understanding of the activities to be undertaken, or because they find class exercises tedious and uninteresting, or because they have not had enough practice in using the new concept. All these problems can be minimized by providing interesting and varied practice in repetition, analysis, and communicative transfer.

NOTES

[1]Wilga Rivers, *Teaching Foreign Language Skills,* 2nd ed. (Chicago: Univ. of Chicago Press, 1981), p. 98.

[2]John Carroll, "Current Issues in Psycholinguistics and Second Language Teaching," *TESOL Quarterly,* 5 (1971), 102–12; Constance Knop, "Three Parts to a Grammar Lesson," (unpub., Univ. of Wisconsin, Madison, 1974); Philip D. Smith, Jr., *Second Language Teaching: A Communicative Strategy* (Boston, Mass.: Heinle and Heinle, 1981).

[3]R. Fischer, "Inductive-Deductive Controversy Revisited," *Modern Language Journal,* 63 (1979), 98–105.

[4]Frank Grittner, *Teaching Foreign Languages,* 2nd ed. (New York: Harper, 1977).

[5]Constance Knop, *Toward Free Conversation and Communication in the Foreign Language Classroom* (Madison, Wisc.: Wisconsin Dept. of Public Instruction, 1977).

[6]_____, *Teaching a Second Language: A Guide for the Student Teacher,* Language in Education: Theory and Practice, Vol. 3 (Washington, D.C.: Center for Applied Linguistics, 1979–80).

[7]James M. Hendrickson, "Error Correction in Foreign Language Teaching: Recent Theory, Research, and Practice," *Modern Language Journal,* 62 (1978), 387–98.

[8]Earl W. Stevick, *Memory, Meaning, and Method* (Rowley, Mass.: Newbury, 1976).

Reading in the Foreign Language Classroom: Focus on Process

Janet King Swaffar

This section presents techniques that any adult reader, regardless of text, method, language level, or language, can apply to achieve comprehension of a text.[1] The techniques are predicated on the assumption that a reader comprehends a text by actively and analytically restructuring information rather than by passively registering information in the mode of the text. The research and theory supporting the notion that reading comprehension results from analytical processing has a venerable tradition, which is currently enjoying a renaissance.[2] The most recent descriptions of the process are emerging primarily in psycholinguistics and discourse analysis. In identifying the inadequacies of the passive reading model, this literature shares several fundamental assumptions that serve as significant points of departure for this paper.

1. Active control of isolated structures and vocabulary does not guarantee reading comprehension. Such grammatical elements remain unrelated until they are integrated into the communicative framework, the message of the text.[3]

2. The ability to translate from the foreign language to the native language is not, in itself, a guarantee of reading comprehension.[4]

3. The use of the who, what, when, and where questions is not an efficient way to foster or check reader comprehension of a text because they isolate new bits of information and thereby remove them from their meaningful context.[5] Such questions may actually interrupt the reader's efforts to put segments or details of the text into a meaningful whole. Only the analytical or inferential why question (why does the reader agree or disagree?) calls for interpretation of meaning. Hence students who can answer the who, what, when, and where recognition questions are frequently unable to frame a response to the why question if it demands an analysis of information only implied in the text.

4. To categorize the reading task as a "skill"—unrelated to listening, speaking, and writing tasks—teaches and reinforces a distinction that may

129

well be unproductive in a communicative setting.[6] If reading is taught as a separate skill, classroom practice focuses on the isolated surface detail of the text (who, what, when, and where questions). Only if reading is taught as part of the total language learning process will classroom practice correlate reading to meaning.

To illustrate this distinction, assume a skills classroom treatment of the fable "Der Wolf und das Lamm."[7]

> ### The Wolf and the Lamb
> Phaedrus (first century after Christ)
>
> Once a wolf and a lamb came to the same stream, for they both were thirsty. The wolf drank upstream, the lamb downstream. Then the wicked robber began an argument: "Why are you sullying the water where I am drinking?" To that the woolly animal responded fearfully: "Please, Wolf, how can I be doing that? The water that I drink comes downstream from you to me." The power of truth silenced the wolf a moment. But immediately thereafter he began anew: "Six moons ago you have insulted me, Lamb!" To that the lamb countered anxiously: "I wasn't even alive then!" "Quite right, it was your father who abused me!"
> With that he seized the lamb and killed it.

Measures of a "successful reading" of this text in a skills framework are based on recognition and recall of vocabulary and grammar forms. Consequently, exercises and examinations rely heavily on the who-what-when-where questions, such as "Where do the wolf and the lamb drink?" and "What does the wolf say to the lamb?," as well as on vocabulary glosses followed by reinforcement drill. Student attention is drawn to disassociated parts of the textual message but not to the interrelationship, the developed meaning, of those parts: structures and vocabulary are removed from their original context. As a result, the language that originally belonged to a text is presented and practiced as a formal paradigm instead of as part of a larger message.

A process approach focuses on the larger message of a text. Text assignments are devised so that students will identify vocabulary and grammar forms as redundant or as variants of a central idea. To avoid presenting isolated functions out of narrative context, the assignments stress inference and analysis in conjunction with recognition and recall. To maintain and draw on the meaning structure of the text, assignments reveal the interrelated functions of vocabulary and grammar in the narrative context. Assignments that fulfill these criteria—relating vocabulary and syntactic features to the total narrative message—are of two major types: (1) semantic categorization (e.g., please identify other words for wolf and lamb, the words that refer to water, the words that describe various ways of speaking, etc.) and (2) syntactic categorization (e.g., pick out of the text the words [nouns] that stand for the following pronouns; the verbs in the present tense, the past, and the present perfect.)

The semantic categorization exercise, grouping words for wolf and lamb, connects authorial sympathies and imagery (woolly animal, robber) to the focal figures of the text and alerts students to implied levels of association. In the syntactic categorization exercise, grouping verb tenses, the grammatical structure of the text is revealed as integral to its meaning. Students will discover the consistent use of simple past for narrative and present tense for dialogue characteristic of the fable genre. The only exception to this pattern occurs after the polite conversation has ceased and the wolf tries to legitimize his intentions by fabricating an excuse to kill the lamb ("Six moons ago you have insulted me, Lamb!"). At this point, the wolf uses the present perfect for the first time. In effect, the shift in tense is the purely syntactical signal that the lamb's situation is hopeless. Such correlations between syntactical changes and changes in implied meaning are frequent and prominent in unedited texts of all kinds, a feature that, if noted, can facilitate reader comprehension. In addition, studies conducted in the past two decades indicate that a learner's efforts to schematize or connect textual information enhance recall significantly.[8] To test this assertion, the reader need only conduct in class one of the process exercises designed for the German fable and subsequently ask students to reconstruct the story from memory. The degree of recall, not only of main ideas but also of grammatical and semantic detail, is generally striking.

Skills approaches, then, focus on language forms: their purview is largely restricted to passive identification of isolated meanings, such as replication of grammatical forms and substitution of vocabulary. In contrast, a process approach regards language learning as an analytic activity; its emphasis is ideational, focused on the meaning or message conveyed by the text. Consequently, all language tasks are viewed as integral parts of a multifaceted whole at whose center is the informational core of communication that is being conveyed.

For those unfamiliar with a process approach to reading, three objections may present themselves that deserve consideration: (1) How can students comprehend a text without knowing all the parts? (2) How can students acquire new vocabulary and structures if they are not learning them explicitly—in paradigms and vocabulary lists? and (3) Even if advanced foreign language students could profit from this approach, how can beginners, first- and second-semester language learners, read texts containing vocabulary and structures with which they are largely unfamiliar?

The first question goes to the heart of reading in *any* language: how do we derive meaning from texts? Emphatically not, say many experts in this field, by identifying words: "Text can be comprehended only if it is read for meaning in the first place: reading to identify words is both unnecessary and inefficient."[9] And ". . . [M]eaning identification is generally a prior operation to word identification because it reduces word uncertainty and therefore permits word identification on minimal visual information."[10]

Such a definition of reading for meaning seems to belie suppositions of current language teaching practice and anticipates our second question: how can we acquire language without explicitly acquiring vocabulary and structures? Reading theorists invert this question to answer it, maintaining that a communicative context must give meaning to structures and vocabulary functions *before* isolated words and syntactic patterns can be meaningful.[11] Moreover, the ability to identify the meanings of words and to recall those words actually seems to be facilitated by meaningful context.[12]

The notion of the necessity of meaningful context suggests a way to resolve the third objection: how can beginning language learners identify meaning while commanding only a slight knowledge of the foreign language? The classroom resolution to this objection depends on the age of the learners. Very young children cannot identify complex meanings because they lack cognitive maturity and extralinguistic reference. Adult readers of English (age fourteen or over), however, bring to any foreign language text a wealth of background knowledge and experience with which to undertake the core task, the necessary first step in the reading process: the formulation of a reading hypothesis.[13] Adults can look at the German version of "Der Wolf und das Lamm" and note, "This is one paragraph long, contains dialogue, and the animals seem to be doing the talking. The words *Wolf* and *Lamm* are like English." The adult reader may then infer, "I'll bet this is a fable." Armed with this hypothesis, our adult learner can proceed to confirm or disconfirm the fable theory and decide whether this is a fable with a traditional moral or a bizarre or humorous variant, such as a Kafka fable.

Such reasoning and its supporting research suggest that to teach reading using the assumptions of a process approach, both instructional strategies and reading exercises must focus on the informational structure of the text. Unless such details interfere with comprehension of information structure, teachers must encourage students to be unconcerned about isolated morphological segments or knowledge of each word in the text.

In natural sequence, the classroom and learner tasks that enable reading for meaning are those which:

1. *Preview:* ask the students to create a reading hypothesis based on preliminary identification of text type and subject matter. (This is a _____ [poem, essay, newspaper article]. It is about the movie *The Tin Drum.*)

2. *Weight:* establish an intrinsic textual focus that correlates redundancies in vocabulary and structures with the preestablished reading hypothesis. (Identify all the words and phrases that refer to the making of the movie *The Tin Drum.*)

3. *Organize:* ask students to trace and reconstruct the linguistic and semantic patterns that expand the focus and reinforce the message of the text. (Identify those words and phrases that criticize the way *The Tin Drum* was

made and those that praise it. Decide which type of observation predominates.) These activities correlate with the natural hierarchy of thought processes that the successful reader in the native language uses to read fluently.[14]

The first contact with the text is inferential, making preliminary hypotheses about subject matter and genre (It is one half sheet of ditto paper in my office mailbox; it's probably a memo; or, There's a list of verb forms; what follows is probably a grammar description). After making initial inferences, the reader uses analytical thought processes to confirm or disconfirm the inferences.

For example, the office memo can be quickly confirmed if the heading has "To" and "From," if it contains the words "employees are advised," and if it is signed by your boss. To make an inference about genre, the reader will, as in the office memo illustration, generally rely on external features, such as headings, pictures, and format. To make an inference about subject matter, the reader will have to skim for four or five key words (predominantly nouns) that are an identifiable aggregate, a group of words comprehended by the reader as meaningfully related, as the propositional core of the text.[15]

Such previewing prepares the student of any language for fluent reading. How, then, may one implement previewing tasks in the classroom?

The Previewing Processes: Genre and Subject Matter

To establish a preliminary framework for reading, it will be necessary to discuss initial inferences before students begin to read an out-of-class reading assignment. As part of the assignment procedure in class, students take one or two minutes to scan the first two or three paragraphs, picking out format features such as illustrations, pagination, and titles (genre preview) or picking out key words such as names and dates (subject matter preview). If the text is, for example, a journalistic report on riots in England, the class finds and possibly underlines names of heads of state or geographic locations and references to destruction that indicate whether the time is the past or the present. Next, books are closed, and then key words recalled by the class should be written on the board or on a transparency. Using this preliminary list, the class decides if all the words are relevant and if any relevant words are missing. Such a discussion creates, in effect, a reading hypothesis. The class as a whole agrees about what to expect.

In actual practice, the identification of genre and subject matter of a new reading assignment should take no more than five minutes at the end of the class hour. It is the optimal preview exercise for reading since it represents a structured attempt to give the class a working hypothesis about the text. If we accept Smith's definition that meaningful reading occurs when reader prediction is confirmed in the process of continued contact with the text, then such preview strategies should reflect intuitive or learned preview strategies of successful readers.[16] The objective of these strategies can be characterized as the effort of correlating subject matter with genre.

After one or two practice sessions, students generally find it easy to correlate genre with subject matter. It is helpful to refer them to the primary types of texts they will be reading. Such a vocabulary list in the foreign language serves both as a guide to students and as a basis for classroom discussion:

Distinctive Genre Types

1. Information
   Articles, reports (e.g., in a magazine)
   Lists (e.g., a menu)
   Tables (e.g., a train or bus schedule)
2. Descriptions
   A concrete description of a person, an object, a visual scene
   A technical description (e.g., a grammar)
3. Advertisements
   Ads (e.g., in a magazine)
   Ads (e.g., in a newspaper)
4. Instructions
   Recipes
   Games
   Construction (e.g., for a paper airplane)
   Assignments, exercises
5. Opinions
   Essay
   Theory
6. Conversations
   Interviews, dialogues
   Monologues
   Sermons, prayers
   Speeches, lectures
7. History
   Biography, autobiography
   Historical analyses
8. Stories or narratives
   Fables
   Fairy tales
   Anecdotes
   Short stories
   Novellas
   Novels

9. Poems
    Songs
    Choral works
    Hymns
    Lyrics
10. Dramas
    Radio plays
    Theatrical works (e.g., comedies, tragedies, operas)
    Scripts for films, tv programs

The genre can often be identified by means of visual characteristics of the text, such as titles, illustrations, and statistical tables.[17]

After establishing genre, students need guidance in anticipating the text's logical development. It is at this point that the integration of genre and subject matter begins. Actually, by establishing genre, students have already identified the probable rhetorical grammar of the text, the stylistic markers that predict the flow of ideas and the constraints within which those ideas can be developed.

As an example, let us assume that the class is working with our fable about the wolf and the lamb. Once students recognize that they are dealing with a fable, they need little knowledge of the target language to know that the text contains the following features as present($+$): $+$ figures, $+$ action, $+$ dialogue, and $+$ visual scene. The students' extrinsic knowledge—their familiarity with fables in the English language—further suggest to them that the text, as a fable, will probably have $+$ chronology and $+$ fiction. Having thus identified which features the text as a fable can potentially develop, students will now be able to weight and organize the information in their reading assignment.

By way of contrast, let us assume that the class is previewing an essay. The students will probably find none of the genre features of the fable, since most essays lack the following features ($-$): $-$action, $-$dialogue, $-$visual scene, $-$fiction. It should be noted that minus features frequently render a text more difficult for the foreign language reader, because the reader finds no visual references or extrinsic information about the world that can be applied to the text.[18]

From Inference to Analytic Thought Processes: Weighting and Organizing

Initial identification of genre and subject matter prepares students for fluent reading—that is, for fuller comprehension achieved through analysis of multiple levels of textual meaning. In previewing, students have isolated a first level, the global presuppositions of genre and subject matter, which can now be confirmed and elaborated in confronting the text on various other levels of content and form, depending on the reader's intent. As a preliminary to fluent reading, the class has hypothesized about the informational boundaries of the text and the rhetorical patterns that structure that information. It is now ready to assess the way the textual language is organized and weighted by the author. Previewing has delineated the information available in the text. Further reading identifies the systematizing or the authorial structuring of that information. Correlating textual information with authorial structure, or, as it is more commonly known, authorial point of view, is the process by which the reader achieves comprehension or reads for meaning: using analytical processes (systematic weighting and organizing) instead of relying solely on recall or recognition.

In the classroom, the implementation of a simple but radical departure from the usual recall and recognition questions (who-what-when-where questions and multiple choice, for example) is essential. To foster true analytic processing in reading, neither recall nor recognition are sufficient. Students can only comprehend a text through an active confrontation with it, in which they select elements of the textual language and then organize and weight those elements into meaningful patterns.

In the fable "The Wolf and the Lamb," the students who selected and grouped the verbs according to the present, past, and present perfect tenses can now analyze the systematic groupings and decide whether or not a pattern correlates that syntactic level with a semantic level of the text. The juxtaposition of these two levels will, in turn, open a range of implied meanings (part of the total implication structure of the text) that students can discuss in simple language drawn almost exclusively from the text. Having understood that there is a pattern, students are prepared to respond to an analytic why question: Warum spricht der Wolf plötzlich im Perfekt? Raten Sie mögliche Gründe. (Why might the wolf have started talking about prior events in the perfect tense?) A range of answers is available in simple text-based language that nonetheless conveys complex implications: He wants to be in the right (justification of actions); He wants to demonstrate his authority (recourse to authoritarian threats); The lamb is supposed to be afraid (intimidation of the lamb); He thinks this is what wolves do (standard bully tactics, working himself up to feel self-righteous in killing the lamb).

The Reading Process: Weighting and Organizing Factors

Two fundamental tasks help readers locate authorial systematizing of information in the text: locating information groupings and identifying the authorial point of view indicated by the weighting of that information. The source of language for these assignments need only be the text, as has been demonstrated above. In classroom practice, both tasks demand no more of the student than reading aloud those segments of the text whose language fulfills the particular requirement. Cognitively, however, students will be asked to do more than recognize information as they did in the preview: they have to analyze it. Establishing the organizing and weighting of textual information is an active analysis, a critique of the structure of the text. In assessing the relative balance or imbalance of information or argumentation, the students are a short step from confronting the question of whether they agree or disagree with the author's presentation.

The first task is to establish, through examination of textual language, the logical groupings of information in terms of continuity-sameness (general to specific, small to large, etc.), chronology-sequence (first, second, third; from the end to the beginning; etc.), and instrumentality (because of x, y results). These are the organizational factors available to the author. If we assume that reading for textual message will be done more accurately if analysis is conducted with a minimum of reader contamination—without the intrusion of opinions and information not expressed in the text—then organizational assignments must be structured so that students examine the language of the text that anticipates distinctive authorial patterns. Three kinds of assignments are useful to foster student analysis of textual language without recourse to text-extrinsic language:

1. Assignments that ask students to select textual references to continuity or discontinuity, sameness or difference. Students will cite or list statements, words, or phrases that reveal, for example, shifts or contrasts in visual scene or in action or behavior of characters. References to such shifts are bound closely to the grammar of the text and include tense indicators (e.g., the old lady in "Frau Prümm erzählt" reflects on her childhood and present life in clearly alternating shifts of tense) and coordinating or subordinating conjunctions that connect a group of reflections ("and," "since," "because") or perhaps separate them ("but," "on the contrary"). An exercise based on the text "Frau Prümm erzählt" (see app. A, p. 142) asks the students to group the statements where Frau Prümm is speaking about the past:

Assignment: Orientation

Identify where Mrs. Prümm speaks of the past.

Possible Answers: "I had silver spoons," "My daughter-in-law stole four hundred marks," "I put my pension money under the sugar bowl."

(An additional example is included with the text in app. A.)

2. Assignments that ask students to select textual references to chronology or sequence of events. Events can be listed, for example, in the order in which they are mentioned. This textual chronology can, in turn, be contrasted with a sequence of the actual order in which events must have occurred. As in the first assignment, the location of textual chronology-sequence is in grammatical detail—most often in the consistent pattern of

temporal references or adverbial expressions ("in 1974," "later," "afterwards," etc.) A sample assignment for "Frau Prümm erzählt" asks students to locate the actual sequence of events that is not self-evident in the narrative structure of the text:

Assignment: Orientation—Time

Put the following in chronological order:

——The daughter-in-law is supposed to have stolen money.

——Mr. Prümm dies.

——The children crawl around Mr. Prümm.

——Mrs. Prümm puts the money under the sugar bowl.

3. Assignments that ask students to group textual references in terms of instrumentality or linked phenomena of any sort: that is, to reveal the ways in which people, objects, or events influence or connect with one another explicitly or implicitly. An example of such an assignment for the "Frau Prümm erzählt" with possible answers is:

A. Find Mrs. Prümm's references to death. For example: "there . . . [participating] in the glory of God."

Possible answers: "Fear . . . that's a laugh," "I wish I were up there already."

B. Identify the experiences in her life that explain the attitude expressed in these opinions. For example: "My daughter-in-law stole 400 marks."

Possible answers: "Two years and he was dead and I was alone," "I can't sleep."

The information falling under at least one of the three organizing factors (continuity, chronology, and instrumentality) must be determined before the students begin the second fundamental task, the assessment of authorial point of view: an analysis of authorial weighting given to the three organizing factors.

Assignments that prepare students for this assessment will require them to refer to their knowledge of the world, to the extrinsic information they bring to the text. Before readers can identify language that suggests negative or positive feelings or note vital omissions in reasoning and information, they must have personal standards for making such judgments. This prerequisite reemphasizes that the assignments here apply only to reading done by adults.[19] But particularly for adults it is vital to distinguish between an impressionistic, unsubstantiated judgment and a judgment based on textual evidence. The two judgments may be the same, but the pedagogical value of the assignments is their focus on the active *processing* of information rather than on "correct" conclusions per se. There are at least seven or eight ways Frau Prümm expresses dissatisfaction with her life. Identifying *any* three or four prepares the student to draw correct conclusions about the larger implications of the text.

The organizing assignments exemplified above must be tailored to the text in question (to genre or subject matter). For any text, however, one or more of the following weighting assignments will provide the basis for subsequent reader judgment or conclusions about the authorial point of view: (1) analyzing authorial objectivity or subjectivity as manifested in textual language; (2) determining whether textual language is critical or uncritical regarding the subject matter; (3) assessing whether textual language is positive or negative regarding the subject matter; (4) locating the relative balance or imbalance of information in the text, as well as possible omissions or extraneous data or arguments.

As an example, let us assume that a first-semester class has been asked to read Wolf Wondratschek's "Aspirin" (see app. B, p. 145). Students will have identified this short text in the preview phase as a love story that refers to two people as "she" and "they," German "sie." The organizing assignment consists of (1) grouping singular and plural references to "sie" (syntactical organizing to locate consistency), and (2) correlating language that refers to the ages of the two persons and the probable setting of the story (semantic organizing to locate consistency). The weighting assignment is to analyze two important author omissions: the absence of personal names and of the pronoun "he."

The reading assignments exclude a number of possible organizational considerations, such as chronology or instrumentality, that are less overt in the language of this particular text. Similarly, assignments examining such weighting features as author objectivity and critical versus uncritical or positive versus negative stance were eliminated as less revealing than those based on inclusion and omission. Inevitably, the tasks assigned elicit subinterpretations, deemphasizing less significant features and directing attention to others. But while the assignment is narrowing a student's field of activity, it does not prescribe a student's response. The tasks are open-ended in the sense that they encourage variability among individual student answers.

In contrast, the nonopen who-when-what-where questions restrict student discourse on both the informational and the organizational levels. They are teacher rather than learner questions. Or, as Hatch and Long state:

> Teachers' questions are usually not genuine questions at all, but pseudo-questions whose real function is to make students display knowledge (which the teacher already has) or to reveal that they lack a given piece of information.[20]

To be sure, the process reading assignment described does restrict examination of information by focusing on "sie" singular or plural rather than, for example, on what happens first, second, or third. But the assignment lets the *student* organize and weight the information, allowing for a considerable range of acceptable observations. For example, in the "Aspirin" weighting assignment, it would not be "wrong" for a student to decide to organize the information in the text around *any* of the hypotheses in the semantic organization assignments (see app. B). The purpose of the exercise is not so much that a student arrives at a prescribed "right" answer or a particular conclusion; rather it is to guide the student to use textual language in the clarification or development of that conclusion, a process that can be valid at *widely different levels of linguistic and interpretive sophistication.* Or, as Clarke and Silberstein conclude: "We must construct reading tasks which reward students as much for trying as for getting the correct answer."[21]

Student A who contrasts singular and plural references in "Aspirin" may not have the level of insight of student B, who points out that references to thinking ("She thinks about Rome") or personal appearance ("She has pretty hands") are exclusively "hers" and not "theirs." Yet student A is not "wrong" for failing to perceive these implications. Successful answers to a process assignment will reflect individual perceptions of the various levels of meaning available in most texts and, as such, will correspond to the students' maturational and cognitive levels.

In the task assigned for "Aspirin," meaning is derived exclusively from examination of textual detail. After students categorize or list dominant textual features, they are ready to proceed from the organization of the text (consistency, same or different) to the weighting of those informational groups. Only now can students determine what is more or less important to the author. Only after grouping the two "sie" functions in their various textual realizations can the class discuss whether or not the use of "sie" singular and plural is indicative of a statement about the people or relationships in the text. The class can compare, for example, whether anything "she" does or thinks has its equivalent in what "they" do or think. Students may disagree whether the young woman's relationship with the young man reflects a differentiated "other" or whether that anonymous plural represents merely an extension of the woman's own self-centered universe ("What is more important, he [er] or she [sie]? How does the text substantiate your answer?"). Before either conclusion is reached, however, the class will have identified recurrent informational and grammatical detail as a textual pattern conveying meaning.

Demonstrably, then, the reading process assignment, even for beginning students, allows the teacher's role to be relatively nondirective and nonprescriptive. "Right" and "wrong" will be a question of amassing evidence instead of pinpointing an isolated correct answer. The teacher's task is to guide students rather than to stand in absolute judgment of their success or failures. As any literary critic knows, interpretations of the meaning of a text will vary, at least to some degree. Process assignments do not exclude the natural richness available in the many levels of textual language on which students may draw. By reason of this natural linguistic richness, unedited readings are more accessible to students even when the texts are judged to be more difficult because of their unknown structures and vocabulary.[22] The redundancies and the real-world context of unedited readings enable students to apply many types of prior knowledge in identifying possible meanings of a text.[23]

With process assignments, the teacher automatically structures class discussions of readings. The entire class, including the teacher, engages in a dialogue about the constituents of the text. The linguistic task for students is simple. To provide a minimal correct answer, they need only read aloud. Their evidence may well be redirected or modified by more linguistically advanced peers in the class, but in the absolute sense ordinarily implied by an incorrect response to the who-what-where questions, a student's answer can never result in total failure.[24] Unless a student is completely unresponsive, some evidence that a student locates can be incorporated into the class's analysis. Ideally, throughout this process the teacher serves only as a monitor, as a resource person confirming and disconfirming the class's reconstruction through a broader knowledge of the language. The teacher need no longer be the absolute authority about what a text means.

Conclusions

Classroom approaches that focus on reading as a process have multiple implications for foreign language teaching. They offer, first, a consistent structure for comparative analysis of texts in the classroom. In providing students with instruction and guidance about how to read for meaning in the target language, the classroom teacher is making optimal use of group interaction.[25]

Second, the process approach offers both students and instructors considerable variety. After the class as a group has developed confidence about the reliability of its reading strategies, even unedited texts can be selected, according to the needs of specific interest groups or individuals.

Third, the process approach emphasizes the importance of reader purpose in undertaking to read a given type of text. Encouraging students to relate their particular interests to their knowledge of German enhances their learning. The knowledge that a chemistry major brings to bear on a scientific text, for example, will greatly facilitate that reader's comprehension of the material. Training in tasks that capitalize on this prior knowledge has motivational as well as cognitive value.

Fourth, the process approach increases freedom of text selection. Students who use this approach need not be restricted to graded readings.[26] Practical reasons beyond the technical assessments of comprehensibility argue in favor of making the transition from simplified to authentic texts as rapidly as possible. Unsimplified texts come closer to approximating the real linguistic world that the foreign language learner is preparing to confront. The sooner students are exposed to authentic language, the more rapidly they will learn that comprehension is a function not of understanding every word but of developing strategies for selecting and identifying multiple verbal and nonverbal cues, strategies essential in both oral and written communication.

The inherent advantage of a process approach is therefore clear: it presents reading as an adult activity, as an active analysis in which students expand their conceptual and informational horizons.

APPENDIX A

"Frau Prümm erzählt" is a text included in *BASIS: A First-Year Course in German.* The text is intended for second-semester students. The preview and orientation exercises below are part of the students' text.

[Exercises]

Preview: "Mrs. Prümm Narrates"
(In class)

Genre: _____

Main figures: _____

Time: _____ past and present_____

Read the first paragraph of the text very quickly (thirty seconds)! While reading, note five words that seem important to you. Then close your books, and, on the basis of the words you have selected, the class will attempt to construct a sentence or sentences that express our initial ideas about the text.

Mrs. Prümm Narrates

Katrine von Hutten

That little witch, my daughter-in-law. She never learned to knuckle down.

My index finger is getting bigger and bigger. Thirty years ago, in my mid-fifties, I started noticing that the children were as afraid of my index finger as of a giant. What should I do? I do my best. When Tina torments Niki, well then I interfere. Children have to play fair. The stronger one shouldn't be allowed to beat up the little fellow. I watch out and give Tina a box behind the ears when she beats up on Niki.

The roll here with butter, I've been carrying it around with me all morning. It's so hard for me to get anything down. I don't have any appetite. But you *have* to eat, otherwise you'll lose strength. People who don't eat die, my mother used to say. *She* managed it. My, how I look forward to seeing mama and papa again.

But my daughter-in-law, I told Richard the moment he brought her in the house, and it wasn't even a year after the wedding before he says to me, "Why did you let that happen, that was a mistake. I needed somebody like you who could really get the job done." "Richard," I answered, "my dear Richard, I told you right from the beginning, but you knew better. It's your life not mine."

My husband, he was a good man. We were like children together, in joy and in sorrow. He worked for the railroad, a boilermaker! One day they pulled him out, half dead, what a day that was. The way he lay there broken and half dead and the way the bed linen looked! I had to wash it three times before it was white again. The children crept around him and cried, "Papa, Papa!" Next thing we knew, he had too many white blood cells. Where that came from! Two years and he was dead and I was alone. We were like children together, always laughed but accomplished a lot, a lot accomplished.

If I'm afraid of dying? That's really a joke. After all, I have my faith. One closes one's eyes in this world and opens them in the next, in the glory of God. My, if I didn't have my faith! It's terrible when one doesn't know what one has. I had silver spoons for Sundays. My daughter-in-law stole four hundred marks from me, I'm absolutely certain about that. I had put my pension money under the sugar bowl. She was there to clean, there wasn't anyone else around. Mrs. Piper said, "It's just unbelievable."

There were twelve children at home, four boys and eight girls: Emil, Kettchen, Lina, Heinrich, Karl, Konrad, Hanna, Mariechen, Margret, Josepha. . . . people thought our father was crazy, always wanted more. Mariechen died between Saturday and Monday, three years old. Mother washed at night or she worked in the fields. We had to have money! There were three of us to a bed, there were even children in bed with grandmother. Last year we had five burials. My mother was always pregnant. She'd come from a well-to-do family, they had six horses.

We helped from the time we were small. We harvested potatoes, in the summer the blueberries, whatever there was. We picked and sold camomile, that was good for fifty cents and that meant a loaf of bread. I also racked when the farmers were bringing in their clover, I knew how to take advantage of a situation. We gathered dandelions for the rabbits on the country paths. The only thing we couldn't do was accept food from people, mother spanked us when we did that and said, "There's plenty to eat at our house!"

We were twelve children at home. Sunday morning our mother always had cooked potatoes on the stove, potato pancakes. Even today I still would rather eat potatoes. The kitchen and we kids and our mother reeked of cooking oil. After breakfast, our father always went to the cemetery to visit his mother. My, how devoted he was to his mother. She was truly a lovely woman. Her name was Emma.

Those were the days. She worked from dawn to late into the night, my mother and I did too, for that matter. From dawn to dusk. Knit a shirt, sewed skirts, darned and mended for the children, she came from sturdy stock. In the morning I took the children to the nursery, the little one on one arm, the other one by the hand, the basket with lunch tucked under my arm, and then I went down to work in the munitions plant, an hour's walk, the entire length of Heidelberger Street. I was there for three years, compulsory service. We made things there, big round things … cartridge shells. My how we worked, worked our fingers off. At home that just continued into the night. Oh yes, we went through a lot. Once my husband came to the factory and said, "Wife, come home now." To which I said, "Why should I come home? I have my work cut out for me here." I went home, there's my Gisela with a temperature of 105 and screaming convulsions for over an hour. I never experienced anything like that again.

But anything is better than this being alone now, this hard old age.

I don't like to think about the past. In the past, a lot of things were better. You knew where you stood, it wasn't a madhouse like today. I don't know what to say about the way things are today. Back then there was always work, more work than you could finish.

We need some rain. The chives look so shaggy. In early March they really shot up nice and green, long as my finger.

Oh, if only I could walk! I'd show the whole world. My entire life, I only did good, they will all testify to that. And now this old age. I can just make it into the bedroom and the kitchen, and pain day and night. If I were only buried and done with it. All the burial arrangements have been made for me. Four hundred marks. None of my relatives will come. And all the things I did for them. I helped them all. Arranged the wedding for my daughter, arranged all the weddings, and no one even stops to visit. It's as if one just didn't exist.

If I could just get around, then I could visit my people. It's hard, this business of being alone. I wish I were already up in heaven.

I hate the nights. They are so long, so long! And I can't sleep anyway. I turn from one side to the other and nothing helps. I spend the whole night looking at the clock. It's a cuckoo clock from the Black Forest, my Konrad gave it to me for my fiftieth birthday. Sometimes at night I feel he is there right next to my back. When I turn over, then he has turned over at the same time and lies next to my back on the other side. I wake up ten times at night because of my bladder, I have to urinate. I would just like to know what wrong I have done in my life. Last year we buried five people!

SOURCE: *Eleven-Thirty: Tenement Stories* (Zürich: Artemis, 1974).

ORGANIZING QUESTION

Using phrases from the text, select statements appropriate for each category.

	FEATURES	RESULTS
Frau Prümm's childhood	(example) twelve children at home	work from dawn to dusk
Married life		
After husband's death		
Currently		

APPENDIX B

The story "Aspirin" is included in *BASIS* as a first-semester text.

Preview: "Aspirin"

(In class)

Genre: _____

Main figures: 1. _____

2. _____

We will quickly read through the text once (thirty seconds)! In the process please mark down five words that seem important to you. Then we will close the books and construct a sentence that conveys the main theme of the text.

ASPIRIN

Wolf Wondratschek

She has a pretty face. She has pretty hair. She has pretty hands. She would like to have prettier legs.

They take walks. They step on wood. She lies down on her back. She hears the radio. They point to airplanes. They are silent. They laugh. She likes to laugh.

They don't live in the city. They know how deep a lake can be.

She is thin. They write letters to each other and write that they love each other. She changes her hairdo sometimes.

They don't talk with each other between the shorts and the main feature film. They argue about little things. They embrace each other. They kiss each other. They lend records to each other.

They have themselves photographed. She thinks about Rome. She has to promise to eat more at the swimming pool.

They sweat. They have open mouths. They often go to adventure films. She often dreams about them. She imagines what it is like to love. She tries out her first cigarette. They tell each other everything.

She has difficulty remaining calm at the front door. She washes herself with cold water. They buy soap. They have birthdays. They smell flowers.

They don't want to have any secrets from each other. She doesn't wear stockings. She borrows a sunlamp. They go dancing. They exaggerate. They sense that they are exaggerating. They love photographs. In photographs she appears somewhat older.

She doesn't say that she wants a lot of children.

They wait all day for the evening. They answer together. They both feel good. They give in. She pulls her sweater over her head. She opens her skirt.

She buys pills. Fortunately, there are pills.

SOURCE: *The Day Used to Start with a Gunshot Wound* (Munich: Hanser, 1970).

SYNTACTIC ORGANIZATION QUESTIONS

Assignment: Verb Subjects

In the story "Aspirin" the subject of every v^a [the inflected verb] is the word "sie." Sometimes "sie" is in the singular and means "she."
Example: [Subject]

Sie has a pretty face.

Sometimes "sie" is in the plural and means "they."
Example: [Subject]

Sie write letters. . . .

1. Underline every v^a that is inflected in the singular.
2. Circle every v^a that has a plural inflection.
3. What is the plural reference to "sie" (i.e., which persons are represented by the plural pronoun)?

Assignment: Orientation

1. Speculate about whether the people in this story are young or old. Which segments of the text substantiate your opinion?
2. The location of this story is probably:
   a. a farm in Africa
   b. a large city in Western Europe or the United States
   c. a small village in Brazil
   d. a suburb of a large city in Western Europe
   Find those segments of the text that substantiate your opinion.

Notes

[1]The substance of this paper reflects thinking and teaching practices developed at the University of Texas, Austin, between 1977 and 1980 and supported by a grant from the National Endowment for the Humanities. Major contributions to the research and materials on which this paper is based were made by G. Truett Cates (now at Austin Coll., Sherman, Tex.), Betty Nance Weber, Phyllis Manning, Margaret Woodruff, Don S. Stephens, John Pustejovsky, and Nancy Zeller. My particular thanks go to Katherine Arens and Inge C. Schwerdtfeger for discussions and guidance in writing this section.

[2]Within the last year, journals such as the *Modern Language Journal, Canadian Modern Language Review, Foreign Language Annals, Language Learning, System, TESOL Quarterly,* and *Zielsprache: Deutsch,* whose previous attention to reading had been relatively limited, have in virtually every issue featured articles on aspects of reading a foreign language.

[3]See Frank Smith and Deborah Lott Holmes, "The Independence of Letter, Word, and Meaning Identification in Reading," in Frank Smith, ed., *Psycholinguistics and Reading* (New York: Holt, 1973), pp. 50–69.

[4]In a discussion of the difficulties of teaching a foreign language for general as opposed to more restricted and clearly defined purposes, Richard Alexander provides a number of examples suggesting that, in part, "the word-for-word translation approach was preprogrammed to complicate the reading process unnecessarily" (p.

117), "A Learning-to-Learn Perspective on Reading in a Foreign Language," *System*, 8 (1980), 113–19.

[5]For a thorough analysis of the inadequacies of the "wh" questions in establishing comprehension of textual meaning, see June K. Phillips, "Second Language Reading: Teaching Decoding Skills," *Foreign Language Annals*, 8 (1975), 227–32; and *A Study of the Applicability of Task Analysis Methodology and Learning Hierarchies in Second-Language Reading*, Diss. Ohio State Univ. 1974. For similar conclusions about native speakers, see also R. C. Anderson ("Comprehension," *Review of Educational Research*, 42, No. 2 (1972), 145–70), who expands the analysis of the deficiencies of traditional questions by comparing responses to verbatim and paraphrase questions about reading passages.

[6]H. G. Widdowson illustrates, in *Teaching Language as Communication* (Oxford: Oxford Univ. Press, 1978), why current distinctions among skills are unproductive in a communicative framework: "speaking and writing are said to be active, or productive skills whereas listening and reading are said to be passive or receptive skills. . . . I want to suggest that although it might be convenient to represent the language skills in this way when considering usage [linguistic competence], it is not specifically helpful, and indeed might be positively misleading, to represent them in this way when considering use [performance]. The terms aural/visual and productive/receptive refer to the way language is manifested rather than to the way it is realized in communication" (p. 57).

[7]This text and exercises, as well as those included as the appendixes of the present article, are drawn from G. Truett Cates and Janet K. Swaffar, *BASIS: A First Course in German* (unpub., © 1979). This fable is presented as part of the first semester's work for high school or college students.

[8]Janet L. Mistler-Lachman, in her study "Levels of Comprehension in Processing of Normal and Ambiguous Sentences," *Journal of Verbal Learning and Verbal Behavior*, 11 (1972), 614–23, concludes that "an additional 'inferential' step was suggested as a component of deep comprehension" (p. 622). Her later study, "Depth of Comprehension and Sentence Memory," *Journal of Verbal Learning and Verbal Behavior*, 13 (1974), 98–106, expands these earlier conclusions:

> The operation of a levels-of-processing model has been less clearly specified, but presumably would hold that the system immediately enters a processing level appropriate to the task demands. Deeper tasks are handled at deeper levels, and deeper levels are characterized by better memory for the input. (p. 105)

The effect of logical processing on language recall in the native language has also been confirmed by David R. Olson, in his paper "Language and Thought: Aspects of a Cognitive Theory of Semantics," *Psychological Review*, 77, No. 4 (1970), 257–73, where he concludes: "it is shown by reference to the role of semantics in a transformational grammar that semantic decisions are not determined by either syntactic or semantic selection restrictions but by the speaker's knowledge of intended referent." See also Richard P. Honeck, "Interpretive versus Structural Effects on Semantic Memory," *Journal of Verbal Learning and Verbal Behavior*, 12 (1973), 448–55; S. A. Bobrow and G. H. Bower, "Comprehension and Recall of Sentences," *Journal of Experimental Psychology*, 80 (1969), 455–61; and Morris Moscovitch and Fergus I. M. Craik, "Depth of Processing, Retrieval Values, and Uniqueness of Encoding as Factors in Recall," *Journal of Verbal Learning and Verbal Behavior*, 15 (1976), 447–58.

[9]Smith, *Psycholinguistics and Reading,* p. 66.

[10]Smith, *Psycholinguistics and Reading,* p. 60. Mark A. Clarke and Sandra Silberstein conclude that teachers of second language students should have as a major goal "to give our students practice and encouragement in using the minimum number of syntactic/semantic clues to obtain the maximum amount of information when reading" (p. 50); from "Toward a Realization of Psycholinguistic Principles in the ESL Reading Class," in R. Mackay, B. Barkman, and R. R. Jordan, eds., *Reading in a Second Language: Hypotheses, Organization, and Practice* (Rowley, Mass.: Newbury, 1979), pp. 48–65.

[11]This premise is gradually finding support in second language research, e.g., "General exposure to the language in communicative situations is therefore relevant to performance requiring attention to either meaning or form" (390), Ellen Bialystok, "The Role of Conscious Strategies in Second Language Proficiency," *Canadian Modern Language Review,* 35, No. 3 (1979), 372–94; Herbert W. Seliger, in "On the Nature and Function of Language Rules in Language Teaching," *TESOL Quarterly,* 13, No. 3 (1979), 359–69, found "no relationship . . . for 'good' [linguistically complete] and 'bad' [incomplete or 'rule-of-thumb'] rules and quality of the learner's performance of the task" (p. 359), because the concept behind a rule dominated in memory.

[12]See Smith, *Psycholinguistics and Reading,* pp. 60–62; P. A. Kolers, "Reading Is Only Incidentally Visual" in K. S. Goodman and J. T. Fleming, eds., *Psycholinguistics and the Teaching of Reading* (Newark, Del.: International Reading Assoc., 1969); and Clarke and Silberstein, who assert that

> more information is contributed by the reader than by the print on the page. That is, readers understand what they read because they are able to take the stimulus beyond its graphic representation and assign it membership to an appropriate group of concepts already stored in their memories. (p. 48)

[13]For a more complete discussion of reading hypotheses, see Frank Smith, *Understanding Reading: A Psycholinguistic Analysis of Reading and Learning to Read* (New York: Holt, 1971), esp. p. 24; and Aaron S. Carton, "Inferencing: A Process in Using and Learning Language," in Paul Pimsleur and Terence Quinn, eds., *The Psychology of Second Language Learning: Papers from the Second International Congress of Applied Linguistics* (Cambridge: Cambridge Univ. Press, 1971), pp. 45–48.

[14]Kenneth S. Goodman, "Psycholinguistic Universals in the Reading Process," in Smith, *Psycholinguistics and Reading,* describes the efficient reader as follows:

> He accomplishes this [efficient reading] by *sampling,* relying on the redundancy of language, and his knowledge of linguistic constraints. He *predicts* structures, *tests* them against the semantic context which he builds up from the situation and the ongoing discourse, and then *confirms* or disconfirms as he processes further language. (p. 23)

Foreign language teachers, however, may have to realize that not all students read efficiently in their native language. James Coady, "A Psycholinguistic Model of the ESL Reader," in Mackay et al., notes that: "We have only recently come to realize that many students have very poor reading habits to transfer from their first language, and thus, in many cases, we must teach reading skills which should have been learned in first language instruction" (p. 12).

[15]The distinction between the propositional content of an utterance and its illocutionary force (the mode in which these propositional facts are presented, such as

questioning, demanding, entreating) is most usefully made by John L. Searle in "Propositions," in his book *Speech Acts: An Essay in the Philosophy of Language* (Cambridge: Cambridge Univ. Press, 1969), sec. 2.4.

[16]Smith, *Understanding Reading.*

[17]This chart of *Textarten* is drawn from Cates and Swaffar.

[18]For a discussion of the relation between textual features and readability, see Helen G. C. Chapman, "Criteria for the Selection of Short Prose Fiction to Be Used in Level II (Intermediate) Foreign Language Classes," Diss. Univ. of Texas 1975. In actual classroom practice, we have found that the following list of features is useful in characterizing the major genres indicated on the chart of *Textarten*. Students given the list and the *Textarten* can draw on this vocabulary during the classroom preview session to work out a particular genre's organizing and weighting features prior to the actual reading of an assignment:

1. +/− *figures* Are characters discussed or do they speak for themselves? Can students list them or cite characteristic behaviors?
2. +/− *dialogue* Do the people speak to one another? To themselves?
3. +/− *visual scene* Is a place or object depicted that the reader can visualize concretely?
4. +/− *action* Do the people or other groupings do anything, or does something happen to them?
5. +/− *fiction* Is this text completely invented by the author, or is the text about actual people and events?
6. +/−*chronology* Do events occur in any temporal order, and does the text reflect that chronology faithfully or vary it and if so, how?
7. +/− *specificity* Is the text about a specific topic or specific person, or is it about a general topic or a type of people? For example, is it about one family's struggle with inflation or about one juvenile delinquent, or is it about the economy or child rearing in general?

[19]In regard to the present study's restriction to adult learners, see Bialystok, "Conscious Strategies in Second Language Proficiency." Her study was unable to ascertain whether or not inferencing strategies would definitively influence language learning:

> In this case, no claim may be made about the role of inferencing—it neither discriminated among the criterion tasks nor facilitated general performance. . . . Both a better instrument for measuring inferencing and a task placing greater stress on general communicative meaning need to be developed. (p. 392)

Inferencing plays a large role in the present study's weighting tasks and requires adult knowledge of the world to facilitate learning with maximum efficiency. Bialystok's sample consisted of Canadian adolescents from fourteen to seventeen years old. The possibility exists that her research instrument for evaluating inferencing was not defective—but that the level of maturity of her subjects made distinctive results difficult to obtain for this strategy.

[20]Evelyn Hatch and Michael H. Long, "Discourse Analysis, What's That?" in Diane Larsen-Freeman, ed., *Discourse Analysis in Second Language Research* (Rowley, Mass.: Newbury, 1980), p. 18.

[21]Clarke and Silberstein, p. 49.

[22]For a detailed discussion of the advantages that unedited texts may have for foreign language learners see J. Honeyfield, "Simplification," *TESOL Quarterly,* 11, No. 4 (1977), 431–40.

²³For a discussion of the importance of a meaningful and authentic real-world context for classroom execises, see Widdowson, particularly pp. 79–82 and 88–91.

²⁴Additionally, the "wh" questions do not correspond to real-world discourse forms. In this sense, process assignments reduce the artificiality of classroom discourse. As Widdowson remarks:

> We are not, in normal circumstances, required to submit ourselves to interrogation after having read something, knowing at the same time that the person putting the questions already knows the answers. To cast comprehension exercises in the form of questions only tends to emphasize the artificiality of the enterprise and so to prevent the learner from adopting the kind of attitude which will encourage the development of the reading ability. (p. 96)

²⁵Colin Harrison and Terry Dolan, "Reading Comprehension: A Psychological Viewpoint," in Mackay et al., pp. 13–23, support the value of group confirmation of reading conclusions:

> What we do say is that no reader will learn from a text unless he actually engages with it, and that these activities [class discussions] seem to encourage this engagement or reflection in a way that individual silent reading may not. . . . The task in developing reading comprehension is to encourage a vital response rather than a mechanical or unchallenged one. Our belief is that in a fluent reader the critical and reflective response is internalized; what group reading activities offer is an externalization of the process of critical reading, which can be shared and enjoyed by those who take part, and which is potentially a valuable learning experience, since it offers the poorer reader models and strategies which he can use in his own private reading. (p. 23)

²⁶For over two decades, the criteria for grading readers have been the focus of a largely unresolved controversy. For an analysis of the current stage in this discussion, see Renate Schulz, "Literature and Readability: Bridging the Gap in Foreign Language Reading," *Modern Language Journal,* 65 (1981), 43–53.

Teaching Writing in
the Foreign Language Curriculum

Claire Gaudiani

Foreign language faculty have an outstanding contribution to make to the improvement of literacy. They should support their English faculty colleagues, who currently shoulder most of the burden. At all levels of FL instruction, elementary through advanced seminars, FL faculty can guide students through the process of learning to write well. For writing is indeed a process, not an event. Therefore well-designed writing assignments move through stages under the teacher's guidance. Good writing skills are not, at least in the Indo-European language groups, language specific. In simple terms, good writing focuses on the word, the sentence, and the paragraph. At the level of the word, writers consider issues like suitability, specificity, clarity, and nuance. Choice of words also involves selection among parts of speech. A preponderance of nouns or adjectives or verbs affects the final project. At the level of the sentence, writers weave words into meaningful syntactical arrangements. Simplicity, complexity, and variety are among the concerns at this level. Each word choice in a syntactical arrangement limits the options for the rest of the sentence. Finally, the level of the paragraph involves sorting, ordering, and organizing the information. Introductory or topic sentences followed by developmental sentences build toward the summary sentence and thus create an accessible, standard format for paragraphs. Therefore practice in writing in FL courses both supports growing communication competence in the FL and benefits the students' literacy in English.

NOTE: Since each workshop offered a seminar on writing, I include this adaptation of a chapter from my book *Teaching Composition in the Foreign Language Curriculum* (Washington, D.C.: Center for Applied Linguistics, 1981), which grew out of an article published in *French Review,* Dec. 1979. Workshop participants changed their style of teaching writing more than they did any other single curricular area covered during the grant period. My book deals more extensively with the suggestions made here and offers a sample syllabus, composition topics, model essays, an introductory packet, and practical ways to manage corrections.

The current and welcome concern for oral proficiency has induced many FL faculty to reduce the amount of writing they demand of students. I urge a reexamination of this now long-standing trend. Well-designed writing assignments throughout the FL curriculum help build oral proficiency. Most of us believe that writing practice in English increases students' capacity to use English. The same logic holds for the effect of writing practice in a second language, even though in the English class students have a grasp of eighty percent or more of the grammar and in a foreign language class that percentage is radically lower. I have found that constant practice in expressing original thoughts in a second language—in writing and rewriting, revising and editing—strengthens students' abilities to use the second language and to write English.

The following approach to teaching writing in the foreign language classroom aims to strengthen student literacy in English while building composition skills in the foreign language. The prototype composition course assumes a class of fifteen to eighteen fourth- or fifth-semester foreign language students, although some of them might actually be freshmen. Their major fields cover the spectrum available at a large university. While originally developed for the French section, the course structure adapts easily to composition classes in other languages. The various elements transfer as well to composition segments of combined composition and conversation courses. The most significant adaptation involves designing substantial writing and rewriting components to strengthen the language skills of elementary- and intermediate-level foreign language students. The approach could be further adapted for use in advanced language, literature, and culture courses. This essay presents the prototype course. Specific remarks about adaptation occur in the conclusion.

Overview

The composition course demands frequent (weekly) writing and provides in-class editing of student compositions. The class reads and discusses one another's essays, not only correcting any grammar errors but also noting elements of style and organizational strategy, using either English or the target language or a mélange of the two. The class offers suggestions to the writer. In peer groups, students practice making increasingly sophisticated and syntactically complex sentences. Students also practice writing well-developed paragraphs and structuring paragraphs into essays. The editing process gradually sensitizes students to nuances in choice of vocabulary and syntactical arrangements. Ultimately the course provides a grounding in the elements of prose style.

The objective of the text-editing approach, stated to students at the outset, is to help them learn to express themselves coherently in the target language and to become sensitive to the dynamics of good expository writing in general. Students should expect to develop the ability to express their thoughts effectively in correct and well-structured prose. The systematic weekly study of grammar and vocabulary indicates that these indispensable tools help students achieve the course goal. Learning to write is not, however, simply learning another set of grammar or spelling rules, nor is it creating translations of complex sentences.

Student commitment to regular writing assignments in a foreign language forms the core of the approach. Ideally, students write compositions each week, keep daily journals, and rewrite each piece until they achieve a level judged satisfactory by them and by the teacher. From midterm on, students alternate between writing compositions one week and reading a short selection from a prose masterpiece in the foreign language the other week. After studying this text, they write two-page papers in English analyzing the author's prose style and then attempt to imitate that style in foreign language compositions of their own. In my experience, these one-page pastiches in a foreign language, coupled with the prose style analyses in English, advance students' understanding of what goes into good writing.

Three notions about learning and writing underlie the text-editing approach to teaching FL composition:

1. Teachers should try to write assignments *with* students whenever possible. It is easy to forget how hard writing is. One way for teachers to remain close to this task is to write with their students, even if only a few times each semester.

2. Students must understand and accept the course goals. Each student receives a packet of materials including course goals, syllabus, a sample grammar midterm exam, and some midterm and final course evaluations to help establish a serious, mutually supportive atmosphere. Writing is a lonely activity. Students will redouble their efforts during their hours of solitary writing if they feel a spirit of collaboration and know they can expect specific reactions to their work from their colleagues and their teacher. The ambiance in the classroom is therefore a vital element in the success of the method.

3. While adapting certain elements from English composition teaching methods, FL teachers must remain aware of the large differences between English and FL composition skill building.

As foreign language teachers transform English composition methods to the needs of their students, questions arise about using the foreign language in writing class. The major goal of composition instruction is to strengthen students' writing skills. I have found it practical to use the foreign language as a secondary skill in class discussions and editing sessions. I realize foreign language teachers may differ with me on this sensitive issue. The possibility of using the foreign language to teach writing would be affected by the size of the class as well as by students' proficiency levels. Frankly, the capacity of the teacher to conduct the class easily in the foreign language also counts.

The basic composition course, designed for a three-session week, works well if students receive a new composition subject at the first session of the new week. At this session, five or six students receive ditto masters onto which they type or write their final drafts. Others copy their compositions onto regular paper. Students hand in final drafts at the second session of the week and should follow a set form when putting their names, the due date, the composition title, and the draft number on each page. They keep pocket folders for their writings. First and second drafts as well as predrafts should be kept clipped together. Each new draft to be evaluated is accompanied by previous work on the topic.

The first compositions range from 50 to 100 words. The second and third pieces should approach 150 words. Clearly these limits will vary depending on what each teacher deems appropriate. I make no suggestions to my classes about paragraphing or sentence design for the first assignment. Specific suggestions about the organizational schema occur during the text-editing sessions in the early weeks of class. The first three topics assigned elicit autobiographical information in a readable expository style.

By the third or fourth week, I find it best to give students the opportunity to experiment with different ways to approach the writing task. Some make detailed outlines. Others may prefer to make a "shopping list" of main ideas or key words. For several weeks students consider, select, and experiment with predraft schemas that may facilitate the actual writing process. For some, a rigid outline may stultify thought and therefore the flow of ideas and language in their compositions. For others, the outline is a "Guide Michelin" that helps them find the best in themselves and avoid getting lost. Each writer must eventually discover a personal strategy to write effectively. By the fourth or fifth week, I request that the compositions be structured into at least three or four paragraphs and that students hand in the preliminary material that supported the writing of the compositions along with their first drafts. If they wish to continue appending this material to later work, I will review it. I do not, however, insist after this first experience.

The fifth essay, two or three times the length of the first, is usually organized into three, four, or more paragraphs. The sixth week combines the prose style analysis in English and the pastiche in the foreign language. In the seventh week the class returns a regular composition assignment. In the eighth, tenth, and twelfth weeks students do English prose style analyses and foreign language pastiches. In the ninth, eleventh, and thirteenth they are assigned regular writing topics. The length of the essays in the second half of the course usually grows to a page or two, but rarely beyond.

Class Participation: Teamwork

All students must participate in the class editing sessions and the grammar review, which takes place during the third session of each week. Since work goes on in small peer groups and study pairs as well as in class discussions, all students have opportunities to become active contributors. Besides banishing (or at least reducing) boredom, active participation by all class members reinforces the basic philosophy of the course. The class works as a team. We all have a stake in one another's progress. We have embarked on the common project of improving writing. Editing texts together is a mutually supportive and instructive activity. All benefit. All contribute. Reinforcing mastery of grammar has the same qualities about it. No team member has the right to benefit without contributing. I find that the atmosphere during text editing helps mitigate some of the isolation of the writer's task and gives students a better sense of commitment to the learning experience, to their classmates, and to the teacher.

A spirit of teamwork grows from the high degree of class participation and peer group work. This spirit grows even stronger if the teacher reduces competition among class members for grades. Students must not feel that they are competing with one another. They progress at their own rate. Grading standards do not ever provide for a curve. On any given assignment, half the class could receive A's or F's. In the absence of intrastudent competition, criticism becomes a way of helping the student writer to produce better rewrites.

Composition Topics

I found it helpful to focus the first three weeks of topics on autobiographical content. Since the writer in the foreign language composition class will embark on all the standard (and very taxing) tasks of English composition without the native command of grammar, topics should not challenge students to draw on unfamiliar content areas. I organize composition topics to facilitate student expressiveness and at the same time elicit certain grammatical constructions. For instance, the first topic might ask students to describe their present lives. A second would ask for a description of their lives at age eight, including one striking incident from that period. A third might concern the students' plans for five years hence, including some of their hopes and fears about the future. A command of the "facts" involved frees students to concentrate on expression and organization of the content. At the same time, the second topic necessitates comprehension of the interplay between imperfect and present perfect tenses. The third encourages use of the future and the subjunctive. All the while, of course, standard forms of pronouns, prepositions, relative pronouns, idiomatic expressions, and the like remain important.

I do not explain my objectives in choosing topics until the end of the first three weeks. In the early phase of writing, I want students to discover how choice of subject determines the need for certain grammatical constructions. They have usually experienced their teachers' insistence on grammar rules; I want to reverse the process and have them discover the need for rules themselves. After this "breaking-in" period, my objective in selecting topics changes. No longer keyed to the need for specific grammatical competencies, choice of topic now centers on variations in style and tone of compositions. Students in the foreign language class usually demonstrate less awareness of style and tone than of grammar. I explain these later objectives so that students can begin to associate foreign language composition writing with improved writing skills in general.

By the fourth week, students have written three different compositions, one each week. They have written first drafts and finished drafts, and they have rewritten the drafts at least once. They are ready to move away from autobiography, but I prefer to use "bridge" topics for two weeks before moving away from the self-centered subjects. Any subject that elicits the writer's opinion about some familiar issue or item serves. I avoid polemical subjects this early in the semester, especially since argumentation poses stylistic challenges for which students should first be prepared through a pastiche exercise. Discussions of social, environmental, or cultural problems often contain complexities that few students can tackle skillfully at this level. I have found that the best transitional topics are brief descriptions and personal aesthetic evaluations of a prose piece or poem, a picture or a slide, or a piece of sculpture.

The students have worked hard, and by the fifth week their writing skills have increased significantly. They responded very positively to my fifth composition assignment, which was to return to their first compositions, expand the theme, and make the essays more sophisticated by using their newly acquired skills. Text editing in class, rewriting, weekly grammar lessons, and sentence-embedding exercises have greatly improved students' writing competencies in the foreign language. When they return to their entry-level composition and rework it, they experience ease and confidence. The psychological boost of this assignment often reinforces students' efforts to continue working and improving.

By the sixth week the topic can take students directly to a description and analysis of a complex issue. Depending on the age, interests, and proficiency level of students, the topic may concern a school or campus situation, a regional or national issue, or perhaps even an ethical controversy. The objective is to have students lay out and analyze the facets of an issue without taking sides. Students move from week four and its call for concrete description and personal assessment to week six, where the topic is more abstract and their choice of words and organizational strategies should indicate balance and fairness. Again, with each assignment in weeks four, five, and six, I explain briefly my rationale for the selection of the topic.

In-Class Text-Editing Process

Each week the bulk of class time centers on reading, reviewing, and editing mimeographed copies of student compositions. Students each receive a packet of five or six triple-spaced, typed, and duplicated compositions, which they correct by hand as the editing process moves forward.

Instead of relying on contrived materials, this approach centers the learning experience on the students' writings. The texts are meaningful because the students create them, not because textbook writers claim that they are. I have found that students respond positively to learning from their own efforts.

Students benefit from class editing in five ways: (1) their efforts to correct and enrich texts enhance their attention in class; (2) they broaden vocabulary and syntactic experience through note taking and discussion of options; (3) their handwritten notes and packets of corrected compositions provide an additional reference tool for their writing assignments; (4) they become more aware of the complex dynamics of good writing; and (5) they learn where to suspect errors in their own writing.

Finally, class editing creates a comfortable context for students' writing. Writing is communicating. If the communication is intended for classmates, not strangers, there is no need to fictionalize the audience. This group has some common ties but is not composed of intimate friends. Class members demand more development and specificity in the written work than do parents or close friends, who receive more personal, elliptical communications. As editors, students learn to use tact, seek clarity, and anticipate well-organized communications while remaining both independent and sympathetic. The good will and mutual respect of the class unit remain signal factors in the success of the class editing process.

The editing process begins with the student-author reading aloud the composition in the ditto packet. The process then continues through five steps.

1. *Comprehension of meaning* The class seeks an explanation for any new or unfamiliar vocabulary and responds to confusion sometimes caused by either incorrect or complex syntax.

2. *Correction of grammar* Once everyone understands the composition, the teacher reads each sentence individually, requesting that the author or a classmate provide any needed grammatical corrections.

3. *Analysis of prose style* When the composition is free of grammatical errors, the instructor asks that the class reread the piece silently and then comment on the style. Initially, students notice sentence length and repetition of the same vocabulary and syntax. The teacher asks students to suggest solutions to inadequacies of the unsophisticated style. Gradually, over the course of the semester, the instructor teaches students to consider more elements of prose style.

4. *Analysis of organization* Students are asked to reflect on the use of paragraphing and of topic and summary sentences.

5. *Overview and synthesis* Finally, the class offers general comments on the composition as a written communication.

Teachers will need to develop confidence in guiding the class editing process. It is useful to list the five categories above on an index card for reference. After the author has finished reading his or her work, the teacher can commend a particular strength in the composition. Then the instructor proceeds, by asking questions, to elicit student responses under each of the headings.

Teachers should begin with some encouraging remarks to establish a supportive atmosphere that builds self-confidence for all participants. Being supportive does not mean the teacher cannot be demanding. Students will learn early in the course what level of achievement is expected of them. Teachers can praise honestly and urge improvement firmly. Students tend to follow the instructor's lead in their own comments. They begin by responding positively to some aspect of the text. Once protocols like politeness and sensitivity to individual differences have been established, students practice looking for and commenting on the strength of a work before searching for errors.

Mutual confidence builds gradually. Mutual respect and a sense of humor can greatly enhance the students' experience in the classroom. I continue to stress the importance of classroom atmosphere, because I believe it can fulfill three important functions. (1) If we agree that writing is a lonely task, the class forms a supportive but critical "family" to share the difficulties and the victories surrounding this process. (2) The ambiance created helps ease students' natural fears of making mistakes, receiving criticism, and perhaps looking foolish. Mistakes provide learning opportunities for everyone—offering new insights, reviewing previously learned information, verifying confusing rules. Errors no longer isolate or embarrass the student but become a natural part of the learning process. (3) The class creates an appropriate audience for student writing. This kind of experience with the discipline involved in developing composition skills is likely to teach students about the process of writing in any language.

Early in the semester, text editing takes a long time. I have preferred to proceed slowly and really teach students how to edit. Typically, while individual writing improves and students begin to understand the scope of their writing task (style, organization, and content as well as grammar), the class is also becoming more proficient at editing. These three kinds of improvement naturally affect the pace at which the class can proceed later on in the semester.

Teachers can prepare for the slower pace by asking only three or four students to put their work on ditto masters each week for the first two or three weeks. Then, as the pace of class editing picks up in the third or fourth week, four or five compositions can be included in the editing packet. The main reason for doing text editing is to teach students how to organize thought into good writing. Doing this job well is more important than completing the packet of work for the day or week. Class editing is an inefficient way to correct compositions. It is an effective way to nurture good writing skills.

Evaluating Compositions

Composition teachers often spend a crushing number of hours correcting students' work—a rewriting task that students would profit from by doing themselves. Alas, despite teachers' fine work, students often look over corrections quickly and file the composition, or, if they come to a conference, they may listen (*a*. approvingly, *b*. admiringly, or *c*. patiently) while teachers review the corrected papers. If it is true that one learns to write by writing and that writing is an isolated task, students should revise alone. Consequently, I advocate the following approach to evaluating student writing:

1. The teacher should circle all errors and place a squiggly line under awkward or inappropriate usage or perhaps simply place a check mark on the line with an error.

2. The teacher should make general remarks about the style: the adequacy of the topic, development and summary sentences, the use of logical connectives, the level of sophistication, repetitiveness in vocabulary or syntax, and so forth.

3. The teacher should comment on the content. For example, do the facts support the conclusions? Can the reader follow the development easily?

4. The teacher should give separate grades for grammar and vocabulary use, stylistic technique, organization of material, and content.

The four grades focus students' attention on the important aspects of composition. Each grade should have equal weight. I give 5 for the best work and 1 for the least adequate work in each category. The total of the categories divided by four yields a number, which I convert to a letter grade: 5 = A, 4 = B, 3 = C, 2 = D, 1 = F.

In summary, students find on their compositions three kinds of evaluative markings. Those on the text indicate location and types of problems (or triumphs). The four-part grid offers a specific assessment of the composition. Finally, the teacher's personal comments about the text help the students in a more detailed way. I always make an effort to compliment the strengths of compositions, even when grades are poor. Students must feel some hope, and I think it is better to grade honestly and firmly, and comment kindly, than to inflate grades in an effort to soothe egos.

Rewriting Compositions

Students may rewrite an infinite number of times. The first rewrite must be handed in within two weeks of the day the composition was due, others in a maximum of one-week intervals. This prevents students from storing four or five compositions and rewriting all of them during one weekend. Writing skills develop as they should, in progressive stages, when essays are rewritten one at a time. In addition, composition topics interlock and focus on certain objectives that should be mastered before proceeding to subsequent stages.

Rewriting all assignments is an important facet of learning to write well. I encourage rewriting by canceling the first grade and giving the second grade and canceling the second and giving the third. Students need to experience writing as a process of recommitting themselves to clear thinking and improved communication.

In rewriting, the students themselves must develop the correct syntax after errors are pointed out. They work their own transformations of grammar and learn to resolve difficulties using the reference tools at their command. Testing procedures safeguard against the inflation of grades on rewrites for the purpose of giving students encouragement.

I correct rewrites the same way I do originals. Sometimes, especially in the beginning, no substantial improvement occurs in the writing, and so none occurs in the grades. Students must never feel that any halfhearted second draft will receive a better grade. To merit a reading, the rewrite must be attached to the original copy of the composition. I compare the two drafts, isolate difficulties unresolved in the second effort, and recommend dictionary or grammar book work to remedy problems. All future rewrites arrive marked as such—#3, #4, and so on—and stapled on top of earlier versions.

Rewriting compositions gives students confidence in their ability to solve problems in their writing. It also gives them experience in using dictionaries and grammar books as reference tools. In very mundane terms, they practice again and again the art of finding meaning.

Prose-Style Analysis and Pastiche

Casually, from the first text-editing session, I encourage students to begin noticing style and making lists of elements of style in their notebooks.

Students seem to respond better if they develop the list through individual or group observation than they do if they receive a list from the teacher. The objective of studying style is to give students additional tools to vary and strengthen their writing techniques. The more they notice independently, the more they will have absorbed for their future use.

By midsemester students have mastered enough grammar to express themselves correctly, if inelegantly, in the foreign language. As a result, I can begin to intensify the focus on style through a variety of exercises, beginning with two new types of writing assignments. Students read short passages in the foreign language and prepare written analyses of the text's characteristic lexical, syntactic, and organizational patterns. Some classes are advanced enough to write in the target language; otherwise, students write these analyses in English. Students then choose a topic and treat it in the style of the assigned author. These models, or pastiches, are judged (in part, at least) on their stylistic resemblance to the original reading assignment. Early efforts at both assignments usually show how unaccustomed students are to considerations of style.

Specifically, during the second session of week five, the class reads the piece that it will use for the pastiche exercise. Students who have spent five weeks editing one another's prose tend to respond enthusiastically to the task of reading a passage free from grammatical problems. This class period focuses naturally on style and organization. I suggest that students refer to the list of stylistic elements they have been developing in their notebooks.

The writing assignment for week six involves reading a selection and writing an analysis in English or the foreign language and a pastiche in the foreign language. The analysis forms the basis of the student's foreign language composition.

HELPING STUDENTS WRITE PROSE-STYLE ANALYSES

In composition class, the study of excellent texts offers several advantages. Not only do students gain exposure to fine writing and all its myriad elements, but they also avoid the mechanistic view of writing that may result from studying isolated constituents of composition.

I point out to students that just as each person has a unique handwriting, each writer has a unique style—a personal way of writing that relates to his or her identity. At the same time, however, style is not a mold that predetermines the final product. It is not withheld from some and bestowed generously on others. The act of writing is an act of exploration, a process with many stages, and style develops naturally from this process.

Students become aware of style by reading a variety of works. I have used Voltaire and Sartre to illustrate cognitive or expository language, Flaubert and Zola for fictional prose styles. Including some excerpts from popular magazines and current newspapers has much to recommend it. Popular writings too have definable styles.

We begin our discussions of styles with a brief definition of purpose. What does the author wish to accomplish? What genre has been selected? What constraints does this choice impose on vocabulary and organizational structure? What freedoms does it permit?

We then look at the overall organization of the text. What information is presented first, last, and so forth? Is the passage built inductively (moving from details to generalities) or deductively (moving from concept to specific illustrations)? What is the position of the narrator or narrative voice with respect to the subject matter? How does the author handle transitions from idea to idea, from one perspective to another?

These questions lead us to some global considerations of presentation strategies. Is the passage primarily descriptive or analytical? Does the author rely on dialogue to convey information or to define characters? Are examples used to illustrate ideas or to introduce them? Most students perceive that their answers fall into three general categories: syntax, vocabulary, and overall impressions.

ANALYSIS OF SENTENCE STRUCTURE

I have found that the sentence is the unit of writing that foreign language students most readily fasten onto as the object of initial analysis. They describe without difficulty and in some detail the characteristics of an author's sentences.

In general, the key characteristics of sentences to be noted are as follows:

length

presence, absence, and type of subordination

strategies for logical connectives, whether simple accumulation or complex causality

word order, the presence or absence of inversions

ANALYSIS OF VOCABULARY AND VERB TENSES

Once students can identify these various syntactic elements successfully, I encourage them to consider the vocabulary choices of the author. The presence or absence in each text of adjectives and adverbs, the use of concrete or abstract, or general or specific nouns are basic characteristics that are easily discerned. So, too, are the choices of verb tenses and the presence or absence of personal pronouns, proper nouns, and the like. Even beginning analysts of prose style can readily pick out the lexical domain from which certain vocabulary choices are made.

Another important element of stylistic analysis is the recognition of figurative language. Many who regularly talk of "saving" or "spending" time fail to realize that these constructions prefigure the metaphor "time is money," an equivalency largely absent in most Romance languages. Yet once made aware of the pervasiveness of this linguistic phenomenon, my students have generally been able to perceive both implicit and explicit metaphorical constructions and to speculate on the ends to which such figures of speech are used by various authors.

The major questions, then, in dealing with the analysis of individual words and vocabulary choices are:

Is the vocabulary general or specific?

Is it concrete or abstract?

Is it drawn from a particular field, such as a technology or psychology?

How are verbs and pronouns treated?

Is there a preponderance of adjectives or adverbs?

Is the language literal or figurative?

ANALYSIS OF PATTERNS

Having established the syntactic and lexical items as key elements in the analytic process, the class is encouraged to consider the unique combination of these elements offered by the individual text. We begin by expanding individual observations, such as those about verb tenses, to find the overall pattern verb tense usage. Similar expansions of vocabulary observations to include the entire text allow conclusions on the overall approach of the author. Is the writing casual? formal? emotionally charged? dispassionate? ironic?

We then explore the notion of sentimentality in writing, as a strategy writers use to solve certain problems, such as developing sympathy for the protagonist, creating different time periods in the protagonist's life, or suggesting satire.

The discussions of tone, point of view, and so forth flow naturally from careful readings of brief passages, once the basic elements of vocabulary and syntax have been analyzed. These observations, in turn, prepare the way for writing the pastiches, the success of which depends greatly on the ability of students to grasp these global considerations of style.

HELPING STUDENTS WRITE PASTICHES

Although writing pastiches, like writing prose-style analyses, hardly qualifies as an innovative approach to teaching composition, it offers foreign language students three signal advantages. It puts students in close contact with exemplary prose in the foreign language and may improve both their writing and their reading abilities. It heightens their awareness of certain stylistic devices by having them imitate these techniques. It sets them at a distance from their own language, permitting them to compare related construction in both languages.

Each time I have taught the course, students have remarked that their reading has been permanently affected. They say that they take less for granted in written works. In the close readings they do to prepare pastiches, they come to see that almost any passage of good writing would yield an interesting analysis of the use of language. Reading well and writing well can hardly be separated, and this composition course brings them together. Pastiche writing demands more than recognition of the stylistic elements. Students must relate the elements to one another and to the effect they have on the subject and on the reader. Students go beyond a catalog of devices and become sensitive to larger issues. They must abstract the principles and exemplify them in their writing.

Writing pastiches offers other advantages to students of composition. Whereas up to week six, students have received a composition topic and written in their own best style, the pastiche assignments reverse the process. The class has a given style under consideration for the week. The students choose whatever topic seems to them appropriate. Therefore, beyond paying attention to reading and to active use of specific syntactic arrangements, students perceive the relation of the subject of an essay to its style (content and form). I prefer to let students discover these issues as they work on their first pastiches. Students regularly show gratifying imagination and sensitivity in their selection of topics relating to the author's style and point of view.

In helping students to produce good pastiches, as in other segments of this course, the teacher should guide, let students discover, and then affirm or adjust their conclusions. This is not a course in formal rhetoric. By watching how professional writers use language and then experimenting with these same tools in pastiches, apprentices test their abilities and make progress as well—much to their teacher's satisfaction. The second satisfaction for teachers comes when some of the specific stylistic elements discovered and manipulated in the prose-style analysis or pastiche produced one week appear "naturally" in the student's regular composition the following week.

Pastiches are handed in with prose-style analyses and are also treated as regular compositions for text editing and grading. Marking students on grammar, style, organization, and content has a slightly new meaning on these assignments. Style and organization become very important in assessing a pastiche. A good composition that bears little resemblance to the master text cannot receive as high a grade as one that does capture something of the style of its model, even though the student has used decent grammar. Somehow, by removing grammar errors from center stage, students begin to see other factors as equally important.

CLASS EDITING OF PROSE-STYLE ANALYSES AND PASTICHES

Three prose-style analyses of masterworks and three pastiches should be duplicated and stapled into packets. All students should keep copies of their own prose style analyses to compare and contrast them with the perceptions offered by other students. The students whose papers have been duplicated read their analyses, and the class carries on with its normal editing work, correcting and analyzing them as compositions. I stress to students the importance of writing excellent expository prose in the style analyses whether the class writes in the foreign language or in English. The style of the analysis is as important as the content. The class members proceed, then, to consider the student's perceptions of the elements of style found in the master text. The students can compare these judgments with their own and note any elements they may have missed.

After two or three prose-style-analysis readings and discussions at the first session of the week, the class goes on to read the pastiches at the second session. By the time students have discussed the style thoroughly they show particular sensitivity to efforts to imitate the model in pastiches. They can pick up the elements in the pastiche that resemble those in the master text. Because they have all worked (and struggled) with the same assignment, they are familiar enough with the original text to appreciate their colleagues' attempts to use these elements in their writing.

Grammar Study

Having worked on editing compositions during the first two sessions of the week, the class spends the third session reviewing grammar. At home students prepare one full lesson from a textbook covering intermediate grammar in twelve to fourteen weeks.

Students in foreign language classes know how dearly their teachers want them to learn grammar. In the composition class a subtle change in the teacher's attitude toward grammar can, in my experience, enhance students' desire to learn it. The task of writing demands a decent grasp of basic grammar. To write well necessitates continual improvements in grammar skills. In the foreign language composition course, I insist on being a resource to students embarked on the task of learning to write, and I teach grammar only as the students express a need for it. This attitude works in the composition course but is less appropriate in an elementary or intermediate language class. Students are less aware of what they need in order to use the language well. As students begin to write a great deal, they often sense gaps in their knowledge of grammar. They receive graded compositions marked only with indications of problems and not neatly corrected in full by their teacher. With the grammar book, they must now try to improve and correct their compositions. It has typically taken two or three weeks for my students to realize that they could use our Friday grammar time wisely by getting help from me on the grammar chapter under consideration for that week.

Vocabulary Study

Each grammar chapter contains a vocabulary list. Students who wish to write well need to increase the number of words at their disposal. I ask students to master the vocabulary list and, once a month or so, I give a ten-minute quiz on the words covered since the last vocabulary quiz. Students should keep a section of their notebooks just for vocabulary.

Sophistication of Syntax and Sentence Embedding

While students work on improving grammar skills, the time spent on sentence-embedding exercises strengthens the constructions they use in their first few compositions. Afterwards, these exercises continue to be useful in showing students how to produce more sophisticated syntax. Students work together in groups of two and three to modify and lengthen and finally combine short structural units. They manipulate these units and explore the ways in which English and the foreign language achieve the same meaning through varied syntactic and lexical arrangements. All sentences are read and corrected before class time ends. This provides instant reinforcement of students' efforts. In learning how to create sophisticated syntax, students must not come to feel that longer, more complicated sentences are preferable to shorter, simpler ones. Their pastiche work will eventually substantiate this fact.

During grammar days, students may be asked to list on the blackboard all the ways to achieve sentence combination in English. Often it is best for the class to develop a list of linking words, especially if the students have had poor training in English grammar. Their list will include, for instance:

Conjunctions: *and, but*
Adverbs: *where, when*
Relative pronouns: *that, which, who, whom*

Typically, I ask that students use one of the duplicated compositions for week one or two as a starting point for sentence combining. The class breaks into small groups and attempts to reorganize some of the simple short sentences of the composition to create more sophisticated pieces of prose. I save particularly good samples of previous classes' compositions and have students rework these as well. The advantage of this approach to sentence combining is that students are always manipulating the grammar in the context of a whole piece of writing. They are less likely to make the mistake of simply telescoping a set of sentences.

Student teams can either read their reorganized compositions aloud or, when time permits, write them on the board. In the beginning, the teams show surprise at the various correct ways a composition's problems can be solved. The teacher can often explain briefly why some combinations are incorrect or infelicitous. Discussing the sentence combining in English will permit the teacher to compare and contrast elements of subordination in English syntax.

Grammar study forms a significant part of the composition course. One day a week is devoted to "old-fashioned" review of rules, practice on written exercises, and work on sentence combining and transforming. In addition, each text-editing class involves adjustments, manipulation, and correction of grammar used in the compositions. When confusion arises about a correction, a swift grammar explanation can be made orally or on the board. The midterm and final grammar exams attest to the signal importance of mastering grammar. Nonetheless, this course focuses on the use of grammar in the context of written communication.

Journals

In addition to writing weekly compositions and studying grammar, students keep a journal. They make one entry for each class day, writing simple, short paragraphs on any subjects they choose. Typically, as they feel more relaxed with the language, students lengthen their entries. Journal keeping helps students overcome the fear of committing pen to paper. It also helps them grow confident about describing daily life, emotions, and events in their second language.

Students should buy small notebooks with sixty or fewer pages and not larger than 8″ × 6″. These notebooks can be easily kept in pocket folders and brought to class each day. They are also easy for the teacher to collect and handle. Students can write only on the right-hand page, leaving the left side for rewrites, should they be necessary. I have found this system better than having the rewrites done elsewhere. Students create facing texts of the same entry, and they and the teacher can correct entries easily.

Evaluation of journals can be organized in a number of ways. In classes of fifteen to eighteen students, journals can be collected two at a time each class day on a rotation basis. I circle errors and return the *cahiers* for rewrites of any pages that receive a minus or a check. Only plus grades do not require rewrites. In larger classes, where correcting journals poses an impossible burden on faculty, teachers can simply read and then offer a general evaluation of eight or ten entries at one time. Teachers can also reduce the quantity of corrections by asking students to write summaries of their journal pages after every two or three weeks of journal keeping. The teacher then reviews the individual entries cursorily and checks the summaries more thoroughly. Of course, the teacher still signals simple errors instead of actually reworking sentences with mistakes.

I always write a short set of comments at the end of my corrections covering a given section. Having circled errors just as on compositions, I take a moment to give students a general assessment of their growing fluency. I try to mention two or three developing strengths while also, of course, remarking on the areas that need continued effort. Personal communication with students has particular importance in this course because of the quantity of work expected. Students often write notes to me in their journals in English or in their second language. Some notes include questions about syntax that seem to cause them repeated difficulty. Others are simply personal messages or the students' reactions to class or to their progress in writing. These unassigned missives are, of course, not corrected.

Testing and Grading

Testing in this composition course involves two hour-long in-class themes and a one-hour test. The final exam consists of a one-hour in-class theme and a one-hour grammar transformation and translation test. These five evaluations verify progress toward the course goal, and the five grades make up forty-five percent of the final grade. Compositions count forty-five percent, and journals and class participation five percent each. No rewrites are permitted on tests.

IN-CLASS THEMES

At the end of week five, students come to class with a dictionary only. The teacher gives a topic assignment, and students write a three- or four-paragraph, 100–150-word essay in the foreign language. This first performance should count five percent of the final grade, while the one done at the end of week ten should count ten percent. The in-class theme section of the final exam should count ten percent of the final grade. I use the same method for marking these tests as I do for the regular compositions; however, there are no rewrites for credit. This testing experience lets students see how they are progressing toward one of the course goals: being able to write a short piece of readable prose in a reasonable amount of time with the aid of a dictionary.

GRAMMAR TESTS

Learning grammar is hard work. The discipline of memorization rarely fills learners with joy. Grammar must be learned, however, and while this course gives students numerous ways to study, practice, verify, and reinforce their learning, they must show their level of mastery through two "old-fashioned" grammar tests.

Many forms of testing will meet this need for verification. I prefer translations or fill-ins in paragraph contexts for several reasons. Students have been manipulating language from English to the foreign language in the text-editing class. Their grammar classes have elicited the same kind of crossing from one language to the other as they compare and contrast ways to express thoughts using similar syntactical forms in each language. Finally students have become accustomed to using language in context; thus I object to individual sentences, each cut off from the others and unrelated to anything else on the test. Testing of grammar should correspond to the expectations and experience of students. Both the midterm and the final grammar tests should count ten percent each toward the final grade.

GRADING

Grading should reflect the philosophy and goals of the course. The compositions help build writing skills, and the three in-class themes verify the development of these skills. The major course goal is met most distinctly in these two activities; consequently, together with the daily journal, they account for seventy-five percent of the class grade. The acquisition of grammar skills supports the primary course goal and, through test performances and students' willingness to participate in class, results in twenty-five percent of the final grade. In all, testing counts forty-five percent, balancing the forty-five percent given for composition writing. Of course, many variations are possible.

Grading in a composition course is, as all agree, very difficult and to a large extent subjective; however, it offers important guidance to students. I find they usually have confidence in the teacher's judgment but appreciate a clear statement of the mechanics of how evaluative decisions will be made.

STUDENT PERSONAL ASSESSMENT STATEMENTS AND EVALUATIONS

While it has been common practice in recent years to encourage student evaluations of courses and instructors at the end of the semester, I have found it advantageous to use personal assessment statements at the beginning of each course. Assessment statements inform the instructor about each student's orientation to the course. They also increase students' awareness of the learning process and help the instructor integrate each student into the class and establish an ongoing process of evaluation.

Writing assessment statements benefits students by directing their attention early in the semester to basic questions relating the course to their personal situations. In my experience, many students have not thoroughly explored these questions for themselves in advance and consequently suffer certain frustrations and disappointments as the course proceeds. Writing a personal assessment statement encourages students to consider different aspects of their commitment to a given learning experience. (See p. 53 of my book *Teaching Writing in the Foreign Language Curriculum* for a list of questions.)

Assessment statements give teachers a basis for a continuing evaluation of students' work. I keep the assessment statements in individual folders, in which I return each student's test after it has been marked. Using the information in their assessment statements, students then evaluate their progress since the last test. I encourage students to evaluate the course and my teaching after each test. This information helps me improve my techniques during the semester and get immediate feedback on my methods instead of waiting for final course evaluations.

Midterm as well as final evaluations of the course by students and teachers support its collaborative, teamwork-oriented philosophy. I often use the same open-ended evaluation form both after week seven and at week fifteen. Writing well is, as I have repeated, a lonely and difficult task. By letting students evaluate the structures that support this task, teachers can improve the structures where possible, explain (and commiserate) where changes are unfeasible, and permit a practical release of pressure resulting from a challenging course.

Many elements of the prototype composition course described above are already part of the FL curriculum. Few approaches to teaching a discipline are wholly new. Most FL programs would, nonetheless, benefit from increasing the writing component of all their courses. Teachers need not fear that this change must mean terrible increases in the time needed to correct compositions. Nurturing writing skills relieves teachers of the burden of rewriting for students. For instance, students can read each other's first drafts and edit them as part of their weekly work. Teachers will then receive much better second drafts that take less time to correct. In addition, many useful tactics can help teachers control the volume of corrections. (See pp. 50–51 in *Teaching Writing in the Foreign Language Curriculum.*)

By the end of the first year of college language at the latest, students should, I believe, be capable of summarizing their readings of specially prepared passages. I suggest assigning this task once every two weeks to the whole class and using the text-editing approach to review and comment on student summaries.

Intermediate levels of grammar courses can often use adaptations of the first four or five assignments listed in the model composition course. Naturally, if students have had writing in their elementary classes, they will be even more ready for these tasks. Text editing of the short essays students write, even just once a month, can offer a welcome and productive break in the grammar course routine. Sophisticated versions of the writing suggestions for the elementary level can direct students' attention to elements of good writing like varied syntax and the avoidance of needlessly repetitious vocabulary.

Upper-division courses should call for a minimum of one or two typed pages of expository writing every two weeks. These essays could be used for literature class discussions. Topics could be on subjects suitable for formal or informal class debates, and the essays could be read and used as position papers. This approach is particularly useful in culture, civilization, and conversation courses. Ultimately, students in the class might form an editorial group and read, edit, and select from among their final drafts the best of their works for a writer's journal.

Committing FL students to more writing assignments builds fluency and literacy in English and the target language. It convinces students that they can express the same thoughts in a variety of ways in their new language and develops critical thinking skills. It helps transform a classroom into a learning community and ultimately creates vital connections between FL faculty and colleagues in English departments.

The Fifth Language Skill:
Understanding the Culture

Howard Lee Nostrand

Language training can contribute both to personal development and to a more compassionate world society. Teachers must meet the challenge to make that contribution in the most significant and the most exciting way.

By focusing on the international and cross-cultural dimension, language study can strengthen a characteristically flat side of American education. Today more than ever, in trade and diplomacy, we must listen, negotiate, persuade—and that means meeting other persons in their own language, literally as well as figuratively. We consequently need knowledge not only of the words they use but also of the values and beliefs that shape their lives.

Quite apart from effective communication across cultures, moreover, just to live our own culture at its best means being open to other cultures and being aware of the relativity of our way of life. Here again, a second language and culture have a unique function. For the understanding of any phenomenon consists of *experience of* it and *knowledge about* it. The way to experience how other cultures can differ from ours is through the language of at least a second culture; and the knowledge to put with the experience is knowledge of the underlying culture patterns. Thus the cultural element in language study is not only essential for successful communication; it is also our subject's most broadening, most humanizing influence on the inner life of the learner.

The American Council on the Teaching of Foreign Languages (ACTFL) defines language competence not just as oral comprehension, speaking, reading, and writing; it includes a fifth skill, sociocultural competence. These five skills are the focus of the Stepladder project, a long-needed effort of ACTFL and other American language associations to achieve nationwide consensus on a core of performance objectives for the successive stages of language learning. (See pp. 184–94.) Progress since World War II—advances in research, cooperation between the Educational Testing Service and the British Council, the elaboration of standards by govern-

172

ment agencies, and the like—has made the project possible. (See Judy Liskin-Gasparro's article, p. 215.)

The core objectives will leave ample room for different emphases yet will achieve advantages such as are obtained in other countries by a ministry of education: namely a manageable succession of challenges to the learner, classes in which the teacher can count on basic elements of preparation in common, a subject-matter standard for teacher preparation, and a way for the profession to resist "misassignment" of teachers to a language they have not learned. For all these purposes, so unevenly attained in our country at present, the sociocultural element is vital, and it can be defined just as deliberately as the other four skills.

So much for defining the challenge to make our subject the most significant possible. What about our other objective, to make our contribution exciting? Here again the foreign culture is a main resource: students today have become more interested in life styles than in literature or even in language for its own sake. Only when they discover that a language and literature express how the bearers of a culture live and what they live for do students grow excited about these fields of study.

The key strategic idea is motivation, and it pays to conceive the idea broadly: to project ourselves into the minds not only of students—ours and those whose interest we can awaken or reawaken after a bad experience—but also of other groups whose cooperation we need. Our fellow teachers in the social sciences, as well as in the arts, will have a higher regard for our subject if they know how the field of foreign language study has broadened and if we show appreciation for the importance of their fields. Reciprocal guest lectures and multidisciplinary discussions or lecture series are good resources. Topics for term papers that cross lines between fields can be proposed to language or literature students and likewise to students in science, art, business, and technology courses.

Administrators and advisers can be motivated. They want their institutions to educate for participation in the real world; we can convince them that we contribute to that mission. In the business and banking community some at least want broadly educated employees and citizens. More than a few want personnel for international business. In our feeder schools, advisers, administrators, and parents can be motivated, on the basis of their interests, to let children begin a language while they still have the physical capacity to imitate speech spontaneously. It is in our interest to help develop serious FL programs for school and preschool children. Motivation begins at home, but it need not stop before it reaches a whole community. The "Bonjour Seattle" experiment analyzed in *Foreign Language Annals* (14, No. 4 [1981], 299–305) offers some practical outreach suggestions.

The appeal to motivation builds a constituency far more solidly than language requirements do. In the long run requiring students to take a language protects mediocrity and alienates the captive audience, as happened in the 1960s. So easy it is, and so deadening, to answer the question "Why study a language?" with "Because colleges require it."

Students are attracted by some elements of the substantive case that can be made, first, for the value of language training to the individual. The "Copernican step" beyond an ethnocentric mentality is made possible through the combined *experience of* and *knowledge about* how cultures differ. A hobby for pleasure and service, language study makes one available for a wider range of job opportunities, able to learn more languages if needed, because one has become a practiced and self-confident language learner. Second, in a world whose insecurity is a worry for every young person and whose need for communication and understanding is desperate, language study has a value for society. A long study, *Interfutures,* reported in 1979 by the Organization for Economic Cooperation and Development, makes evident that the leaders and electorates of the developed countries will largely determine which of six scenarios will face the world by the year 2000. Since the desirable outcomes require informed and far-sighted decisions, the worst scenarios are the likeliest: antagonism between the developed and developing nations resulting from exploitation, cutthroat competition among the producers of industrial goods and services. The stakes ahead motivate one to get involved in shaping one's future situation.

How to Select What to Teach

Anyone who teaches "the fifth skill" must confront the question of how to select from the infinite aspects of a culture. I suggest we be guided by three considerations: what our students want; what they would want if they knew what we know; and our local strengths and limitations.

When at the beginning of a course I ask students today what they want to accomplish, nearly all answer that they want to communicate and to learn about the people. A simple questionnaire can elicit more reflective answers, but, even so, students' perceived needs cover only the surface. Even the Stepladder definitions of performance objectives, from rating one (mere survival skills) to five (native characteristics), tell only what an examinee is able to do, not how a student is to achieve the competence.

I wager that the most effective way for an outsider to progress in the sociocultural competence is to study, and to experience through the language, situations such as one would meet socially or professionally, always relating the attitudes and behavior encountered to the main themes of the culture.

By "main themes" I mean something more precise and demanding than the term may suggest. I have defined the term and explained how it reconciles sociological with anthropological theories in "The Emergent Model of a Sociocultural System" (*Contemporary French Civilization,* 2, No. 2 [1978], 277–94). The "emergent model" is an inventory of behavior patterns and institutions, organized into subsystems (cultural, societal, and ecological) so as to favor the conversion, when we know enough, from an inventory to a model showing the dynamic relations among the parts. The introduction to this article explains that three items in the cultural subsystem constitute the culture's "ground of meaning," that is, the mental furnishings that give to an utterance, an event, or a situation the culturally conditioned meaning it has for a member of the culture. The three elements are the culture's value system, its cognitive style, and its world picture, which is made up of presuppositions about the nature of humanity, society, and the world. It is interesting that what Americans prefer to call presuppositions, or simply assumptions, an audience at the College de France voted to call "the existential premises" of a people.

A "main theme," as I am using the expression, means one of a culture's major values, with its definition enlarged to include the habits of mind and the assumptions an outsider must be aware of in order to grasp what the value means for the culture bearer. The value is bound to be an emotionally charged concept, for it is not just a criterion for making judgments and choices but a feeling of how something *ought* to be. If the value is thwarted in favor of some opposite, the culture bearer feels annoyed.

Examples of values that differ enough to cause friction even between historically related cultures are the American achievement-success orientation, veiled in other cultures by modesty (hypocrisy?); the French pride in their *intellectualité;* the Hispanic *dignidad,* so easily offended, with the not uncommon result of a lifelong *resentimiento.*

An example of differing habits of mind, or cognitive styles, is the American or Persian "case-particular" tendency to regard each object of attention as discrete and self-dependent; the Russian or ancient Roman tendency toward a synthesis, a closed system, so that what does not fit is "deviationism"; and in between, the French propensity for an open sort of synthesis. The French mind perceives the relationships of an object as part of its definition, but the synthesis is less than total and is expected to evolve. (See my article "French Culture's Concern for Relationships: Relationism," *Foreign Language Annals,* 6, No. 4 [1973], 469–80.)

An example of differing assumptions is the American readiness to trust others—a factor in the nation's capacity for large-scale organization and delegation of authority—versus the more usual pattern of distrust, except for a small group of proved friends, separated from "the others" by a sharp line of demarcation.

Literature, language, social institutions, everyday events, even dialogues designed for language practice become illuminating and exciting revelations of a mentality when one relates behavior to the culture's "ground of meaning," its main themes. Social scientists have long refrained from contributing much to the knowledge needed for this approach. The reluctance is being overcome, however, by practical needs of effective cross-cultural communication and by disillusion with the narrowly positivistic conception of science. An early breakthrough, still of value, was Robin Williams' *American Society: A Sociological Interpretation,* whose third edition (Knopf, 1970) has one hundred pages on the value system. One of the benefits of our working together on educational applications is to stimulate the social science research, basic as well as applied, that is needed for all cross-cultural relations.

Let me not leave the subtopic of what the student needs to know without facing the question of how to deal with the variations in a culture, particularly the differences according to social class. For European cultures the most sensible solution is to take the middle class (in Latin America, the bulk of the upper class) as the point of entry, mentioning the old aristocracies and the urban and rural working classes where the differences are worth knowing. The same solution—a selected reference point—can be applied to other variations: for regional differences, choosing the world-standard dialect and the prestige subculture; for age groups, the generation in power, with special attention paid in our classes to the students' age-mates.

Finally, selecting what to teach involves the consideration of our own local strengths and weaknesses. Some teams of teachers will be strong in direct experience of a people's everyday life; others in the history of its literature. Either background provides illuminating manifestations of the culture's main themes. Whatever the strength, an effort is needed to present both the ordinary life and the historic achievements of the people. The ordinary life students will encounter as travel and contact increase; the historic achievements are often the ideal substance for the sort of discussions that lead to a warm, congenial rapport.

Some local situations will require emphasis on careers, for which the needed composite background may have to come partly from neighboring colleges and from the community. Where such knowledge is lacking, there remains an untapped local resource. Many professors, especially those in small colleges who are free from the publish-or-perish syndrome, are inactive in research for the very good reason that they see the unimportance of piling up more of the same stuff they produced in graduate school. The methods of attack they learned, however, are useful for investigating topics such as cross-cultural conflict and resolution, career needs, literary examples of main themes, and ways of presenting cultural material, as well as for evaluating materials as means to the Stepladder standards of competence. Theodore Mueller at the University of Kentucky found some interesting presumptive evidence simply by comparing French classes that had and had not studied a dozen purported main themes of French culture: Watching a comedy of Jules Romains the experimental group laughed, while the control group did not, at certain points where a French audience laughs. Neither high-level comedy nor low-level farce, the play represents an intermediate level of culture-related humor. Its characters are comic because they pretend to *intellectualité* without having the requisite *formation culturelle.* One can become excited by research when one knows it is meaningful. And research never hurts promotion.

How to Inform Ourselves

It is practicable even in a busy life to find out what has already been done on a topic selected for teaching or research. A first source that saves time, the culture section of the *ACTFL Annual Bibliography of Books and Articles on Pedagogy in Foreign Languages* cites American and foreign journals that provide leads. A librarian can suggest resources locally available or accessible by computer.

True, one has to touch too many bases to find out what is known on any given point. For each of the foreign cultures, there is a need to simplify access to rich but dispersed documentation. Anyone can help in developing a coordinated system that will enable all of us to be more efficient. One procedure, which is gradually producing results in France—and now, in Quebec—began with a proposal that the American Association of Teachers of French create a national commission on ethnography. As chairman of that commission, later as just a member, I was able to convene five annual meetings of representatives of the dozen or so main French agencies. None of the agencies felt it could arrogate to itself the position of *chef de file,* with the result that none could convene the others—an example of the need for outside and inside observers of a culture to work together. By the fourth meeting, there was widespread recognition of regrettable overlaps and lacunae in the services offered. At the fifth, a coordinating committee of the agencies was created, and one of them was empowered to convene further meetings in the absence of the outsider. That project has reached the stage of asking teachers and researchers to name the descriptors they would like to be able to use, as the French and Quebecois agencies computerize their bibliographies and consolidate their operations. We are working toward the ideal situation where one will be able to see a full or selective bibliography on a computer, place an order, and receive the wanted documents from a center in North America. The 1984 convention of the Fédération Internationale de Professeurs de Français is to review the progress and invite other francophone countries to join in. This procedure and the resulting thesaurus of common descriptors can be adapted to any language community.

How to Present the Descriptive Knowledge Selected

Let me begin with three general suggestions, then comment on the ways to introduce cultural material into the beginning, intermediate, and advanced courses.

First, I assume that all the class contact time after the first half-hour will be spent in the target language. Practice in the interaction between live speakers is necessary but scarce, even with all the practice that recorded cues can evoke. When I use a word that cannot be inferred by the students, I insert an English word parenthetically; but the utterance is in the target language.

Second, I recommend playing down the (inevitable) contrastive interest as far as possible and leaving translation until the advanced stage of learning. Then a highly reflective exercise can bring to conscious formulation the differences in mentality: by that time one can interrogate one's experience to speculate *why* a case-particular mind enumerates "a,b,c,d," while in a relational culture one says "from a to d, passing through b and c."

The reason for playing down the contrastive is that we want the learner to experience how the foreign culture makes sense in its own terms. To learn each element of it as an extrusion from our system—"They do that, we do this"—merely confirms the student's ingrained suspicion that while our culture has a center, *is* the center, the other just goes off in all directions. In studying a culture, just as in learning a language, there are the two results to choose between, which Nelson Brooks called compound and coordinate systems. The compound system is a mixture centered in one's native culture. Far preferable are two (or more) coordinate systems, not uncoordinated but each with its own independent ground of meaning. This is the result that most enriches life. The learner retains a home culture but understands the other from within and so is able to conform to its social conventionalities without culture shock.

The third general suggestion is to vary the devices and activities in class, selecting from those which exploit the apparent fact that we are an organism programmed for learning language in conjunction with other than verbal behavior. We learn words and constructions not alone but in situations that excite curiosity or the urge to speak or that carry some other emotional charge. (For a partial list of devices, divided between those conducive to *experience of* and *knowledge about* a culture, see my "Empathy for a Second Culture: Motivations and Techniques," in Gilbert Jarvis, *ACTFL Review of Foreign Language Education No. 5, Responding to New Realities* [Skokie, Ill.: National Textbook, 1974], pp. 263–327.)

For the beginners' course, one can choose a textbook that at least gives uncoordinated elements of the culture. Criteria for evaluating this aspect of textbooks are proposed on p. 181.

Homework in English, consisting of thought questions in a sequence, can be used to stimulate reflective analysis of cultural material, beginning with a first dialogue. But it is surprising how much beginners can soon understand in the foreign language when the subject is as basic as human values. After all, the great religions have conveyed their main concepts with a minimum of vocabulary.

As early as it becomes practicable, a main resource is brief comment and discussion based on the material studied—including the language. Even phonology, the great sound shift that put English out of step with the European languages, or Grimm's law, is fascinating and conduces to an attitude of understanding.

Beginning with the elementary level, short projects can be proposed that develop an individual interest, acquaint a student with the library, and strengthen the contribution of the language course to liberal education. (On pp. 15–17, culture capsules are suggested, with sample tests.) At the second-year level, literature and periodicals can supplement the textbook. The situations used in class can be more natural and can include foreign guests.

Literature is a gold mine. The values it manifests include elegant expression, logical organization, and, in fiction, the observation and analysis of behavior. The habits of mind, of which the author is often unaware, show through such procedures as the "a,b,c,d" versus the "a to d" forms of enumeration, which in turn relate back to either the Greek time concept, linear, or the Roman *tempus,* basically a period of time marked by beginning and end. The assumptions of a culture show through all kinds of attitudes toward the world and toward people. For example, the Spanish expression *tener confianza con alguien,* "to be at ease with a person," involves the whole gestalt of the distrusted outside world with which one tries to deal obliquely, through an intermediary common acquaintance.

Periodical literature gives occasion to distinguish among ideologies in a culture and to show how the coherence of a rationale may be valued, to the disparagement of our case-particular mentality.

In the advanced literature course, whole major works can be studied, and their conception shows a culture's characteristics on a larger scale. A scene of a play, for a case-particular culture, is a basic building block. A relational culture sees a play as a whole organized in facets, or acts, and a new scene marks no more than the movement of a character on or off the stage.

If a culture course or a senior-year seminar does not provide a recapitulating synthesis of main themes, the advanced literature course can assume this function without neglecting the place of literary works in their other great context, world literature as a universal form of human creativity.

The culture course may well develop the historical dimension as well as treat the present in the context of history. This course can, if necessary, be taught in English so as to include history majors and can serve as a flagship course for an alternative undergraduate major or minor program of area study. David Pinkey, a historian, and I have given together a ten-week junior-level course, The Making of Contemporary France, meeting five days a week. Much of the reading can be done in French, and on two of the five days the discussion groups meet separately in French or English. In three lectures a week, the historian goes as far back as is necessary for the topic of the week, while at least one lecture deals with the present. Topics have included centralization, class structure, education, the status of women, the revolutionary tradition, national security, industrialization, and urbanization. Students write a midterm paper relating two of the prior topics and a more broadly synthesizing final paper.

The language-and-area sequence at the University of Washington has been conceived to build competences by whatever means, on campus or abroad, rather than in prescribed courses. A survey of course offerings in related departments discovered many courses that permitted at least a term paper applying the content of the instruction to France. In any college, even in those progressive institutions that have opened up the departmental structures, one can find possibilities of cross-disciplinary cooperation that our departmentalized mentality has hidden from us.

Your Career

The recommendation to develop the teaching of the "fifth skill" requires a label, that in the short range it may be injurious to a career, given the academic peer-group pressure against innovation and the current social backlash against teaching the relativity of cultures and value systems. But our nation is increasingly realizing that our comfortable, familiar ethnocentrism is itself injurious to our diplomacy, our balance of trade, our global prestige—in short, to the national interest. Moreover, ethnocentrism puts a straightjacket on the self-fulfillment and civic adequacy of individual Americans. How should one reconcile the short-range danger and the long-range opportunity? I can remember when Latin-American literature, then linguistics, were disparaged specialties. Fads vanish, needed innovations remain. The resolution lies, I believe, in cautious persistence. So I would advise, proceed with circumspection and with empathy for one's less venturesome colleagues and superiors. But proceed!

Martin Luther King had a profound insight that "those whom we want to change, we must first love". There *is* a universal humanity, at a level of generality above the differences among cultures and subcultures, just as there is coherence in a culture above the level of individual differences. By putting cultural differences and similarities in their place at the middle level, we can avoid antagonizing those who see the universal or the individual level as preeminent. In this perspective, cross-cultural understanding is a main hope of shaping this dangerous world to make possible the realization of elemental human values.

Criteria for the Cultural Component of Foreign Language Textbooks

Significance

1. Will the situations presented interest the expected students? Would students be likely to encounter similar situations?
2. Are the culture patterns selected those that the students need to know? Does the book cover the material of the appropriate step on the ACTFL Stepladder? (See pp. 193–94. For a checklist of culture patterns and social institutions, see also "The 'Emergent Model' of a Sociocultural System," *Contemporary French Civilization*, 2, No. 2 [1978], 277–94.)
3. Are the culture patterns presented vividly? Do activities aim at their assimilation?
4. Is the life of today presented authentically and in good balance with the people's historic achievements? Do the language and the grammar rules reflect current usage?
5. Are explanations of culture patterns suggested and clearly distinguished from descriptions of the patterns? Particularly, are the situations interpreted in the light of the culture's central values, habits of mind, and assumptions underlying the culture bearer's behavior?

Validity

1. Assuming that examples are accompanied by generalizations, is overgeneralization avoided?
2. Are dates given for the opinion polls used?
3. Does the author avoid the temptation to indulge in stereotypes (such as "beautiful but dumb") for the sake of humor?

Methods of teaching

1. Is the cultural material, including pictures, made relevant to the language or literature being studied?
2. Are the methods of presentation diversified to avoid monotony?
3. Does the development of the receptive and productive skills strike the proper balance for the expected students?

The Sociocultural Component in the ACTFL Stepladder Project

Preliminary position paper, Howard Nostrand

RELATION OF INSTRUCTIONAL LEVELS TO THE SUCCESSIVE THRESHOLDS OF COMPETENCE

In the case of the speaking-interacting skill, the objectives of the successive learning levels clearly should not follow the sequence of thresholds 1, 2, and so on, because the ungrammatical utterances that achieve survival competence result in habits detrimental to more sophisticated communication.

In the case of the sociocultural competence, to aim first at that threshold level would not be counterproductive for the higher levels of performance if present working theory is valid. If, however, body-language interaction proves to be not incidental but of primary importance, the early conditioning of foreign phrases to wrong kinesics is a major detriment to communicative competence. In any case, it cannot be assumed that the successive thresholds provide the best pedagogical sequence. Furthermore, this sequence should introduce concepts, understanding, from the start—not skill and habits alone. And the early, limited concepts should be so formulated as to permit their incorporation later into more comprehensive generalizations without contradicting them.

RELATION OF CULTURAL SUBSTANCE TO PERFORMANCE OBJECTIVES

The needed nationwide consensus cannot go beyond

1. The sociocultural competence as defined by the Stepladder, and
2. The general human-development objectives:
   a. Understanding of a foreign life style
   b. Application of that understanding to a relativistic perspective on one's own way of life
   c. Moral and aesthetic sensitivity, increased through acquaintance with a people's literature and other arts

The differing approaches to the substance of a culture are not part of the consensus but means to objectives 1 and 2. It is a wager, that a particularly effective means to both sets of objectives is to relate the patterns of behavior and artistic production in a culture to its underlying "ground of meaning": its central values, presuppositions, and habits of mind, or cognitive style. (See pp. 174–77.) This approach, and others, inform educational programs aiming to produce the competences that are to be measured.

Short Projects for an Observer of a Culture, Using Library Resources (and Developing Writing Skills)

1. Leaf through a popular magazine or newspaper, if only through the illustrations and ads. Deduce evidences of attitudes, what is valued, what is assumed, and so forth.

2. For a topic of personal interest, scan the contents of the *Modern Language Journal, Foreign Language Annals,* culture-specific periodicals such as that of the respective American Association of Teachers, and magazines such as, for French, *Contemporary French Civilization, Tocqueville Review,* and *Le français dans le monde.*

3. Use subject-matter bibliographies for a topic easily defined, such as the family, the status of women, religion, politics, the educational system, youth, sports, or a vocation. In English, for example: *Reader's Guide to Periodical Literature, New York Times Index, Psychological Abstracts, Sociological Abstracts, ACTFL Bibliography, MLA Bibliography,* vol. 2. In French, SODEC (see samples in *AATF National Bulletin,* late 1970s and 1980), *Bulletin signalétique* (CNRS), *Bulletin Analytique* (Institute de Sciences Politiques).

   For a brief annotated bibliography of the French language area, see H. L. Nostrand, "Sociocultural Background," in Douglas W. Alden, ed., *A Critical Bibliog. of French Literature,* vol. 6, *The Twentieth Century (Syracuse, N.Y.: Syracuse Univ. Press, 1980),* pp. 95–100. Other sections are valuable for literature, history, and philosophy. For German, see *Bibliographie der deutschen Zeitschriftenliteratur.* For all languages except German, see (looking up the German words to search) *Bibliographie der fremdsprachichen Zeitschriftenliteratur.*

POINTS FOR A SYSTEMATIC METHOD

Use 3" × 5" slips. They are easy to rearrange in a structure to support your conclusions.

Keep a record of the sources you have covered.

Keep a bibliography slip, using a standard form, for every item read or otherwise to be retained (see *MLA Handbook*).

Keep a summary of items read: at top, author and year; in left margin, page references.

Make a slip for each idea that occurs to you as you read and reflect. Use complete sentences. Once you have your thoughts in this objective form, you can criticize the ideas and streamline your expressions of them.

Chapter Five

ACTFL Stepladder to Competence in Five Foreign Language and Literature Skills

Much has been said in the literature about the need to design usable proficiency goals to guide language instructions. Increasingly, foreign language educators have focused on teaching to achieve communicative facility and to meet needs relating to students' lives outside the classroom. But the gains made in recent years are not easily communicated, since there is no common yardstick that conveys information regarding achievement either to others in foreign language education or to consumers of the abilities that students gain through language study. This project, A Design for Measuring and Communicating Foreign Language Proficiency, is funded by a grant from the International Studies and Foreign Language Program of the United States Department of Education. The project addresses the need to develop guidelines that clearly articulate standards of achievement at the various stages of language learning.

ACTFL Provisional Proficiency Guidelines

PROVISIONAL GENERIC DESCRIPTIONS—SPEAKING
(For details on this skill, see pp. 214–20.)

Novice—Low   Unable to function in the spoken language. Oral production is limited to occasional isolated words. Essentially no communicative ability.

Novice—Mid   Able to operate only in a very limited capacity within very predictable areas of need. Vocabulary limited to that necessary to express simple elementary needs and basic courtesy formulae. Syntax is fragmented, inflections and word endings frequently omitted, confused or distorted and the majority of utterances consist of isolated words or short formulae. Utterances rarely consist of more than two or three words and are marked by frequent long pauses and repetition of an interlocutor's words. Pronunciation is frequently unintelligible and is strongly influenced by first language. Can be understood only with difficulty, even by persons such as teachers who are used to speaking with non-native speakers or in interactions where the context strongly supports the utterance.

Novice—High   Able to satisfy immediate needs using learned utterances. Can ask questions or make statements with reasonable accuracy only where this involves short memorized utterances or formulae. There is no real autonomy of expression, although there may be some emerging signs of spontaneity and flexibility. There is a slight increase in utterance length but frequent long pauses and repetition of interlocutor's words still occur. Most utterances are telegraphic and word endings are often omitted, confused or distorted. Vocabulary is limited to areas of immediate survival needs. Can differentiate most phonemes when produced in isolation but when they are combined in words or groups of words, errors are frequent and, even with repetition, may severely inhibit communication even with persons used to dealing with such learners. Little development in stress and intonation is evident.

Intermediate—Low   Able to satisfy basic survival needs and minimum courtesy requirements. In areas of immediate need or on very familiar topics, can ask and answer simple questions, initiate and respond to simple statements, and maintain very simple face-to-face conversations. When asked to do so, is able to formulate some questions with limited constructions and much inaccuracy. Almost every utterance contains fractured syntax and other grammatical errors. Vocabulary inadequate to express anything but the most elementary needs. Strong interference from native language occurs in articulation, stress and intonation. Misunderstandings frequently arise from limited vocabulary and grammar and erroneous phonology but, with repetition, can generally be understood by native speakers in regular contact with foreigners attempting to speak their language. Little precision in information conveyed owing to tentative state of grammatical development and little or no use of modifiers.

Intermediate—Mid   Able to satisfy some survival needs and some limited social demands. Is able to formulate some questions when asked to do so. Vocabulary permits discussion of topics beyond basic survival needs such as personal history and leisure time activities. Some evidence of grammatical accuracy in basic constructions, for example, subject-verb agreement, noun-adjective agreement, some notion of inflection.

Intermediate—High   Able to satisfy most survival needs and limited social demands. Shows some spontaneity in language production but fluency is very uneven. Can initiate and sustain a general conversation but has little understanding of the social conventions of conversation. Developing flexibility in a range of circumstances beyond immediate survival needs. Limited vocabulary range necessitates much hesitation and circumlocution. The commoner tense forms occur but errors are frequent in formation and selection. Can use most question forms. While some word order is established, errors still occur in more complex patterns. Cannot sustain coherent structures in longer utterances or unfamiliar situations. Ability to describe and give precise information is limited. Aware of basic cohesive features such as pronouns and verb inflections, but many are unreliable, especially if less immediate in reference. Extended discourse is largely a series of short, discrete utterances. Articulation is comprehensible to native speakers used to dealing with foreigners, and can combine most phonemes with reasonable comprehensibility, but still has difficulty in producing certain sounds, in certain positions, or in certain combinations, and speech will usually be labored. Still has to repeat utterances frequently to be understood by the general public. Able to produce some narration in either past or future.

Advanced   Able to satisfy routine social demands and limited work requirements. Can handle with confidence but not with facility most social situations including introductions and casual conversations about current events, as well as work, family, and autobiographical information; can handle limited work requirements, needing help in handling any complications or difficulties. Has a speaking vocabulary sufficient to respond simply with some circumlocutions; accent, though often quite faulty, is intelligible; can usually handle elementary constructions quite accurately but does not have thorough or confident control of the grammar.

Advanced-Plus   Able to satisfy most work requirements and show some ability to communicate on concrete topics relating to particular interests and special fields of competence. Generally strong in either grammar or vocabulary, but not in both. Weaknesses or unevenness in one of the foregoing or in pronunciation result in occasional miscommunication. Areas of weakness range from simple constructions such as plurals, articles, prepositions, and negatives to more complex structures such as tense usage, passive constructions, word order, and relative clauses. Normally controls general vocabulary with some groping for everyday vocabulary still evident. Often shows remarkable fluency and ease of speech, but under tension or pressure language may break down.

Superior   Able to speak the language with sufficient structural accuracy and vocabulary to participate effectively in most formal and informal conversations on practical, social, and professional topics. Can discuss particular interests and special fields of competence with reasonable ease. Vocabulary is broad enough that speaker rarely has to grope for a word; accent may be obviously foreign; control of grammar good; errors virtually never interfere with understanding and rarely disturb the native speaker.

PROVISIONAL GENERIC DESCRIPTIONS—LISTENING

Novice—Low   No practical understanding of the spoken language. Understanding limited to occasional isolated words, such as cognates, borrowed words, and high frequency social conventions. Essentially no ability to comprehend even short utterances.

Novice—Mid   Sufficient comprehension to understand some memorized words within predictable areas of need. Vocabulary for comprehension limited to simple elementary needs and basic courtesy formulae. Utterances understood rarely exceed more than two or three words at a time and ability to understand is characterized by long pauses for assimilation and by repeated requests on the listener's part for repetition, and/or a slower rate of speech. Confuses words that sound similar.

Novice—High   Sufficient comprehension to understand a number of memorized utterances in areas of immediate need. Comprehends slightly longer utterances in situations where the context aids understanding, such as at the table, in a restaurant/store, in a train/bus. Phrases recognized have for the most part been memorized. Comprehends vocabulary common to daily needs. Comprehends simple questions/statements about family members, age, address, weather, time, daily activities and interests. Misunderstandings arise from failure to perceive critical sounds or endings. Understands even standard speech with difficulty but gets some main ideas. Often requires repetition and/or a slowed rate of speed for comprehension, even when listening to persons such as teachers who are used to speaking with non-natives.

Intermediate—Low   Sufficient comprehension to understand utterances about basic survival needs, minimum courtesy and travel requirements. In areas of immediate need or on very familiar topics, can understand non-memorized material, such as simple questions and answers, statements, and face-to-face conversations in the standard language. Comprehension areas include basic needs: meals, lodging, transportation, time, simple instructions (e.g., route directions) and routine commands (e.g., from customs officials, police). Understands main ideas. Misunderstandings frequently arise from lack of vocabulary or faulty processing of syntactic information often caused by strong interference from the native language or by the imperfect and partial acquisition of the target grammar.

Intermediate—Mid   Sufficient comprehension to understand simple conversations about some survival needs and some limited social conventions. Vocabulary permits understanding of topics beyond basic survival needs such as personal history and leisure time activities. Evidence of understanding basic constructions, for example, subject-verb agreement, noun-adjective agreement; evidence that some inflection is understood.

Intermediate—High   Sufficient comprehension to understand short conversations about most survival needs and limited social conventions. Increasingly able to understand topics beyond immediate survival needs. Shows spontaneity in understanding, but speed and consistency of understanding uneven. Limited vocabulary range necessitates repetition for understanding. Understands commoner tense forms and some word order patterns, including most question forms, but miscommunication still occurs with more complex patterns. Can get the gist of conversations, but cannot sustain comprehension in longer utterances or in unfamiliar situations. Understanding of descriptions and detailed information is limited. Aware of basic cohesive features such as pronouns and verb inflections, but many are unreliably understood, especially if other material intervenes. Understanding is largely limited to a series of short, discrete utterances. Still has to ask for utterances to be repeated. Some ability to understand the facts.

Advanced   Sufficient comprehension to understand conversations about routine social conventions and limited school or work requirements. Able to understand face-to-face speech in the standard language, delivered at a normal rate with some repetition and rewording, by a native speaker not used to dealing with foreigners. Understands everyday topics, common personal and family news, well-known current events, and routine matters involving school or work; descriptions and narration about current, past and future events; and essential points of discussion or speech at an elementary level on topics in special fields of interest.

Advanced-Plus   Sufficient comprehension to understand most routine social conventions, conversations on school or work requirements, and discussions on concrete topics related to particular interests and special fields of competence. Often shows remarkable ability and ease of understanding, but comprehension may break down under tension or pressure, including unfavorable listening conditions. Candidate may display weakness or deficiency due to inadequate vocabulary base or less than secure knowledge of grammar and syntax. Normally understands general vocabulary with some hesitant understanding of everyday vocabulary still evident. Can sometimes detect emotional overtones. Some ability to understand between the lines, i.e., to make inferences.

Superior   Sufficient comprehension to understand the essentials of all speech in standard dialects, including technical discussions within a special field. Has sufficient understanding of face-to-face speech, delivered with normal clarity and speed in standard language, on general topics and areas of special interest; understands hypothesizing and supported opinions. Has broad enough vocabulary that rarely has to ask for paraphrasing or explanation. Can follow accurately the essentials of conversations between educated native speakers, reasonably clear telephone calls, radio broadcasts, standard news items, oral reports, some oral technical reports, and public addresses on non-technical subjects. May not understand native speakers if they speak very quickly or use some slang or unfamiliar dialect. Can often detect emotional overtones. Can understand "between the lines" (i.e., make inferences).

PROVISIONAL GENERIC DESCRIPTIONS—READING

Novice—Low   No functional ability in reading the foreign language.

Novice—Mid   Sufficient understanding of the written language to interpret highly contextualized words or cognates within predictable areas. Vocabulary for comprehension limited to simple elementary needs such as names, addresses, dates, street signs, building names, short informative signs (e.g., no smoking, entrance/exit) and formulaic vocabulary requesting same. Material understood rarely exceeds a single phrase and comprehension requires successive rereading and checking.

Novice—High   Sufficient comprehension of the written to interpret set expressions in areas of immediate need. Can recognize all the letters in the printed version of an alphabetic system and high-frequency elements of a syllabary or a character system. Where vocabulary has been mastered can read for instruction and directional purposes standardized messages, phrases or expressions such as some items on menus, schedules, timetables, maps and signs indicating hours of operation, social codes, and traffic regulations. This material is read only for essential information. Detail is overlooked or misunderstood.

Intermediate—Low   Sufficient comprehension to understand in printed form the simplest connected material, either authentic or specially prepared, dealing with basic survival and social needs. Able to understand both mastered material and recombinations of the mastered elements that achieve meanings at the same level. Understands main ideas in material whose structures and syntax parallel the native language. Can read messages, greetings, statements of social amenities or other simple language containing only the highest frequency grammatical patterns and vocabulary items including cognates (if appropriate). Misunderstandings arise when a syntax diverges from that of the native language or when grammatical cues are overlooked.

Intermediate—Mid   Sufficient comprehension to understand in printed form simple discourse for informative or social purposes. In response to perceived needs can read for information material such as announcements of public events, popular advertising, notes containing biographical information or narration of events, and straightforward newspaper headlines and story titles. Can guess at unfamiliar vocabulary if highly contextualized. Relies primarily on adverbs as time indicators. Has some difficulty with factors in discourse, such as matching pronouns with referents. May have to read material several times before understanding.

Intermediate—High   Sufficient comprehension to understand a simple paragraph for personal communication, information or recreational purposes. Can read with understanding social notes, letters and invitations; can locate and derive main ideas of the introductory/summary paragraphs from high interest or familiar news or other informational sources; can read for pleasure specially prepared, or some uncomplicated authentic prose, such as fictional narratives or cultural information. Shows spontaneity in reading by ability to guess at meaning from context. Understands common time indicators and can interpret some cohesive factors such as objective pronouns and simple clause connectors. Begins to relate sentences in the discourse to advance meaning, but cannot sustain understanding of longer discourse on unfamiliar topics. Misinterpretation still occurs with more complex patterns.

Advanced   Sufficient comprehension to read simple authentic printed material or edited textual material within a familiar context. Can read uncomplicated but authentic prose on familiar subjects containing description and narration such as news items describing frequently occurring events, simple biographic information, social notices, and standard business letters. Can read edited texts such as prose fiction and contemporary culture. The prose is predominantly in familiar sentence patterns. Can follow essential points of written discussion at level of main ideas and some supporting ones with topics in a field of interest or where background exists. Some misunderstandings. Able to read the facts but cannot draw inferences.

Advanced-Plus   Sufficient comprehension to understand most factual information in non-technical prose as well as some discussions on concrete topics related to special interests. Able to read for information and description, to follow sequence of events, and to react to that information. Is able to separate main ideas from lesser ones, and uses that division to advance understanding. Can locate and interpret main ideas and details in material written for the general public. Will begin to guess sensibly at new words by using linguistic context and prior knowledge. May react personally to material but does not yet detect subjective attitudes, values, or judgments in the writing.

Superior   Able to read standard newspaper items addressed to the general reader, routine correspondence reports and technical material in a field of interest at a normal rate of speed (at least 220 wpm). Readers can gain new knowledge from material on unfamiliar topics in areas of a general nature. Can interpret hypotheses, supported opinions and conjectures. Can also read short stories, novels, and other recreational literature accessible to the general public. Reading ability is not subject-matter dependent. Has broad enough general vocabulary that successful guessing resolves problems with complex structures and low-frequency idioms. Misreading is rare. Almost always produces correct interpretation. Able to read between the lines. May be unable to appreciate nuance or stylistics.

PROVISIONAL GENERIC DESCRIPTIONS—WRITING

Novice—Low No functional ability in writing the foreign language.

Novice—Mid No practical communicative writing skills. Able to copy isolated words or short phrases. Able to transcribe previously studied words or phrases.

Novice—High Able to write simple fixed expressions and limited memorized material. Can supply information when requested on forms such as hotel registrations and travel documents. Can write names, numbers, dates, one's own nationality, addresses, and other simple biographic information, as well as learned vocabulary, short phrases, and simple lists. Can write all the symbols in an alphabetic or syllabic system or 50 of the most common characters. Can write simple memorized material with frequent misspellings and inaccuracies.

Intermediate—Low Has sufficient control of the writing system to meet limited practical needs. Can write short messages, such as simple questions or notes, postcards, phone messages, and the like within the scope of limited language experience. Can take simple notes on material dealing with familiar topics although memory span is extremely limited. Can create statements or questions within the scope of limited language experience. Material produced consists of recombinations of learned vocabulary and structures into simple sentences. Vocabulary is inadequate to express anything but elementary needs. Writing tends to be a loosely organized collection of sentence fragments on a very familiar topic. Makes continual errors in spelling, grammar, and punctuation, but writing can be read and understood by a native speaker used to dealing with foreigners. Able to produce appropriately some fundamental sociolinguistic distinctions in formal and familiar style, such as appropriate subject pronouns, titles of address and basic social formulae.

Intermediate—Mid Sufficient control of writing system to meet some survival needs and some limited social demands. Able to compose short paragraphs or take simple notes on very familiar topics grounded in personal experience. Can discuss likes and dislikes, daily routine, everyday events, and the like. Can express past time, using content words and time expressions, or with sporadically accurate verbs. Evidence of good control of basic constructions and inflections such as subject-verb agreement, noun-adjective agreement, and straightforward syntactic constructions in present or future time, though errors occasionally occur. May make frequent errors, however, when venturing beyond current level of linguistic competence. When resorting to a dictionary, often is unable to identify appropriate vocabulary, or uses dictionary entry in uninflected form.

Intermediate—High   Sufficient control of writing system to meet most survival needs and limited social demands. Can take notes in some detail on familiar topics, and respond to personal questions using elementary vocabulary and common structures. Can write simple letters, brief synopses and paraphrases, summaries of biographical data and work experience, and short compositions on familiar topics. Can create sentences and short paragraphs relating to most survival needs (food, lodging, transportation, immediate surroundings and situations) and limited social demands. Can relate personal history, discuss topics such as daily life, preferences, and other familiar material. Can express fairly accurately present and future time. Can produce some past verb forms, but not always accurately or with correct usage. Shows good control of elementary vocabulary and some control of basic syntactic patterns but major errors still occur when expressing more complex thoughts. Dictionary usage may still yield incorrect vocabulary of forms, although can use a dictionary to advantage to express simple ideas. Generally cannot use basic cohesive elements of discourse to advantage such as relative constructions, subject pronouns, connectors, etc. Writing, though faulty, is comprehensible to native speakers used to dealing with foreigners.

Advanced   Able to write routine social correspondence and simple discourse of at least several paragraphs on familiar topics. Can write simple social correspondence, take notes, and write cohesive summaries, resumes, and short narratives and descriptions on factual topics. Able to write about everyday topics using both description and narration. Has sufficient writing vocabulary to express himself/herself simply with some circumlocution. Can write about a very limited number of current events or daily situations and express personal preferences and observations in some detail, using basic structures. Still makes common errors in spelling and punctuation, but shows some control of the most common formats and punctuation conventions. Good control of the morphology of the language (in inflected languages) and of the most frequently used syntactic structures. Elementary constructions are usually handled quite accurately, and writing is understandable to a native speaker not used to reading the writing of foreigners. Uses a limited number of cohesive devices such as pronouns and repeated words with good accuracy. Able to join sentences in limited discourse, but has difficulty and makes frequent errors in producing complex sentences. Paragraphs are reasonably unified and coherent.

Advanced-Plus   Shows ability to write about most common topics with some precision and in some detail. Can write fairly detailed resumes and summaries and take quite accurate notes. Can write most social and informal business correspondence. Can describe and narrate personal experiences and explain simply points of view in prose discourse. Can write about concrete topics relating to particular interests and special fields of competence. Normally controls general vocabulary with some circumlocution. Often shows remarkable fluency and ease of expression, but under time constraints and pressure language may be inaccurate and/or incomprehensible. Generally strong in either grammar or vocabulary, but not in both. Weaknesses and unevenness in one of the foregoing or in spelling result in occasional miscommunication. Areas of weakness range from simple constructions such as plurals, articles, prepositions, and negatives to more complex structures such as tense usage, passive constructions, word order, and relative clauses. Some misuse of vocabulary still evident. Shows a limited ability to use circumlocution. Uses dictionary to advantage to supply unknown words. Writing is understandable to native speakers not used to reading material written by non-natives, though the style is still obviously foreign.

Superior   Able to use the written language effectively in most formal and informal exchanges on practical, social, and professional topics. Can write most types of correspondence, such as memos and social and business letters, short research papers and statements of position in areas of special interest or in special fields. Can express hypotheses, conjectures, and present arguments or points of view accurately and effectively. Can write about areas of special interest and handle topics in special fields, in addition to most common topics. Good control of a full range of structures, spelling, and a wide general vocabulary allow the writer to convey his/her message accurately, though style may be foreign. Can use complex and compound sentence structures to express ideas clearly and coherently. Uses dictionary with a high degree of accuracy to supply specialized vocabulary. Errors, though sometimes made when using more complex structures, are occasional, and rarely disturb the native speaker. Sporadic errors when using basic structures. Although sensitive to differences in formal and informal style, still cannot tailor writing precisely and accurately to a variety of audiences or styles.

PROVISIONAL GENERIC DESCRIPTIONS—CULTURE

Novice   Limited interaction. Behaves with considerateness. Is resourceful in nonverbal communication, but is unreliable in interpretation of nonverbal cues. Is limited in language, as indicated under the listening and speaking skills. Lacks generally the knowledge of culture patterns requisite for survival situations.

Intermediate   Survival competence. Can deal with familiar survival situations and interact with a culture bearer accustomed to foreigners. Uses behavior acquired for the purpose of greeting and leave-taking, expressing wants, asking directions, buying food, using transportation, tipping. Comprehends the response. Makes errors as the result of misunderstanding; miscommunicates, and misapplies assumptions about the culture.

Advanced   Limited social competence. Handles routine social situations successfully with a culture bearer accustomed to foreigners. Shows comprehension of common rules of etiquette, taboos and sensitivities, though home culture predominates. Can make polite requests, accept and refuse invitations, offer and receive gifts, apologize, make introductions, telephone, purchase and bargain, do routine banking. Can discuss a few aspects of the home and the foreign country, such as general current events and policies, as well as a field of personal interest. Does not offend the culture bearer, but some important misunderstandings and miscommunications occur, in interaction with one unaccustomed to foreigners. Is not competent to take part in a formal meeting, or in a group situation where several persons are speaking informally at the same time.

Superior   Working social and professional competence. Can participate in almost all social situations and those within one vocation. Handles unfamiliar types of situations with ease and sensitivity, including some involving common taboos, or other emotionally charged subjects. Comprehends most nonverbal responses. Laughs at some culture-related humor. In productive skills, neither culture predominates; nevertheless, makes appropriate use of cultural references and expressions. Generally distinguishes between a formal and informal register. Discusses abstract ideas relating the foreign to the native culture. Is generally limited, however, in handling abstractions. Minor inaccuracies occur in perception of meaning and in the expression of the intended representation, but do not result in serious misunderstanding, even by a culture bearer unaccustomed to foreigners.

Near-Native Competence   Full social and professional competence. Fits behavior to audience, and the culture of the target language dominates almost entirely. Has internalized the concept that culture is relative and is always on the lookout to do the appropriate thing. Can counsel, persuade, negotiate, represent a point of view, interpret for dignitaries, describe and compare features of the two cultures. In such comparisons, can discuss geography, history, institutions, custom and behavior patterns, current events, and national policies. Perceives almost all unverbalized responses, and recognizes almost all allusions, including historical and literary commonplaces. Laughs at most culture-related humor. Controls a formal and informal register of behavior. Is inferior to the culture bearer only in background information related to the culture such as childhood experiences, detailed regional geography and past events of significance.

Native Competence   Examinee is indistinguishable from a person brought up and educated in the culture.

Chapter Six

Testing

Redefining and expanding curricular goals suggests modifications in testing students and evaluating programs. In the past, too many discrepancies have existed between proclaimed objectives and their ensuing measurement. This chapter proposes rethinking of testing procedures to parallel the kinds of curricular modifications described in the preceding chapter.

For those planning FLL curricula for expanded needs and purposes, Renate Schulz outlines principles and procedures for testing and evaluation. She proposes a model consisting of four components: (1) preinstructional evaluation of students' personal variables, (2) course-specific achievement testing, (3) overall proficiency testing, and (4) continual program evaluation.

Judith Liskin-Gasparro focuses on contemporary interest in proficiency-based instruction and requirements. She stresses the importance of defining realistic goals for the expanded foreign language curriculum and summarizes advancement undertaken by ACTFL, the Educational Testing Service, and the U.S. Department of Education in the area of oral proficiency assessment in academic settings.

Testing and Evaluation: Suggestions for a Model Program

Renate A. Schulz

"Testing is a highly specialized activity which usually requires a knowledge of statistics and computational skills which most teachers have neither the time nor the overriding desire to master."[1] This statement unfortunately characterizes the attitudes of many teachers on all instructional levels. The apparent disinterest in testing and evaluation is in almost paradoxical contrast to the frequent and regular demands made on practically any educator to make important decisions affecting their students' lives. Our tests affect student placement, grades, self-concept, career choices, degrees, certification, career opportunities, and more. Yet I know of no undergraduate and very few graduate teacher education programs that require a course in the particular problems of testing knowledge and skills acquired in the foreign language classroom.

This paper proposes a model for a comprehensive departmental testing and evaluation program consisting of four components: (1) preinstructional evaluation of students' personal variables, such as aptitude, attitudes, and individual learning styles; (2) course-specific achievement testing; (3) end-of-program, overall proficiency testing; and (4) continual program evaluation.

Preinstructional Evaluation

In discussing preinstructional student evaluation I will not go into details of attitudinal or learning-style measurement. As crucially important as these variables appear to be for foreign language learning, we lack easily usable instruments and guidelines that would enable untrained persons to interpret the test results in these areas. Until research studies provide unambivalent interpretations of test results on those measures, such testing might be better left in the domain of psychologists. Further, determining a student's learning style is most useful if we can individualize instruction to

196

take advantage of a student's preferred mode of learning. Few postsecondary programs offer such an opportunity.[2]

For attitude measurement, one instrument is commercially available: the *Jakobovits Foreign Language Attitude Questionnaire*.[3] Information on student attitudes can, of course, be helpful in course placement if a department has an intensive or accelerated track, since we know that highly positive attitudes toward a culture and toward foreign language study facilitate success in learning another language.[4] If attitudes are measured before and after instruction, the scores can also indicate whether instruction modified attitudes—one of the proclaimed goals of most programs.

Let me elaborate on the measurement of foreign language aptitude. In a survey conducted during 1977, only 1% of the responding 693 departments indicated regular administration of a foreign language aptitude test.[5] Yet aptitude scores can be of considerable usefulness for placement, recruitment, and promotional purposes. What constitutes aptitude—or talent—for learning another language? Researchers have attempted to establish relationships between success in foreign language learning and a number of personal variables, including musical ability, hearing acuity, intelligence, mathematical reasoning, and creativity. Carroll suggests that aptitude is reflected in how much time an individual needs to learn something under optimal conditions of motivation, opportunity to learn, and quality of instruction.[6]

The function of an aptitude test is to predict the statistical chances of success an individual has in learning a foreign language. Two aptitude tests are currently commercially available: the Carroll-Sapon Modern Language Aptitude Test (MLAT), developed in 1955, has a version for upper-level high school students and adults as well as one for elementary school students (EMLAT, 1967); the Pimsleur Language Aptitude Battery (PLAB), developed in 1967, can be administered to junior and senior high school students.[7] The abilities measured by these tests are phonetic coding and auditory ability (sound discrimination, sound symbol association), grammatical sensitivity (awareness of syntactical patterning of sentences and grammatical function of sentence elements), and inductive reasoning ability (identification of patterns of correspondence in meaning or grammatical form). In all three tests, the students must demonstrate memory, reading comprehension in English, learning speed, and, to some extent, knowledge of English vocabulary. The tests are in English (i.e., a student needs no background in another language), and the results are believed to be valid across all languages. The PLAB also takes grade point average and motivation into account in the aptitude formula.

Aptitude scores, if available from all freshmen, can be used by a department to build enrollment. Promising students can be specially contacted and encouraged to take foreign languages early in their studies to give them time to obtain fluency in a second language as a career adjunct skill. If testing all incoming freshmen is impossible, the test could be advertised and given to all interested students during registration week or during the first week of classes. Aptitude scores can be used for placement if a department offers accelerated, honors, individualized, or intensive language learning tracks. Further, in the absence of a diagnostic learning style measure, the information obtained on the various parts of the test can also aid in diagnosing a student's potential difficulties and can indicate the need for special assistance.

Aptitude tests should not be used to select students "out" of foreign languages. First of all, few departments are in a position to discourage anyone from enrolling; second, a score on an aptitude test is no guarantee that the person will succeed or fail in second language study. Like all statistics, aptitude norms are group measures and can only predict statistical probabilities. Other variables, such as attitude, motivation, instructor, instructional mode and materials, or time permitted for learning, influence success.[8] It is not unusual for a student in the lower percentile ranks in measured aptitude to excel in a course. Only if a department has reasons for limiting enrollment should an aptitude test be used for selection purposes. For instance, if the Reserve Officers Training Corps program at an institution wants to give fifteen of the sixty prospective officers enrolled in ROTC a basic proficiency in German and makes only an eight-week summer course available, the department would be justified—indeed wise—to use aptitude scores to find the most promising students.

If aptitude scores are not available, the best other single predictor of success in college foreign language study, as established by a study conducted by Ayers et al., is grade point average (GPA). ACT and SAT scores, although available for most students, do not appear to provide sufficiently high correlations to function as adequate predictors of success.[9]

The myth that only students with a high IQ can learn a second language is, interestingly, not verified by some psycholinguistic research. In a Canadian study, Genesee concluded that "IQ level is not the exclusive or necessarily the most important variable in predicting second language learning succcess."[10] His findings indicate that IQ scores correlate significantly with reading comprehension and control of grammatical structures but not with listening comprehension and interpersonal communication. Genesee summarizes:

> students of different academic abilities are equally able, or nearly equally able, to acquire certain communicational aspects of a second language. The implications of the results of the study are that if the goals of the second language program relate to acquisition of inter-personal communication skills, then students who have low academic or intellectual abilities are just as likely to benefit from exposure to the programs as are students with high intellectual or academic abilities. . . . On the other hand, where the goals of the second language program pertain to proficiency in aca-

demic language skills, then not all students will be equally successful in
the program.   (p. 279)

A persistent problem of most departments is placement testing. Objectives, instructional time, teacher qualifications, materials, and methods used in foreign language education differ widely nationwide on both the secondary and college levels. The only safe assumption to be made about prior language exposure is that the person with an "elementary" language background has sat from between 45 to about 180 instructional periods (depending on whether the student comes from high school or college study) in a class where the language was "taught." Lacking common national standards that define instructional levels in terms of concrete minimal objectives and proficiencies, automatic placement (i.e., counting one year of high school study as equivalent to one semester of college study) is all but impossible.

In the 1977 survey referred to previously, 437 (63%) of the 693 responding departments reported using some type of formal testing for placement. About half of those departments used a locally constructed test, while the other half administered a standardized exam to assess students' prior language background.[11] The predictive validity of placement tests—whether standardized or "home-made"—is not always satisfactory, because (1) students may not be motivated to do well on the test; (2) they may suffer from test anxiety or testing fatigue that impair performance; (3) or they may do poorly only because of the length of time that has elapsed since they studied the language (such students often do well when prior learning gets reactivated).

Studies have been conducted to find the most dependable predictors for successful placement. Dalton and King report that CEEB (College Entrance Examination Board) test scores placed students accurately 80% of the time—at least as reflected by the students' own satisfaction with placement. Other criteria, such as SAT scores, high school percentile rank, number of semesters of high school foreign language study, or high school study of a foreign language other than the one the student was seeking placement in, agreed only in 62% of the cases with student satisfaction in placement. The same study found that high school foreign language grades are not clearly related to accurate placement.[12]

The following standardized tests have been used for placement: College Entrance Examination Board tests, Admission Testing Program (ATP) Achievement Tests, Advanced Placement Program (AP) examinations in language and literature, and College Level Examination Program (CLEP) tests, all available through the Educational Testing Service (ETS) in Princeton, New Jersey. The MLA Cooperative Foreign Language Tests and the Pimsleur Achievement Tests have also been used for placement.[13]

The advantage of a locally constructed placement test is, of course, that it can be geared to specific instructional materials and objectives. The disadvantages are that constructing, administering, and grading the tests are time and energy consuming and that they apparently have no more predictive power than standardized tests that are not based on specific instructional materials. If locally constructed tests are preferable, departments might consider using techniques that have been shown by research studies to be dependable measures of global or integrative language competence. Dictations and cloze tests are examples of such techniques. They are easy to construct, easy to grade, and can easily be based on locally used instructional materials.[14]

Increasingly, departments encourage students with a high school background to continue foreign language study in college by permitting them to enroll in courses above the first introductory term without placement testing. If such a student passes the course with a specified grade (usually B or C), he or she will automatically receive credit for the preceding courses in the sequence, thus essentially receiving college credit (but no grade) for high school study. Such a self-placement procedure works relatively well at the University of Arkansas, where students can be granted up to twelve credits through this process. If a self-placement policy is in effect, however, some preventive measures need to be taken to keep students with extensive high school backgrounds—who might want to repeat the elementary courses for easy A's—out of beginning language instruction. While a thorough review can be beneficial to them, their presence and apparent ease of comprehension discourage and intimidate students without any prior language study. On the first day of classes students can be asked to complete an information sheet that indicates the students' family language background, number of semesters of prior language study, when the language was studied last, whether they have studied any other languages, and whether they have traveled abroad. Armed with that information, instructors then can individually counsel those students who might be incorrectly placed to enroll in a more appropriate course. If students are allowed to return to a lower-level class in case they find the materials too difficult, few will insist on staying in a course against an instructor's recommendations.

Whatever the placement criteria and procedures, a department should inform foreign language programs in local high schools about its policies so that the schools' teachers can articulate their instruction accordingly.

Achievement Testing

Not much needs to be said about achievement testing, since several excellent handbooks provide detailed guidance in the art and science of constructing and evaluating items to test the language skills, knowledge of grammar, vocabulary, pronunciation, and cultural and literary knowledge.[15] I wish, however, to address one important shortcoming in class-room achievement testing: the incongruity between proclaimed course objectives (particularly in lower-level language courses) and the contents of achievement tests. Omaggio, while lauding the advances made in learning theory, teaching methodology, and materials, states that too often curricu-lar revisions are made without concomitant changes in evaluation proce-dures and that the gap between classroom goals and their measurement is increasing rather than decreasing.[16]

A personal experience will illustrate this discrepancy. Some time ago I participated in the evaluation of a foreign language program. The team of evaluators was presented with a highly sophisticated statement in which the institutional goals and objectives had been coordinated with the goals and objectives of the foreign language program. Of the dozen or so program objectives, about one fourth related to cultural insights and awareness, about an equal number had to do with the ability to communicate with per-sons from other cultures, and several dealt with insights into language and communication in general and the improvement of English communication skills in particular. When asked for copies of tests that measured to what extent program goals were being reached, the response was embarrassed silence and excuses. It turned out that the classroom tests (unfortunately, like those in most other departments) required students to transform the present into the past, to write from dictation, to construct grammatically correct sentences from given components, to answer questions based on cues provided, and so forth. Not once did we encounter an item in the final course exams that tested students' ability to communicate, their knowledge of the culture, or their insights into the communication process in general.

The lack of face validity (i.e., the discrepancy between course objec-tives and test) is evident not only in teacher-constructed tests; it is equally visible in the tests—supposedly constructed by specialists—that accompany our commercially available instructional materials. I cannot overemphasize the importance of the classroom test as indicator of the teaching and learn-ing that goes on in a course. The test gives concrete evidence of a teacher's instructional objectives and priorities (conscious or subconscious), his or her view of language and communication, as well as his or her (conscious or subconscious) conception of how languages are learned. On the stu-dents' side the test indicates what is important to learn and to remember, what they should study and emphasize in their review, and, of course, what they have learned.

One other point needs to be raised while on the topic of achievement testing: the need for formative, criterion-referenced testing as well as sum-mative, norm-referenced testing in language courses. Our teaching and testing is still predominantly based on a sequential, behaviorist model of language learning. That is, in each chapter, we teach, practice, test—and as-sume that students will know and retain forever—a number of carefully sequenced and graded phrases, vocabulary items, and grammatical structures without systematic reentry in subsequent chapters. This sequential learning is similar to that expected in a chronologically arranged world history course where Ramses II is followed by Alexander the Great who is followed by Caesar who is followed by Charlemagne who is followed by Napoleon who is followed by Hitler; or in a country-by-country-without-return geography class, where you will never again encounter Afghanistan if you happened to have been absent on the day "it" was "taught."

Unfortunately, student "output" is not identical to teacher "input," and language learning is not a strictly sequential process. It resembles more a spiral process, where components are constantly reentered, reviewed, enlarged on, forgotten, reentered, reviewed, enlarged on, and so forth. (See the model below.) Our teaching and testing need to allow for this reentry processing in language acquisition. One way this can be accomplished in testing is through formative, criterion-referenced testing procedures. Such testing assumes that (1) specific objectives underlie each test, and (2) each objective needs to be mastered to a certain degree before a student progresses to new material. Criterion-referenced tests are, therefore, essentially evaluated on a pass-fail basis (though the "pass" can, of course,

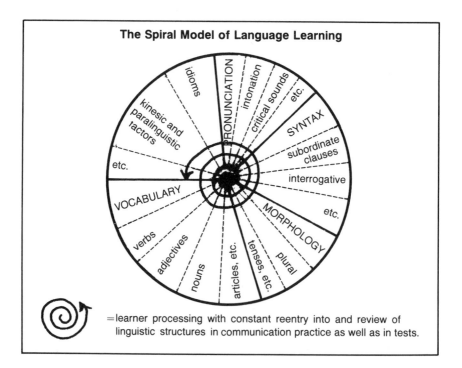

The Spiral Model of Language Learning

= learner processing with constant reentry into and review of linguistic structures in communication practice as well as in tests.

distinguish among excellent, good, or average performances). Such testing also assumes that students are permitted to retake a test (or parts thereof), if they have not yet mastered whatever is being tested. This type of testing is the basis of an individualized, self-paced program.

Summative, norm-referenced testing, on the other hand, compares a student's achievement with the achievement of classmates or with norms derived from testing large national, regional, or institutional samples. The information derived from a formative, criterion-referenced test is: Mary has or has not mastered adjective endings. The information derived from a summative, norm-referenced test is: Mary ranks fifth in a class of thirty in her ability to decline adjective endings.

Practically any test can be used for formative or for summative purposes. Both types of tests have their place in the foreign language class. If, during the term of instruction, the test is to serve diagnostic, pedagogical purposes, students should be allowed to retake it until they can demonstrate sufficient mastery of the skills tested. At the end of a course, a summative test is in order; it provides a summary assessment of students' learning, ranks their achievement, and compares it with results achieved in similar courses by other students.

Proficiency Testing

The lack of valid and reliable procedures and instruments for testing foreign language proficiency is probably the profession's most serious evaluation problem. Proficiency, as opposed to achievement, testing is not related to specific course content. Rather, it indicates the overall ability a student has acquired by whatever means (e.g., formal instruction, self-study, travel or study abroad, contact with speakers of the target language). Our profession is in dire need of a battery of criterion-referenced proficiency tests through which we can establish minimal national standards for our graduates, for our teachers, and for those persons who need to use their foreign language skills for careers in government, commerce, and industry. In addition, we need to establish what constitutes realistic, desirable "proficiency" at various levels of instruction and find means of measuring that construct reliably in an educational setting.

Among the many problems of testing language proficiency are the difficulties encountered in devising tests that truly sample communicative abilities, establishing criteria for measuring, and dealing with time and cost constraints in administering such tests, since at least oral proficiency needs to be tested individually. Achieving objectivity in evaluations and training persons to administer and score such tests present further problems.[17]

In response to recommendations made by the President's Commission on Foreign Language and International Studies, ACTFL, in collaboration with the Educational Testing Service and government language training agencies, has attempted to adapt the Foreign Service Institute (FSI) oral proficiency interview for use at the secondary and postsecondary levels of language instruction. Judith Liskin-Gasparro discusses this adaptation in the next section.

The advantages of the FSI oral interview are (1) the exam achieves high face validity by examining candidates in a natural, communicative situation; (2) the ratings, performed by specially trained and experienced evaluators, provide a reliable measure of a candidate's oral proficiency; and (3) the result of the exam (i.e., the rating based on five proficiency levels) is clearly and meaningfully defined in terms of actual, real-life competencies.[18]

Another promising development in proficiency testing is the *Zertifikat Deutsch als Fremdsprache (ZDaF),* an internationally used test of proficiency in German, developed by the Goethe Institute in collaboration with the Volkshochschulverband (Association for Continuing Education) of the Federal Republic of Germany. In the United States the examination is, unfortunately, available only in German. In the Federal Republic similar tests are available for Spanish and French. In contrast to the FSI oral interview, the *ZDaF* measures proficiency in all four language skill areas separately and has a written part (approximately three hours) and an oral part (approximately fifteen minutes). The test measures reading and listening comprehension by multiple-choice questions based on written and spoken texts; writing ability by a letter to be written by the student according to specific instructions and by a multiple-choice cloze test; and speaking proficiency by the student's performance in a short, structured interview on a selected topic and in a number of simulated communicative situations where the student has to make a situationally appropriate response to the cue given by the test administrator. Several United States institutions are making the *ZDaF* available to students and are reporting very satisfactory results not just in student achievement but also in public relations and visibility for the department.[19]

Program Evaluation

Some guidance in program evaluation can be obtained from Jarvis and Adams, *Evaluating a Second Language Program.*[20] I do, however, wish to point to two major weaknesses that I have encountered repeatedly in my experience as program evaluator at several secondary and postsecondary institutions: the lack of comparative statistics on student achievement and proficiency and the lack of feedback from graduates.

Most of us, at some time or other during our careers, have gone through the tedious, time- and energy-consuming process of administration-mandated program evaluation. We have composed voluminous documents listing the courses taught, the staff, their training and accomplishments, enrollment statistics for each course, and the number of graduating majors and minors a year. We also calculated student-teacher ratios and FTE course loads for instructional staff; we inventoried functional (and nonfunctional) hardware and software as well as the library holdings; we listed films, lectures, festivals, and other "extracurricular" community involvement and service activities. Evidence of scholarly activity of the faculty is provided by their publications and by their presentations at meetings of learned societies. Service to the community is implied in outreach programs. But in the area of student learning—the major function of the university—supportive evidence is often missing.

In the 1977 survey referred to earlier, only 27% of the respondents reported giving regular, systematic, summative, departmental achievement tests.[21] A number of departments with large multisection undergraduate courses do not even give common final examinations to all sections of one course. Each instructor (often an untrained and inexperienced teaching assistant) devises his or her own summative test, in spite of the need for each language course to be carefully articulated with the next. In my opinion this practice borders on educational irresponsibility. Only 13% of the responding departments administered a standardized test, such as the MLA Cooperative Test, College Board Achievement Tests, National Teacher Examination, or the Graduate Record Exam, for comparison of their students' achievement with national norms. The nineteen institutions selected by that study as particularly "successful" could document their success mainly by citing enrollment increases; only one could provide evidence of increasing student achievement.

Evaluation of learning *must* be part of the measurement of program effectiveness. But not only do few departments systematically collect comparative achievement or proficiency data (either comparative within the program from year to year or comparative with national or regional norms); fewer yet attempt to collect evidence of program effectiveness from graduates after they leave the institution. By asking questions such as: Did they find jobs in their major area of study? Did they continue with graduate training? Did they feel adequately prepared for work or graduate study?, departments can gain important information. Admittedly, it is difficult in our mobile society to keep in touch with former students. Perhaps an annual departmental newsletter that requests an update of students' addresses could facilitate a periodic survey (every five years?) of recent graduates' opinions and suggestions regarding program effectiveness.

Conclusion and Recommendations

Testing and evaluation must be a priority in foreign language departments, with attention given to the congruity between objectives, both instructional and program, and required test performance by students. "Teaching for the test" is not wrong, provided the test requires a valid sampling of knowledge and skills to be mastered in a course. As much as possible, departments should make available aptitude tests and diagnostic tests of learning styles to help students assess their capabilities and to help teachers provide personalized help. Departments need to give formative, criterion-referenced tests to permit students to gain mastery of specific discrete-point knowledge and skills as well as summative, norm-referenced tests to measure final course achievement and to compare, over time, student learning and effectiveness of instruction. Since academic grades or credits are poor indicators of proficiency, departments need to support actively national efforts to standardize and improve proficiency testing, and they should incorporate these tests into their curriculum as soon as available.

A visual representation of the proposed evaluation model may help departments in assessing current practices and in planning and implementing improved evaluation procedures in the future.

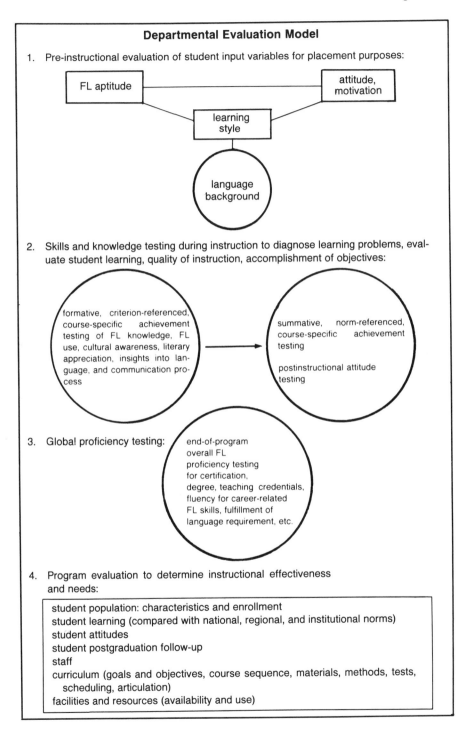

Departmental Evaluation Model

1. Pre-instructional evaluation of student input variables for placement purposes:

> FL aptitude — attitude, motivation
>
> learning style
>
> language background

2. Skills and knowledge testing during instruction to diagnose learning problems, evaluate student learning, quality of instruction, accomplishment of objectives:

> formative, criterion-referenced, course-specific achievement testing of FL knowledge, FL use, cultural awareness, literary appreciation, insights into language, and communication process
>
> → summative, norm-referenced, course-specific achievement testing
>
> postinstructional attitude testing

3. Global proficiency testing:

> end-of-program overall FL proficiency testing for certification, degree, teaching credentials, fluency for career-related FL skills, fulfillment of language requirement, etc.

4. Program evaluation to determine instructional effectiveness and needs:

> student population: characteristics and enrollment
> student learning (compared with national, regional, and institutional norms)
> student attitudes
> student postgraduation follow-up
> staff
> curriculum (goals and objectives, course sequence, materials, methods, tests, scheduling, articulation)
> facilities and resources (availability and use)

Notes

[1]Ronald Mackay, Bruce Barkman, and R. R. Jordan, eds., *Reading in a Second Language: Hypotheses, Organization, and Practice* (Rowley, Mass.: Newbury, 1979), p. ix.

[2]Readers interested in the measurement of learning styles might want to consult Helen S. Lepke, "Assessing Individual Learning Styles: An Analysis of Five Instruments," *Foreign Language Annals*, 11 (1978), 657–68; and the following articles in Renate A. Schulz, ed., *Personalizing Foreign Language Instruction: Learning Styles and Teaching Options* (Skokie, Ill.: National Textbook, 1977): Derek N. Nunney, "Educational Cognitive Style: A Basis for Personalizing Foreign Language Instruction," pp. 1–14; Helen S. Lepke, "Discovering Student Learning Styles through Cognitive Style Mapping," pp. 15–20; and Harry Reinert, "ELSIE Is No Bull! or, On Utilizing Information concerning Student Learning Styles," pp. 21–28.

[3]Copies can be obtained from the Northeast Conference on the Teaching of Foreign Languages, Box 623, Middlebury, VT 05753.

[4]Robert C. Gardner and Wallace E. Lambert, *Attitudes and Motivation in Second-Language Learning* (Rowley, Mass.: Newbury, 1972).

[5]Renate A. Schulz, *Options for Undergraduate Foreign Language Programs: Four-Year and Two-Year Colleges* (New York: MLA, 1979), p. 9.

[6]John B. Carroll, "Learning Theory for the Classroom Teacher," in Gilbert A. Jarvis, ed., *The Challenge of Communication* (Skokie, Ill.: National Textbook, 1974), pp. 113–49.

[7]All three tests are available from the Psychological Corp., 757 Third Ave., New York, NY 10017.

[8]See Carroll, "Learning Theory for the Classroom Teacher."

[9]Jerry B. Ayers, Florinda A. Bustamante, and Philip J. Campana, "Prediction of Success in College Foreign Language Courses," *Educational and Psychological Measurement*, 33 (1973), 939–42.

[10]F. Genesee, "The Role of Intelligence in Second Language Learning," *Language Learning*, 26 (1976), 278.

[11]Schulz, *Options for Undergraduate Foreign Language Programs*, p. 9.

[12]Starrette Dalton and Larry D. King, "Foreign Language Placement: An Alternative Validation Procedure," *Educational and Psychological Measurement*, 34 (1974), 915–21.

[13]The MLA Cooperative Foreign Language Test in French, German, Italian, Russian, and Spanish are available in two difficulty levels (intended for administration after two and four years of high school study) from Addison-Wesley Publishing Co., South St., Reading, MA 01867; the Pimsleur Modern Foreign Language Proficiency Tests in French, German, and Spanish are available in two difficulty levels (intended for administration after one and two years of high school study) from the Psychological Corp., 757 Third Ave., New York, NY 10017.

[14]In cloze procedure testing every nth word is deleted from a passage of running prose and replaced with a blank of standard length. The student must complete the text by supplying the missing words that logically fit the meaning of the passage. See, for instance, John W. Oller, Jr., "Cloze Tests of Second Language Proficiency and What They Measure," *Language Learning*, 23 (1973), 105–18; and Joseph A.

Wipf, "Selective Deletions with Multiple Cues: A Variation of the Cloze Procedure as a Technique for Teaching and Testing Reading," *Unterrichtspraxis,* 14 (1981), 208–11.

[15]See, for instance, John L. D. Clark, *Foreign Language Testing: Theory and Practice* (Philadelphia: Center for Curriculum Development, 1972); David P. Harris, *Testing English as a Second Language* (New York: McGraw-Hill, 1969); and Rebecca M. Valette, *Modern Language Testing,* 2nd ed. (New York: Harcourt, 1977).

[16]Alice C. Omaggio, "Priorities in Classroom Testing for the 1980s," *Proceedings of the National Conference on Professional Priorities, November 1980, Boston, Mass.* (Hastings-on-Hudson, N.Y.: ACTFL Materials Center), pp. 47–53.

[17]See Walter H. Bartz, *Testing Oral Communication in the Foreign Language Classroom,* Language in Education: Theory and Practice, No. 17 (Arlington, Va.: Center for Applied Linguistics, 1979); and section on evaluation in *Proceedings of the National Conference on Professional Priorities,* pp. 40–54.

[18]For an explanation of the Foreign Service Institute rating procedure, see Rebecca M. Valette, *Modern Language Testing,* 2nd ed. (New York: Harcourt, 1977), pp. 157–60. See also Howard T. Young, "On Using Foreign Service Institute Tests and Standards on Campuses," in James Frith, ed., *Measuring Spoken Language Proficiency,* (Washington, D.C.: Georgetown Univ. Press, 1980); and the chapters by Clark, Graham, Lowe, Reschke, and Sollenberger in John L. D. Clark, ed., *Direct Testing of Speaking Proficiency: Theory and Application* (Princeton, N.J.: Educational Testing Service, 1978).

[19]Gerd K. Schneider, "The Place of 'Zertifikat Deutsch' in the German Curriculum," paper presented at the 96th annual convention of the Modern Language Association of America, N.Y., Dec. 1981; see also Oliver Finley Graves, "The *Zertifikat Deutsch als Fremdsprache:* An Alabama Experience," *Unterrichtspraxis,* 13 (1980), 211–16. Departments interested in more information on the *ZDaF* should contact one of the regional branches of the Goethe Institute.

[20]Gilbert A. Jarvis and Shirley J. Adams, *Evaluating a Second Language Program,* Language in Education: Theory and Practice, No. 19 (Arlington, Va.: Center for Applied Linguistics, 1979).

[21]Schulz, *Options for Undergraduate Foreign Language Programs,* see note 5, p. 9.

Proficiency Testing, Classroom Testing, and National Standards

Judith E. Liskin-Gasparro

"Communication in its most simplistic form is the exchange of information by two parties."[1] This is what language instruction and language learning are all about—the acquisition of the ability to communicate, to transmit information in another tongue. As video technology replaces the printing press as the foremost medium of communication, the skills of active communication, of listening and speaking, become increasingly more important.

Until recently, modern language education espoused the goals and methods of classical language instruction—the development of literacy skills, primarily reading, the ability to translate, and a knowledge of grammar. It was thought that the mental discipline required to memorize and apply grammatical rules was in itself highly desirable and that reading literary texts in another language was the ultimate goal of language study.

Oral skills long had a very low priority in most foreign language programs. It is notable that the concerns of national security, raised by World War II and later by Sputnik I, stimulated more practical foreign language instruction. Then the great innovations of the 1960s, the advent of the audiolingual approach and the establishment of the NDEA institutes, changed the face of language teaching in this country.

Some twenty years have passed since the heyday of NDEA and audiolingualism, and we still find that most students leave high school and college unable to communicate in a foreign language. The promise of audiolingualism, the ability to communicate with native speakers of another language, has not been realized. The audiolingual approach emphasized memorization of dialogues and manipulation of structures in drills with the expectation that these discrete pieces of knowledge would serve as building blocks for creative language use. Over time, however, experience showed that students were most likely to simply retain these bits and pieces of language in their discrete form, without being able to integrate them into the language as a whole. There was no natural leap from these memorized lines in artificial contexts to creative language use in real contexts.

At the same time, many promises were made about what miracles the audiolingual approach could work. Perhaps the most serious shortcoming of the language movement of the 1960s were these unrealistic promises of "fluency," "bilingualism," and "native-like pronunciation." It was eventually realized that no methodology, texts, or equipment could possibly turn out "fluent" or "bilingual" speakers after four or even six years of foreign language instruction.

Defining realistic goals for foreign language study may be the single most important task of foreign language educators in the 1980s. The fact is that second language learning takes much longer than people think. Studying a foreign language is akin to studying a musical instrument or gymnastics; the skills involved in competent performance take many years of energetic practice and hard work. The academic subject most similar to foreign languages in this regard is mathematics. No one expects students to be proficient at mathematics after two or three years of study; indeed, students study mathematics for almost the entire twelve years of their elementary and secondary school careers just to become conversant with the basic uses of mathematics in daily life.

Measuring Language Proficiency

How, then, do we measure how much foreign language an individual actually knows? What are the standards, and what instruments can be used? Most classroom tests are achievement tests, that is, tests that assess to what degree students have mastered the content of a course of study. They usually test discrete structural and lexical items. National examinations, such as those developed by the College Board, ETS, and the American Associations of Teachers of German, French, and Spanish, are generally achievement tests. Results are expressed as percentages of correct answers or as scaled scores that compare students to one another.

As Jones points out, language testing after World War II became more a science than an art.[2] Multiple-choice and fill-in questions gave tests higher reliability and became the local and national norm. Examinations requiring free responses, such as essays or taped speech samples, were eschewed both on scientific grounds (the test-retest reliability was relatively low) and on practical grounds (such tests are time-consuming and expensive to evaluate).

More recently, the foreign language teaching and testing professions have shown renewed interest in integrative, or proficiency-based, instruction and evaluation. Although the 1960s goal of "functional bilingualism" is now seen as unrealistically high, it is still possible to reorient instruction toward training in practical communicative ability in addition to linguistic accuracy and skill.

In the United States today language study outside traditional academic settings is burgeoning. Classes in the proprietary language schools and adult education programs are virtually teeming with adults who want to learn another language for purposes of travel, career, or personal enrichment. Most are former high school and college language students who all have the same complaint: "I took (two, three) years of (French, German, Spanish) and I can't say a thing." This interest in foreign language study, along with the report of the President's Commission on Foreign Language and International Studies and its call for increased national foreign language competence, is all the more reason to reconsider the goals and evaluation methods of foreign language instruction.

There is tremendous interest now around the country in proficiency-based instruction, also referred to as instruction for "communicative competence." A proficiency-based approach takes into consideration not only the linguistic accuracy of an utterance but also the success of the speaker in communicating the desired information. Nevertheless, this approach stresses communication *through* language, not *in spite of* language. Smiles and gestures may get you a hotel room in Brussels or a meal in Caracas, but language, not nonverbal signals, is required for communicative competence.

While most wide-scale test development has tended to be rather conservative, United States government agencies have for the last thirty or so years been developing, refining, and using a proficiency-based performance test, conducted as a face-to-face interview, to measure the ability to speak a foreign language. This procedure—known variously as the oral proficiency interview, the FSI interview test, and the ILR (Interagency Language Roundtable) test—has measured speaking ability against descriptions of language use of professional adults in government service. Since 1956 the government's oral interview test has qualified 60,000 State Department and other government employees to fill posts in some sixty languages around the world with a recognized and readily understood proficiency label (S-2, S-3, etc.).

Among nongovernment agencies, Educational Testing Service was the first to adopt the interview and government definitions. Under contract from the government, ETS used the system for a number of years to train the examiners who certified the language proficiency of Peace Corps volunteers. Outside the government, ETS has also trained examiners to test and certify the language proficiency of bilingual and ESL teachers in California, Florida, Illinois, New Jersey, and Texas.

How does the oral proficiency interview work? In the classic government test one or two testers conduct a face-to-face interview with a candidate for ten to thirty minutes. The resulting speech sample is rated on a scale of 0 (no functional ability in the language) to 5 (ability equivalent to that of an educated native speaker of the language), with pluses given for performances stronger than halfway to the next level. The ratings (there are twelve in all) are properly thought of as ranges rather than as points on the scale, since each rating can cover a breadth of weaker and stronger performances.

The language functions, subject-matter areas (content), and accuracy requirements for each level are set forth in the government's Spoken Language Proficiency Definitions, as follows:

Elementary Proficiency

S-1 *Able to satisfy routine travel needs and minimum courtesy requirements.* Can ask and answer questions on very familiar topics; within the scope of the very limited language experience can understand simple questions and statements, allowing for slowed speech, repetition or paraphrase; speaking vocabulary inadequate to express anything but the most elementary needs; errors in pronunciation and grammar are frequent, but can be understood by a native speaker used to dealing with foreigners attempting to speak the language; while topics which are "very familiar" and elementary needs vary considerably from individual to individual, any person at the S-1 level should be able to order a simple meal, ask for shelter or lodging, ask for simple directions, make purchases and tell time.

Limited Working Proficiency

S-2 *Able to satisfy routine social demands and limited work requirements.* Can handle most social situations including introductions and casual conversations about current events, as well as work, family and autobiographical information; can handle limited work requirements, needing help in handling any complications or difficulties; can get the gist of most conversations on nontechnical subjects (i.e., topics that require no specialized knowledge); and has a speaking vocabulary sufficient to respond simply with some circumlocutions; accent, though often quite faulty, is intelligible; can usually handle elementary constructions quite accurately but does not have thorough control of grammar.

Professional Proficiency

S-3 *Able to speak the language with sufficient structural accuracy and vocabulary to participate effectively in most formal and informal conversations on practical, social and professional topics.* Can discuss particular interests and special fields of competence with reasonable ease; comprehension is quite complete for a normal rate of speech; general vocabulary is broad enough that rarely has to grope for a word; accent may be obviously foreign; control of grammar good; errors virtually never interfere with understanding and rarely disturb the native speaker.

Representational Proficiency

S-4 *Able to use the language fluently and accurately on all levels normally pertinent to professional needs.* Can understand and participate in any conversation within the range of own personal and professional experience with a high degree of fluency and precision of vocabulary; would rarely be taken for a native speaker, but can respond appropriately even in unfamiliar situations; errors of pronunciation and grammar quite rare; can handle informal interpreting from and into the language.

Native or Bilingual Proficiency

S-5 *Speaking proficiency equivalent to that of an educated native speaker.* Has complete fluency in the language such that speech on all levels is fully accepted by educated native speakers in all of its features, including breadth of vocabulary and idiom, colloquialisms, and pertinent cultural references.

It is important to note that the levels are not equidistant points on a scale. There is no mean score. The distance between levels 0 and 1, for example, is much smaller than the distance between levels 1 and 2, which in turn is still smaller than the distance between levels 2 and 3. The distance between level 3 and level 4, in terms of both quantity and accuracy of language and probable time needed to reach each level, is so great that it is frankly impossible for people to achieve level 4 proficiency through classroom instruction.

Development of an Oral Proficiency Scale for Academic Use*

Until quite recently, the oral interview was virtually unknown to the academic profession. In 1979 interest in using the interview test to assess language proficiency of students in secondary schools and colleges sprang up in several quarters, sparked in part by the recommendation of the President's Commission that national goals for language study be formulated. It was recognized that the government proficiency scale, covering the whole spectrum of speaking ability, had limited applicability to academic language learners. Most students, even those who had spent a summer or a year abroad, would receive ratings below level 3 on the ILR scale.

John B. Carroll, in a study reported in *Foreign Language Annals* (1 [December 1967], 131–51), looked at the foreign language proficiency of senior majors of French, German, Russian, and Spanish. Most were rated 2 or 2+. Since most students of foreign languages are not majors nearing graduation from college, it seems safe to assume that secondary school and college foreign language teachers will be primarily interested in ILR levels 0 and 1.

---

*This section is adapted from ch. 1 of the *ETS Proficiency Testing Manual,* 1982.

The ILR scale as it is used in the government makes provision for five definable ranges of proficiency between levels 0 and 2: 0, 0+, 1, 1+, and 2. As previously discussed, these ranges are not equidistant from each other but rather represent increasing increments of proficiency as one moves up the scale. Thus levels 0 and 0+ are relatively close to each other, while the gap between levels 1+ and 2 is relatively great. An informal study conducted by ETS, in which oral proficiency interviews were administered to approximately thirty secondary school Spanish students, confirmed the intuition that the descriptive ranges were so far apart that the scale did not effectively discriminate among students whom teachers would judge to be significantly different in oral ability.

The Foreign Service Institute held a series of three Testing Kit Workshops in 1979–80 for approximately seventy college teachers of French and Spanish. The faculty members were introduced to the ILR system of oral proficiency assessment and were trained to interview and rate. Support was offered by mail and telephone to the professors when they returned to their campuses and began to test their students.

One major result of both the informal ETS study and the FSI workshop was consensus on the need to expand the lower end of the ILR scale to make it more applicable to students in traditional academic environments. Teachers wanted more points between levels 0 and 2 so that they could register improvements in performance that were not great enough to earn a different ILR rating.

While the FSI was conducting its workshops, ETS was approaching the question of an academically oriented speaking scale from another perspective. In response to expressions of interest from the British Council, the English Speaking Union, and German and Japanese agencies, ETS sponsored a small conference in June 1979 to discuss the possibility and desirability of establishing a "common yardstick" (or yardsticks) to describe performance in one or more language skills. At this conference and in subsequent meetings, participants discussed descriptive scales of language proficiency developed in various countries and by international agencies, such as the Council of Europe, and prepared new draft scales. On the basis of these initial activities, ETS requested and received funding from the International Research and Studies Division of the U.S. Department of Education for a project entitled "A Common Metric for Language Proficiency." The principal result of this project was the development of an expanded lower end of the ILR scale. Specifically, draft descriptions were written for three ranges between levels 0 and 1 and three ranges between levels 1 and 2.

Most recently, leadership in oral proficiency assessment in academic settings has been assumed by the American Council on the Teaching of Foreign Languages. ACTFL had also received a grant from the International Research and Studies Division of the U.S. Department of Education for work in the area of language proficiency. The project seeks to define language-specific proficiency-based goals of instruction for the four language skills and culture. The ETS Common Yardstick oral interaction definitions, which dovetailed with the ACTFL project, were turned over to ACTFL for further refinement and for field testing when the Common Yardstick project came to an end in December 1981.

ACTFL in turn asked Pardee Lowe, Jr., of the ILR to investigate the validity and accuracy of the ETS descriptions. Assisted by funds and professional collaboration from ETS, Lowe designed a research project for French and Spanish to determine (1) whether independent raters would rank in the same order (weakest to strongest) a group of tapes known to be at the same ILR level and (2) whether tapes known to be at a given ILR level could be separated according to the expanded intralevel descriptions. As of this writing, preliminary findings are as follows: (1) it is indeed possible to make fine distinctions among linguistic performances at a given ILR level; (2) experienced testers will agree on these distinctions; and (3) the expanded intralevel descriptions are accurate descriptions of linguistic performance.

These expanded descriptions have been termed the "ACTFL/ETS Provisional Speaking Definitions." Under a grant to ACTFL from the U.S. Department of Education entitled "Professional Development: Oral Proficiency Testing and Rating," the definitions were taught for the first time in February 1982 to a group of thirty college teachers of French and Spanish. A second workshop in February 1983 extended the same training to professors of German and Italian.

Levels 0, 1, and 2 have for academic use been renamed Novice, Intermediate, and Advanced. It was decided to truncate the scale at level 3, designating as Superior all speech samples at levels that the government would term sufficient for professional purposes.

At this writing, participants in the ACTFL Oral Proficiency Assessment Project have interviewed and rated large numbers of students. The taped interviews have been evaluated for accuracy of rating and effectiveness of elicitation techniques. The participants had direct and frequent contact with the ETS and ILR trainers and with ACTFL for the remainder of the academic year.

Newly funded projects and proposals by ACTFL to the U.S. Department of Education, to the Fund for the Improvement of Post-Secondary Education (FIPSE), and to the National Endowment for the Humanities plan to extend the work in proficiency assessment to other languages, include secondary school and community colleges in the efforts, and turn the focus from techniques of oral proficiency assessment to the implications of these techniques for curriculum in foreign language classrooms and to proficiency in other language skills and in culture.

Teaching Oral Proficiency in the Classroom

The government oral proficiency interview, even with the academically oriented ACTFL-ETS modifications, will be nothing more than an interesting new test unless it can be related to the goals and methods of classroom teaching. Any discussion of tests and testing should begin with some basic questions:

1. What are the goals of each of my courses? What do I want students to be able to *do* with the language after one semester, two semesters, or four semesters of study?
2. Are these the same goals that the students have? Are they expecting to "speak like a native" after two semesters?
3. Am I teaching them what I want them to learn?
4. Am I testing them on what I teach?

These questions, basic as they may be, are not easy to answer. Although language proficiency has generally been a stated goal of language instruction for years, the meaning and degree of this "proficiency" have not been clearly defined. In many institutions proficiency means the number of courses taken or the score obtained on the College Board Achievement Test or on a placement-exemption examination. The University of Pennsylvania, under the leadership of Barbara Freed, assistant dean for languages, has taken a giant step toward a proficiency-based language requirement and away from a time-based requirement. By expecting students to complete the language requirement by attaining a particular level of proficiency rather than by taking a given number of semesters of study, the department has recognized that what counts is linguistic performance, not simple persistence.

The importance of testing what is taught cannot be overemphasized. Students, especially today, tend to be extremely pragmatic. If they think that something will not be tested on the final exam, chances are they will choose not to study and not to learn it.

If the testing of functional language skill is adopted by the academic teaching profession—a likelihood supported by recent activity in this area—then it will be necessary to do more in the classroom to teach functional language ability. Experience in testing secondary school and college students indicates that level 1 (Intermediate in the ACTFL-ETS nomenclature) proficiency is a realistic and laudable goal for most students. Students who reach level 1 can survive in the target language. They can create with the language, combining and recombining the pieces they have mastered to carry on a simple conversation. They can describe persons or everyday objects in short sentences; they can ask and answer questions; and they can get themselves into, through, and out of an everyday situation (giving directions, inviting a friend to a party, getting a room in a hotel, buying stamps at the post office). In fact, the ILR level 1 description can be separated into a series of "can do" statements. An expanded version of these statements might well constitute an outline of an intermediate language course.

Can ask and answer questions on highly familiar topics

> weather
> calendar (day, month, year)
> time
> names of objects
> family members
> daily activities

Can enumerate in short sentences; give simple descriptions

> persons (height, hair color, eye color, relationship, profession, etc.)
> objects (function [simple], size, shape, color, etc.)
> clothing (name, size, color)
> house (number and names of rooms, contents of rooms, colors, etc.)

Can order a simple meal

> knows basic courtesy formulas to use with waiter
> names of foods
> numbers and prices

Can ask for shelter or lodging

> availability
> requirements of room (number of persons, private bath, etc.)
> price
> method of payment

Can ask for simple directions

> knows vocabulary for left, right, straight, corner, stop sign, etc.
> advice on modes of transportation
> time needed to reach destination

Can make purchases

> color
> size
> price

There is a natural tension in language teaching between training for linguistic correctness and training for sheer communicative ability ("getting the message across"). Individuals who learn their languages in academic programs traditionally become more linguistically correct speakers, strong in grammar but relatively weak in fluency and vocabulary. Those who learn a language in the target country without formal training often become "street" speakers—very strong in fluency, in certain areas of vocabulary, and perhaps in pronunciation, but weak in grammar. Since foreign language teaching does not aim to produce speakers of pidgin-French or pidgin-German, teachers need to combine "skill-getting" exercises and instruction in conjunction with "skill-using" activities.[3]

Teachers are very familiar with typical skill-getting activities—homework assignments, exercises, drills, vocabulary practice, and so forth. Mastering discrete building blocks of language is very important if students' linguistic ability is to progress beyond the point of "Me Tarzan, you Jane." It is, therefore, fully appropriate that some classroom testing be devoted to determining whether students are learning the material being taught through the skill-building activities. If, however, a goal of a language course is that students progress to the point of Tarzan's introduction of himself to Jane, students have to engage in skill-using activities in the classroom. They have to be instructed in how to use the language to communicate basic needs and information, such as those sketched out in the expanded level 1 description above. Conversational exercises and activities need to be set up in such a way that students are required to supply the details themselves, filling in the bare outline (supplied by the teacher) by their own creative efforts. The teacher can set the stage, offer a few suggestions, and let the students take it from there.

The oral interview at level 1 requires examinees to show that they can successfully get into, through, and out of everyday situations. Skill-using activities in the classroom should make extensive use of such situations. For example, a student is handed an index card containing the following instructions (in English, in order not to give away the necessary vocabulary):

> You call a friend to invite her to a party.
> Include the following:
> 1. Day, time, and place
> 2. Who will be there
> 3. Type of party
> 4. Directions to your house
> 5. Ask her to bring cheese or
>   a bottle of wine.

Two students could take the roles. Both would have to ask and answer questions and demonstrate the ability to handle level 1 functions. There are many such situational conversations, even at this relatively low level.

Testing speaking ability is clearly more time-consuming and more subjective than the multiple-choice tests scored by computers. The oral interview at level 1 or lower can be administered by an experienced tester in less than ten minutes. Even so, ten minutes a student adds up to a lot of time, especially if the interview or like procedures become regular classroom practices. But if we believe that speaking is important, then time has to be made for it to be taught and tested.

Short of face-to-face interview between teacher and student, conversational situations among groups of students can be set up so that the speech of several students can be evaluated at the same time. (Telling students ahead of time that they will be graded in large part on the amount they speak will contribute notably to the success of the procedure.) Two excellent publications, *Oral Communication Testing: A Handbook for the Foreign Language Teacher,* by Cathy Linder, and "Testing Oral Communication in the Foreign Language Classroom," by Walter H. Bartz (see bibliography), offer sound information and advice on question types and scoring for oral tests.

In a test that measures students' ability to communicate, discrete errors cannot be the primary criterion for scoring. The government's level 1 proficiency description, for example, contains the following accuracy requirement: ". . . errors in pronunciation and grammar are frequent, but can be understood by a native speaker used to dealing with foreigners attempting to speak the language." For students at this level, then, only the basics of structure and syntax are required, just enough for them to make themselves understood to a sympathetic native speaker. In fact, errors that show that a concept has been mastered, even if the exception has not, might be cause for celebration at this level and would certainly be less serious than errors of basic syntax that would make it hard for the student to be understood by a native speaker. For example, a student who says "la problema" in Spanish has demonstrated understanding of the major principle of gender identification of nouns, even if he or she has not yet learned that certain words of Greek origin ending in -*ema* are masculine. A much more serious error would be something like "C'est Jean que je vais avec" (It's John I'm going with), a sentence that might well confuse a native speaker.

The government oral proficiency test holds great promise for foreign language instruction not just as a way to evaluate speaking ability but also, to use ACTFL's terminology, as a stepladder of student progress. Carefully designed speaking tests can provide both benchmarks of progress and diagnostic information on areas that need improvement. For example, students who have been in language courses for several years and have learned to conjugate verbs in many tenses may still only be able to ask and answer simple questions in the present tense. Such information can be very useful to teachers in helping them decide how much and in what order material should be presented. The potential for insights into the teaching of functional language ability is the real value of the oral interview.

Notes

Helen L. Jorstad, "Testing as Communication," in Gilbert A. Jarvis, ed., *The Challenge of Communication,* ACTFL Foreign Language Education series, vol. 6 (Skokie, Ill.: National Textbook, 1974), p. 223.

²Randall L. Jones, "Testing: A Vital Connection," in June K. Phillips, ed., *The Language Connection: From the Classroom to the World,* ACTFL Foreign Language Education series, vol. 9 (Skokie, Ill.: National Textbook, 1977), p. 238.

³Rebecca M. Valette and Cathy Linder, "Measuring the Variables and Testing the Outcomes," in June K. Phillips, ed., *Building an Experience—Building for Success,* ACTFL Foreign Language Education series, vol. 10 (Skokie, Ill.: National Textbook, 1979), pp. 213–14.

Chapter Seven

Six Successful Change Strategies Based on the Four-Stage Model

Edited by Carol Herron

This chapter concentrates on what an individual faculty member can do to bring about the political, professional, and personal changes that must accompany any redirection foreign language and literature teaching takes. The papers in this chapter force us to think of how we can make an impact on the college, the students, and the community to bring about desired changes. Six authors, all participants of the 1979 or 1980 workshops, discuss potential developmental activities, implemented in their schools, in a variety of areas: curriculum remodeling, new approaches to management and growth, professional "networking" with foreign language educators at the college and high school levels, and the pursuit of external funding. The goal is to help equip us with innovative ideas crucial for engagement and growth in the decades ahead.

William Cipolla establishes the basis and development for curriculum modification. He is concerned with ensuring well-taught elementary language classes that, in turn, may alleviate the attrition rate in the upper-level literature courses. He details the issues involved in adopting and implementing the Dartmouth Intensive Language Model at a small private four-year college.

Expanding the horizons of faculty and curricula is at the heart of Marie Tollerson's report. Motivated by a steady decline in foreign language enrollments at the historically and predominantly black college where she teaches, Tollerson decided to implement a new program based on integrated study in business administration, cooperative education offering undergraduates work experience in their professions, and foreign languages. Described are student activities during the four-year career-oriented program, the summer study-abroad component, course content, and possibilities for faculty development through travel abroad to study foreign commerce and culture.

Theresia Reimers discusses the opportunities and potential problems associated with the use of various types of educational technology in the foreign language classroom. She presents an overview of available technologies, including language laboratory facilities, video, and computer-assisted instruction. Speaking as a chairperson, she also describes a major change in foreign language departmental structure and stresses the administration's support for faculty development and the importance of building a professional network with workshop participants and other colleagues.

Esperanza Gurza discusses the progress the foreign language department has made, under her direction as chair, toward resolving some of the problems she reported in her carry-over work plans. She outlines new approaches to departmental management and student growth in enrollments, student services, intramural and extramural public relations, and effective utilization of faculty.

Lynn Herkstroeter looks to the immediate future to suggest how we may broaden the base of support for our discipline through improved professional "networking" and public relations. She proposes ways of informing administrators of the values of foreign language study, of working with high school teachers in the area, of organizing community activities for National Foreign Language Week, for a foreign language day, and for a poetry recital contest. The publication and distribution of a foreign language journal newsletter to high schools and colleges throughout Michigan is also highlighted.

In the last report Bette Hirsch sets forth her strategies in pursuing external funding and her subsequent successful efforts to obtain an NEH consultant grant. She also focuses on curriculum changes that occurred as outgrowths from the consultant grant and from her participation in the workshop. Hirsch concludes by discussing the development of closer relations with the administration, the community, and other professional foreign language educators in the county by using the local and school press to publicize departmental activities, forming a county-wide foreign language educators association, and establishing a foreign language information center on campus. (See Hirsch's contribution, as director of one of the pilot groups in the collaborative professional development project, p. 284.)

We hope to speak for all those involved in the 1979 and 1980 workshops in saying that the true value of the sessions lies not only in the immediate benefits derived but more especially in the longer-term impetus the workshops may have provided for the advancement of language and literature teaching.

Building from the Bottom Up

William F. Cipolla

I am not sure at exactly what point we knew that our problem was greater than dwindling enrollments, that it was, in a sense, greater than our own survival as language teachers. ("We" refers to Eulalia Cobb and me, the entire full-time French Faculty of our department.) To be sure, we had seen it happening. First there was the erosion in the requirement. At least we had managed to retain a one-year obligation, but that had led to a disastrous reduction in the number of second-year students. Where, we asked ourselves, would we get the students to inhabit our treasured advanced courses? Who would lovingly listen as I peeled back the layers of Mallarmé's language? Who would be able to utter a string of comprehensible words carrying at least a sign of intelligent recognition?

You have probably been there. You probably know the signs. After a few semesters, surprisingly few, one comes to appreciate the slightest responses: sentence fragments, mangled tenses, finally a grunt or a nod evokes an encouraging smile. You find yourself making your important points in English. Before long those literature courses get frighteningly scarce. Cancellation because of underenrollment was running to thirty-five percent. We took the defensive, built into the schedule the possibility of loss. We juggled commitments, foresaw eventualities, insured our loads in the light of the worst.

Easy analyses: The students have changed. They are no longer interested in serious literature. They have become "career-oriented." Those who do sit in our language classes are there to acquire a marketable skill, a weapon to penetrate that elusive job market in "international commerce." I tried to picture Susan H. or Jeff A., pimply, awkward, behind a broad desk in a towering high-rise conducting business in several tongues. My imagination failed me; I began to ask them questions.

What I found out came as a shock but not a surprise. How could we have been so blind? Yes, indeed, times had changed, but the real problem was not that our students had lost interest in literature. It was far more serious than that, worse even than the fate of our jobs. The problem was that they couldn't read. Neither French nor, *horreur,* English. A difficult sentence became impossibly arcane when the subtleties of tense and structure were passed over out of ignorance. There is pleasure in labor, I thought, only when it bears fruit out of barren land.

We set about to remedy the situation. Since we still had a requirement, the disease showed its symptoms at the top. The advanced courses were most vulnerable to extinction; we were losing our Moyen Age and Renaissance students regularly. The course on Symbolisme depended on the panache of the teacher. It would work if you performed relentlessly, every hour of the semester. But when we questioned our students, we found out that the task was not beyond their intelligence or their interest, but it was beyond their skill, and we realized that the solution was to build from the bottom.

It took courage to face reality. We loved our big courses. That love had put us where we were, but it could keep us there no longer. We had given the bulk of language instruction to part-time help, though, increasingly, because of cancellation at advanced levels, we were doing most of that teaching ourselves. What was needed was to train students hard, to put them in the *manège,* to crack the whip without having a whip. We called Dartmouth.

The keystone of our revitalized program would be the Dartmouth Model. To get the program, we needed a strategy. One did not simply announce to one's dean that the college ought to spend $12,000 or $15,000 out of a tenuous budget just so students could ape phrases invented by an extravagant New England professor. We calculated carefully. We invited a colleague from a nearby institution where an intensive program had met with success. We applied for grant money. We convinced the dean of our commitment. We went to the FLL development workshop in San Francisco. We went to Dartmouth to observe and consult. We showed our dean that we were in touch with a network stretching from coast to coast and that, in short order, he would be able to point with pride to a mark we would put on the map.

It worked. After the dean, we took on the faculty. At our small four-year school, curricular decisions are subject to faculty vote.[1] Gently we approached our colleagues; we wooed them with the high seriousness of our cause. In March, a few months after we had made our decision, we won. We had our program. Intensive French, adapted from the Dartmouth Model, was to be a reality at Western Maryland. We set ourselves to the laborious task of implementation.

We foresaw serious problems. In our department three majors were possible: French, German, and Spanish. Only French was to be taught intensively; intensively was the only way French was to be taught. How could we convince students to submit to eight hours of classroom work two semesters in a row for eight credits, when they could do six hours of German or Spanish, spend three hours in the classroom, and still fulfill their requirement? We gambled. We already knew that the student who wanted simply to complete a requirement was not the one who interested us. We wanted those who would love French enough to go on, to populate those lonely seats in our tiny upper-level classrooms. We advertised the program: three hours of master class, three hours of drill, two hours of lab, eight to ten hours of out-of-class preparation.[2] It sounded forbidding, even to us. To our surprise enrollments became the least of our problems. We developed a waiting list after filling four sections, twenty-five students each. We could even replenish the group after the inevitable "drops."

It was those drill sections that still gnawed at our guts; we had no graduate students to call on for help. Would our own juniors and seniors, whose shortcomings and lack of skills we had woefully complained about, be up to the task? We planned our workshop as they do it at Dartmouth. A week before classes resumed in September, our upper-level students would spend three days learning the techniques: eye contact, finger snapping, one-pump handshakes to show their pleasure at a correct response. On the third evening we set up a jury. Each participant would lead a ten-minute drill; the faculty would rate them according to categories they had already used to rate one another during the group critiques that followed each session. The students' enthusiasm floored us; we had forgotten what a powerful force it is to be able to use what you have learned. These students were amply qualified to perform the necessary tasks; they took their roles seriously; they would be getting paid to help others learn what they knew.

So far, so good. When the new semester began in September (1980), we had four master classes of twenty-five students each, and ten drill sections averaging ten. It was an ideal distribution, and to ensure it, we had that waiting list of those who had signed up too late. What could go wrong?

Before the drop-add period was over, we had lost more than twenty students and had exhausted our waiting list. Over the next few weeks we lost ten more. By the beginning of the second semester, we had dwindled from one hundred to just under seventy. Could we convince the dean not to cancel a master class? After all, we had promised twenty-five a section. We bargained. We gave up a popular course in French conversation and dropped back to eight drills, in return for keeping our four master classes. We were disappointed but not despondent. Besides, something else had begun to happen.

Natural selection had set in. Those students who had stayed with us were beginning to speak French, real French. They began to ask, Could they be considered for drill positions? What were their chances of studying abroad? Would they be ready by their junior year? We advised them to take the newly created third semester of intensive French, to go on into composition and conversation, to attend the workshop just for the practice. We invited some of them, the really good ones, to try out.

The interest we had generated by instituting intensive French was not restricted to the campus community. Inquisitive calls came from neighboring colleges; high school teachers wanted to visit our classes. We sent program descriptions to the homes of all new students who applied for admission so that their parents, who paid the tuition, could read about what we were doing. In the past we had received, in a typical year, two to five inquiries about majoring in French. This year by the end of March, we had already received almost twenty. Were we doing what John Rassias was doing on tv? We assured them we were; we hoped they would give us serious thought.

So far our strategy seems to be paying off. We have created a new interest in French among a small but competent group of students committed to mastering the language. We are reshaping the major program to allow for the greatest possible flexibility in combining language study with another field. New courses in composition, conversation, and translation are developing a reliable audience. Given a first-year student with little or no background in French, we are now confident that we can produce a skillful language user in four years.

The future remains uncertain. For the moment our offerings in French literature taught in French are minimal. We teach literature in translation and culture courses in English to many enthusiastic students who would never find their way into a French-speaking classroom. These courses secure our teaching loads. What remains to be seen is whether the new skills in language will naturally generate a greater demand for literature in the original. For that we must simply wait. In the meantime I am enjoying the chattering I hear in the halls while sitting at my desk waiting for class. Much of it is now in French.

Notes

[1]Western Maryland College is a private four-year liberal arts institution with an enrollment of 1,300. The student population is mostly white, middle-class, suburban, graduating in the top third of their high school class.

[2]For a detailed description of the program, please contact the author. At Western Maryland we use John Rassias, *Le Français* (New York: Harper, 1980). Though other texts can be adapted to intensive instructional methods, we have found that for sheer abundance of first-rate drill and exercise material, Rassias' book works best.

A Program of Integrated Study in Business Administration, Cooperative Education, and Foreign Languages

Marie Tollerson

The development of this new program of study was motivated by the decline in interest in foreign languages. LeMoyne-Owen College had eliminated its foreign language requirements for graduation.[1] The result was a steady decline in enrollment in foreign language courses.

I decided to try to implement a new program based on the change that was occurring all across the United States—the application of foreign language study to other professions. LeMoyne-Owen had two advantages—a popular and comparatively new program in business (established in 1972) and a growing cooperative education program (established in 1975) to ensure work experience in a student's profession before graduation.

Step 1

The foreign language curriculum was redesigned to include two tracks: one with emphasis on the traditional literary studies,[2] the other with emphasis on the study of the language itself. The latter would prepare students to use a foreign language as a complement to other majors or would lay the foundations for further studies in interpretation and translation. The new program obviously centers on the second track.

During the first year (preferably the freshman year), students take elementary and intermediate grammar courses. They are encouraged to take part in the foreign language dramatic productions. The first month of the summer trimester they take a course in intensive elementary conversation.

The second year, students take advanced grammar and professional French or Spanish (oriented toward the student's chosen profession). They attend the spring three-day cultural workshop (funded by ICA, the International Communications Agency) conducted by Fulbright scholars from abroad. (A limited number of guests from the Memphis community are invited to attend.) May is again devoted to a course in intensive conversation. In July and August students who have maintained at least a C average in foreign language courses and have the approval of their departments study abroad. As part of their second year of study, students purchase a cultural text (written on an intermediate level) that is to be read during the year and discussed in foreign language club meetings. They must also participate in the annual foreign language dramatic presentation.

The third and fourth years, students take professional French or Spanish for one hour of credit each trimester they are on campus. Students have already requested that these final courses be kept at three hours. This extension, however, will depend on faculty availability.

The scope of the program is limited by the size of the foreign language faculty (one person). Obviously, colleges with larger faculties can develop considerably broader programs. If student demand increases, the program at LeMoyne-Owen will be expanded.

Step 2

Sashikant Thakur, who had been involved with international business programs at the State University of New York and who had much experience in the field of international business, volunteered to help develop the program. Working around the foreign language minimum, he designed a business marketing model so that the marketing sequence can be easily replaced by courses in administration, accounting, and so on. All the courses listed in the business marketing sequence are already in the curriculum of LeMoyne-Owen so that no new faculty or additional courses need be added.

Step 3

It is the responsibility of the Office of Cooperative Education at LeMoyne-Owen College to find suitable professional job placement for students enrolled in the program. Following the intensive conversation course at the end of the freshman or first year, students are sent out for their first work experience from June through August. Anytime after their study period abroad (the second summer), the students are sent out for the second time for practice in their prospective professions. The third cooperative education experience, it is hoped, will be abroad.

Steps 1 and 2 of this program have been realized. The foreign language program has been adopted and is in operation. The business sequence is being followed. ICA awarded LeMoyne-Owen College the funds necessary to send the first contingent of students and faculty advisers abroad in the summer of 1981 for further study of the languages and cultures of France and Mexico. The business internships abroad still need to be established, although some contacts have been made.

In 1982 another incentive was added. We were finally able to establish a cooperative education slot in Mexico. Whenever necessary, one or two students of Spanish who have a good command of English teach English to Mexican adults in Saltillo. The students receive special training for this assignment from Juanita Williamson and Marie Tollerson. Negotiations are in progress to find a similar slot for the French students.

An additional aspect of the program has been retraining for the foreign language faculty. I have returned to France for two consecutive summers (with some financial aid from LeMoyne-Owen) to study French commerce and culture. There are courses offered in many parts of France. Those interested should write the French consulate or professional societies for a listing. Below are three suggestions:

Alliance Française
101, boulevard RASPAIL
75270 Paris, France

Mademoiselle Renée BOUTON
Centre Malesherbes
108, boulevard MALESHERBES
75017 Paris, France

Centre International des Etudes Françaises
Université Catholique de l'Ouest
Boite Postale 808
49005 Angers, France

Conclusion

Since the award from ICA, enrollment in foreign language courses at LeMoyne-Owen has increased greatly (from classes of 5–8 to classes of 25–31). We are attracting some of the best students from all departments, although business majors remain the most numerous. Some attrition is expected, of course. But judging from the ability of the students we still expect that advanced and professional language courses will have between ten and fifteen students a class.

The first courses in professional French and Spanish are being designed now. Present plans require:

1. That the class uses one of the profession-oriented texts now on the market.
2. That each student establishes a dummy corporation or institution that will interact with other dummy corporations and institutions represented in the class. For example, an engineering student would establish a company, correspond with a banking student to arrange financing, hire a marketing student to handle advertising, and, finally, construct and explain in the target language class a proposed engineering project.

3. That, as students advance in the professional courses, the department will subscribe to relevant professional journals from abroad. Students will use them for oral and written reports and as a means of acquainting themselves with the advanced vocabulary and real problems of their prospective professions.

We continue trying to broaden the base of our community support. We have an agreement with the black business community to maintain some scholarships once ICA funding ends in exchange for the establishment of a center on campus for the study of black business. We also launched a special campaign fund that we hope will bear fruit. We have already received one scholarship from a national black women's group called The Links, Inc. and were able to add one more student to the summer traveling list.

Notes

[1] This requirement has been partially restored. All humanities majors must now take at least eight hours of a foreign language.

[2] From a realistic point of vew, we do not expect foreign language literature majors in the future. If the language track expands, survey courses may be offered as a part of culture study.

Hollins College: Strategies for Development

Theresia E. Reimers

Hollins College is a small (about 975 students) liberal arts college for women. Although we have not had a language requirement for several years, there is considerable interest in foreign study. We have two study-abroad programs: a one-year program in Paris and a semester program in London. Each program enrolls from fifty to fifty-five students, thirty to thirty-five from Hollins and about twenty from other colleges. We usually have at least one student a year at a Goethe Institute in Germany; the student takes two eight-week courses and receives credit for one semester and a short term. Students also take part in programs in Spain and in the Soviet Union.

Since my participation in the workshop several changes have occurred in our department that reflect the positive attitude of our administration: (1) at our request a major change in the departmental structure was made; (2) there has been generous support for faculty development; (3) we have been able to make experimental curriculum modifications with minimal procedural difficulty; and (4) we have been able to modernize our language laboratory and to begin the use of video both in the classroom and in the laboratory. The most obvious change is the organizational one: beginning next fall the language department will be split into two separate departments: the French department (with a new chair) and the German, Russian, and Spanish department (of which I remain chair). The language laboratory is separate, under my direction, and has a separate budget. The administration made a wise choice in the chair of the French department, and relations between the two new departments are cordial.

We lost the battle of the language requirement for various reasons. The main reason for the decision, which was voted on by the College Legislature (composed of both faculty members and students), seemed to be that having a language requirement would be a serious handicap in recruiting new students.

The Russian faculty was reduced to one half-time person, although the major in Russian studies survives. Despite the cut in faculty the administration has been supportive of the language departments. Believing with us

232

that our Russian professor is too good to lose, the administration generously offered to send him with his family to a Goethe Institute in Germany for the summer to brush up his German so that he can teach half-time German in the fall. He and I took part in a Rassias workshop (also at the college's expense), an experience we both found exhilarating, exhausting, and profitable.

Individually paced instruction is, I believe, the primary reason German has survived and prospered. The approach has its pitfalls: it is time-consuming for the instructors, and it is a trap for the students who think they can do the whole course during the last week of the semester.

We have been using materials developed by the Army Language School of Monterey and will supplement them next year with the new Goethe Institute texts. Students are compelled to listen and respond to the cassettes; there is no other way they can study. In the first semester all examinations are oral. Students have the option of either using the language laboratory or using the cassettes on their own machines. The language laboratory is much more popular since we remodeled one room: there are no carrels; the machines are secured to a long table along one wall and to two round tables. Thick carpeting, draperies, cork on the walls, and acoustical tile on the ceiling keep the room quiet. The atmosphere is informal and cheerful; the chair seats are upholstered to be comfortable (but not too comfortable). The laboratory is operated on the library system and is open to students from 7 a.m. to 11 p.m. The machines are Sony model RC 87; the quality is excellent, even for music. The quarter-track format greatly simplifies the problems of tape duplication: cassettes recorded for or on these machines are compatible with any other machines, so students can use the same tapes in the laboratory or on their own machines.

In addition to the new laboratory room we have acquired video equipment. My use of it experimentally during the first semester was so successful that I spent a good part of my sabbatical semester developing new materials. I am concentrating on developing materials for video because there is little material available and because I am familiar with the technical aspects of production. It would be foolish to disregard twenty years of experience in photography and film to begin at the beginning with computers. The possibilities of the use of video on all levels are limited only by the time one has to develop ideas. Because our students have grown up with television, they readily take to video as a means of language learning, but their expectations with respect to technical quality are fairly high.

The greatest challenge is on the elementary level; one cannot use existing laboratory materials without rethinking them completely in visual terms. How can we make German grammar memorable? Apply the Rassias principle of making it so ridiculous students cannot forget it? We hope to find out whether they remember prepositions that take the accusative or the dative case better when they have been taught by the pink panther (use of dimensional animation). We believe that we can save production time by adapting some animation sequences to teach either German or Russian grammar with different sound tracks. This will require sophisticated editing equipment that we will get in September.

There is some good material available on video from the German education tv network, but the quantity is limited. A serious problem with French video is that French tv makes almost no material available in American (National Television Standards Committee) format. We make video materials available to students on the library system, but they have to sign for a key to a video room.

Attempts to get computer materials have met with frustration, with the exception of Russian. The program from Dartmouth is being translated for our computer and should be ready by fall. The Ohio State program in German is still not available in a computer language we can use and is not expected to be available in the near future. PLATO is simply too expensive. We got a computer game for the Apple in Spanish, but it did not prove exciting or useful. Although the materials available for microcomputer in German are fragmentary and not very promising, we have ordered a couple of grammar drills and will see how they work out. I passed up *German: Read and Translate* since my basic approach is speak and do *not* translate.

Innovative teaching techniques have helped keep Russian and German alive at Hollins. The cost in instructors' time and energy is high, but the results are rewarding. Our colleagues in the other languages are interested but wary; they know I spent the better part of my leave behind a video camera or in front of a monitor. Next fall I shall teach the German film course in English in addition to my German courses; it keeps up my enrollments and is relatively undemanding. Second semester I shall teach the Western tradition (Machiavelli through Jung); one cannot exist on grammar and video alone. Short term I shall offer Intensive Beginning German, German Literature in Opera, and (probably) Editing Videotape.

The Russian culture course continues to be a great success, and the elementary course promises to be more attractive to students with the new functional-notional orientation and the use of the computer. We intend to do a cooking series on video in Russian and German, and we hope to interest our colleagues in participating. I made the first tape recently, doing both the cooking and the camera work to show how easy it is.

An important result of the workshop has been the "networking" of participants; the continual exchange of ideas, problems, and solutions. Since the workshop, I have attended the Northeast Conference each year and the Ohio State Conference on Individualized Instruction. These stimulating and profitable meetings offer the opportunity to hear papers about new developments in one's field (I attend every presentation on video and computers) and to meet colleagues with similar interests.

University of Puget Sound: Strategies for Development

Esperanza Gurza

I want to discuss the progress we have made toward resolving some of the problems outlined in the carry-over work plan I completed at the conclusion of the workshop. The problems included low enrollments and student services, intramural and extramural public relations, and effective utilization of faculty. The following progress has been made:

Student Enrollments and Services

There is a 20.6% increase in FL registration this fall (1981) as compared with last fall. Since credit registrations are up 7.3% overall at the university, our enrollment figure represents an actual FL gain of 13.3%. The increase was the result of several steps:

1. Negotiations were carried out with the director of advising so that foreign language faculty were allowed to reserve ten places each in an FL section to accommodate freshman advisees, instead of creating special sections for them.

2. We talked with administrators, personnel in the advising and career planning offices, and other faculty advisers about the need to encourage students to take FL courses.

3. We encouraged the politics and government department to legalize and advertise an interdisciplinary major that had existed only in their books. It involves six units of one foreign language. It has now been approved by the curriculum committee and is to appear in the new edition of the university bulletin.

4. Two members of our department have been attending meetings of the study-abroad consortium to which our university belongs, in the hopes of initiating programs requiring or highlighting the study of FLL. A semester in Salamanca, Spain, is now planned for spring 1983 with a possible semester in alternate years in Mexico. We hope to see programs developed for students of French and German.

5.   We have worked with the career development office regarding internships for FL students. Some have been arranged and other opportunities are being explored. The possibility of doing internships abroad was proposed by us and is being investigated also.

6.   We have begun a campaign to encourage our FLL seniors and recent graduates to apply for Fulbright Scholarship grants. For the last four years every grantee in our university has been a student of German. We are now urging deserving students in French and Spanish to apply. Our faculty counsels students about possibilities and provides guidance during the application period.

Intramural Public Relations

1.   Besides making the efforts outlined above, we have been agreeing and even offering to lecture to classes in other disciplines and to speak to groups of students with special interests (such as honor societies).

2.   We have volunteered for university committees, both regular ones, such as curriculum and academic standards, and ad hoc committees, such as one considering alternate interim proposals.

3.   We worked with the Asian Studies Committee to develop a cooperative proposal for hiring a part-time adjunct to teach Japanese 101 and 102 next year. We succeeded in having the Asian studies program increase its requirements by two courses in Japanese or any other appropriate language, with the possibility of one of the courses being linguistics, which is also in our curriculum.

4.   Through the work and the leadership of a member of the FL department who is interested in African literature, we cosponsored with the departments of English and religion and with Pacific Lutheran University a visit of an African scholar. The success of the visit brought us considerable recognition from colleagues across campus.

Extramural Public Relations

1.   We have met twice with the FLL department of our neighboring Pacific Lutheran University to discuss matters of common concern and to open up the possibility of future cooperation.

2.   We met with the Tacoma public school's FLL teachers to plan and carry out a Secondary School Day as a part of our 1981 Foreign Language Week celebration. Over two hundred junior and senior high school students came to our campus for one afternoon to put on skits, songs, and dances related to their FL study. We were supported by the Office of Admissions, which provided the refreshments for this occasion.

3. We celebrated the 1981 Foreign Language Week with exhibits in the library, foreign films, a lecture on a literary subject by a professor from Central Washington University, and an FL festival featuring students and faculty as artists, directors, and actors. Our public relations office got good publicity for the affair in local and regional newspapers.

4. Throughout the spring of 1981, we offered a free foreign language film festival, which also received some publicity.

5. We are sponsoring an FL contest at each local high school to select its best student of French, German, and Spanish for a day-long visit on our campus this fall.

6. A meeting with the Tacoma public schools' FLL teachers is scheduled for the end of this month to plan 1982 Foreign Language Week activities and to discuss the contest (5).

Faculty Development

1. A faculty exchange program was arranged between one of our professors and the assistant director of the Pomona Modular Academy program in Paris, with full cooperation of the administrators involved. Both kept their salaries from their institutions, thus facilitating the issuing of an immigration permit for the French counterpart.

2. With the administration's help a one-year's leave of absence without pay was granted to an FL tenured member who had not been able to complete the Ph.D., and a full-time replacement was hired.

3. Copies of speeches and papers that come across my desk regarding FLL needs, program development, or pedagogical suggestions are now circulated among the members in our department.

Building Local Support for Foreign Languages

Lynn Herkstroeter

Saginaw Valley State College is a four-year state institution in Michigan with approximately 4,000 students, eighty percent of whom commute. It has no foreign language requirement, though students may count four credits of language for their humanities requirements. Since the college is in an urban, blue-collar community, there seems to be low interest in foreign languages and cultures. There is, therefore, a strong need to make the public aware of their importance.

After returning from the NEH workshop in San Francisco, 1980, I had many new and exciting ideas about teaching, curricular changes, and public relations. Perhaps it mainly inspired me to mobilize those in my college and community to do more to promote foreign languages. This report deals primarily with our efforts in public relations.

At the San Francisco workshop I had become familiar with the report of the President's Commission on Foreign Language and International Studies. Since the document states unequivocally the urgent need for training Americans to understand foreign languages and cultures, I distributed copies of it to the deans, vice-presidents, and president, encouraging them to discuss it with my department. Copies of the report were also placed on reserve in the library. Subsequently I led a discussion of the topic at a faculty association meeting. These activities seemed especially important because the college is now revising its general education requirement. My serving on a committee to formulate a proposal for the new requirement should help us to ensure the inclusion of an international studies component.

With respect to the community at large, my major strategy has been to work with the high school teachers of foreign language. Three years ago we founded the Saginaw Valley Foreign Language Association, an organization for foreign language teachers within a thirty-mile radius of the college. We had the faculty secretary telephone the area schools to obtain the names of potential members. Generally the organization meets informally three times a year to discuss common concerns, such as the report of the President's Commission and topics concerning education, business, and diplomacy. The association also initiated a letter-writing campaign to Michigan legislators.

In addition, our group planned community activities for National Foreign Language Week. Teachers were asked to relate what types of events they were planning in their schools and what had worked well for them in the past. Among events planned were international dinners, skits, contests, and days for ethnic dress. Two high school teachers, serving as coordinators, distributed a calendar of events to the media and to other teachers.

At the time the *Saginaw News,* our local newspaper, printed an article of mine about the President's Commission report, and as a result, I was interviewed on television for a local public affairs program.

Our organization met again in May to discuss local concerns, such as millage tax failures and program cuts in some districts. We drafted letters to local school boards to deplore cuts in foreign language programs and to stress the importance of FL study.

Among our departmental activities for community outreach are Foreign Language Day, the Poetry Recital Contest, and *Alethea,* our journal-newsletter. Foreign Language Day has been an annual event in our area in early November for six years. Generally five hundred to six hundred students from area high schools attend. Activities include poster, skit, song, and dance contests; ethnic songs and dances by natives or professionals; displays about foreign cultures; foreign films; and sale booths for items made by our students. Local newspapers and television stations have come to cover the event.

The Poetry Recital Contest takes place yearly in early spring. The best students in each high school are asked to memorize a poem from a selection that we furnish. Two upper-division and two lower-division awards are made in each of four languages: French, German, Polish, and Spanish. Parents and teachers of the participating students are encouraged to attend.

Our journal-newsletter, *Alethea,* features stories, articles, and poems by students and faculty in our department. It is published once each semester and is sent to high schools and colleges throughout Michigan as well as to other interested parties. Currently we distribute about 1,400 copies. At state or even national foreign language meetings, I often hear favorable comments about *Alethea.*

Members of the Department of Modern Foreign Languages have also been active in student recruitment. We have spoken at high schools, met with high school counselors, and volunteered to counsel students during freshman orientation. We have prepared pamphlets about out department, and we make ourselves available for placement testing of incoming students.

Establishing effective public relations is time-consuming. Most of us have heavy teaching loads, boring committee work, and little time for research. We may wonder why we should spend even more time advertising foreign languages. Yet community support can be a real asset. If people know you or know of you, they are more likely to sign up for your classes. Furthermore, high school teachers may send you students, especially those who want to continue language study in college. Administrators are likely to be impressed if you are respected in the community. They like getting favorable media coverage for the college, and it is hard to cut a program that has public support. Admissions offices also welcome departmental efforts. Activities such as Foreign Language Day bring students to the campus. Even if the students do not become foreign language majors, they may well attend the institution you helped publicize to study in other fields.

In September 1980 foreign languages at Saginaw Valley State College showed substantial increases in enrollment, more than double the number of new students at the college. It would seem that our efforts in public relations have not been in vain.

Cabrillo College: Strategies for Development

Bette G. Hirsch

Cabrillo Community College of Santa Cruz County is located seventy-five miles south of San Francisco and has 12,000 students and 1,250 language students each semester. In the main, California's public schools have received no local funding since the passage of Proposition 13 in 1978. Our money comes from the state and is based on enrollment. Small classes risk cancellation; teaching assistant hours are limited; part-time teaching positions cannot be consolidated into full-time ones. Rooms are difficult to obtain during the prime hours, and no new buildings are planned. Although the county is growing, the college and our department show no growth and little change.

Master teachers at the 1979 workshop gave me many ideas for enhancing our program in such areas as outside funding, curriculum remodeling, and creative management. I wanted to share the information I had received and to inspire others at my college. I hoped we might redirect our energies to solve problems and explore new possibilities. It was clear to me that involvement at the decision-making stage is crucial; participation in a plan makes the newness less threatening and increases motivation.

I sent a summary of my notes and ideas from the workshop to all department members and to certain members of the administration in January 1980. We held a departmental meeting in February to discuss the material and to establish priorities for development and change at Cabrillo.

After this meeting, I spoke about our plans to the academic dean, the head of the library, and the counseling division chairman. These meetings contributed to the success of our efforts by making it known that our department was involved in the finest of national programs, that we were considering making innovations, and that we cared about the campus-wide results of our actions. Departmental involvement in goal formation allayed faculty fears of "What will I be forced to do?"

Now committed to development, we wanted to find out more about the Rassias Dartmouth method and see whether it could be adapted to a community college program. We were interested in hearing more about computers. We wanted to reach out more effectively to the high school students and teachers in our county. We were interested in examining our curriculum in the light of national trends and a changing student body. But we lacked money to visit other schools, to get training or even introductions to various new methodologies, or to hire an expert to guide us. And so we decided to look to outside resources as presented during the workshop. We eventually applied for an NEH consultant grant. In October 1980 we learned that we had been awarded a grant of $7,314 and that Carmen Chaves McClendon was to be our consultant.

McClendon visited us first that November and then in March of 1981. She helped us focus on our needs more clearly. She shared with us some happenings and alternative methodologies in foreign language teaching. She spoke with our administrators and the governing board and other faculty, both about foreign languages in the United States and about the creativity she perceived in our department. She was able to obtain promises of support from our academic dean and our college president for developing the use of computer-assisted instruction (CAI), for setting up a foreign language information center, for preparing a foreign languages and careers brochure for publicity and outreach to the community, for hiring teaching assistants to implement the Rassias program, and for encouraging our budding County Foreign Language Educators Society. (See p. 284 for details on this organizational effort.)

Part of the grant can be used for faculty travel. We have accordingly visited innovative programs in Sacramento, California (the Rassias model at American River Community College), in Riverside, California (Rassias training session and CAI at Loma Linda University), and at Dartmouth College (CAI and Rassias).

Perhaps the greatest change since we have been awarded the grant is our visibility on campus. We are not doing much that is radically different. We have always had a healthy program (eight languages offered; twenty-four instructors) and a staff committed to fine teaching. But now, suddenly, many people know what a good job we are doing. The president speaks of our creative work at the governing board meeting and mentions our fine work in a letter sent county-wide. The organizers of an interdepartmental forum on the future of the humanities at Cabrillo invite me to participate. Money requested for projects (e.g., shelves for an information center, a career brochure, a conference) is often approved. Administrators see merit in putting money in places where it gets results.

Another more subtle benefit lies in our bettered self-image. The enthusiasm and the new ideas generated by the consultant and the off-campus visits dramatically changed feelings about work and effectiveness. Although $7,314 is not very much, it has changed our position on campus as a department and mine personally as one instructor who also holds a grant.

In addition to helping us find outside funding, the workshop provided models and approaches that we could apply to Cabrillo's curriculum. I admired John Rassias' intensive language method and I sought ways to implement it at Cabrillo. We discussed the method, saw the Rassias videotapes, sent members to other campuses to view the program working, and gained support from administrators for a trial run. We adopted the Rassias text (fall 1980), and I received training in the method while at Dartmouth (Jan. 1981). I helped arrange for Rassias to give a West Coast workshop on his method (March 1981), which many of our faculty attended. A follow-up questionnaire ascertained much interest in attending a full training program on the West Coast. Rassias gave one at Stanford University (Sept. 1981), where I assisted him as a trainer, and our faculty again participated.

Howard Nostrand's suggestions about including cultural information in beginning language classes and presenting a culture course as an option to advanced students are compelling. I reexamined first- and second-year texts with this focus and now have offered a new contemporary French culture course, which proved popular.

Claire Gaudiani's description during the workshop for her composition course was most helpful. I proposed a similar course to our curriculum committee, and it was accepted. It was offered in the fall of 1981.

Computer-assisted instruction is another innovation introduced to us. We knew of the availability of terminals and microcomputers on campus, but almost none of our foreign language faculty had any background in the field. To gain some computer literacy, I took a course in the BASIC language and corresponded with others developing foreign language software. The administration has supported our efforts to create or adopt some foreign language computer programs.

Finally, the workshop presented practical department management and professional growth approaches. We have adopted or are developing six of them.

1. We attempt to have frequent articles explaining our new courses, department activities, and achievements of language students and faculty appear in our campus newspaper, faculty journal, local newspapers, and in memos to our deans, president, and governing board.

2. A brochure detailing foreign language courses as career preparation has been developed and is available on campus and in the county.

3. The workshop and our consultant have provided models for community outreach. We are interested in establishing contact with our county community, particularly its large Spanish-speaking population. Several of our instructors are working in this area (e.g., planning January and summer tours that include the community, studying ways to bring the Spanish-speaking community into our classes, and working with an organization devising ways to keep high school students in school).

4. Improving communication with other foreign language professionals in our county has long been a goal. Ideas of the workshop and of our consultant led to my forming a County Foreign Language Educators Association.

Our initial meetings have brought together teachers of elementary, junior high school, high school, community college, and university classes. We view this group as a future asset to our county's foreign language offerings.

5. The idea for a foreign language information center was presented in the workshop. We have not yet obtained grant monies to launch a center as originally envisioned but have been able to begin one in a limited manner. The College Career Center allocated us a corner, and we have collected and consolidated resources often requested by students. This material includes career information, catalogs of summer foreign language programs here and abroad, year-long language programs at the undergraduate and graduate levels, travel brochures, and notices of community cultural events and county job needs. There is space for students to read foreign periodicals that have been placed there. We have held our first annual Foreign Languages and Careers workshop in this area. We sense that the center will meet the needs of our diverse student body and bring us new students.

6. Several of our instructors have become active in regional and national professional organizations, another suggestion of the workshop. We have helped to organize meetings in our area during which expert teachers and theorists have discussed current pedagogical methods, such as PEFL, TPR, Lozanov, and the Natural Method.

The 1979 NEH Workshop has seeded much change at Cabrillo College. After a period of information sharing and goal formation, we have made progress in curriculum development, professional growth, department management techniques, and acquisition of outside funding. At a time of economic retrenchment, it is still possible to be innovative in a California community college.

PART THREE

Future Directions

Chapter Eight

Securing Outside Funding

General Information

College and university departments constantly change curricula, build programs, and update faculty skills. Most of this work proceeds without outside support as part of the institution's business. When projected changes go beyond the resources designed for routine growth and development, additional support becomes necessary. Any proposal to bring in outside support will focus on why the project exceeds the limits of routine change, that is, why outside support is needed. What will be the results of the project? How will it improve the teaching and learning process for faculty and students? How will the department evaluate the new program? And very important, how will the project continue in the postfunding period? Many of these questions will be answered as the project develops if the department uses a guide like the one suggested on pp. 80–82. Good planning for curricular change greatly eases the burden of grant writing. In fact, as noted in that section, the strategies for planned changes can be used as the outline of a grant proposal unless the funding agency prefers applicants to use its own form.

Most of the suggestions in this chapter concern projects for department and curriculum development. Faculty seeking fellowship funds for their scholarly activities should see pp. 258–61 in particular.

Generally letters of support from academic officers should accompany grant proposals. These letters should not only express the officers' understanding of the project and enthusiasm for it but also indicate how the project complements other institutional efforts and goals. In addition, any constituencies mentioned as potential participants should submit letters of support. For instance, if your project is to run a workshop for regional FL faculty, show your plans to some regional faculty early in the development process. Discover their level of interest, entertain their suggestions, and keep them abreast of your progress. Then invite them to write letters of support. Or, if other departments in your institution figure prominently in the project, administrators or concerned faculty should write letters of support for that section of the proposal.

Another section of the proposal should contain the résumés of all those who will work in the project, including the project director. Additional suggestions for formulating grant proposals are in chapter 2. Note especially the sections on creating a schedule of activities and duties and on preparing the budget and budget narrative (pp. 78–79).

Before considering (or reconsidering) a search for grant support a novice in the field needs some basic information to avoid the pitfalls.

FAILURE

Prepare to fail. We begin with this notion because it simply is a commonplace in grant seeking. But failure should cause only fleeting disappointment. The shame is not in failing—only in not trying. The pursuit of outside funding becomes more competitive every day, so only a fool expects to win easily. Everyone who competes learns a great deal in the process. To avoid being discouraged, always bank on some failure and try to place a grant proposal in the hands of several agencies at once. If two agencies accept the project, you can always negotiate; you can take partial funding from each source or accept one and tell the other you will return later with a request for assistance on a subsequent part of the project. More likely, you will not receive multiple grants. The grant process is different from the process of publishing a manuscript. Agencies accept and encourage joint application and joint funding. Humanities faculty typically make far fewer grant proposals in their professional careers than do their colleagues in the sciences and social sciences. Consequently, the rejection of a proposal does more psychological damage to humanities faculty and departments. Increasing the number of grants made increases the chances of receiving support and blunts the impact of any single rejection.

When a grant proposal is rejected, ask if reviewers' comments are available. They can sometimes help you strengthen the proposal for a subsequent competition. Also ask if the program officer advises resubmission of the project at a later time.

"TURN-AROUND TIME"

Prepare for an extended "turn-around time." This is the time needed from application deadline to announcement of results. For NEH grants, the turn-around time may be as short as six months; for other proposals eighteen months may be standard. Some private foundations decide quickly how they will respond to a proposal. Be sure to do academic planning with turn-around time in mind.

TEAMWORK

Create a team effort right from the beginning. "Lone Rangers" do receive outside funding, but their lives are difficult when funding for a departmental project comes and they have not enlisted sufficient help from their colleagues. If you create a team, giving important jobs and incentives to your colleagues, the project will be stronger and its impact more widespread than if it is known as your "baby." (See pp. 69–70, 92–93 for information on team building.)

READ CAREFULLY

After the computer data-base search explained below has provided you with realistic sources, get in touch with the program officers of the foundations or agencies. Get all the latest information on the competitions you are eligible to apply for. Once you have the information in writing, make sure you understand the application procedure, deadlines, and the review process. Follow directions scrupulously and refer back to them often. Ask for a ratio of proposals funded to proposals received and whether or not reviewers' comments will be available. Find out the average size of grants given in the recent past. Find out if the program officers read preproposals (early draft versions of the grant proposal). You may also ask if the agency can send brief descriptions of recent projects it has funded. Some agencies may send copies of successful applications (without budget information). These publications often contain fine suggestions that you can use to strengthen your program. For instance, a community outreach or student involvement element may fit perfectly with the rest of your plan but simply had not occurred to you.

GRANTS OFFICERS

Many institutions now have grants officers, who can offer substantial assistance but may also pose certain dangers to faculty efforts to secure funding. Usually these professionals know how to discover sources of funding, write well, can help organize a grant proposal, and know the special interests of specific foundations and the regulations of government agencies. Some institutions require faculty to inform the grants officer before seeking outside funding. Although the officer is most often a first and best ally in securing outside support, some faculty have had trying experiences in their grants offices. Let their experiences benefit the rest of us. Some grants officers try to take over projects. In one case, a small request for consultant assistance and some released time to set up an FL center was redesigned by a grants officer into an enormous proposal with large expenditures for computers and software. The project was judged overambitious by the funding agency, and the whole grant was rejected. The grants officer may have seen a chance to piggyback a few other institutional needs onto a project that looked promising. Funding agencies often see through this attempt, and the original project suffers. Make sure some academic officer outside the grants office will remain your ally in getting the project *you need* through the grants office.

Grants officers often travel to Washington and other funding meccas. If they take your project along, give them a written statement about how *you* see the project developing (see strategies for planned change, ch. 2). This statement should include your name and telephone number at the office and at home. Most often program officers who deal with grants at foundations and agencies come from specific disciplines in the humanities. They will often appreciate having access to the faculty member likely to direct the project and likely to have more complete information on it than the grants officer does.

Incidentally, in your contacts with program officers, pay close attention to the suggestions they offer but avoid losing the project to a reformulation that may suit a foundation but would not suit your faculty and students. Organize notes carefully before calling a program officer. Not only do officers appreciate succinct discussions with applicants, but also the notes they take will reflect your notes and will create a better in-house record of your project for future reference.

If a grants officer helps write your project, be certain you and the officer both understand that plain English works best. Avoid jargon and pretentious phases.

Before the grant goes out, make sure you can live both with the assignments it gives you and with the budget. If you get the grant, you will find yourself responsible for evaluation reports that must address expectations raised by the proposal. Commit yourself only to what you can and will do.

STUDENT CONSTITUENCIES

As much as possible involve interested students in the process of grant seeking. They can help do data-base searches and send draft letters to agencies, and they can read and help edit early versions of the proposal. This excellent experience instructs them in the importance of good critical thinking, clear writing, meticulous care in final draft preparation, and attention to deadlines and specifications. Science majors often see their faculty preparing grants. Humanities majors would benefit greatly from participating in our efforts to secure funds for research and development.

Data-Base Research

This section guides departments in researching resources of funding for foreign language and literature programs. The humanities cannot realistically expect large increases in public (federal) funding during a period of economic retrenchment. Thus no one can overemphasize the importance of maintaining a variety of sources of support, public and private. The term "support" in this chapter refers to funding for curriculum development, faculty development, symposia, and project grants; grants to support construction or renovation of facilities; grants to individual faculty members for travel and research (fellowships and awards); and funds for study and travel abroad.

The first part of this section explains the basic mechanisms for locating public and private funding sources for individual scholars or institutions. Included are directions on how to conduct a data-base computer search and a search of printed reference materials. The second part contains a sample data-base search for FLL funding presented in an annotated bibliographical format. This list of private and public agencies that invite funding proposals from individual foreign language educators and their institutions does not pretend to be comprehensive but should help get you started in finding sources. The bibliography and the information in the first part should provide a basic reference to support a more complete search that you may undertake in the future.

HOW TO CONDUCT A SEARCH

1. Lockhead Information System (known as the Dialog System)
2. A Systems Development Corporation (known as Orbit)
3. The Bibliographic Retrieval Services (known as BRS)

All three systems are available in the reference department of the library at Emory University, where this research was conducted. You may find one or all of these systems in the library or, perhaps, in a computer center on your campus. A skilled technician will normally be on hand to help you run the data-base search, for which a fee is charged. Prices vary according to the system you are using and the data base you are consulting. Many schools subsidize these searches; you should check on this before you begin your work. Others may charge a service fee in addition to the actual cost charged by the vendor, so there will be a wide variation in cost.

Once you know that you have access to one of the computer systems mentioned above, you will need to consult the existing, pertinent data bases. The major data bases that pertain to awards, foundations, and grants and that are programmed into the computer systems mentioned above include:

1. ERIC (available through Dialog, Orbit, and BRS)
   ERIC is the complete data base on educational materials from the Educational Resources Information Center. It is concerned with identifying the most significant and timely education research reports and projects.
2. FOUNDATION DIRECTORY (available through Dialog)
   The Foundation Directory provides descriptions of over 3,500 foundations that have assets of $1 million or more or that make grants of $100,000 or more annually. The private foundations that qualify for inclusion account for nearly ninety percent of the assets of all foundations in the United States and eighty percent of all foundation giving.

3. FOUNDATION GRANTS INDEX (available through Dialog)
    The Foundation Grants Index contains information on grants awarded by more than four hundred major American philanthropic foundations. Information on grants actually given by foundations is useful in determining types and amounts of grants awarded since foundations seldom announce the availability of funds for specific purposes. Grants to individuals and grants of less than $5,000 are not included.

4. GRANTS DATABASE (available through Dialog and Orbit)
    Grants Database is the source to more than 1,500 grant programs available through government (federal, state, local), commercial organizations, associations, and private foundations. The academic discipline(s) for which grants are available are given with each program.

5. NATIONAL FOUNDATIONS (available through Dialog)
    National Foundations provides records of all 21,800 United States foundations that award grants regardless of the assets of the foundation or of the total amount of grants it awards annually. Approximately 17,000 small foundations excluded from coverage in the Foundation Directory because their assets total less than $1 million are listed in National Foundations. Since many of these foundations restrict their donations to local or regional recipients, community organizations with local projects will find this data base particularly useful.

In the index guide for use of all of these data bases, you will find a list of key words or descriptors that the technician will key into the system to limit your search, for example, modern languages, Greek, Latin, fellowships, grants, awards, financial support for college faculty. The descriptors vary from data base to data base.

If you have neither access to a system nor funds to support the research, you can still search through printed materials. In fact, most of the data bases mentioned above have a corresponding printed source.

1. The corresponding printed sources for ERIC:
    Current Index to Journals in Education. Vol. 1– . New York: CCM Information Sciences, 1969– . ($150 a year)
    Resources in Education. Vol. 1– . Washington, D.C.: U.S. Government Printing Office, 1966– .($42.50 a year) (Known as *Research in Education* until 1975).

2. The corresponding printed source for FOUNDATION DIRECTORY:
    Foundation Directory. 7th ed. New York: Foundation Center, 1979. ($36 a year)

3. The corresponding printed source for FOUNDATION GRANTS INDEX:
    Foundation Grants Index, 1970/71– . New York: Foundation Center, 1972– . ($27 a year)

4. The corresponding Printed source for GRANTS DATABASE:
    Grants Information System. Scottsdale, Ariz.: Oryx Press, 1974– . ($375 a year)

5. There is no printed counterpart for NATIONAL FOUNDATIONS data base.

Other reference sources may be found in your library or in the university development office. (See insert below.) Listed below are the other printed materials that we used in our search.

1. *Annual Register of Grant Support.* 14th ed. Chicago: Marquis Academic Media, 1980–81.
2. *Foundation Grants to Individuals.* 2nd ed. New York: Foundation Center, 1979.
3. *Taft Foundation Report.* Washington, D.C.: Taft, 1980.

These sources are all indexed according to fields of interest. For example, in the *Taft Foundation Reporter,* we looked under Arts and Humanities, Language Education, Faculty Development, Graduate Education, Educational Research, and Building and Construction. In the *Foundation Grants to Individuals,* we used the key words fellowships (Arts and Humanities), graduate scholarships, awards, prizes, and grants through nominations. For the *Annual Register of Grant Support,* we used the descriptors Humanities (languages and literature), international studies and research abroad, higher education projects and research, educational projects and research general, and scholar aid programs in all disciplines.

Many graduate research libraries now publish information on funding sources or have this information available in the reference section. The following information on file at the Van Pelt Library, University of Pennsylvania, suggests the range of assistance possible from the graduate library nearest you. All this information can serve you immediately as you search for sources and prepare to organize your project and write your proposal. Generally it is inadvisable to write a proposal until the selection of sources has been narrowed to an appropriate number and until you have made contact with the program officer at the foundation or agency.

Bibliography on Funding Sources

SUBJECT HEADINGS

The following is a list of suggested subject headings for use in the main card catalog. They are selected from the Library of Congress *List of Subject Headings* which may be consulted on the shelf adjacent to the card catalog.

Education—Finance

Endowments—U.S.

Endowments—Directories—Periodicals

Grants in aid—U.S.

Grants in aid—Handbooks, Manuals, etc.

Proposal Writing in the Social Sciences

Funding Sources Bibliography (*cont.*)

Research Grants—U.S.—Bibliography—Directories

Research Grants—U.S.—Periodicals

Subsidies

GUIDES TO THE LITERATURE

Sheehy, Eugene P. *Guide to Reference Books.* 9th ed. Chicago: American Library Assn., 1976.

A comprehensive annotated guide to reference books. Bibliography of funding sources located in the sections entitled "Social Sciences—General Works—Foundations and Philanthropic Organizations" and "Social Sciences—Education—Fellowships and Scholarships."

Woodbury, Marda. *A Guide to Sources of Educational Information.* Washington, D.C.: Resources Press, 1976.

The chapter on government and financial information lists prime sources of government and foundation funding in education.

Foundation Directory. 8th ed. New York: Foundation Center, 1981.

Levitan, Don. *Selected Bibliography on Grantsmanship.* Monticello, Ill.: Council of Planning Librarians, Exchange Bibliography 641, 1974.

An annotated bibliography including information on private and public sources of funding, as well as resource material on all facets of grantsmanship.

White, Virginia P. *Grants: How to Find Out about Them and What to Do Next.* New York: Plenum, 1983.

A basic guide to information on all aspects of grantsmanship. Contains a bibliography on proposal writing and various appendixes on types of grants, how to apply for them, and how to get them.

DIRECTORIES

Annual Register of Grant Support. Chicago: Marquis Academic Media Annual.

A comprehensive guide to grant support, programs of government agencies, foundations, corporations, and professional organizations. A classified arrangement with several appendixes.

Arlett, Allan, ed. *A Canadian Directory to Foundations and Other Granting Agencies.* Ottawa: Assoc. of Universities and Colleges of Canada, 1973.

Includes grants from private and government sources on both the provincial and federal levels. There is no minimum asset or grant figure necessary for inclusion. Listing is alphabetical by foundation, with various indexes. Some coverage of American funding sources.

Dewey, Richard E. *Federal Funding Data,* including *Manual on Development of Proposals and Directory of Government Funding Programs.* New York: National Jewish Welfare Board, 1972.

Directory of Pennsylvania Foundations. Philadelphia: Free Library of Philadelphia, 1978.

Lists foundations in Pennsylvania by geographical area. Includes an index to subject interests of foundations. (Many states have similar publications.)

Directory of Research Grants. Scottsdale, Ariz.: Oryx, 1975.

A compilation of information on grant support from government as well as private foundations and corporations. Organized by academic discipline.

Foundation Center Source Book. Comp. by the Foundation Center. New York: Columbia

Funding Sources Bibliography (*cont.*)

University Press, 1975–76. 2 vols.
> Gives documentation on large grant-making foundations.

Foundation Directory. 8th ed. Comp. by the Foundation Center. New York: Foundation Center, 1981.
> Includes all nongovernment and nonprofit foundations that have assets of $1,000,000 or more. Arranged geographically, with personal name, subject field, and corporate title indexes. Introductory material provides excellent information on foundations in general and their operation.

Foundation Grants Index. Comp. by the Foundation Center. New York: Columbia Univ. Press. (Annual or bimonthly) (School of Social Work Periodicals)
> This index forms the removable section of the bimonthly *Foundation News.* The cumulations from these bimonthly issues comprise the annual volume. It is a list of currently reported grants arranged alphabetically by state, then foundation name. Additional indexes of grant recipients, and key words and phrases taken from grant descriptions.

The Grants Register. London: St. James Press; New York: St. Martin's. Every two years.
> A listing of grants, fellowships, and grants-in-aid from government and private sources. Especially good for postgraduate students requiring further professional training. A-Z arrangement by grantor. Contains useful foreign addresses.

Guide to European Foundations, prepared by the Giovanni Agnelli Foundation. New York: Columbia Univ. Press, 1973.
> Provides information on foundations primarily in Western European countries. Arranged geographically.

List of Organizations Filing as Private Foundations. Comp. by the Foundation Center. New York: Columbia Univ. Press, 1973.
> A transcription of 30,000 organization names as they appear on the microfilm of the 1970 returns supplied by the Internal Revenue Service.

McClellan, Georgia. *Fellowship Guide for Western Europe.* 2nd ed. Pittsburgh: Council for European Studies, 1971.
> A publication for American graduate students, faculty, and researchers in the social sciences and humanities seeking funds for study or research in Western Europe. Arranged by country and discipline.

PMLA. Annual Directory Issue, September.
> A detailed section entitled "Fellowships and Grants" appearing in the annual directory issue includes those institutions, organizations, and foundations that concentrate on funding for the humanities and social sciences.

GUIDES, HANDBOOKS, MANUALS

The Bread Game: The Realities of Foundation Fundraising. Rev. ed. San Francisco: Glide Publications, 1981.
> A useful guide for the grant seeker, combining friendly advice with warnings of the pitfalls of the grant process.

Brodsky, Jean, ed. *The Proposal Writer's Swipe File.* Washington, D.C.: Taft Products, 1973.
> A style manual containing twelve samples of professionally written grant proposals.

Dermer, Joseph. *How to Raise Funds from Foundations.* New York: Public Service Materials Center, 1972.
> A manual suggesting practical approaches to the theory and reality of securing foundation grants.

Funding Sources Bibliography (*cont.*)

————. *How to Write Successful Foundation Presentations.* New York: Public Service Materials Center, 1975.

Instructive manual detailing all procedures in communicating with the foundation, from the writing of the appointment letter to the letter of renewal.

Fellowship and Grants of Interest to Historians. Washington, D.C.: American Historical Assoc., 1976.

An alphabetical listing of grants and fellowships in the field of history. Concluding pages of pamphlet provide general hints on grant applications and securing the grant.

Grantwriting Guide for Social Workers. Ann Arbor, Mich.: Campus Publishers, 1972.

A general introduction to grantwriting, not solely for social workers. Includes guidelines for grant seekers in both private and government sectors.

Hall, Mary. *Developing Skills in Proposal Writing.* Corvallis, Ore.: Office of Federal Relations, Oregon State System of Higher Education, 1971.

"A primer for individuals faced with the task of preparing a proposal. It deals specifically with applications to federal government agencies but much of the content is equally appropriate for requests to private foundations, industry and state agencies."

Hill, William J. *A Comprehensive Guide to Successful Grantsmanship.* Denver: Grant Development Institute, 1972.

Focuses on the how-to's of winning grant support. Provides insight into all areas of grantsmanship, includes tips on writing applications, proposals, and letters.

COMMENTARIES

Cuninggim, Merrimon. *Private Money and Public Service.* New York: McGraw-Hill, 1972.

Examines the role of foundations in American society by presenting various attitudes of Americans toward philanthropy. The author defends foundations against criticism from the public.

Hillman, Howard. *The Art of Winning Foundation Grants.* New York: Vanguard, 1975.

Margolin, Judith B. *About Foundations.* Comp. by the Foundation Center. New York: Foundation Center, 1975.

Useful facts for grant seekers. The booklet describes the Foundation Center's many services and publications. Includes a glossary.

Whitaker, Benjamin. *The Philanthropoids: Foundations and Society.* New York: Morrow, 1974.

An analytical study of foundations, including their history, economic and political roles in society. Contains bibliographies, charts, and graphs.

U.S. GOVERNMENT PUBLICATIONS

U.S. Office of Management and Budget. *Catalogue of Federal Domestic Assistance.* Washington, D.C.: U.S. Government Printing Office, 1976.

A comprehensive listing and description of federal programs, including grants, loans, and scholarships, that provide assistance or benefits to the American public. Issued annually with semiannual updates. Indexed by subject, agency, and program category.

U.S. Office of the Federal Register. *Federal Register.* Washington, D.C.: Superintendent of Documents.

Daily reports, with a monthly index, of regulations, legal notices, and announcements of programs and grants from federal agencies.

U.S. Office of the Federal Register. *U.S. Government Manual, 1976–77.* Washington,

---

Funding Sources Bibliography (*cont.*)

D.C.: Superintendent of Documents, 1976.
The official handbook of the federal government describes the purposes and programs of most government agencies and lists administrative staff. Revised annually.

NEWSPAPERS, PERIODICALS, NEWSLETTERS

The Chronicle of Higher Education. Baltimore: 1966– .
Published weekly during the academic year, this newspaper contains campus notes, legislative activities, book reviews, and announcements of grants, gifts and bequests.

Foundation News. New York: Council on Foundations, 1960– .
A bimonthly journal incorporating news and feature articles on the latest developments in foundation philanthropy, pending legislation, book reviews, conference and meeting announcements. The removable section contains *Foundation Grants Index.* (See p. 000.)

Higher Education and National Affairs. Washington, D.C.: American Council on Education.
A weekly newsletter listing legislative developments of interest to higher education, grant announcements, and news of colleges and universities.

Government agency bulletins and pamphlets describe policies, activities, and programs, and include deadline dates for grant proposals. Agencies include National Endowment to the Arts, National Endowment for the Humanities, National Institute of Education, and National Science Foundation.

When checking periodical indexes, such as *Readers' Guide, Social Sciences Index,* or *Business Periodicals Index,* for articles on funding, the following subject headings are used:
Foundations, Charitable and educational
Grants-in-aid
Research Grants

Regional Library of the Foundation Center of New York is located in the Social Sciences and History Department of the Free Library of Philadelphia, Logan Square. It is a noncirculating reference collection of specialized materials dealing with foundations, fund raising, and philanthropy. These materials are available to researchers who come to the library. There is no telephone service. Open Monday through Friday, 9–5. (Contact the Foundation Center of New York for information on the regional library nearest you.)

POSSIBLE SOURCES OF FUNDING

A list of over eighty possible funding organizations was compiled after consulting several sources: ERIC Database, FOUNDATION GRANTS INDEX Database, and the following printed materials: *Annual Register of Grant Support, Foundation Grants to Individuals,* and *Taft Foundation Report* (see p. 253).

Each of the funding organizations was reached individually in a letter in which we asked for their permission to cite them in this section of the book. The agencies included in the annotated bibliography all granted permission. This bibliography is divided into two main categories of private and public funding. Each of these categories subdivides into support to individuals, support to institutions, and support to institutions and to individuals. These citations do not, of course, guarantee that a grant proposal in the field of foreign language and literature will receive funding. The sponsoring agencies only acknowledged their willingness to accept for possible consideration projects dealing with our discipline. You will note that many of the funding sources establish restrictions on eligibility and areas of interest. Many of the programs that you may locate on your own will have similar restrictions. These restrictions change over the years and so should not be considered permanent. We suggest that you write to any organization that shows promise for your needs and ask for information on deadlines of application and proposal procedures. We also added a section of possible sources of funding that may yield support for your program.

Private Funding Sources: To Individual Scholars

(See the most recent September issue of *PMLA* for up-to-date information on funding for foreign language study. Faculty seeking individual grants should write for a booklet called *A Selected List of Fellowship Opportunities and Aids to Advanced Education.* Copies are available from the Publications Office, National Science Foundation, 1800 G Street, NW, Washington, DC 20550.)

American Association of University Women (2401 Virginia Ave., NW, Washington, DC 20037) offers fellowships at the doctoral and postdoctoral level. Postdoctoral fellowships normally will not be awarded to women who have received the doctorate within the past three years or for revision of the dissertation. It is expected that a doctorate fellowship will be used for the final year of doctoral work and that the degree will be received at the end of the fellowship year. No restrictions on age, academic field, or place of study. Period of award is for twelve months, and amount of award is based on cost-of-living and other expenses related to the project.

American Council of Learned Societies (228 E. 45th St., New York, NY 10017), a private, national representative of the humanities, offers several categories of fellowships and grants for scholars whose research programs have a predominantly humanistic emphasis: postdoctoral fellowships, fellowships for recent Ph.D. recipients, study fellowships in fields different from scholar's field of specialization, grants-in-aid in support of individual research including travel expenses, travel grants for participation in international congresses and conferences abroad, area studies supported jointly by the ACLS and the Social Science Research Council in Eastern Europe, Africa, China, Japan, Korea, Latin America, the Near and Middle East, South Asia, Southeast Asia, and Western Europe.

Canadian Embassy, Faculty Enrichment Program (1771 N Street, NW, Washington, DC 20036) supports postdoctoral study and research grants relating to Canada in order to develop new courses on some aspect of Canadian studies that will subsequently be offered at home institution. Monthly stipend for a period of no more than six months.

The French-American Foundation (680 Park Ave., New York, NY 10021) is not a direct source of funding but a source of information for nonacademic programs.

German Academic Exchange Service (New York Office, 535 Fifth Ave., Suite 1107, New York, NY 10017) offers various kinds of support: doctoral and postdoctoral grants for study and research in the Federal Republic of Germany (DAAD programs), academic study tours in Germany for professors and students affiliated with an American university, summer language courses at Goethe Institute for undergraduates or graduates enrolled at a U.S. university (must have completed one year of college German), three-week summer course at a German university of applicant's choice (must have completed at least three years of college-level German). Most awards include stipend for tuition and fees, partial living expenses, travel subsidy.

Germanistic Society of America (Institute of International Education, Study Abroad Programs, 809 United Nations Plaza, New York, NY 10017) offers program support for study of German abroad.

George A. and Eliza Gardner Howard Foundation (Box 1867, Brown Univ., Graduate School, Providence, RI 02912) offers rotating fellowships for different disciplines. Foreign language category scheduled for support in 1982–83, then again three years later. Stipends will range from $5,000 to $12,000 for one year to support persons engaged in independent projects.

Institute of International Education, Division of Study Abroad Programs (809 United Nations Plaza, New York, NY 10017) offers study abroad opportunities for individuals in many different countries.

Institute for Research in the Humanities (Univ. of Wisconsin, Old Observatory, Madison, WI 53706) invites applications for postdoctoral fellowships tenable at the institute. Candidates must have a doctoral degree and must intend to pursue research in some aspect of the humanities. In general, the institute is interested in developing research in history, philosophy, and language and literature. Stipends will be approximately $13,000.

International Research and Exchange Board (655 Third Ave., New York, NY 10017) administers research exchange programs with the socialist countries of Eastern Europe and with the USSR: research grants, language training programs, travel grants for senior scholars for the purposes of consultation and for lecturing.

The Japan Foundation (Suite 570, Watergate Office Bldg., 600 New Hampshire Ave., NW, Washington, DC 20037).

Sibley Fellowship Committee, United Chapters of Phi Beta Kappa (1811 Q Street, NW, Washington, DC 20009) awards the Mary Isabel Sibley Fellowship alternately in the fields of Greek and French. Both fields are broadly interpreted: language and literature for French; language, literature, history, archaelogy for Greek. The award is made annually and carries a stipend. Candidates must be unmarried women between 25 and 35 years of age, hold the doctorate or have fulfilled all requirements for the doctorate except the dissertation. They must plan to devote full-time work to research during the fellowship year.

Social Science Research Council (605 Third Ave., New York, NY 10016) offers doctoral fellowships and postdoctoral grants for research in both the social sciences and the humanities. A certain number of awards are available for research to be carried out abroad: Africa, Asia, Latin America, the Caribbean, the Near and Middle East, Western Europe.

South Atlantic MLA (Drawer CA, University, AL 35486) offers SAMLA Studies Award. Write for more information.

Tinker Foundation, Inc. (645 Madison Ave., New York, NY 10022) offers postdoctoral fellowships to further understanding among peoples in the United States, Latin America, Spain, and Portugal, providing scholars interested in Latin America and Iberian Studies the opportunity to do research in social sciences, marine sciences, and international relations. Annual stipend and travel expenses for field research are included. Applicants must have completed doctoral studies no fewer than three years but no more than ten years prior to the time of application.

Wesleyan University Center for the Humanities (95 Pearl St., Middletown, CT 06457) offers two Mellon Fellowships a year; requires residence, participation in the work of the center, teaching of one course a term in undergraduate general humanities education. Scholars and teachers whose interests bear on any of the following fields are encouraged to apply: art history, literature, history, philosophy, religion, literary theory.

Institut Français de Washington (141 Dey Hall, Univ. of North Carolina, Chapel Hill, NC 27514) offers several awards in French language, literature, and history. The Gilbert Chinard Scholarships support two $750 awards for maintenance (not travel) during research in France for a period of at least two months. These scholarships are in the fields of French history and literature and are available to candidates in the final stage of the Ph.D. dissertation or who have held the Ph.D. no longer than six years before application. The Gilbert Chinard Literary Prize is an annual prize of $1,000 for work in the history or criticism of French literature. The prize will be awarded to a North American scholar for a book in its manuscript form, written in English or French. Manuscripts should be recent and unpublished, or accepted for publication and not yet printed. The Gilbert Chinard Prize in French History is attributed through the intermediary of the Society for French Historial Studies (annual prize of $1,000). The selection is made by a committee nominated by the society. The Gilbert Chinard Pedagogical Prize of $500 is awarded for the best article on a pedagogical problem in the teaching of French. Selection is first made by the *French Review;* final decision is taken by a committee designated by the institute.

The Lady Davis Fellowship Trust (P.O. Box 1255, Jerusalem, 91000, Israel) offers awards for study, research, or teaching on graduate, postdoctorate, or professorial levels at the Hebrew University of Jerusalem and the Technion-Israel Institute of Technology, Haifa. The Lady Davis fellowships are open to candidates irrespective of race, creed, sex, or nationality. The fellowships are tenable for a period of one year or two years, and the grant for fellows defrays the cost of travel, tuition fees (where applicable), and reasonable living expenses in Israel.

Private Funding Sources: To Institutions

Association of American Colleges (1818 R St., NW, Washington, DC 20009). Project Lodestar, supported by a grant from the Andrew W. Mellon Foundation, is a national effort to find the best ways in which institutions of higher learning can attack issues related to liberal learning. By providing consultants for institutional advisory teams, the project assists participating institutions in renewing liberal learning and in strengthening institutional structures to support it. The project began in the 1979–80 academic year and will continue over a four-year period. Institutional needs that have already been addressed by advisory teams are enrollment planning, articulation projects between community colleges and four-year institutions, a review of undergraduate curriculum, the development of interdisciplinary programs following departmental reorganization, review of general education distribution requirements, and the implementation of a general education core requirement over a four-year period. Institutional cost-sharing of 50% is expected and usually falls between $3,000 and $4,500 depending on the size of the advisory team and nature of the problem. Project Quill is a program of direct grants to support the development of innovative programs aimed at assuring that career-oriented students receive adequate instruction in liberal learning. Projects should relate to liberal learning for future professionals or liberal learning for working adults. Awards range from $1,000 to $10,000. Proposals may be initiated by faculty, administrators, staff, or students but must be authorized by chief executive officer. Joint proposals by several persons, departments, or cooperating institutions are encouraged.

Educational Foundation of America (16250 Ventura Blvd., Room 445, Encino, CA 91346) makes grants for specific projects in the broad area of undergraduate higher education. An informal letter of inquiry or a brief preliminary proposal will usually be sufficient for staff to determine whether proposal research falls within the interests of the foundation. In the past, some grants have been awarded to institutions for purposes of curriculum development.

The Kresge Foundation (P.O. Box 3151, West Big Beaver Road, Troy, MI 48084) offers grants limited to the support of building construction, renovation projects, or purchase of major movable equipment having a unit cost of not less than $50,000. The foundation does not generally grant initial funds or total project costs. Grants are usually made on a challenge basis. Typically, the successful applicant has already raised some money, and a grant is awarded for a portion of the remaining funds.

Olin Foundation, Inc. (299 Park Ave., New York, NY 10017) makes grants to private colleges and universities for the construction of academic buildings and libraries. The foundation generally undertakes to pay the total cost of the new facility, including equipment and furnishings. In the past, building grants have been made for the construction of arts and humanities facilities.

The Pew Memorial Trust (c/o Glen Mede Trust Co., 229 S. 18th St., Philadelphia, PA 19103) often receives proposals to support humanities research. Write for further information.

Rhode Island Foundation (957 N. Main Street, Providence, RI 02904) offers grants to support humanities research. Write for further information.

Sid W. Richardson Foundation (2103 Fort Worth National Bank Bldg., Fort Worth, TX 76102) offers grant and project support for language and literature study limited to institutions in Texas.

Private Funding Sources: To Individuals and to Institutions

Exxon Education Foundation (111 West 49th St., New York, NY 10020) offers intermittent, restricted funding to foreign languages through their international studies program and high-leverage grants for faculty and program development.

Ford Foundation (320 East 43rd St., New York, NY 10017) offers limited number of grants to support activities to ensure excellence in higher education and educational systems generally. The foundation encourages global projects. It will support work concerning immigrants and refugees and work that aims to improve understanding of American foreign policy issues.

Rockefeller Foundation, Humanities Division (1133 Ave. of the Americas, New York, NY 10036) offers fellowships and project grants to support humanistic scholarship intended to examine the social and cultural issues of the contemporary world.

Public Funding Sources: To Institutions

U.S. Information Agency, Office of Private Sector Programs (400 C Street SW, Washington, DC 20547) provides selective assistance and grant support to nonprofit organizations that enhance America's competence in world affairs through greater understanding of other societies—their peoples, values, cultures, and aspirations. Proposals for grant support must fall within one or more of the following categories: advancing basic cultural knowledge, enhancing the international competency of Americans in positions of public and private leadership, encouraging an international perspective, and encouraging institutions and professional organizations to add an international dimension to their members' understanding and work. USICA support for projects will not normally be extended for a period longer than three years and will not be awarded to projects that mostly involve research.

Public Funding Sources: To Individuals and Institutions

The National Endowment for the Humanities (Old Post Office, 1100 Pennsylvania Ave. NW, Washington, D.C. 20506, tel. 202 786-0373). Foreign language and literature departments will benefit in a number of ways from the changes brought to the Education Programs Division of NEH by the new NEH chairman, William T. Bennett, and Division Director Richard Ekman. In the November 1982 issue of *Humanities,* Ekman described some of these changes and the philosophy and intent that stimulated them:

> The national effort now underway to restore high standards of achievement in American education will succeed only when teachers and curricula place intellectual demands on students. That simple reality is the basis for new categories of support in the NEH division of Education Programs.
>
> The Division's purpose remains the improvement of teaching and learning of the humanities in the nation's institutions of formal education. But rather than emphasizing curriculum change as the principal means to achieve that goal, the new categories will support a wide variety of efforts to increase the effectiveness with which the humanities are taught in existing programs.
>
> There is much excitement about education today—an anticipation of important changes resulting from a new pursuit of excellence. And although the United States is a country that has consistently valued education as a matter of national pride, the strength of this new commitment is awesome.
>
> What teachers and scholars have told us at the Endowment about the critical issues they are facing in education has shaped our ideas for the changes in the Endowment's education programs. The new categories are responses to those who wish to require of their students more writing, more difficult reading, and more ambitious degree requirements in history, in philosophy, in the languages and literatures of foreign cultures, indeed, in any of the humanities disciplines.
>
> Put simply, the Endowment will respond most favorably to proposals which are designed to increase both the quality and quantity of humanities study required of students. The Endowment recognizes that this goal can be reached by many routes. The new program guidelines, therefore, are clear about the aims of education in the humanities but are flexible about the means to achieve them.
>
> The reorganized Division contains five areas, each of which has a dis-

tinctive concern. The first is to improve instruction in the central disciplines in undergraduate education. The Endowment will support efforts to strengthen introductory courses in the humanities, on the premise that first experiences with the humanities shape students' attitudes toward further coursework. It will help departments and programs build excellence in an individual field, in the belief that Endowment support should offset economic and demographic challenges to institutional survival and bolster existing structures. It will assist the efforts of institutions that have made a commitment to extend the humanities throughout the undergraduate curriculum, on the grounds that coherent education is a necessary pre-condition for real learning to occur.

The Endowment will also support exemplary projects in undergraduate and graduate education that promise to be of significance to a large number of colleges and universities. The support of "model" projects is, these days, a particularly cost-effective way of improving humanities education since fewer resources are required to emulate such projects than to reinvent them.

A third concern is improving humanities instruction in elementary and secondary education. The Division will support the establishment of institutes for teachers of history, literature, languages, and other disciplines to deepen their understanding of their fields and the most effective ways of teaching them. The most important changes in this area will be the placing of more emphasis on the commonly taught subjects and less on enrichment in other subject areas; more emphasis on substance and less on pedagogy; more emphasis on teachers and less on materials that attempt to be "teacher proof."

The aim of the Division's fourth area is enhancing humanities instruction for nontraditional learners. This area was established to assist educational as well as cultural institutions that have widened access to the humanities through nontraditional approaches. It will support projects that increase the intellectual rigor or decrease the unit cost of nontraditional humanities instruction.

For example, a university's continuing education division that has developed television courses may obtain support for efforts to improve those courses and to offer them more efficiently.

The Division will also award grants that prepare teaching materials from recent research, including that which has been supported by the Endowment's Research and Fellowships Divisions.

We expect that these forms of support will help restore the humanities to a central, rather than peripheral, role in education. This approach is predicated on the view that history, philosophy, literature, languages and the other humanities disciplines are both a body of ideas and texts of lasting significance and a set of methods and skills with utility well beyond the fields in which they are initially learned.

In general, the Division's changes involve a movement away from curriculum development as the only or best means of strengthening humanities study and a movement toward fortifying existing disciplines and programs through a variety of activities that may include, for example, faculty development seminars, improved sabbatical leave programs, changes in degree requirements, and the hosting of scholars-in-residence.

I believe that these new programs will strengthen the humanities in American schools, colleges and universities and will further encourage educators who are reviving their commitment to educational excellence.

PROGRAMS AND GUIDELINES

1. Central disciplines in Undergraduate Education. Grants support costs associated with strengthening the teaching of the humanities in colleges and universities. Applications should show evidence of activities, plans, and commitments to improve the quality, rigor, and coherence of offerings in the humanities Eligible applicants: Two- and four-year colleges, universities, nonprofit technical schools, and other post secondary institutions.

    Improving Introductory Courses. Grants support institutional plans to give introductory courses a more central place in the curriculum and to make the first experiences of undergraduates in the humanities more effective.

    Promoting Excellence in a Field. Grants support plans to improve the quality of all the courses and faculty in a specific discipline or field.

    Fostering Coherence throughout an Institution. Grants support plans to improve the total program of offerings in the humanities in an institution.

    Contact: Assistant Director or Program Officer for one of the three programs named above. Tel. (202) 786-0380.

2. Humanities Instruction in Elementary and Secondary Schools. Grants support institutes and projects designed to improve the teaching of history, foreign languages, literature, and the other humanities in elementary and secondary schools. Eligible applicants: Public and private elementary and secondary schools, school systems, colleges and universities, and other nonprofit educational organizations.

    Institutes for Teachers. Provide opportunities for teachers of history, languages, literature, and other humanistic disciplines to learn more about their fields and the most effective ways of teaching them by studying under the direction of leading scholars and master teachers.

    Collaborative Projects. Provide partial support for joint university-school system projects of varying sizes designed to strengthen the curriculum and teaching in the basic disciplines of the humanities.

    Contact: Assistant Director, Humanities Instruction in Elementary and Secondary Schools. Tel. (202) 786-0377.

3. Exemplary Projects in Undergraduate and Graduate Education. Grants to promote the development and dissemination of projects in the humanities which are likely to have significance to a large number of institutions. Eligible applicants: Colleges and universities, nonprofit academic and professional associations, and other institutions or agencies serving higher education.

    Feasibility Grants. Assist institutions to refine and evaluate programs or materials which have the potential for national dissemination.

    Major Projects. Provide for direct dissemination activities such as conferences, workshops, and institutes and for the preparation of teaching materials.

    Contact: Program Officer, Exemplary Projects in Undergraduate and Graduate Education. Tel. (202) 786-0384.

4. Humanities Programs for Nontraditional Learners. Grants support efforts to improve the quality and rigor of humanistic education offered to new types of learners through cost-effective means. Eligible Applicants: Colleges, universities, educational consortia, libraries, museums, and other cultural institutions.

    Contact: Program Officer, Humanities Programs for Nontraditional Learners. Tel. (202) 786-0384.

5. Teaching Materials from Recent Research. Grants support preparation of teaching materials based on recently completed scholarly research. Although Endowment-funded research is of particular interest, the program is also open to other applicants. Eligible Applicants: Organizations and individuals possessing the capability to achieve the program's purposes.

    Contact: Program Officer, Teaching Materials from Recent Research. Tel. (202) 786-0384.

Foreign language and literature faculty will quickly see that their departments will be able to apply for funds under "Promoting Excellence in a Field." They should also consider collaborating with colleagues in other departments to improve humanities curriculum at the introductory level and across the total program of offerings. Foreign language and literature courses should be a carefully designed component of institutional projects at both levels. In fact, at each point in the rest of the revised guidelines, FLL faculty will discover ways to strengthen their own curriculum while also achieving additional goals: outreach to the schools, to adult learners, and to a larger regional or national public.

The Office of International Education (U.S. Department of Education, Washington, DC 20202) offers grants, fellowships, awards for expanding the international and global dimensions of American education and for promoting awareness of other cultures. Seven programs for individuals and institutions are conducted primarily within the U.S.: the International Studies Centers Program (to institutions), the Research Program (to institutions and individuals), the Graduate International Studies Program (to institutions), the Undergraduate International Studies Program (to institutions), the Citizen Education for Cultural Understanding Program (to public and private agencies and organizations), the Foreign Curriculum Consultant Program (to institutions), and the Foreign Language and Area Studies Fellowship Program (to institutions for graduate studies). Six programs for individuals and institutions are conducted primarily overseas: the Faculty Research Abroad Program (to institutions), the Doctoral Dissertation Research Program (assistance to graduate students), the Group Projects Abroad (to institutions for training, research, curriculum development), the Seminar Abroad Program (to individuals), the Teacher Exchange Program (awards to individuals to teach abroad), Special Bilateral Projects (support to individuals for projects with other nations to support short-term institutes, research seminars, and exchanges).

The Fund for the Improvement of Post-Secondary Education (400 Maryland Ave., SW, Room 3123, Washington, DC 20202). A well-known source of support for education, F.I.P.S.E. tends to concentrate on programs with broad replicability outside the institutions that created them. Grants vary from about $10,000 to $150,000 a year for projects lasting from one to three years. The fund collects all proposals that significantly improve learning opportunities.

State-based NEH Committees (see addresses on pp. 268–71). Many FL faculty have had excellent success building fine projects with the help of the state programs. These projects must focus on bringing humanities programs to constituencies not served in the regular academic curriculum. Write Dr. Alain Ranwez, Box 26, Dept. of Foreign Language and Literature, Metropolitan State Coll., Denver, CO 80204, for information on his project with the Colorado Committee.

State Department of Education. Do not overlook this agency in seeking sources for funding. Again, many FL faculty have both received help and provided important support to their state's FL teachers using funds from the State Department of Education.

Possible Additional Sources of Funding

J. S. Abercombie Foundation (P.O. Box 27339, Houston, TX 77027)

Belgian American Foundation (420 Lexington Ave., New York, NY 10017)

Robert Sterling Clark Foundation (100 Wall St., New York, NY 10005)

Gladys Krieble Delmas Foundation (40 Wall St., New York, NY 10005)

Educational Exchange Service (Nassestrasse 8 Postfach 2240, D-5300 Bonn 1, Federal Republic of Germany)

Max Kade Foundation (100 Church St., Room 1604, New York, NY 10007)

Luso-American Education Foundation (P.O. Box 1768, Oakland, CA 94604)

Charles E. Merrill Trust (P.O. Box 488, Ithaca, NY 14850)

Ministry of Education, ICETEX (Apartado Aero 5735, Bogota, D.E., Colombia)

National Humanities Center (P.O. Box 12256, Research Triangle Park, NC 27709)

National Humanities Faculty (1266 Main St., Concord, MA 01742)

Phi Sigma Iota, The Foreign Language Honor Society (National Executive Office, Hamilton Coll., Clinton, NY 13323)

Rome Prize Fellowships (American Academy in Rome, 41 East 65th St., New York, NY 10021)

S & H Foundation (Sperry & Hutchinson Bldg., 330 Madison Ave., New York, NY 10017)

Alfred P. Sloan Foundation (630 Fifth Ave., New York, NY 10020)

Société des Professeurs Français en Amérique (22 East 60th St., New York, NY 10570)

DeWitt Wallace Fund (c/o Reader's Digest Assoc., Inc., Pleasantville, NY 10570)

Addresses of State-Based Humanities Councils

ALABAMA
Committee for the Humanities in
    Alabama
Box A-40
Birmingham-Southern College
Birmingham, AL 35204
(205) 324-1314

ALASKA
Alaska Humanities Forum
429 D Street, Room 211
Loussac Sogn Bldg.
Anchorage, AK 99501
(907) 272-5341

ARIZONA
Arizona Humanities Council
112 N. Central Ave., Suite 304
Phoenix, AZ 85004
(602) 257-0335

ARKANSAS
Arkansas Endowment for the
    Humanities
Remmel Bldg., Suite 102
1010 W. 3rd St.
Little Rock, AR 72201
(501) 663-3451

CALIFORNIA
California Council for the
    Humanities
312 Sutter St., Suite 601
San Francisco, CA 94108
(415) 391-1474

COLORADO
Colorado Humanities Program
601 Broadway, Suite 307
Denver, CO 80203
(303) 595-0881

CONNECTICUT
Connecticut Humanities Council
195 Church St.
Wesleyan Station
Middletown, CT 06457
(203) 347-6888

DELAWARE
Delaware Humanities Forum
2600 Pennsylvania Ave.
Wilmington, DE 19806
(302) 738-8491

DISTRICT OF COLUMBIA
D.C. Community Humanities
    Council
1341 G Street, NW, Suite 620
Washington, DC 20005
(202) 347-1732

FLORIDA
Florida Endowment for the
    Humanities
LET 468
Univ. of South Florida
Tampa, FL 33620
(813) 974-4094

GEORGIA
Georgia Endowment for the
    Humanities
1589 Clifton Rd., NE
Emory Univ.
Atlanta, GA 30322
(404) 329-7500

HAWAII
Hawaii Committee for the
    Humanities
2615 S. King St., Suite 211
Honolulu, HI 96826
(808) 947-5891

IDAHO
Assoc. for the Humanities in Idaho
1409 W. Washington St.
Boise, ID 83702
(208) 345-5346

ILLINOIS
Illinois Humanities Council
201 W. Springfield Ave., Room
    1002
Champaign, IL 61820
(217) 333-7611

Addresses of State-Based Humanities Councils (*cont.*)

INDIANA
Indiana Committee for the
  Humanities
4200 Northwestern Ave.
Indianapolis, IN 46208
(317) 925-5316

IOWA
Iowa Humanities Board
Oakdale Campus
Univ. of Iowa
Iowa City, IA 52242
(319) 353-6754

KANSAS
Kansas Committee for the
  Humanities
112 W. Sixth St., Suite 509
Topeka, KS 66603
(913) 357-0359

KENTUCKY
Kentucky Humanities Council, Inc.
Ligon House
Univ. of Kentucky
Lexington, KY 40508
(606) 258-5932

LOUISIANA
Louisiana Committee for the
  Humanities
1215 Prytania St., Suite 535
New Orleans, LA 70130
(504) 523-4352

MAINE
Maine Humanities Council
P.O. Box 7202
Portland, ME 04112
(207) 773-5051

MARYLAND
Maryland Committee for the
  Humanities
516 N. Charles St., Room 304–
  305
Baltimore, MD 21201
(301) 837-1938

MASSACHUSETTS
Massachusetts Foundation for the
  Humanities and Public Policy
237-E Whitmore
Administration Bldg.
Univ. of Massachusetts
Amherst, MA 01003
(413) 545-1936

MICHIGAN
Michigan Council for the
  Humanities
Nisbet Bldg., Suite 30
1407 S. Harrison Rd.
East Lansing, MI 48824
(517) 355-0160

MINNESOTA
Minnesota Humanities Commission
Metro Square, Suite 282
St. Paul, MN 55101
(612) 224-5739

MISSISSIPPI
Mississippi Committee for the
  Humanities, Inc.
3825 Ridgewood Rd., Room 111
Jackson, MS 39211
(601) 982-6752

MISSOURI
Missouri State Committee for the
  Humanities
Loberg Bldg., Suite 202
11425 Dorsett Rd.
Maryland Heights, MO 63043
(314) 739-7368

MONTANA
Montana Committee for the
  Humanities
P.O. Box 8036
Hellgate Station
Missoula, MT 59807
(406) 243-6022

Addresses of State-Based Humanities Councils (*cont.*)

NEBRASKA
Nebraska Committee for the
  Humanities
Cooper Plaza, Suite 405
211 N. 12th St.
Lincoln, NE 68508
(308) 474-2131

NEVADA
Nevada Humanities Committee
P.O. Box 8065
Reno, NV 89507
(702) 784-6587

NEW HAMPSHIRE
New Hampshire Council for the
  Humanities
112 South State St.
Concord, NH 03301
(603) 224-4071

NEW JERSEY
New Jersey Committee for the
  Humanities
73 Easton Ave.
New Brunswick, NJ 08903
(201) 932-7726

NEW MEXICO
New Mexico Humanities Council
1712 Las Lomas NE
Univ. of New Mexico
Albuquerque, NM 87131
(505) 277-3705

NEW YORK
New York Council for the
  Humanities
33 W. 42nd St.
New York, NY 10036
(212) 354-3040

NORTH CAROLINA
North Carolina Humanities
  Committee
112 Foust Bldg.
UNC-Greensboro

Greensboro, NC 27412
(919) 379-5325

NORTH DAKOTA
North Dakota Humanities Council
Box 2191,
Bismarck, ND 58502
(701) 663-1948

OHIO
Ohio Program in the Humanities
760 Pleasant Ridge Ave.
Columbus, OH 43209
(614) 236-6879

OKLAHOMA
Oklahoma Humanities Committee
Executive Terrace Bldg.
2809 Northwest Expressway, Suite
  500
Oklahoma City, OK 73112
(405) 840-1721

OREGON
Oregon Committee for the
  Humanities
418 S.W. Washington, Room 410
Portland, OR 97204
(503) 241-0543

PENNSYLVANIA
Pennsylvania Humanities Council
401 N. Broad St.
Philadelphia, PA 19108
(215) 925-1005

PUERTO RICO
Fundacion Puertorriquena de las
  Humanidades
Box S-4307
Old San Juan, PR 00904
(809) 723-2087

RHODE ISLAND
Rhode Island Committee for the
  Humanities
463 Broadway
Providence, RI 02909
(404) 273-2250

Addresses of State-Based Humanities Councils (*cont.*)

SOUTH CAROLINA
South Carolina Committee for the
 Humanities
17 Calendar Court, Suite 6
Columbia, SC 29206
(803) 738-1850
SOUTH DAKOTA
South Dakota Committee on the
 Humanities
University Station, Box 35
Brookings, SD 57007
(605) 688-4823
TENNESSEE
Tennessee Committee for the
 Humanities
1001 18th Ave. S.
Nashville, TN 37212
(615) 320-7001
TEXAS
Texas Committee for the
 Humanities
1604 Nueces
Austin, TX 78701
(512) 473-8585
UTAH
Utah Endowment for the
 Humanities
10 W. Broadway
Broadway Bldg., Suite 900
Salt Lake City, UT 84101
(801) 531-7868
VERMONT
Vermont Council on the
 Humanities and Public Issues

Grant House, P.O. Box 58
Hyde Park, VT 05655
(802) 888-3183
VIRGINIA
Virginia Foundation for the
 Humanities and Public Policy
One-B West Range
Univ. of Virginia
Charlottesville, VA 22903
(804) 924-3296
WASHINGTON
Washington Commission on the
 Humanities
Olympia, WA 98505
(206) 866-6510
WEST VIRGINIA
Humanities Foundation of West
 Virginia
Box 204
Institute, WV 25112
(304) 768-8869
WISCONSIN
Wisconsin Humanities Committee
716 Langdon St.
Madison, WI 53706
(608) 262-0706
WYOMING
Wyoming Council for the
 Humanities
Box 3274-Univ. Sta.
Laramie, WY 82701
(307) 766-6496

Chapter Nine

Professional Collaborative Development Programs

Academic faculty members, like doctors and lawyers, need opportunities for professional development during their active careers. These opportunities help ensure that the level of practice in the professions reflects the best current research and wisdom. In addition, these opportunities provide more advanced professionals with a way to assist new colleagues in making the transition from graduate training to regular practice while enabling newly trained members to try their skills under the guidance of their experienced colleagues. Lawyers and doctors, like academic faculty members, attend state and national conventions as well as special-interest conferences designed to expose them to current research in their fields. Unlike faculty, though, most doctors and lawyers also belong to local professional societies, such as county bar associations and county medical groups. These societies serve several purposes. They help keep professionals up-to-date. They bring colleagues in the same region into closer contact with one another, developing confidence for professional consultations. They are an expression of the corporate concern professional people have for maintaining high standards. For instance, it is in the best interest of doctors that medicine be practiced responsibly and well in their area. Most professionals in a given region are eligible to meet in the county medical or bar associations, regardless of their clientele or the kind of medicine or law the professional practices. Academic faculties, especially foreign language and literature faculties, will benefit enormously from adopting this model of professional development from the medical and legal professions.

Rising travel costs and shrinking departmental budgets have prevented many faculty members from attending national conventions. Some cannot even attend regional language conferences unless they are included in the program. To reduce costs, many college libraries have stopped subscribing to foreign language journals with low user frequency. Many foreign language faculty teach increased loads because tight budgets have prohibited hiring, even in schools where enrollments have increased. All these factors conspire to make ongoing faculty development more difficult to achieve just when it is most important. For instance, in response to the President's Commission, the ACTFL Stepladder project has produced descriptors of proficiency levels for each of the five skills: reading, writing, speaking, listening, and culture. These standards must affect classroom teaching. Oral proficiency testing and improvements in the teaching of writing and reading will help students develop language skills. Many institutions are restoring or increasing language requirements. It is imperative that these and other indications of growth become familiar to foreign language and literature (FLL) teachers at all levels as quickly as possible.

Since January 1981 I have helped establish three pilot collaborative faculty development groups. One operates in a community college, one in a major state university, and one in a small private liberal arts college. These teams provide models for academic analogues of local medical and bar associations. They appear to succeed in unifying the members of the profession in a region into a cohesive, collaborative group. Like the societies of other professions, local faculty associations provide a forum for continual professional development. Through numerous workshops, seminars, training courses, and regular society meetings, members keep up-to-date on the latest developments in their fields without having to travel great distances and without expenditures of scarce money and time. Most important, however, these associations enable members of a profession to establish continual dialogues, to exchange ideas, methods, and developments, and to create a critical body of common interests and expertise. The existence of these local academic groups attests that, like doctors and lawyers, faculty can work together to develop a sense of responsibility for the level of professional practice by peers in their locale.

The three pilot programs offer the additional benefit of unifying FLL teaching faculty of all educational sectors within a locale. Traditionally, those teaching the same discipline and using largely the same methods have tended to stratify their professional meetings. Whereas grammar and high school faculty may attend professional meetings with their college and university colleagues, they often attend different sesssions. The sense of real collaboration and mutual respect across educational sectors is rare. Equally rare is the spirit of group responsibility for the level of professional practice in a given locale. The academic profession remains fragmented along institutional lines. With notable exceptions, we have neglected to promote collectively and consistently the professional development of our colleagues.

Lack of collaboration among grade school, secondary, and postsecondary FLL faculty has often made it difficult for students to move from high school foreign language classes to the college and university foreign language classes. The lack of communication among the foreign language faculty at all educational levels has led to confusion over what students know or should know as they progress from one level to the next. It has hindered faculty in their efforts to ascertain students' proficiency levels, to organize effective classes, and to test students with varying levels of proficiency and preparations.

Professional responsibilities include the obligation not only to produce scholarly work but also to provide the best FLL education to students and continuing professional education for fellow teachers. The establishment of collaborative professional development groups enables faculty to fulfill these obligations. Integrated FLL programs that meet monthly or bimonthly and include faculty from all levels stimulate dialogue among teachers and lead to the organization of programs that provide continuity for FLL students. The professional-update teams exchange methodologies, materials, and means of testing and, like county medical and bar associations, keep members abreast of current literature, trends, approaches, and events. These groups meet the specific needs of local members and help them solve their special problems. Most important, however, the groups strengthen the commitment of foreign language teachers to their own development, to the needs of their students, to one another, and to their discipline.

How large should the local faculty professional development association be and who should belong to it? While each area will have unique features, a group larger than forty or fifty could be unwieldy. The group should include foreign language faculty from all the languages and from all educational sectors: grammar and high schools, community colleges, four-year colleges, and universities. Both full- and part-time teachers should be represented, as should those oriented toward literacy and pedagogical research and those who focus on teaching. Members would meet monthly or bimonthly.

Ideally, the first half of each meeting would consist of a time-saving version of the "journal reading" practiced among scientists. Faculty members would volunteer to read and prepare abstracts on the articles in various journals. In a five-minute presentation, one person would describe the contents of an autumn *Modern Language Journal;* another, an autumn *ADFL Bulletin;* another, an autumn *Foreign Language Annals. French Review, Hispania, Unterrichtspraxis,* among others, should also be covered by group members. After each presentation, the speaker would pass out a one-page copy of his or her remarks with a bibliography. Each quarter another group of members would report on the contents of the journals. In less than one hour and with modest effort, colleagues would bring each other up-to-date. Moreover, the journal reading session exposes specialists in one language to useful developments in the study of other languages. Language teachers have a great deal in common. Journal reading offers an efficient and intelligent use of time at local professional development meetings.

The second half of each meeting might focus on a presentation related to a current concern of local teachers. The group may have designated any one of a number of issues as worthy of a one- or two-year collaborative investigation. Perhaps faculty will look into ways to improve students' global perspectives through FLL classes or ways to improve student literacy through FLL study. At some meetings, faculty might hold a panel discussion of several books or articles on the topic. At others, faculty might teach segments of a model class or describe new materials they have used or developed.

In time these topics help local faculty recognize the need to make long-range plans to assist one another. Whole groups might see substantial improvements in the quality of teaching in their classes that relate to the central theme. Growing expertise in the groups should also attract well-deserved administrative support from teachers' institutions as well as interest from the community. As the level of professional practice improves, all colleagues will benefit. The local professional development association will have achieved its purpose.

How to Set Up a Collaborative Professional Development Group

Regardless of differences in institutions and regions, certain basic steps guided the formation of all three collaborative development teams. These procedures may prove useful to other faculty intending to establish local groups. First, faculty need to secure support for the idea. As a consultant and project director, I have taken the idea of local professional groups to more than sixty institutions in the past two years. Enthusiasm usually greets the notion instantly. Groups have begun to establish themselves all over the country. I suggest that individual faculty members present the idea to their colleagues and to the administrators of their institutions. If sufficient interest and support exist, the initiators should seek endorsements, recommendations, and suggestions for faculty and administrators, who should receive invitations to the first meeting. This step is of great value in forming the team. In addition, having the endorsement of one's administrators and colleagues helps in securing further support for the plan.

Instead of beginning with departmental colleagues, some faculty prefer to begin with public school officials, secondary school teaching faculty, and administrators and foreign language faculty from other postsecondary institutions in the area. Endorsements that emerge from these persons give the broad base of support needed for a program committed to the establishment of a collaborative and integrated group of professionals.

Another way to begin is to get in touch with two high school teachers, a public school official, and a postsecondary faculty member or administrator about setting up an ad hoc committee to study the idea of a professional-update group. This group can draft a short general proposal concerning the objectives, function, and structure of such a group and recruit further support for it.

Once initial support has been secured, a steering or ad hoc committee of especially interested colleagues should meet. The members of the committee should represent both the schools and the postsecondary sectors. If possible, both teaching faculty and administrators should participate in the ad hoc committee. The major purpose of this committee is to draft a proposal that outlines the goals, structure, and size of the professional development program, elaborates a strategy for reaching and recruiting all those who can benefit from this program, and anticipates the first meeting. A well-organized collaborative plan is crucial and must precede all other efforts. A half-baked project will fail to inspire either enthusiasm or loyalty in other faculty, but a well-structured, carefully formulated proposal will indicate the potential for faculty to help one another. Furthermore, in refining and clarifying the local needs and goals of teachers, the proposal helps define the pertinent issues both for the committee and for prospective members. (See NCSU proposal, p. 281.)

One of the difficulties some FLL faculty report from their NDEA Institute experience concerns precisely the lack of a collaborative spirit. University faculty dominated many institutes. These new attempts to establish local professional development teams will have an excellent chance for success if they are truly collaborative. If these teams wish to establish direct, continual, and supportive contacts among members of the profession, collaboration must play a dynamic role in the first stage of the whole process. Including high school teachers and school officials from the initial phase on minimizes the risk of alienating any group from the project.

After the committee has drawn up a general proposal and made preliminary plans for the first meeting, it should venture, armed with the plan, to expand its base of support. The best contacts to establish are with public school officials, high school, college, and university faculty and administrators, and officials at the Department of Education. They may not only provide endorsements and encouragement but also yield further contacts; listings of all the foreign language teachers in a given area; possible publicity through newsletters, newspapers, and conferences; and ideas on how best to reach all potential participants. Some administrators might support the program by offering credit or released time to faculty members who attend the meetings. Such incentives and administrative support make participation in the program more attractive.

Recruiting teachers takes careful planning. A letter of invitation to the first meeting should be sent to all FLL faculty within a reasonable driving distance. The letter should explain the need for the group, state the group's function and goals, and include a short description of the structure and purpose of the first session. A good recruitment program also includes letters to principals and deans of local schools explaining the objectives of the project and asking them to encourage their faculty to attend. A public-service notice in local newspapers will alert interested faculty to the meeting.

Beyond sending invitations, letters, and notices, however, ad hoc committees of all three pilot groups stressed the importance of establishing personal contacts with as many of the invited faculty as possible. Each group noted that most of the teachers who had received a letter that was followed by a phone call or a visit came to the meeting. Those who only received a letter were less likely to attend. Personal contact increases the likelihood of faculty attendance because it shows the concern and commitment of the organizer. It also gives the prospective member the opportunity to raise pertinent questions and thus helps both organizer and prospective participant see the need for local professional educational opportunities for faculty. The time invested by the ad hoc committee members in developing the initial group ensures a solid, broad base of support for the project.

The first meeting should take place at a centrally located point—possibly a local hotel or the institution that arranged the session. This meeting, described in detail by each of the three pilot groups, provides the opportunity for the participants to meet socially, to discuss the challenges they face in common as professionals, and to explore how the structure and goals of a local association can best serve their needs. The group should also prepare the schedule and agenda for the next meeting. Participants might volunteer for such assignments as reporting on some topic of common interest or reviewing a book or an article from a professional journal. Someone may arrange for a speaker. Other participants should work on ways to encourage foreign language faculty who did not attend to come to the next meeting. Everyone should have some role to play. In the spirit of collaboration vital to this venture, the college and university faculty should avoid dominating the proceedings.

As a follow-up to the first meeting a letter should be sent to all those who attended. Each participant and administrator designated by teachers should receive a copy of the minutes of the meeting and a letter thanking him or her for support and cooperation. This courtesy will not only keep them informed of the group's activities but may also aid in anchoring support for their faculty's involvement in the project. A letter and a copy of the minutes should go to the invited faculty who did not attend. Again, a committee member may see the usefulness of personally encouraging these individuals to attend the next meeting. The committee should investigate all avenues for publicizing the project. A short article on the group and its objectives in a local newspaper or in a newsletter will stimulate additional interest among FLL teachers in the region.

In publicizing the second meeting the group should give particular attention to faculty who did not attend the first one. If feasible, when scheduling meetings, the group may consider convening at different locations. Rotating sites spreads responsibility among members and spares some members the problem of always traveling the same distance.

During the second and subsequent meetings the collaborative effort truly becomes apparent. Working together to solve immediate problems and to meet future needs encourages teachers to help one another organize special events, such as an area-wide training session for oral proficiency testing. Members who participate in workshops around the country may report their experiences to the local group. Others can take assignments to research and report on new developments, approaches, and techniques in areas such as methodology, proficiency testing, and second-language acquisition. Colleagues can arrange to visit one another's classes, set up presentations or tutoring by their students, plan demonstrations, and address local business and civic groups. These and other activities can be pursued concurrently with the group's two major activities: sharing current research and studying a common topic together.

The second half of this paper consists of reports from the three pilot professional-update teams concerning their experiences in establishing themselves. One team is based at a large state university in an urban setting, another at a community college in California, and another at a small private liberal arts college in a rural area. The project directors—Arlene Malinowski, Bette Hirsch, and Charles Byrd—worked with me in turning this idea for local professional development into a functioning reality. While the overall goals of the three teams are the same, differences in demographics, educational emphasis, and geographic location have exposed each team to different advantages and difficulties. Regardless of these differences, however, they share the objective of ongoing professional development of their members.

The approaches and expectations of the teams differ most with regard to the specific needs and interests of their student populations—college-bound or vocationally oriented—and to the needs specific to the geographical locations and structures of the educational systems. The reports document these differences and the respective approaches. The information they contain can guide other faculty who decide to initiate local collaborative professional development programs.

A Report on Collaborative Professional Development at North Carolina State University

Arlene Malinowski

The Collaborative Professional Update Project began at NCSU in the spring of 1981. Under the guidance of Claire Gaudiani, an ad hoc committee was formed consisting of two area (Wake County) high school teachers, two NCSU faculty members (the department head and me), and the foreign language consultant for Spanish from the State Department of Public Instruction. A proposal was drafted, guidelines were drawn, and goals were defined; letters of endorsement were secured from the chancellor, provost, school deans, and public school administrators.

In late August 1981, at the first general high school faculty meeting of the school year, all Wake County foreign language teachers were invited to participate on the collaborative professional development update team. Few volunteered, but with the help of the foreign language coordinator for Wake County high schools, Jane Smith, I was able to convince several interested faculty members. The team therefore consisted of eight high school faculty from Wake County and eight faculty members from NCSU.

The first meeting of the update team was scheduled for 15 October 1981. (Subsequent meetings were planned for 19 November, 17 December, 18 February, 18 March, 15 April 1981–82.) The necessary arrangements were made: the dean's conference room was reserved for our use; coffee and tea were made available; a reminder, along with a copy of the agenda, was sent to each member. A guest speaker, William Hilliard from the Wake County Medical Society, was also invited to address the team. The purpose of the first meeting was to orient the group to the task and responsibilities of collaborative professional development. One way of doing this was to share with members the information contained in the original proposal and to discuss with them the idea for the project as Claire Gaudiani had conceived it; another way was to hear from our invited speaker, who represented the medical profession. His participation, I feel, was

279

very important at that first meeting; it helped to set the professional tone that we wish to maintain. We also decided, at that first meeting, to elect officers to ensure effective functioning of the group.

The update team has now met four times. The meetings, which are two hours long, have the following general format:

Members of the team make announcements concerning community events or special programs sponsored by their respective institutions. Their projects are discussed and future activities are planned.

A period of open discussion follows. The topics that have been treated under this heading will serve to illustrate some of the major areas of interest of the group: (a) problems facing high school and college foreign language teachers in Wake County; (b) ascertaining students' perceptions of the learning of foreign languages; (c) a behind-the-scenes look at secondary-and college-level foreign language instruction (team members formed groups according to teaching level and shared methods and materials); (d) drafting a questionnaire to solicit information from other universities concerning foreign language requirements; (e) the role of the placement test in measuring language proficiency and the need for goals clarification and assessment in foreign language teaching, learning, and testing. (We provided members with a preliminary list of guidelines for goals clarification that I wrote up following a telephone conversation with Barbara Freed at the University of Pennsylvania.) Subcommittees are formed when appropriate.

The update portion of the meeting consists of reports of the literature in the field of second-language acquisition and foreign language pedagogy by individual team members. Reports are generally done by volunteers and an effort is made to encourage both high school and college faculty to participate at each update session. Topics are chosen for timeliness and relevancy. A sample of our update activities includes (a) a review of the book *The Tongue-Tied American* written by Congressman Paul Simon; (b) a discussion of some recent articles in the *FLA* on promoting communication in the classroom; (c) an introduction to *Der Unterrichtspraxis;* (d) a review of some recent articles on the correction of students' errors in oral production. Included on the March agenda are the reports "Silent Way" and "Lozanov Method."

The Collaborative Professional Development Update Project is fulfilling a need that has been recognized for some time now at NCSU, as the enthusiasm and support of the team members, faculty at large, and the administration attests. Worthy of note is a perceptible increase in interest and concern about our role as professionals and our responsibility to the community for effective foreign language teaching in the schools and universities. A sense of comradery is developing among the team members; we are getting to know one another well, as friends, and we are more and more willing to share our feelings of competency or inadequacy, our classroom failures as well as our successes. Members want to learn more about the language-learning process and about ways of enhancing their classroom performance. In addition, the update team at NCSU is particularly enthusiastic about a future project that has been planned: the construction of an evaluation instrument to measure language proficiency at the college level. This "homemade" placement test, designed by both high school and college faculty, may be among the first of its kind. It is, to my mind, a striking example of professional collaboration.

Professional Development Update
(Sample Project Proposal)

For the past five years the Department of Foreign Languages and Literatures at North Carolina State University has demonstrated its keen appreciation of the need for increased contact and cooperation with the high schools and junior high schools of Wake County. Under the direction of Department Head Alan Gonzalez, several attempts have been made to stimulate a dialogue between high school and university faculty: secondary school foreign language teachers have been invited to campus for informal social gatherings; departmental faculty members have been encouraged to participate in the organization of workshops on cultural topics to be presented in high school classrooms; and, since 1980, the department has sponsored a quite successful Foreign Language Festival, which has brought to campus several thousand enthusiastic local high school students—accompanied by their equally enthusiastic teachers—to perform in talent competitions in the foreign language arts. These activities, whose usefulness has been acknowledged by high school teachers, principals, and coordinators, have served to initiate the dialogue and, at the same time, have made more evident to all involved the desirability of establishing and maintaining channels of direct and continuous communication between the university and the secondary schools.

As director of the university teacher education program, I have had frequent opportunity to meet and speak with high school teachers. Often almost in desperation, they have asked me how we, at the college level, conduct our foreign language classes—what type of tests we administer, what we expect of entering students, what we require of them during the semester—and how they might more effectively design their courses to prepare their students better for foreign language study in college. That this urgent interest demanded a well-conceived response we all recognized; the fundamental question was how we should go about bridging the gap. Earlier this year it was suggested that a one-day workshop would allow high school and faculty teachers to meet to share methods and materials; as a one- day activity, however, with no guarantee of follow-up, it was understood that this workshop would be a far from adequate solution to the problem.

When Claire Gaudiani presented us with her plans to institute, nationwide, a coordinated high school and college faculty development project and invited the department at North Carolina State University to take part in the work, we eagerly accepted, appreciating the relevance of the project, as she outlined it for us, to the obligations we were attempting to fulfill. Following her instructions, Gonzalez and I asked two high school teachers and a member of the Department of Public Instruction to form with us an ad hoc committee to draw up a proposal for an ongoing two-year professional development program to be carried out by a team of NCSU faculty members and Wake County high school teachers.

Drafted on 24 March, the proposal contains the following major points:

1. The team will be composed of eight to ten interested faculty members from the Department of Foreign Languages and Literatures at NCSU, and ten to twelve foreign language teachers from four high schools and two junior high schools in Wake County. The entire foreign language faculty at each institution will be apprised of the project; it is expected, however, that there will be few volunteers during the initial stages. The selection of members from the secondary schools will be made with the assistance of school principals, and the Foreign Language Coordinator for Wake County Public High Schools, Jane Smith. The university team members will periodically report on the activities of the group at departmental faculty meetings. Reports of the work of the update team will reach all foreign language secondary school teachers through school faculty meetings, the monthly newsletter, and the first-of-the-year workshop meetings attended by all Wake County high school teachers.

2. The team will meet on a prearranged schedule for a period of two hours, four to six times a year. One of the seminar rooms on the NCSU campus will be reserved for these meetings.

3. The meetings will serve as a forum at which college and high school faculty can assess their needs, discuss their main pedagogical concerns, and engage in cooperative professional interaction. The following aims have been outlined by the committee:

(a)To establish a set of realistic objectives that college and high school teachers can work with in their language classes; particularly to define competencies and levels of achievement that would ensure smoother transition from junior high school to high school, and from high school to college.

(b)To discuss the role of foreign languages in the world, in the United States, and in the state of North Carolina and to explore ways of better serving students' vocational interests and needs.

(c)To keep abreast of new trends and approaches in foreign language teaching, through regular review of pertinent literature, as found in *Foreign Language Annals, Modern Language Journal, ADFL Bulletin, French Review,* and *Hispania.* Team members will be expected to share the tasks of reading about and reporting on recent developments. At least one hour of each meeting will be devoted to this important professional activity.

Curriculum improvement, while expected to be a long-range result of this enterprise, is not, it should be noted, an immediate concern. The objectives of this cooperative effort, rather, are to ensure professional growth, to improve teacher effectiveness, and to achieve productive collaboration between high school and college teachers.

The success of this project can of course only be guaranteed if the team is composed of individuals personally committed to the joint effort of articulation. Since participation in the group will require extra preparation time, it is hoped that the professionals involved will receive recognition for their work. The committee is requesting that high school teachers be awarded two continuing education units each year for their participation and that university faculty members be granted released time (the amount and kind to be agreed on in each case in consultations with the department head). Letters of endorsement for the project are being sought from Chancellor Joab L. Thomas, Assistant Provost Murray S. Downs, Dean Carl J. Dolce, of the School of Education, Dean Robert O. Tilman, of the School of Humanities and Social Sciences, Jane Smith, and the principals of Cary Senior High School and Enloe Senior High School, John Stevens and Leon Herndon.

Responses to this proposal are welcome.

Professional Update Program, Cabrillo College

Bette Hirsch

Cabrillo, where I have headed the French program since 1973, is the community college of Santa Cruz County. Located seventy-five miles south of San Francisco, it has 12,000 enrolled students and 1,250 foreign language students each semester. Our county is a blending of coastal resort towns, agricultural valleys, mountain villages, and comfortable middle-class suburbs.

In February 1980, shortly after I attended the 1979 Workshop for Development of Foreign Language and Literature Programs in San Francisco, our foreign language instructors met at my request, discussed a packet I had prepared from the workshop, and established priorities for development and change in our department. These goals included an exploration of the Dartmouth Intensive Language Method (DILM) and other curricular changes (computers, culture courses, etc.), the establishment of a foreign language career center, and more efficient ways to reach out to the foreign language teachers and students in our county.

During the past decade, our foreign language department attempted increased contact and cooperation with the secondary schools and the university in Santa Cruz county (UCSC). Our instructors spoke to high school audiences about our program, gave slide shows at the junior and senior high schools, organized regional conferences for professional growth, and participated in Cabrillo-UCSC workshops. Secondary school teachers served on our hiring committees and held part-time positions on our faculty (as had UCSC professors). These contacts were sporadic at best, and though useful in initiating dialogue, they had not established channels of direct and continual communication among secondary schools, the university, and the community college.

In spring 1980 I applied for and next fall received a NEH consultant grant. Our consultant, Carmen McClendon, shared models she had developed for use in Mississippi that had involved college and secondary school teachers in ongoing professional activities and summer training workshops.

In early 1981 Claire Gaudiani presented to me her plans to institute a coordinated nationwide high school and college faculty development project. On the basis of my work with her in the two workshops and her knowledge of our county and college goals, she asked Cabrillo to be one of the institutions across the country pioneering a model program entailing collaborative effort among county teachers of foreign languages. I viewed the project as highly relevant to our identified goals and in line with suggestions of the President's Commission on Foreign Languages and International Studies, and thus I accepted the challenge.

I began by discussing the idea at a department meeting to ensure support for the venture. Next I spoke with our college president (at some schools an academic dean would be the appropriate choice). I believe that it is important for administrators to hear at the beginning stages about a major faculty project. They then can often make helpful suggestions and feel some partnership and involvement with the faculty. If I later need support, I have a greater chance of receiving it from them.

Our president, John Petersen, offered to have Cabrillo host the first meeting of what he saw as a needed group and to help me reach administrators if I got a poor response from any of the six area high school districts. He also gave me a county publication listing all teachers. This guide was invaluable, since no lists of foreign language teachers are available in California or even in our county.

Other department members and I telephoned foreign language instructors at UCSC, at the public junior high schools and high schools, and at private elementary and secondary schools. An ad hoc steering committee brought representatives from each type of school to Cabrillo (centrally located in the county and presenting no parking difficulty in the afternoons) on 29 April. Before this first meeting, I prepared a three-page memo about the goals, structure, and functioning of a county educators' association. Realizing that our collaborative team would be unique in its focus on the needs of Santa Cruz county, I suggested that we might address such questions as:

1. What kind of professional update group would work?
2. What were the specific needs of area teachers?
3. How often would county meetings be held? where? when?
4. Who would be invited to attend?

During the ad hoc committee meeting we agreed on certain guiding principles:

1. Ours would be a truly collaborative group. Wherever we teach, we face similar situations and can comfortably meet as a cluster of professionals committed to one another, to our students, and to our discipline.

2. We might emulate the model of a county medical society that meets

quarterly, hears papers, discusses important county issues, shares advice, and reports on current research.

3. We would make an initial commitment to meet at specified times for two years and then to evaluate the group and its effectiveness.

4. A typical county meeting might include:

    a. One hour of reviews of important articles in such journals as the *ADFL Bulletin, French Review, Foreign Language Annals, Hispania, PMLA,* and *Modern Language Journal,* concerning current research in pedagogy. Articles would be assigned to update teams for presentation.

    b. One hour of discussion of a specific current problem or theme (such as innovative curriculum approaches, global education, career information, student literacy, enrollment patterns, testing for proficiency). This hour might be led by county members or by an outside speaker.

The objectives of this cooperative effort would be to ensure professional growth, to improve teacher effectiveness, and to achieve productive collaboration among elementary, secondary, and postsecondary foreign language educators. We further hoped that the continuing process of involvement of these professionals would serve as a model to neighboring counties and promote foreign language education.

Some specific goals of the ad hoc group emerged to organize conversation groups with native speakers in the county; to organize foreign language camps for high school students; and to aim for better articulation among the different levels of education.

The steering group organized publicity for the first county meeting, helping to distribute a prepared announcement and to make telephone calls to each school a few days before a meeting. These calls are important to a successful attendance. Once a commitment is given to attend and to spread the word, it is much less likely that the person will stay at home.

Our first county meeting was held on 29 May. It had been organized to foster socializing (name tags, cookies and punch, comfortable carpeted room). Brief introductions were followed by a goal-setting session and then by a lecture and discussion led by James Asher of San Jose State (whose work on the psychology of language was featured in last August's *Psychology Today*).

Those attending included fifteen people affiliated with Cabrillo College, three with UCSC, four with junior high schools, seven with public high schools, two from a private high school, one from an adult education program, four from elementary programs, and several students and retired teachers. The very fact of so many language teachers from the county sharing ideas and resources was quite exciting.

At the second county meeting we sat in a circle and in turn told of ourselves, our departments, and our goals for the group. Those with special interests circulated sheets to form subgroups (language camp, conversation groups, National Foreign Language Week activities, etc.). We discussed the adoption of one theme for the next two years but found no enthusiasm or consensus on this idea. There was strong agreement, though, about the importance of staying up-to-date on the professional literature—even on journals outside the languages we teach. Since we recognized that few of us have time for such reading, we accepted the concept of forming teams to report during future meetings. Our next meeting will include reports from update teams covering journals of the French, Spanish, German, Russian, and Chinese professional organizations.

The group voiced strong interest in having a demonstration of the Dartmouth Intensive Language Method and hearing about its implementation at Cabrillo College. This will be done during our new meeting, scheduled to be held at UCSC.

During the past nine months, our "baby," a collaborative professional group of foreign language educators in Santa Cruz County, has been conceived, nurtured, and born. Some immediate results are evident.

1. Approximately forty foreign language instructors in the county from more than fifteen schools now know one another.

2. This knowledge in and of itself has stimulated strong support within the group—support that is especially important in a county isolated from both the San Francisco and Monterey areas, in which nothing of this kind exists.

3. There is definitely a promise of future interaction and a desire to reach the other fifty or so who have not yet joined us.

4. Clearly we are taking our own responsibility for keeping up-to-date, and we are meeting on the basis of our discipline, not on artificial lines of status.

The Cabrillo College model of the coordinated faculty development project, though in its infancy, is growing and is definitely meeting some important needs in Santa Cruz county.

A Professional Collaborative Team: The Holston Language Association

Charles W. Byrd, Jr.
Emory and Henry College

The professional update group that I initiated in our area is located in the mountains of southwest Virginia and northeast Tennessee. It includes teachers from high schools, community colleges, and four-year colleges. The area is geographically isolated and sparsely populated, and these factors affected the development of our group.

The idea to form this group came to me last spring from Claire Gaudiani. At her suggestion, I met with two high school teachers whom I knew to discuss what kind of organization would respond to our local needs. I think it is worthwhile to mention two points here: first, it is a good idea to write a proposal, even if only for local consumption, because the writing forces refinement of ideas; second, it is important to involve high school teachers from the beginning. Otherwise, they may feel excluded from the leadership of the group and might look to the college teachers for absolute guidance. This is not the idea behind a collaborative approach.

In addition to meeting with the two high school teachers, I also talked with the two county supervisors of high school foreign language teachers and with my academic dean. All three replied in writing with their encouragement and support for the project. Early administrative support is also important.

The size of the group envisioned in the original planning of the ad hoc committee, consisting of the two high school teachers and me, was to be limited to those in two counties, so that no one would have to travel more than thirty miles to attend meetings. Driving at night in the mountains is difficult. The pool of possible teachers included fourteen from the high schools and thirteen from the postsecondary level. This total of twenty-seven seemed a manageable group. Owing to potential travel difficulties, we decided to limit the number of meetings to two a year. We hoped eventually to increase the number to four.

To organize the first meeting, I sent a letter to all the foreign language teachers in the designated area. Those of us on the ad hoc committee also

288

talked to the teachers with whom we came into regular contact. With a couple of exceptions, the teachers who had received oral and written invitations attended the first meeting. Personal contact has proved important in recruiting members.

We also received encouragement from the public school administrators. In particular, one county's supervisor offered one-half day of in-service credit to those of his teachers who attended our first meeting.

On 24 September 1981 we held our first meeting. Fourteen teachers were present, representing a good mix of levels and schools, but we were disappointed that only one teacher came from Smyth County. The poor attendance from Smyth County was due to the lack of personal contact before the meeting. One of my tasks before our next meeting is to visit that county's foreign language supervisor and individual teachers to encourage their participation.

We conducted little business at the first meeting. Instead, we spent most of our time getting to know one another and talking about our common problems. The enthusiasm of those present and our feeling of collegiality were encouraging. I think that the emphasis of the ad hoc committee on shared problems and concerns encouraged a free exchange among teachers from all levels of education.

We decided at this first meeting that our organization should be kept simple, and accordingly we elected only a secretary to inform people about our next meeting and to take care of the necessary correspondence. I was elected to that post, partly because I had helped to start the group and partly because I had access to copying equipment at my college—my department's budget can absorb those costs. We also discussed several projects that we might undertake.

Perhaps the most surprising result of the first meeting was the desire of all present to have a second meeting soon and not to wait until the early spring. Therefore we decided to meet again in six weeks, in early November.

The follow-up to the first meeting took public and private forms. In the first, the area newspapers—both county weeklies and a city daily—ran articles on the organization of the Holston Language Association. This coverage gave us public exposure and even aroused interest among teachers outside our original area. Both high school and college teachers telephoned me to find out how they could be included.

The private follow-up consisted of personal letters. I sent one letter containing abbreviated minutes of the meeting to those who had attended, and I sent another to teachers who had been invited to the first meeting and who had failed to come. Unfortunately, none of them attended the second meeting either. I concluded that we need to meet people in person and not to rely totally on correspondence. In this age of junk mail, the telephone and interview are much more powerful influences than letters.

Our second meeting, held on 12 November 1981, was different in format from the first. Whereas the first had been in a public restaurant with a buffet dinner, the second was in the home of a colleague from my college. Everyone contributed to the dinner, and we mingled more informally and in a much more relaxed fashion than we had the first time. After an hour of eating and talking, we settled down to discuss our future direction. We decided that we must try to make our group larger in order to have a critical mass of interests and expertise.

I will say parenthetically that this decision by the group had been forecast by one of my colleagues in my college's department of education. I had spoken with him between our two meetings to get his advice about the politics of the public schools. He happens to be a mathematician who is active in a regional mathematics association, and he gave me several valuable suggestions about group size, people's willingness to travel further than I had expected, and the need to emphasize pedagogy in our work. I encourage all those intending to organize a group to get in touch with the teachers of education in their schools. Teachers of education have a different perspective on the problem and a different set of contacts in the public schools.

Our group also discussed methods of recruitment for our spring meeting, and we decided that each of us would take the responsibility of talking to people we knew personally and encouraging their participation. It happened conveniently that someone in the group knew someone in every area into which we hoped to expand. After these personal contacts were made, I promised to send a letter of invitation, which was received more warmly than earlier ones had been.

We also discussed our future activities. We will investigate the holding of a regional language fair, publish a newsletter and compile biographic and professional fact sheets, share successful classroom methods and techniques, and I hope, review the professional pedagogical literature. At the moment, some of the teachers do not seem interested in the last activity, but I think they will change their minds when they see the usefulness of journal reading to their own classroom teaching.

I have encountered several obstacles in setting up this organization. First, everyone is busy and has little time for yet another school-related activity. In addition, the high school teachers often have divided loyalties between a foreign language and another subject (often the other subject is their area of major interest). Both these problems can be overcome, at least with some teachers, through personal visits and encouragement and with the active support of the public school administrators.

Second, the area covered by our organization means that some must travel a considerable distance. I think that two or three meetings a year held in a central location will help solve this problem.

A third obstacle, which was stated by one of the public school administrators in his letter of reaction to my original proposal, is the possibility of college domination in the group. The group's organizers must stress the collaborative spirit of the group by encouraging high school participation and leadership from the beginning. For example, high school representatives should be members of the organizing committee. High school teachers should also be asked for advice frequently. These efforts will create an atmosphere of comradeship. One final way to broaden the group's appeal is to discuss foreign language education in other than an exclusively college-bound context. If we really do believe that foreign language study has the value we profess it does, we must not forget that many students in our high schools will never attend college. They need and benefit from foreign language study too.

The final problem that I will mention has no easy remedy. There are jealousies and rivalries among the teachers from the same level of instruction. One high school teacher was miffed because I did not include her on the original ad hoc committee. By stressing the commonality of the problems that we face and the desire for shared solutions, I hope that in time these jealousies will subside. Rivalries among college faculties also exist. Some can be avoided if the meeting places are moved frequently and if the direction of the group is truly a joint process. A little tact is in order.

In any case, the Holston Language Association is alive and well, preparing for its next meeting. We will come together at the home of a colleague from yet another college and attempt to organize a regional language fair. We are looking forward to working together and helping one another like peers and colleagues.

Project Update

As this book goes to press, the NEH project called "Strengthening the Humanities through Foreign Language and Literature Studies" (EH-20237-82) has received substantial additional financial support from the Rockefeller Foundation. Application packets were requested by 850 faculty. More than 127 colleges and universities and more than 346 school systems collaborated on making applications. Eighty teams have now been selected and are establishing regional centers in accordance with the provisions of the grant project. Teams applying for participation in the project had to show that the members of local steering committees came from the schools and postsecondary institutions and represented the commonly taught languages. For further information on this project write:

Project Director's Office
Strengthening the Humanities through Foreign Language and Literature Studies
C.G.S.
210 Logan Hall
University of Pennsylvania
Philadelphia, PA 19104

Chapter Ten

A Case for the Study of Literature in Foreign Languages

The new curriculum currently developing in many foreign language and literature departments involves courses and concerns relatively uncommon in higher education twenty-five years ago. For instance, courses in foreign languages for careers indicate a concern for the practicality and usefulness of foreign language study. Among other things, these courses represent the faculty's attempt to answer the question "What can I *do* with a foreign language?" Courses on the world of language (see pp. 26–27) introduce the general concepts of linguistics, semiology, and anthropology and show a concern for broader content in FLL classes. In many departments, efforts are under way to redesign the introductory and intermediate language courses to achieve proficiency levels measurable by tests like the ACTFL-ETS oral proficiency test. I hope this book helps nurture fruitful developments.

Where is the study of literature in the midst of all this change? The vast majority of faculty in the discipline continue to be trained primarily to teach literature. In most of the more than two hundred four-year institutions I have worked with in the past four years, enrollments in literature courses were reported as low, dropping to or holding at levels below those of enrollments twenty to twenty-five years ago. I believe that strengthening the teaching of literature is the next major issue in our profession, and I hope that this need receives the same kind of attention, creativity, and—if necessary—funding that have poured into career-oriented language courses and proficiency test development. The profession needs a national survey on the quality, content, and form of curricula in postsecondary foreign language literature courses.

Faculty interested in improving the study of literature will want to refer to *Interrelations of Literature,* edited by Jean-Pierre Barricelli and Joseph Gibaldi. They may also wish to write to the Education Programs Division of the National Endowment for the Humanities, Old Post Office, 1100 Pennsylvania Ave. NW, Washington, DC, 20506, for a description of recently funded projects that concern the teaching of foreign literatures. The

MLA Division on the Teaching of Literature may also offer some suggestions.

Since in many institutions fewer students seem to be taking literature courses, it seems appropriate to make some remarks on enrollments. College-level study of literature in foreign languages depends largely on the quality of high school foreign language preparation. Few students who begin foreign language and literature study as freshmen have the time to develop language proficiency adequate to the task of reading literature in the language. The more selective undergraduate institutions have seen a less precipitous decline in enrollments in foreign language literature courses precisely because a higher proportion of their students arrive at college with sufficient linguistic skills to enter the departmental program at the advanced composition or introductory literature course level. Even those students who neither major nor minor still have time to take advanced courses while pursuing their other interests. Many study abroad. All of them experience their foreign language courses at an intellectual level comparable to that experienced in their other college courses, unlike the students who begin or rebegin language study at the introductory level, where intellectual content is necessarily minimal and skill-building aspects are often frustrating, tedious, and reminiscent of high school. If college foreign language faculty wish to increase enrollment in their literature programs one possible way is to try to enhance the quality and quantity of foreign language instruction in the high schools.

This remains, in my view, one of the most important areas of responsibility for every college and university faculty member in our field. High school faculty have little occasion to use the languages they teach with speakers who use those languages well. Teachers with whom I have worked express frustration and embarrassment at their lack of language proficiency. Financial exigencies and scheduling problems often force them to teach languages they studied only cursorily. They teach many hours each day and are burdened with an array of ancillary duties that absorb their time and energy. In-service days that should offer them the opportunity to converse in the language they teach or review new methods and texts are often given over to discussing classroom management or to counting books or performing other tasks unrelated to their subject areas. College and university faculty all over the country should, I believe, offer to collaborate with high school teachers in the region to ensure that the best teaching goes on at both levels (see p. 272 for a description of the national project I initiated to establish this kind of interaction).

Even if we were to succeed in our efforts to promote and improve foreign language study in the schools, what would incoming students prepared for advanced courses find in colleges and universities? Little creativity has been invested in the design of most literature courses. Many are watered-down versions of the graduate courses faculty themselves took as students.

Many are circumscribed by the availability of texts. Perhaps the profession has been so busy in the past fifteen years defending the study of foreign languages that few have put their efforts into articulating the reasons for studying literature. We must begin this task and do it well, or in many institutions—even those with foreign language requirements—the teaching of literature in languages other than English is going to all but disappear. In 1990, will only the most selective institutions teach the great texts by Goethe, Flaubert, Dante, and Cervantes in their original languages? This is not an idle question, because students are not the only ones who are withdrawing from FL literature courses.

In two large well-known public institutions where I have done consultancies in the past two years, the deans have encouraged study of foreign languages and cultures as a practical asset to their students' future lives. They have also said, however, that the study of literature in foreign languages is "esoteric" and therefore nonessential to their curricula. Both institutions had adequate student enrollments, a burgeoning commitment to technology, and a strong orientation to practicality. The foreign language departments were willing to teach a range of "practical"—that is, career-oriented—foreign language courses and submit themselves and their students to the strict accountability of oral proficiency testing. For this, the deans admired and appreciated the faculty. The language major and the study of FL literature, however, did not seem to fit the deans' plans for the future. These two institutions may be isolated cases. I hope so, but I fear that they are not.

The study of literature in foreign languages in not esoteric. The case to be made here has three parts. The first is the same as the case made for the study of literature in English. The second and third address specifically the benefit of studying a piece of literature in its original language, but since I wish to respond to the "deans," I will not dwell on the aesthetic or even the philosophical reasons that make up the first part. As faculty in the humanities, we would probably agree that the study of literature, regardless of the language, plays a central role in the development of a thoughtful citizenry knowledgeable in the human cultural treasury of ideas, traditions, and values. Students should read literature to learn how to enjoy good writing. Good writing, as I. A. Richards says, contains appraisals of human existence. It reminds readers that certain specific as well as certain general questions continue to matter. The systematic study of literature teaches us how to interpret relational systems, avoid simplistic thinking, develop judgment and taste. It combines cognitive activities like classification, discrimination, and exploration of facts and consideration of the nature of evidence with imaginative activities that reproduce for readers the sensuous experience of the text in mysterious ways. The study of literature develops critical thinking and problem-solving skills. Iris Murdoch explains that literature engages the reader's whole personality, that it is both mimetic, imitating reality, and anamnestic, stimulating our memory of what we did not know we knew. We are entertained and educated. We learn to know others and ourselves, grow in tolerance, and experience private consolation.

As educated people, we all know these reasons for studying literature in any language. But students reading literature in a *foreign* language labor to possess the text in certain striking ways. They experience heightened sensitivity to the choice of words, to nuances of meanings, to syntactic variations, and to the organizational strategies of the text. Every word matters. The labor students must expend frustrates them yet also indicates to them the kind of precision and dedication that could be spent (and often is not) on reading in their own language. They experience more clearly the stages inherent in coming to understand a text. Once the efforts made on the linguistic level begin to bear fruit, the student quickly perceives the inadequacy of that level as the ultimate one. The next question is, "So what? What does this *mean?*" The labors begin anew. The student must struggle with the linguistically comprehensible text to discover answers at the philosophical, metaphoric, contextual, and personal levels. The text lures the reader to engage intellectually, to exert that discipline of mind that abjures simplistic answers but recognizes simplicity. Is this an esoteric effort to be reserved for an intellectual elite? I think not, and for very practical reasons.

At the most pragmatic level, the foreign language text, like any piece of literature, becomes a problem to solve. But in dealing with foreign language texts, students can take nothing for granted. Being less familiar with the language, culture, history, and author, the student must exercise a wide range of skills. Primary among them are the capacities to develop, test, and affirm or recompose hypotheses; to recognize patterns of internal logic and external implications; and to draw conclusions from evidence. In short, the foreign language text trains students in some of the most taxing problem-solving skills required for work in the modern world.

If the study of literature in foreign languages can make a significant contribution to students' development of problem-solving skills, it also has another practical aspect. It can make a crucial contribution to cultural literacy. Students cannot develop real proficiency in a language without studying the texts that use the language to transmit the culture's important ideas. Despite the deans' encouragement of language study at the elementary and intermediate levels, the suppression of literature and culture courses deprives language study of a *content.* The deans I have referred to, and many others, have been tricked by a myth widespread in educational circles during the past ten years. It concerns literacy. This myth says that literacy is independent of content: that people can learn to read and write and speak well regardless of the texts selected to teach them. But "literacy," as E. D. Hirsch comments, "implies specific contents as well as formal skills. . . . Part of our skill in reading and in writing is skill not just with linguistic structures but with words. Words are not purely formal counters of language; they represent large underlying domains of content. Part of language skill is content skill" ("Cultural Literacy," *American Scholar* [Spring 1983], p. 164). Hirsch makes a daring suggestion that a national board be convened to exert leadership in developing a broad list of literary works for study at different grade levels, to create, that is, a common canon with enough leeway "to yield local freedom but also to yield a measure of commonality in our literary heritage." To support his suggestion he calls, ironically enough, on evidence from the foreign language and literature curriculum where, Hirsch believes, there is common recognition of the relation between linguistic proficiency and translinguistic cultural knowledge.

> To get very far in reading or writing French, a student must come to know facets of French culture quite different from his own. . . . National culture always had this "foreignness" with respect to family culture alone. School materials contain unfamiliar materials that promote the "acculturation" that is a universal part of growing up in any tribe or nation. Acculturation into a national literate culture might be defined as learning what the "common reader" of a newspaper in a literate culture could be expected to know. That would include knowledge of certain values (whether or not one accepted them), and knowledge of such things as (for example) the First Amendment, Grant and Lee, and DNA. In our own culture, what should these contents be? Surely our answer to that should partly define our school curriculum. Acculturation into a literate culture (the minimal aim of schooling; we should aim still higher) could be defined as the gaining of cultural literacy. (p. 166)

The study of literature, then, is definitely not esoteric. Real literacy in any language depends on knowledge, therefore on texts both literary and otherwise. The degree to which foreign language classes depend on literature and significant textual content in courses is being used to support suggestions for improvement of the English curriculum. Is this the moment to step away from the study of literature in foreign language courses? I think not. Such a moment could never be justified in institutions where faculty and administrators believe that they share responsibilities for an academically sound enterprise.

As foreign language and literature faculty reshape the curriculum in the future, we will need to remember our calling as faculty in the humanities and resist the temptation to convert every few years to a new denomination in the always modern "church of what's happening now." The study of foreign literatures is one of our central responsibilities. It will remain one and deserves our best efforts to make it as fruitful as possible for the students whose linguistic skills, cultural sensitivities, and career ambitions we nurture in other areas of the foreign language and literature curriculum.

Bibliographies

General

Entries marked with an asterisk are especially appropriate to use for book reviews designed to inform administrators about the FLL discipline.

American Council on the Teaching of Foreign Languages. *Proceedings of the National Conference on Professional Priorities,* November 1980.

Baker, Reid, ed. *Teaching for Tomorrow in the Foreign Language Classroom.* Skokie, Ill.: National Textbook, 1978.

Barricelli, Jean-Pierre, and Joseph Gibaldi, eds. *Interrelations of Literature.* New York: MLA, 1982.

Barrows, Thomas S., Stephen F. Klein, and John C. D. Clark. *What College Students Know and Believe about Their World.* New Rochelle, N.Y.: Change Magazine Press, 1981.

Born, Warren C., and Kathryn Buck, eds. *Options for the Teaching of Foreign Languages, Literatures, and Culture.* New York: American Council on the Teaching of Foreign Languages, 1978.

Brod, Richard I., ed. *Language Study for the 1980s.* New York: MLA, 1980.

*Delattre, Edwin J. "The Humanities Can Irrigate Deserts." *Foreign Language Annals,* 11 (1978), 7–8.

Edgerton, Mills F., Jr. "On Knowing a Foreign Language." *Modern Language Journal,* 64 (1980), 222–27.

Gaudiani, Claire. "Student Personal Assessment and Goal Statements." *ADFL Bulletin,* 10, No. 1 (Sept. 1978), 37–39.

Grittner, Frank, ed. *Careers, Communication, and Culture in Foreign Language Teaching.* Skokie, Ill.: National Textbook, 1974.

*Hammond, Sandra B., and William D. Sims. *Award-Winning Foreign Language Programs.* Skokie, Ill.: National Textbook, 1981.

Hancock, Charles R. "Second Language Study and Intellectual Development." *Foreign Language Annals,* 10 (1977), 75–79.

Krashen, Stephen. *Second Language Acquisition and Second Language Learning.* New York: Pergamon, 1981.

*Lambert, Richard D. "Language Learning and Language Utilization." *ADFL Bulletin,* 13, No. 1 (1981), 7–11.

McLane, Kathleen, and Alice Omaggio. "ERIC Documents on Foreign Language Teaching and Linguistics." *Modern Language Journal,* 41 (1977), 340–63.

*Marshall, Geoffrey. "Applications as Tea Leaves: The NEH and the Teaching of the Humanities." *ADFL Bulletin,* 11, No. 1 (Sept. 1979), 31–34.

*President's Commission on Foreign Language and International Studies. *Strength through Wisdom: A Critique of U.S. Capability.* Washington, D.C.: U.S. Government Printing Office, 1979.

Rivers, Wilga. *Speaking in Many Tongues: Essays in Foreign Language Teaching.* Rowley, Mass.: Newbury, 1972.

Seigneuret, J. C. "Bucking the Trend." *ADFL Bulletin,* 10, No. 2 (Nov. 1978), 28–31.

*Simon, Paul. *The Tongue-Tied American: Confronting the Foreign Language Crisis.* New York: Continuum, 1980.

*Stevick, Earl. *Teaching Languages: A Way and Ways.* Rowley, Mass.: Newbury, 1980.

Management

Barricelli, Jean-Pierre. "Managing a Zoo: The Total Foreign Language Department." *Profession 81.* New York: MLA, 1981, pp. 37–42.

DuVerlie, Claud. "Climbing the Ladder of Institutional Priorities." *ADFL Bulletin,* 12, No. 2 (Nov. 1980), 4–7.

────── and Alan S. Rosenthal. "How to Prosper during a Foreign Language Crisis." *ADFL Bulletin,* 12, No. 1 (Sept. 1980), 17–22.

Gaudiani, Claire. " 'Cultivons notre jardin': Strategies for Building the Foreign Language and Literature Program." *ADFL Bulletin,* 11, No. 3 (March 1980), 39–44.

Melcher, Robert. "Roles and Relationships: Clarifying the Manager's Job." *Personnel,* May–June 1967, pp. 33–43.

Moss Kanter, Rosabeth. "Changing the Shape of Work: Reform in Academe." *Current Issues in Higher Education,* 1979. Published by American Assn. for Higher Education.

Curriculum Planning

Grittner, Frank. *Student Motivation and the Foreign Language Teacher: A Guide for Building the Modern Curriculum.* Skokie, Ill.: National Textbook, 1977.

Higgs, Theodore, ed. *Curriculum Competence and the Foreign Language Teacher.* ACTFL Foreign Language Education Series, vol. 13. Skokie, Ill.: National Textbook, 1982.

Schulz, Renate A. *Options for Undergraduate Foreign Language Programs.* New York: MLA, 1979.

Communicative Competency

Alexander, Richard. "A Learning-to-Learn Perspective on Reading in a Foreign Language." *System,* 8 (1980), 113–19.

Bartz, Walter H. *Testing Oral Communications in the Foreign Language Classroom.* Language in Education: Theory and Practice, vol. 1. Arlington, Va.: Center for Applied Linguistics, 1979.

Hosenfield, Carol. "A Learning-Teaching View of Second Language Instruction." *Foreign Language Annals,* 12 (1979), 51–54.

————"A Preliminary Investigation of the Reading Strategies of Successful and Nonsuccessful Second Language Learners." *System,* 5, No. 2 (1977), 110–23.

McCoy, Ingeborg R. "Means to Overcome the Anxieties of Second Language Learners." *Foreign Language Annals,* 12 (1979), 185–90.

Schmelzer, Henry. "The Associational Method in Language Learning." *Foreign Language Annals,* 12 (1979), 129–35.

Schulz, Renate A., and Walter H. Bartz. "Free to Communicate." In June K. Phillips, ed. *Perspective: A New Freedom.* ACTFL Foreign Language Education Series. vol. 7. Skokie, Ill.: National Textbook, 1975.

————, ed. *Teaching for Communication in the Foreign Language Classroom.* Skokie, Ill.: National Textbook, 1976.

Reading

Compiled by Janet K. Swaffer
University of Texas, Austin

ARTICLES THAT SUBSTANTIATE READING PROCESS CLAIMS

1. Teaching in Target Language

Alexander, Richard. "A Learning-to-Learn Perspective on Reading in a Foreign Language." *System,* 8 (1980), 113–19. In presenting research on effective reading strategies, Alexander finds that translation "was preprogrammed to complicate the reading process unnecessarily" (p. 117) at initial learning stages.

Cates, G. Truett, and Janet K. Swaffar. *Reading a Second Language.* Language in Education: Theory and Practice, No. 20. Arlington, Va.: Center for Applied Linguistics, 1979. Particularly pp. 4–7 discuss comprehension strategies that foster reading and classroom discussions in the target language and the lexical and grammatical advantages of such exposure.

2. Advantages of Authentic or Unsimplified Texts

Honeyfield, J. "Simplification." *TESOL Quarterly,* 11 (1977), 431–40. A discussion that suggests that simplification of texts makes readings more difficult by eliminating natural redundancies of language.

Schulz, Renate. "Literature and Readibility: Bridging the Gap in Foreign Language Reading." *Modern Language Journal,* 65 (1981), 43–53. A complete discussion of factors to consider in grading readings and of the difficulties in determining levels of difficulty of texts.

3. Advantages of Adult Materials

Strevens, Peter. "The Nature of Language Teaching." In Jack C. Richards, ed. *Understanding Second and Foreign Language Learning, Issues and Approaches.* Rowley, Mass.: Newbury, 1978. A discussion of the motivational factors that influence success and failure in foreign language students, emphasizing interest in materials.

4. Appropriate for Any Level of Adult Learner (Process Approach as an Adult Activity)

Clarke, Mark A., and Sandra Silberstein. "Toward a Realization of Psycholinguistic Principles in the ESL Reading Class." In Mackay, Barkman, and Jordan, eds. *Reading in a Second Language.* Rowley, Mass.: Newbury, 1979, pp. 48–65. Based on psycholinguistic evidence, a presentation of the conceptual apparatus of the adult learner as applied in classroom strategies for reading comprehension.

Goodman, Kenneth S. "Psycholinguistic Universals in the Reading Process." In Frank Smith, ed. *Psycholinguistics and Reading.* New York: Holt, 1973. A discussion of the reading hypotheses that an adult language learner is able to form because of cognitive maturity and strategies for comprehension that can be applied in first or second language reading.

Smith, Frank, and Deborah Lott Holmes. "The Independence of Letter, Word, and Meaning Identification in Reading." In *Psycholinguistics and Reading,* pp. 50–69. A discussion of the communicative framework into which an adult learner must integrate both meaning and grammatical detail of a text before understanding can occur.

Swaffar, Janet K. "Reading in the Foreign Language Classroom: Focus on Process." *Unterrichtspraxis,* 14, No. 2 (1981), 176–99. A demonstration and explanation of reading process strategies in the adult foreign language classroom at various linguistic levels.

5. Comprehension before Production

Asher, James J. *Learning Another Language through Actions: The Complete Teacher's Guidebook.* Los Gatos, Calif.: Sky Oaks, 1977. A description of the classroom implementation of the total physical response approach to FL teaching, in which evidence of comprehension precedes all demands for verbal production.

Carroll, John B. "Learning Theory for the Classroom Teacher." In Gilbert A. Jarvis, ed. *The Challenge of Communication.* ACTFL Review of Foreign Language Education, vol. 6. Skokie, Ill.: National Textbook, 1974, pp. 113–49. A review of psychological research suggesting that speech production is based on communicative structures that must be stored in the mind of the speaker (comprehended) before they can be actively used.

Widdowson, H. G. *Teaching Language as Communication.* Oxford: Oxford Univ. Press, 1978. A discussion of the textual features that must be comprehended before the language learner can read for meaning (the "communicative framework" of a text) and classroom implementations of this approach.

Winitz, Harris, ed. *The Comprehension Approach: An Evolving Methodology in Foreign Language Instruction.* Rowley, Mass.: Newbury, 1981. Articles concerning various facets of implementation and research of a comprehension (or process) approach to language teaching.

6. Concentration on Deep-Structure Comprehension before Grammatical Expression (Cognitive Complexity versus Surface Grammaticality)

Mistler-Lachman, Janet L. "Levels of Comprehension in Processing of Normal and Ambiguous Sentences." *Journal of Verbal Learning and Verbal Behavior,* 11 (1972), 614–23. Also "Depth of Comprehension and Sentence Memory." *Journal of Verbal Learning,* 13 (1974), 98–106. Both articles discuss the relation of depth-of-processing and memory for linguistic data, concluding that linguistic input which requires higher-order logical processing for comprehension will be retained and recalled at higher levels than cognitively simple materials will be.

Olson, David R. "Language and Thought: Aspects of a Cognitive Theory of Semantics." *Psychological Review,* 77, No. 4 (1970), 257–73. By reference to the role of semantics in transformational grammar, Olson confirms that both semantic selection and syntactic decisions made by a language user are conditioned by the idea underlying an utterance.

7. Errors Are Natural

Clarke and Silberstein. See sec. 4. Suggests that the emphasis in constructing reading tasks be on the strategies students use in problem solving and not on artificially discrete, single correct answers (esp. p. 21).

Hatch, Evelyn, and Michael H. Long. "Discourse Analysis, What's That?" In D. Larsen-Freeman, ed. *Discourse Analysis in Second Language Research.* Rowley, Mass.: Newbury, 1980. A discussion of "wh-" questions as they restrict student discourse and hence student practice on both informational and organizational levels of language.

Phillips, June K. "Second Language Reading: Teaching Decoding Skills." *Foreign Language Annals,* 8 (Oct. 1975), 227–32.

——. *A Study of the Applicability of Task Analysis Methodologies and Learning Hierarchies in Second-Language Reading.* Diss. Ohio State Univ. 1974. Both studies elaborate on the nature of errors in language acquisition, and particularly with reference to the inadequacy of traditional "wh-" questions as they reinforce an artificial communication environment in the classroom. Errors in such an environment are products of random mismatches between student and teacher, not necessarily a matter of cognition.

8. Clear Conceptualization Is the Precondition for Correct Grammatical Detail (Not the Converse)

Hosenfeld, Carol. "A Preliminary Investigation of the Reading Strategies of Successful and Nonsuccessful Second Language Learners." *System,* 5, No. 2 (1977), 110–23. In this analysis of actual reading strategies, Hosenfeld reveals that the successful reader (as a conceptually adult reader) uses the deep-structure idea of the text to bridge gaps in his or her knowledge of specific items of vocabulary, syntax, or morphology. An unsuccessful reader is impeded by gaps in knowledge of surface detail from comprehension of the text message.

Moscovitch, Morris, and Fergus I. M. Cralk. "Depth of Processing, Retrieval Values, and Uniqueness of Encoding as Factors in Recall." *Journal of Verbal Learning and Verbal Behavior,* 15 (1976), 447–58. A discussion of research which demonstrates that recall of both semantic and syntactical detail is contingent on the cognitive processing of the original information.

EXTENSIONS OF PROCESS THEORIES IN OTHER DISCIPLINES

(with reference to learning and perception models that can serve as bases for interdisciplinary courses coordinated with foreign language study)

Foucault, Michel. *The Archaeology of Knowledge.* Trans. A. M. Sheridan Smith. New York: Harper, 1972. Extends Mach's idea of frame of reference and Whorf's notions of cultural relativity into the concept of the *episteme:* the idea that each culture has only one particular underlying pattern of conceptualization available to it and that these patterns of logical processing are manifested in the logic of social and political institutions. In this context, see also Thomas S. Kuhn, *The Structure of*

Scientific Revolutions (Chicago: Univ. of Chicago Press, 1970), which posits that a true discovery in the sciences causes a deep-ranging shift in the entire pattern of conceptualization of a culture—a shift in its *episteme,* in its innate logical processing model; Jean Piaget, *The Development of Thought: Equilibrium of Cognitive Structures* (New York: Viking, 1975), which explains that certain age groups are incapable of conceptualization along certain patterns (as Foucault claims for historical ages).

Freud, Sigmund. *An Outline of Psychoanalysis.* Trans. James Stachey. New York: Norton, 1949. Whereas Kant concentrated on human logical facilities, Freud added unconscious processing of data to the conscious levels Kant had delimited. Freud posited that we process data according to three models: the functions of our conscious mind (the ego), the patterns inherited from our society (the culture-bound superego), and the needs of our physical organism (the unconscious drives of our id). There are no preestablished harmonies among these systems, so conflicts arise in their data processing: neuroses, dream work, and abreactions are examples of two or three modes of data processing in conflict.

Kant, Immanuel. *Critique of Pure Reason.* Trans. Norman Kemp Smith. New York: St. Martin's, 1965 (esp. bk. 1, sec. 3 of the "Transcendental Analytic," the table of categories). Kant's categories, the basis for all logical processing models, delimit the patterns of logical association of data that all humans use—basic patterns of logical thinking in any field.

Mach, Ernst. *The Analysis of Sensations and the Relation of the Physical to the Psychical.* Trans. C. M. Williams. New York: Dover, 1959 (esp. "Introductory Remarks: Antimetaphysical"). The scientist who was responsible for the concept of frame of reference that led to the formulation of special relativity by Einstein. Here Mach discusses the modes, or frames, of reference in which data are processed by our minds. Depending on which elements of consciousness are addressed, we designate the conclusions we reach in our logical processing of information as referring to psychological realities, objective reality, or the effects of our bodies on our consciousness. In these seemingly different investigations, neither the type of data nor the methods of processing differ but only the frame of reference in which we choose to communicate our results.

Saussure, Ferdinand de. *Course in General Linguistics.* Ed. Charles Bally and Riedlinger Sechehaye. Trans. Wade Baskin. New York: McGraw-Hill, 1966 (esp. pt. 1, sec. 1: "The Nature of the Linguistic Sign"). Specifies the relation of language to perception. In every word or concept (together, the linguistic sign), there is a unification of a signified concept (a mental picture or reference) and a signifier (an arbitrary, culture-bound word). Both data processing and communication depend on this duality of the linguistic sign and may be interfered with on either level (on the level of deep-structure concept reference or on that of surface-structure object reference).

Whorf, Benjamin Lee. *Language, Thought, and Reality.* Cambridge: MIT Press, 1956. Turns the problem of communication and the cultural relativity of data on its head, discussing the way our inherited language becomes our inherited perspective on the world: all our categories of conceptualization depend on our cultural-temporal references, as retained and reflected in our language patterns.

Additional references: Bertolt Brecht, *On Theater;* Jean-Paul Sartre, *What Is Literature?*; Herbert Marcuse, *Studies in Critical Philosophy.* All three deal with the concept of "engaged literature" in different forms: literature that attempts to address, uncover, and potentially alter the patterns of conceptualization of a particular society or age. Brecht: the epic theater forces the audience to think about the cultural norms and socioeconomic conditions that influence its thought. Marcuse and Sartre discuss the realities conditioned in society, the categories of existence that affect all our lives.

Writing

Documents identified by an ED number may also be read on microfiche at an ERIC library collection or ordered from the ERIC Document Reproduction Service, P.O. Box 190, Arlington, VA 22210.

Brown, Rollo. *How the French Boy Learns to Write.* Urbana, Ill.: National Council of Teachers of English, 1963. ED 039 216.

Bruffee, Kenneth. *A Short Course in Writing.* 2nd ed. Cambridge: Winthrop, 1980.

———. "The Brooklyn Plan: Attaining Intellectual Growth through Peer Group Tutoring." *Liberal Education,* 64 (1978), 447–68. This article offers an excellent rationale for peer tutoring as a vehicle to enhance understanding of principles of good writing. It also offers suggestions for teachers on how to guide students in building the skills necessary to criticize each other's work effectively. I recommend that all language teachers read this article.

Comeau, R., N. Lamoureux, and F. Bustin. *Ensemble: Littérature and Ensemble: Grammaire.* New York: Holt, 1977.

Cooper, Thomas. "A Strategy for Teaching Writing." *Modern Language Journal,* 41 (Sept.–Oct. 1977), 241–46.

———, Genelle Morain, and Theodore Kalivoda. *Sentence Combining in Second Language Instruction.* Language in Education series, no. 31. Washington, D.C.: Center for Applied Linguistics/ERIC Clearinghouse on Languages and Linguistics, 1980. ED 195 167.

Corbett, Edward. *Classical Rhetoric for the Modern Student.* New York: Oxford Univ. Press, 1965.

Eastman, Richard M. *Style.* 2nd ed. New York: Oxford Univ. Press, 1978.

Emig, Jane. "Writing as a Mode of Learning." *College Composition and Communication,* 28 (May 1977), 122–28.

Gaudiani, Claire. *Teaching Writing in the Foreign Language Curriculum.* Washington, D.C.: Center for Applied Linguistics, 1982.

Hawkins, Thomas. *Group-Inquiry Technique for Teaching Writing.* Urbana, Ill.: ERIC Clearinghouse on Reading and Communication Skills, 1976. ED 128 813.

Hirsch, E. D. *The Philosophy of Composition.* Chicago: Univ. of Chicago Press, 1977.

Irmscher, William F. *Teaching Expository Writing.* New York: Holt, 1979. This straightforward text discusses issues such as the process of writing and why and how to teach writing. It includes a large section of course planning, teaching vocabulary, syntax, and style and concludes with a section on evaluation.

Krug, Clara. "Promoting a Positive Attitude towards Writing." *Notes on Teaching English,* 9, No. 1 (1981), 10–12.

———. "An Error-Analysis Design for Improving the Writing Skills of College-Level Foreign Language Students." ERIC Clearinghouse on Reading and Communication Skills, 1982.

Lalande, John. "An Error in Error-Correction Policies." *ADFL Bulletin,* 12, No. 3 (March 1981): 45–47. This article argues for more extensive or "total correction" policies against the traditional selective error correction. The author's theoretical justification and his bibliographic entries on both sides of the issue make this an interesting piece for consideration of teachers of writing in FL departments.

MacIntyre, Alasdair. "Noam Chomsky's View of Language." In Mark Lester, ed. *Readings in Applied Transformational Grammar.* New York: Holt, 1979.

Maimon, Elaine P. "Talking to Strangers." *College Composition and Communication,* 30 (Dec. 1979), 364–69. Maimon stresses collaborative learning and the importance of having students write drafts, edit, and write often.

———, Gerald Belcher, Gail Hearn, Barbara Nodine, and Finbarr O'Connor. *Writing in the Arts and Sciences.* Cambridge: Winthrop, 1981.

———, Gerald Belcher, Gail Hearn, Barbara Nodine, and Finbarr O'Connor. *Readings in the Arts and Sciences.* Cambridge: Winthrop, 1982.

Mellon, John C. *Transformational Sentence Combining.* Research report No. 10. Urbana, Ill.: National Council of Teachers of English, 1969. ED 034 752.

Moffat, James. *Teaching the Universe of Discourse.* Boston: Houghton-Mifflin, 1964.

Morton, Jacqueline. *English Grammar for Students of French.* Ann Arbor: Olivia and Hill, 1978. Also available for other languages. Excellent support for English skills.

O'Hare, Frank. *Sentence Combining.* Research report No. 15. Urbana, Ill.: National Council of Teachers of English, 1971. ED 073 483.

———. *Sentencecraft.* New York: Ginn, 1974. This workbook covers fairly elementary levels but is useful as a guide to foreign language teachers attempting to isolate for their students types of sentences and combining techniques.

Rivers, Wilga. "Motivation in Bilingual Programs." In Wilga Rivers, ed. *Speaking in Many Tongues.* 2nd ed. Rowley, Mass.: Newbury, 1976.

Sareil, Jean. *Explication de texte.* Vols. 1 and 2. Englewood Cliffs, N.J.: Prentice-Hall, 1967.

Shaughnessey, Mina. *Errors and Expectations.* New York: Oxford Univ. Press, 1977. This book is especially helpful to foreign language teachers with little or no background in composition teaching. The descriptive bibliography offers specific guidance on readings about the writing process, the learner's situation, grammar and vocabulary, spelling, second language learning, and academic discourse.

Stanford, Gene, and the Committee on Classroom Practices. *How to Handle the Paper Load.* Urbana, Ill.: National Council of Teachers of English, 1979. ED 176 334.

Vinay, P., and J. Darbelnet. *Stylistique comparée du francais et de l'anglais.* 2nd ed. Paris: Didier, 1958.

International Education, Global Outlook, and Culture

Compiled with the help of Humphrey Tonkin

INTERNATIONALIZING THE CURRICULUM

Alger, Chadwick F., and David G. Hoovler. *You and Your Community in the World.* Columbus, Ohio: Consortium for International Studies Education, 1978.

Berryman, Sue, et al. *Foreign Languages and International Studies Specialists: The Marketplace and National Policy.* (Available through ERIC or Rand Corporation: R 2501 - NEH, September 1979.)

Bonham, George W., ed. *The Great Core Curriculum Debate.* New Rochelle, N.Y.: Change Magazine Press, 1979.

———. "What Global Knowledge Is Enough?" *Update I,* Council on Learning, Fall 1979.

Brod, Richard, ed. *Foreign Languages for the 1980s: Reports of the MLA-ACLS Task Forces.* New York: MLA, 1980.

Burn, Barbara. *Expanding the International Dimension of Higher Education.* San Francisco: Jossey-Bass, 1980.

Clark, Beatrice S. "The Infusion of African Cultural Elements in Language Learning: A Modular Approach." *Foreign Language Annals,* 15 (1982), 23–28.

Conner, Maurice W. "New Curricular Connections." In June K. Phillips, ed. *The Language Connection: From the Classroom to the World.* The ACTFL Foreign Language Education Series, vol. 9. Skokie, Ill.: National Textbook, 1977, pp. 95–121.

Council on Learning. *Education for a Global Century: Handbook of Exemplary International Programs.* New Rochelle, N.Y.: Change Magazine Press, 1981.

Geno, Thomas H., ed. *Foreign Language and International Studies: Toward Cooperation and Integration.* 1981 Northeast Conference Reports. New York: The Conference, 1981.

Global Responsibility: The Role of the Foreign Language Teacher. Proc. of Northeast Conference on Foreign Language and International Studies, 1981: Toward Cooperation and Integration. Middlebury, Vt.: Northeast Conference Reports, 1981.

Hanvey, Robert. *An Attainable Global Perspective.* New York: Center for Global Perspectives, 1975.

Hymes, Dell H. "Linguistic Aspects of Comparative Political Research." In Robert J. Holt and John E. Turner, eds. *Methodology of Comparative Research.* New York: Free Press, 1970, pp. 296–341.

Institute for World Order. *Peace and World Order Studies: A Curriculum Guide.* New York: IWO, 1981.

Mestenhauser, Josef A. *Learning with Foreign Students.* Minneapolis: Univ. of Minnesota Press, 1976.

——, and Dietmar Barsig. "Foreign Students as Teachers." Washington, D.C.: National Assoc. for Foreign Student Affairs, 1978.

Michigan State University. *International Education at Michigan State University in an Interdependent World.* East Lansing: Office of International Programs, Michigan State Univ., 1980.

Missionary Training Center of the Church of Jesus Christ of Latter-Day Saints. *Culture for Missionaries: Hong Kong, Taiwan.* Provo, Utah: MTC, 1980.

Muller, Robert. *The Need for Global Education.* Philadelphia: Global Interdependence Center, n.d.

Nehrt, Lee C. *Case Studies of Internationalization of the Business School Curriculum.* St. Louis: American Assembly of Collegiate Schools of Business, 1981.

O'Maley, Patty, and Barbara Jurasek. "International Education at Earlham." *Journal of the National Association of Foreign Student Affairs,* Spring 1982, pp. 13–14.

Project for Global Education. *Organizing for Peace and World Order Studies: A Guide of Strategies and Methods.* New York: Institute for World Order, 1981.

Santoni, Georges. *Contemporary French Culture and Society.* Albany, N.Y.: State University of New York, 1982.

Strasheim, Lorraine A. "Broadening the Middle School Curriculum through Content: Globalizing Foreign Languages." In June K. Phillips, ed. *Action for the 80s: A Political, Professional, and Public Program for Foreign Language Education.* The ACTFL Foreign Language Education Series. Skokie Ill.: National Textbook, 1981, pp. 129–45.

Tonkin, Humphrey. "Language and International Studies: Closing the Gap." *ADFL Bulletin,* 13, No. 1 (Sept. 1981), 13–20.

———, and Jane Edwards. *The World in the Curriculum: Curricular Strategies for the 21st Century.* New Rochelle, N.Y.: Change Magazine, 1981.

Torney-Purta, Judith. "Global Education: An Area for Fruitful Collaboration between Foreign Language and Social Studies." In ACTFL, *Proceedings of the National Conference on Professional Priorities,* November 1980, pp. 35–38.

United States Office of Education. *Task Force on Global Education: Report with Recommendations.* Washington, D.C.: USOE, 1979.

RESOURCE GUIDES

Brown, Walter T. *While You're in Washington and New York, Get Me and My College an International Studies Grant.* New York: Council for Intercultural Studies and Programs, 1982.

———, ed. *The CISP International Studies Funding Book.* 3rd ed. New York: Council for Intercultural Studies and Programs, 1982.

Global Perspectives in Education. *The Organization Resource Directory for Global Education.* New York: Global Perspectives in Education, 1980.

Karp, Basil. "The Global Perspective in Education: A Guide for Undergraduate Teachers." *International Education Review,* 6 (Spring 1981), 5–13.

Project for Global Education. *Annotated Bibliography* (selected books, articles, films, journals, and social change organizations). New York: Institute for World Order, 1981.

United Nations. *Films of the United Nations Family 1980–81.* New York: United Nations, 1980.

———. *Playback: A UN Family Bulletin on Audio Visual Matters.* New York: United Nations.

Wiprud, Helen R., ed. *International Education Programs of the U.S. Government.* Washington, D.C.: U.S. Government Printing Office, 1980.

Wiseberg, Laurie, and Harry M. Scoble, eds. *North American Human Rights Directory.* Garrett Park, Md.: Garrett, 1980.

Whole World Handbook. 6th ed. New York: Council on International Educational Exchange, 1981.

World Future Society. *The Future: A Guide to Information Sources.* Washington, D.C.: World Future Society, 1979.

CULTURE

Henderson, Ingeborg. "Cultural Strategies in Elementary College Language Courses." *Modern Language Journal,* 64 (1980), 190–96.

Ketchum, Ann Duhamel. "The Teaching of French Contemporary Civilization." *Modern Language Journal,* 62 (1978), 3–10.

Nostrand, Howard. "French Culture's Concern for Relationships: Relationism." *Foreign Language Annals,* 4 (May 1973), 469–80.

———. "Empathy for a Second Culture." In Gilbert A. Jarvis, ed. *Responding to New Realities.* ACTFL Review of Foreign Language Education, vol. 5. Skokie, Ill.: National Textbook, 1974, pp. 263–327.

———. "The 'Emergent Model' Applied to Contemporary France." *Contemporary French Civilization,* 2, No. 2 (1978), 277–94.

Seelye, Ned. *Teaching Culture: Strategies for Foreign Language Educators.* Skokie, Ill.: National Textbook, 1974.

Wallace, Anthony. "The New Culture-and-Personality." In *Anthropology and Human Behavior,* Washington, D.C.: Anthropological Society of Washington, 1962, pp. 1–12.

Faculty Development

Gaudiani, Claire. "Professional Collaborative Development Programs." *ADFL Bulletin,* 14, No. 3 (March 1983), 17–26.

———, and Clara Krug. "A House No Longer Divided: Faculty Collaboration across Educational Sectors." *Ram's Horn,* Dartmouth Language Outreach Program, Spring 1983.

Nelsen, William, and Michael Siegal. *Effective Approaches to Faculty Development.* Washington, D.C.: Assn. of American Colleges.

Noonan, John F., ed. *Learning about Teaching.* San Francisco: Jossey-Bass, 1980.

White, Alvin M., ed. *Interdisciplinary Teaching.* San Francisco: Jossey-Bass, 1981.

Testing

Compiled by Judy Liskin-Gasparro
Educational Testing Service

Bartz, Walter H. *Testing Oral Communications in the Foreign Language Classroom.* Language in Education: Theory and Practice, vol. 1. Arlington, Va.: Center for Applied Linguistics, 1979.

Born, Warren C., ed. *Goals Clarification: Curriculum, Teaching, Evaluation.* Reports of the Working Committees. Middlebury, Vt.: Northeast Conference on the Teaching of Foreign Languages, 1975.

Clark, John L. D. *Foreign Language Testing: Theory and Practice.* Philadelphia: Center for Curriculum Development, 1972.

―――. "Measurement Implications of Recent Trends in Foreign Language Teaching." In Dale L. Lange, ed., *Foreign Language Education: A Reappraisal.* ACTFL Foreign Language Education Series, vol. 4. Skokie, Ill.: National Textbook, 1972, pp. 219–57.

Freed, Barbara F. "Establishing Proficiency-Based Language Requirements." *ADFL Bulletin,* 13, No. 2 (1981), 6–12.

Gunterman, Gail. "Developing Functional Proficiency in a Foreign Language." *Foreign Language Annals,* 12 (1979), 219–28.

Jones, Randall L. "Testing: A Vital Connection." In June K. Phillips, ed. *The Language Connection: From the Classroom to the World.* ACTFL Foreign Language Education Series, vol. 9. Skokie, Ill.: National Textbook, 1977, pp. 237–65.

Jorstad, Helen L. "Testing as Communication." In Gilbert A. Jarvis, ed., *The Challenge of Communication.* ACTFL Foreign Language Education series, vol. 6. Skokie, Ill.: National Textbook, 1974, pp. 223–73.

Kalivoda, Theodore B. "Take a Closer Look at Your Students' Communicative Ability!" *Hispania* 68 (Sept. 1980), 539–644.

Linder, Cathy, ed. *Oral Communication Testing: A Handbook for the Foreign Language Teacher.* Skokie, Ill.: National Textbook, 1977.

Schultz, Renate A., and Walter H. Bartz. "Free to Communicate." In June K. Phillips, ed. *Perspective: A New Freedom.* ACTFL Foreign Language Education series, vol. 7. Skokie, Ill.: National Textbook, 1975.

Valdman, Albert, and Marvin Moody. "Testing Communicative Ability." *French Review,* 52 (May 1979), 552–61.

Valette, Rebecca M. *Modern Language Testing.* 2nd ed. New York: Harcourt, 1977.

―――, and Cathy Linder. "Measuring the Variables and Testing the Outcomes." In June K. Phillips, ed. *Building an Experience—Building for Success.* ACTFL Foreign Language Education series, vol. 10. Skokie, Ill.: National Textbook, 1979, pp. 199–232.

Computers

Collett, Michael J. *Computers in Language Teaching.* Canterbury Monographs for Teachers of French, 2. Christchurch, Eng.: Univ. of Canterbury, 1980.

Harrison, John S. "Applications of Computer Technology in Foreign Language Teaching and Learning." In Robert G. Mead, Jr., ed. *The Foreign Language Teacher: The Lifelong Learner.* 1982 Northeast Conference reports. New York: The Conference, 1982, pp. 143–51.

Olsen, Solveig. "Foreign Language Departments and Computer-Assisted Instruction: A Survey." *Modern Language Journal,* 64 (1980), 341–49.

Omaggio, Alice C., et al. "Foreign Language in the Secondary School: Reconciling the Dream with the Reality—Computer-Assisted Instruction." In Robert G. Mead, Jr., ed. *Foreign Languages: Key Links in the Chain of Learning.* 1983 Northeast Conference reports. Middlebury, Vt.: The Conference, 1983, 45–6.

Careers

Church, Jo Ann. "French for Lawyers." *French Review,* 52, No. 3 (1979), 463–70.

Coveney, James, and Sheila J. Moore. *Glossary of French and English Management Terms.* London: Longman, 1972.

LeBlanc, Alfred, and Jeanne LeBlanc. "The B.S. Degree in French Business at the Pennsylvania State University." *Modern Language Journal,* 63 (1979), 41–43.

Lentz, M. M., Hilda Watson, and S. McGuinn. *French in the Office.* London: Longman, 1978.

Communication Activities in Second Language Teaching

Compiled by Barbara Gonzalez
University of Texas, San Antonio

Asher, James. *Learning Another Language through Actions.* Los Gatos, Calif.: Sky Oaks, 1977.

Brown, H. Douglas. *Principles of Language Learning and Teaching.* Englewood Cliffs, N.J.: Prentice-Hall, 1980.

Dominicis, Maria C., and Joseph A. Cussen. *Casos y Cosas.* Dallas: Scott, Foresman, 1981.

Eckard, Ronald D., and Mary Ann Kearny. *Teaching Conversation Skills in ESL.* Washington, D.C.: Center for Applied Linguistics, 1981.

Freeman, G. Ronald. *Intercambios.* New York: Random House, 1980.

Gattegno, Caleb. *Teaching Foreign Languages in Schools the Silent Way.* New York: Educational Solutions, 1972.

Gaudiani, Claire L. "The Participatory Classroom." *Foreign Language Annals,* 14 (May 1981), 171–80.

Gonzalez, Barbara. *Small Group Activities for Second Language Teaching.* ED 152 102.

Herron, Carol. "Foreign-Language Learning Approaches as Metaphor." *Modern Language Journal,* 66 (1982), 235–42.

———. "The Foreign Language Teacher: A Humanist?" *French Review,* 56 (1983), 535–45.

Hubp, Loretta Burke. *Let's Play Games in Spanish.* Skokie, Ill.: National Textbook, 1974.

Joiner, Elizabeth. "Keep Them Guessing." In Elizabeth Joiner and Patricia Westphal, eds. *Developing Communications Skills.* Rowley, Mass.: Newbury, 1978.

Kettering, Judith Carl. *Developing Communicative Competence: Interaction Activities in English as a Second Language.* Pittsburgh: University Center for International Studies, 1975.

Kramsch, Claire J. *Discourse Analysis and Second Language Teaching.* Washington, D.C.: Center for Applied Linguistics, 1981.

Krashen, Stephen D. *Second Language Acquisition and Second Language Learning.* New York: Pergamon, 1981.

Kupferschmid, Gene. *Y tú, qué dices?* Lexington, Mass.: D.C. Heath, 1982.

Lee, W. R. *Language Teaching Games and Contests.* Oxford: Oxford Univ. Press, 1979.

Littlewood, William. *Communicative Language Teaching.* Cambridge: Cambridge Univ. Press, 1981.

Moskowitz, Gertrude. *Caring and Sharing in the Foreign Language Class.* Rowley, Mass.: Newbury, 1978.

Omaggio, Alice C. *Helping Learners Succeed: Activities for the Foreign Language Classroom.* Washington, D.C.: Center for Applied Linguistics, 1981.

Paulston, Christina Bratt, and Howard R. Selekman. "Interaction Activities in the Foreign Classroom, or How to Grow a Tulip Rose." In Joiner and Westphal, eds. *Developing Communications Skills.*

Rooks, George. *Conversar sin parar.* Rowley, Mass.: Newbury, 1982.

Savingnon, Sandra. "Teaching for Communication." In Joiner and Westphal, eds. *Developing Communications Skills.*

Sedwick, Frank. *Conversation in Spanish.* New York: Van Nostrand, 1981. (Also *Conversation in French, Conversation in German,* and *Conversation in Italian.*)

Smith, Clyde R. "Contextualizing Pattern Drills: The 'German Circle Games.'" *Foreign Language Annals,* 14 (May 1981), 203–12.

Stevick, Earl W. *Teaching and Learning Languages.* Cambridge: Cambridge Univ. Press, 1982.

Ur, Penny. *Discussions That Work.* Cambridge: Cambridge Univ. Press, 1981.

Urzua, Carole. *Talking Purposefully.* Silver Spring, Md.: Institute of Modern Languages, 1981.

Valette, Rebecca. "Developing and Evaluating Communications Skills in the Classroom." In Joiner and Westphal, eds. *Developing Communications Skills.*

Westphal, Patricia B. "Moi Tarzan, Vous Jane?: A Study of Communicative Competence." In Joiner and Westphal, eds. *Developing Communications Skills.*

Widdowson, H. G. *Teaching Language as Communication.* Oxford: Oxford Univ. Press, 1978.

Winn-Bell Olsen, Judy E. *Communication-Starters and Other Activities for the ESL Classroom.* San Francisco: Alemany, 1977.

Wright, Andrew, David Betterridge, and Michael Buckby. *Games for Language Learning.* Cambridge: Cambridge Univ. Press, 1979.

Yalden, Janice. *Communicative Language Teaching: Principles and Practice.* Toronto, Ont.: OISE, 1981.

Zelson, Sidney N.J. "Skill-Using, Self-Expression and Communication: Exercises in Three Dimensions." In Joiner and Westphal, eds. *Developing Communications Skills.*

Index